THE SEDUCTION OF ETHICS:
TRANSFORMING THE SOCIAL SCIENCES

The Seduction of Ethics is an ethnographic work about relationships between researchers and research-ethics committees. In this book, Will C. van den Hoonaard looks at formal research-ethics codes and how countless administrators, researchers, scholars, and policy makers are lured into their ambit. In Canada alone, ethics review is a $35 million 'industry.'

What drives this seduction is not only a moral panic and a view of people as vulnerable and needing protection, but also the public's desire for institutional accountability. The result is a systematic change in the way social researchers conduct their work. Students increasingly rely on ethics committees for advice about social research methods, and when such advice issues from committees who have no expertise or knowledge of those methods, social research becomes divorced from its traditions. Social sciences disciplines begin to resemble one another and the richness of conventional social research is lost as researchers try to fit their approach to the technical demands of ethics codes. These inevitable changes are leading to a homogenization and pauperization of social research.

The Seduction of Ethics offers an analysis of the moral cosmology and practices of ethics committees in regard to research and researchers. Using participant observation, records, interviews, and the scholarly literature on the topic, the book explores the research-ethics review process itself. Van den Hoonaard reveals an idiosyncratic and inconsistent world, where researchers employ particular strategies of avoidance or partial or full compliance as they seek approval from ethics committees. In research-ethics committees, he argues, administrative routines often overwhelm thinking about substantive ethical issues.

WILL C. VAN DEN HOONAARD is a professor emeritus in the Department of Sociology at the University of New Brunswick.

OTHER PUBLICATIONS BY THE AUTHOR

The Equality of Women and Men: The Experience of the Bahá'í Community of Canada (with D.K. van den Hoonaard) (2006)

The Ethics Trapeze (special issue of *Journal of Academic Ethics*) (2006)

Walking the Tightrope: Ethical Issues for Qualitative Researchers (editor) (2002)

Working with Sensitizing Concepts: Analytical Field Research (1997)

The Origins of the Bahá'í Community of Canada, 1898–1948 (1996)

Reluctant Pioneers: Constraints and Opportunities in an Icelandic Fishing Community (1992)

Silent Ethnicity: The Dutch of New Brunswick (1991)

WILL C. VAN DEN HOONAARD

The Seduction of Ethics

Transforming the Social Sciences

UNIVERSITY OF TORONTO PRESS
Toronto   Buffalo   London

© University of Toronto Press Incorporated 2011
Toronto Buffalo London
www.utppublishing.com
Printed in Canada

ISBN 978-1-4426-4268-3 (cloth)
ISBN 978-1-4426-1150-4 (paper)

Printed on acid-free, 100% post-consumer recycled paper with vegetable-based inks.

Library and Archives Canada Cataloguing in Publication

van den Hoonaard, Will C. (Willy Carl), 1942–
The seduction of ethics : transforming the social sciences /
Will C. van den Hoonaard.

Includes bibliographical references and index.
ISBN 978-1-4426-4268-3 (bound).   ISBN 978-1-4426-1150-4 (pbk.)

1. Social sciences – Research – Moral and ethical aspects.   2. Social sciences
and ethics.   I. Title.

H62.V348 2011   174'.93   C2011-901392-4

This book has been published with the help of a grant from the Humanities
and Social Sciences Federation of Canada, using funds provided by the
Social Sciences and Humanities Research Council of Canada.

University of Toronto Press acknowledges the financial assistance to its
publishing program of the Canada Council for the Arts and the Ontario
Arts Council.

 Canada Council   Conseil des Arts
for the Arts   du Canada    ONTARIO ARTS COUNCIL
CONSEIL DES ARTS DE L'ONTARIO

University of Toronto Press acknowledges the financial support for its
publishing activities of the Government of Canada through the Canada
Book Fund.

Our civil competencies are resources to warm the world.

–Erving Goffman

Contents

x   Contents

Preface

The audience of twenty ethics aficionados breathed a sigh of relief after they had escaped the 34-degrees Celsius temperature outside. They settled in on their hard plastic chairs. They had come to hear a speaker who had travelled halfway around the world to share his insights about ethics and the social sciences. As the fans rotated, some of the speaker's notes ruffled slightly. He was wearing his van Gogh tie to lighten the mood of his talk. The topic was too serious not to make light of it. His lecture was predictable. He sketched the development of ethics policies in his and other countries and traced the impact of the policies on social research. Even the nature of medical ethics, he found, was troubling, but he only approached this emerging insight with caution. After forty minutes, he put away his notes and cordially invited the audience to offer comments or questions. What transpired then was an unheralded question that betrayed his own pessimism: 'Is there thus no hope for social scientists in the ethics regime?' The speaker was shocked by his inability to phrase a hopeful answer. That question shifted the whole focus of my research . . . and ultimately shaped this book. That question sat on my brain during the thirty-hour trip back home and continued to swell into a daring issue that has occupied my time since then.

Social scientists live in troubled times these days. Much as the repeated warnings of global warming have gone unheeded by politicians and other decision-makers, so, too, has the insistent clamour by social scientists about the grave impact of medical ethics as a template for all research gone unheeded. At best, the clamour is dismissed.

This has not been an easy book to write. Pessimism is not my nature and the years of belief that ethics of social science research will somehow fit into the pantheon of medical ethics have proven illusory.

I, too, failed to listen more closely to the clamour. My habit of offering a vision of coexistence with medical ethics came in the form of public lectures, an edited book, articles, teaching a graduate seminar on ethics in research, and in the shape of my own research on ethics. That one question uttered in the cool shade of a lecture hall forced me to reconsider the book I had planned to write. I, too, have joined the ranks of those who have warned others about the coming defeat of the social sciences by the imposition of medical ethics.

What now? How can I explain my troubling insight to my colleagues and friends whom I have had the privilege of associating with as a trustee of Canada's national ethics guidelines? Will they be insulted with my radical departure from what they have come to expect of me? How will I be able to face my research and interview participants across Canada who have been extraordinarily kind and generous with their time and with their ideas? Pessimism caught me by surprise.

Pessimism is an awful thing to live with. It is the easy way out. It saves not having to come up with a solution. However, I am deeply hopeful that this book will transmute the pessimism into something a lot more worthwhile, maybe even a clue about what we can do. This book is not about dispensing with ethical codes of conduct. Rather, it advocates a system of ethics that speaks to the needs of social researchers.

Acknowledgments

I am compelled to use the metaphor of a seafarer to describe the numerous contributions made by individuals and institutions to the completion of this sojourn on the sea of ethics review. All too often, I saw the horizon of finishing the sojourn, only to be pulled away by other facets of the research. Among the individuals who have contributed to the extensive bibliographic work, I am honoured to include Fern Paul, Rebecca Anderson, Stephanie Bruce, and Anita Connolly. Transcription work fell upon Sarah Noftell, Jennifer Noftell, and Rosanna Paling. Dr Peter Kepros of the UNB Research Ethics Board took a deep interest in the research and opened the means for me to pursue the research in a fitting way. Tricia Jarrett and Tracy McDonald offered superb, often humorous, administrative assistance. Dr Joan Sieber proffered a warm, collegial, and personal friendship. She also shared with me her views about an early draft of *The Seduction of Ethics*. Lehanne Knowlton of the Atlantic Centre for Qualitative Research and Analysis, St Thomas University, helped me to convert my easy-to-handle WordPerfect manuscript to another, less elegant and more convoluted, digital format that seems to be more popular at the moment. I also thank Debbie Poirier of UNB Imaging Services. Beth McAuley, editor for the University of Toronto Press, ought to take credit for catching glitches of grammar, syntax, and anything else that makes the life of an editor so rewarding. Thank you, Beth.

The numerous research participants, and the five Research Ethics Boards that allowed me to sit in on their meetings, provided a wonderful array of insights about the research-ethics process. Their contributions were thoughtful and spoke of their commitment to ethics in research. Given the universal experience of social researchers with ethics-review committees, the reader (or the people whose research experiences I have studied) may inadvertently misappropriate quoted texts to themselves or to others.

A project such as this would not have gotten off the ground without institutional support. First and foremost, I include the Social Sciences and Humanities Research Council of Canada (Grant No. 410-2003-0318). No less important was Therese de Groote of the Secretariat on Research Ethics, whose deep commitment to improving the lot of social researchers in the research-ethics review process is widely known among researchers in Canada. I also thank my co-founding members of the Interagency Advisory Panel on Research Ethics and my colleagues on its Social Sciences and Humanities Working Committee on Ethics. The University of New Brunswick Research Office, as well as the university in general, provided much help.

It is much more difficult to acknowledge the intellectual contributions to the book. I have been in touch with most of the people cited in the study and in the bibliography, thanking them for their own research. Often, we sustained the correspondence over many years (and continue to do so). Chief among them I include Dr Ann Hamilton (Oklahoma), Dr Ted Riecken (University of Victoria), Dr Linda Nugent (UNBSJ), Dr Gillian Ranson (Calgary), Dr Rosemary Clews (St. Thomas University), Drs Cheryl and Dan Albas (Manitoba), Dr Dawne Clarke (St. Thomas University), Dr Larry Wisniewski (Chair of the Department of Sociology at the University of New Brunswick), Dr Christine Halse and Dr Maureen Fitzgerald (both of University of Western Sydney), and Dr Anne Honey of Australia. I am unable to mention the names of students and colleagues who shared with me the letters they received from their ethics committees to whom I am so grateful. A special thanks to Dr Barbara Paterson, Canada Research Chair (Tier 1) in the Faculty of Nursing at the University of New Brunswick, who followed through on her kind and eager offer to read the first full draft of the book manuscript. Her husband, George Feenstra, a theologian by training, offered some keen advice on chapter 15 for which I am grateful. Dr John Mueller of the University of Calgary and Dr Paul Grayson of York University were also kind to comment on an early draft of *The Seduction of Ethics*. To each, I am intensely grateful for the time they have taken out of their busy schedule to read this early draft. Needless to say, I bear full responsibility for any errors, misinterpretations, or questionable conclusions.

I am particularly grateful to Mr Virgil Duff, Executive Editor, University of Toronto Press, for his instantaneous and consistent enthusiasm for the book. I also wish to thank Dr Iara Guerriero for her encouragement and invitation to various World Health Organization conferences in Brazil, which allowed me to develop a number of themes in anticipation of this book. I am especially happy that she managed to come to Canada as a postdoctoral fellow. Dr Luc Thériault kindly read an early draft of my various papers on the subject. A special thanks to the two anonymous reviewers of the Press who, I hope, will find some of their suggestions resonating in the current draft.

There is no question that, above all others, my spouse, Dr Deborah Kestin van den Hoonaard, provided all the essential ingredients to complete this work. She edited the first drafts, proofread subsequent drafts, attended my talks, and offered her own imaginative and substantive reflections about the research-ethics review process. She also sheltered me in her Atlantic Centre for Qualitative Research and Analysis at St Thomas University (Fredericton), which allowed me to pursue the research and writing of this book. I dedicate this work to her, 'Dr Honey II.'

THE SEDUCTION OF ETHICS:
TRANSFORMING THE SOCIAL SCIENCES

1 Introduction

Contemporary national research-ethics regimes for universities are seductive. They pull into their orbit administrators, policymakers, university staff, members of ethics committees, and researchers. This seduction is transforming the very nature and method of social science research. Just as the political, professional, and business realms have become fascinated, even obsessed, with ethics codes as a substitute for the general moral culture, so, too, have research-granting agencies, researchers, and their guardians (universities, administrators) fallen prey to the seduction of ethics. My aim is to record the interactions between researchers and these guardians that account for the pervasive transformation of social research.[1] This transformation has led to the homogenization of social research methods whereby the disciplines within the social sciences are increasingly resembling each other; at the same time, the inherent richness invested in the diversity of the social science disciplines is disappearing, leading to their pauperization. At the outset, it should be made clear that while a research-ethics review plays an important role in reshaping social research, it is by no means the sole factor. There are many other factors within the academic world that have an impact on these changes.

No one disagrees with the need for a culture of ethical conduct, much as everyone agrees that using a Global Positioning System (GPS) is a needful element of contemporary wayfarers. But is it always needful? A number of years ago, a visiting foursome to the Arctic relied on a GPS instrument to find their way across the tundra back to a hamlet. With impressive precision they were able to pinpoint their location on the GPS. Sadly, they still lost their way and had to be rescued by local folks who intimately knew the land. Experienced wayfarers on the tundra know that much depends on knowing where the serpentine creeks and obstructive knuckles are to navigate them and return safely. On such outings, the hamlet can sometimes appear at a distance and then seemingly disappear when the dictates of the tundra landscape must be followed.[2]

Similarly, national research-ethics regimes pinpoint the goals of research ethics: preserving human dignity, confidentiality, and anonymity (to name a few). But for social scientists the challenge lies in following a social-research landscape that is marked by entirely different contours than is the case for biomedical research, which forms the basis of these formal research-ethics codes. Many social scientists get lost in the moral tundra because the signage speaks to biomedical research, as opposed to social research. Still, social researchers are mandated to follow these codes.

As is the case with our fascination with GPS, ethics is a vortex pulling in all kinds of routines, peoples, and activities. Researchers must skip over the details of the terrain, just setting sights on ethics goals. Ann Hamilton, who authored one of the few empirical studies about research-ethics committees, avers that even students 'seemed nearly obsessed with the IRB and its requirements and impact on their research' (Hamilton, 2002: 16). She argues that in the United States, '[i]t can be argued that the Common Rule (45 C.F.R. § 46, 1991) is an instance of social-level delusion, detached from reality, a Baudrillardian (1983) seduction into simulation' (108).

In response to deep concerns among social scientists and other scientists about the research-ethics review process around the world, but especially in the anglophone world, Emma Bell and Allan Bryman (2007: 66, citing Furedi, 2002) exclaim that 'universities have developed an obsession with research ethics driven by risk assessment and a fear of litigation that leads them to act more conservatively than the law requires, being more concerned with the reputation of the university than with the ideals of research.' C. Kristina Gunsalus, one of the most widely cited experts in the field, summarized the current state of research-ethics review as follows: '. . . we have been left with regulations that both under-reach and over-reach, that are both too broadly and too narrowly applied' (Gunsalus, 2003b: 2).[3]

Premise of *The Seduction of Ethics*

The Seduction of Ethics explores the ramifications of national research-ethics regimes for social researchers. It is a study of social regulation:

how rules are applied, used, adopted, adapted to, rationalized, and resisted. It is not a study about the merits or demerits of ethics per se. It does not intend to specify which ethics rules should or should not apply to social research. There are numerous prescriptive reports and studies that deal with those applications (and I will refer to them when the occasion arises).

I want to include a note here about the terms I use in this book to refer to ethics committees. The term 'IRBs' refers to Institutional Review Boards that are charged with approving research deemed ethically consistent with the 'Common Rule' in the United States. The equivalent term in Canada is 'REBs,' Research Ethics Boards, also charged with the purpose of approving research guided by Canada's national research-ethics guidelines, the *Tri-Council Policy Statement on Research Involving Humans (TCPS)*. In England the equivalent body is 'LECs' or 'RECs,' which are Local/Regional Ethics Committees. In Australia, 'HRECs' refer to Human Research Ethics Committees and cover the same purpose. I retain these distinctive monikers to faithfully reflect the ideas and findings in their particular social contexts. Only when my observations exceed national or local boundaries do I use the more germane term 'ethics-review committees,' or simply 'ethics committees.' I also use the simpler term 'ethics review' to denote the longer, less elegant term 'research-ethics review.'

Although I used a variety of methods to examine the interactions between ethics committees and researchers, I primarily used ethnography (appendix A offers details about the research methods I used in this text) as a means of studying these worlds. Some REBs, while still not allowing participant observation during the meetings, were sufficiently interested in my research that they encouraged all of their members (and office staff) to be interviewed. A few others, namely, five (three small, one medium-sized, and one large university), opened their doors to being observed in 'action,' two of which offered a full inspection of their records and applications (with the consent of their researchers). Attending conferences and symposia on ethics in research, especially those sponsored by the National Council on Ethical Human Research (NCEHR) and by the Canadian Association of Research Ethics Boards (CAREB), but also by numerous professional societies, allowed me to observe the debates and issues closely. Over a five-year period, I attended twelve such conferences. In half of the cases, I presented on behalf of the Interagency Advisory Panel on Research Ethics (of which I was a member); in the other half, as someone presenting his research findings. Martin Tolich and Maureen Fitzgerald, researchers engaged in the study of the ethics-review world, offer a description of ethnography as 'boundless, and asking questions, engaging in everyday discussions, and taking fieldnotes [that] is an ethnographer's way of understanding the world' (Tolich and Fitzgerald, 2006: 72). Ann Hamilton elaborates on the purpose of qualitative research that 'implies an emphasis on process and a search for depth of understanding of perceptions, meanings, interpretations, and behaviors, in contrast with the measurement of the quantity, frequency, or even intensity of some externally defined variables (operationalizations, most prominently)' (Hamilton, 2002: 235).

I conducted formal interviews with thirty-one people, which included nine researchers, nine chairs of REBs, six other members of REBs, four staff members in the ethics or research offices, and three senior-level administrators. The longest interview lasted two and a half hours, the shortest was forty-five minutes. All of this material resulted in 444 pages of formal interview data and nearly 1,800 other pages of data. When one considers the overall contacts with the 'research-ethics' landscape, I have reached 270 people, 66 per cent of whom were researchers, 6 per cent REB chairs, 13.6 per cent members of REBs (excluding the chairs), 7 per cent staff in ethics offices, 5 per cent administrators, and one editor of an academic journal. These contacts also include people from the United States, England, Australia, and South Africa. I found research participants in forty-nine universities, as well as in fifteen non-university organizations.

I also convened a focus group at a small university in Ontario, consisting of an REB chair, a member of the REB, and two staff members of the ethics office.

Throughout the length of the research, researchers and members of REBs sent me reports, either of their activities or about the actions taken by their respective academic societies. Of particular interest to me were memos and cases. I undertook textual analyses of these materials.

Finally, I benefitted from my personal experience working inside Canada's national research-ethics regime. Between 2001 and 2005, I served as a founding member of Canada's Interagency Advisory Panel on Research Ethics (PRE); I also served as the first Chair of the Social Sciences and Humanities Working Group on Ethics (SSHWC) from 2003 to 2005. This organizational experience laid an important foundation for my own understanding of the landscape of the national ethics regime.

The Seduction of Ethics, however, betrays my ambivalence about the need for an ethics regime. On some days, I am deeply moved by the helpful and sincere interest research-ethics committees have shown in research – affirming the sense of community. On other days, I am painfully aware of the disservice they can cause. This ambivalence has led me to see two worlds: the world of research-ethics committees and that of the researchers themselves. The former is maintained by procedures and bureaucratic routines, largely unaffected by research practice (Truman, 2003: 1). That world is immersed in the larger culture. It acts upon the social dictates of accountability, responds to a moral panic about research gone off the tracks, and views research subjects as fragile and needing protection by rules of privacy. The latter world consists of unhappy researchers who see their research as constrained and continuously 'produced' through normalization of ethics. To gauge the interaction of these two worlds, one needs to explore the defining characteristics of their communication (Koerner, 2005: 232).

My opening paragraphs have already alluded to a number of researchers engaged in the study of the research-ethics review process, namely, Carole Truman, Martin Tolich, Maureen Fitzgerald, Ann Hamilton, Emma Bell, Allan Bryman, and C. Kristina Gunsalus. For them, researchers are swimming in a sea of discontent, whose tides are produced by the research-ethics process. The discontent manifests itself in a variety of ways. Within the social sciences, as Jack Katz points out, there is a noticeable increase in the discontent and criticism of the power of IRBs that 'appears to be increasing in blogs, academic journals ... and white papers by academic task forces' (Katz, 2007: 808).[4] Canada's own Social Sciences and Humanities Working Committee of the Interagency Advisory Panel on Research Ethics has pointed to the sources of this discontent (SSHWC, 2004). Adam Hedgecoe (2008: 874), himself a proponent of the ethics-review process, claims that ethics review 'has come under attack as never before.' Still another, Rachel Aldred, speaks of 'the new ethical barrage' (Aldred, 2008: 893). Other voices, Yvonna S. Lincoln and William G. Tierney in particular, exclaim these troubling times for researchers: 'As IRBs increase their regulatory functions, the number of "stories" of researcher experiences is increasing. As the stories increase, the sense of frustration, anxiety, and anger appears to increase correspondingly' (Lincoln and Tierney, 2004: 221).

Some have already reported on the fundamental shifts in the social sciences accompanying these dissatisfactions. Social research, according to Robert Dingwall, is moving from the hands of social researchers to journalists, undercover police, or security personnel (Dingwall, 2008: 10). Some anthropologists are moving to the military (e.g., 'Human

Terrain System' research in Iraq) (Glen, 2007), corporations, or into the world of artists where there is no requirement for research-ethics review (E28-M, Fieldnotes: 167).[5] A main worry for artists is about biomedical researchers' themselves moving into narrative studies and writing up ethics policies for artists. Appearing over the horizon for research-ethics review are cultural geography, civil engineering, film studies, research in the new media, art, and theatre (see also Hamilton, 2002: 270).

One notes other impacts of research-ethics review: researchers now exaggerate hypothetical benefits of their research (to secure favourable outcomes of the review process), and research-ethics committees create myths and horror stories and misinterpret past research. The requirement to follow the results of the ethics review of one's research plans, according to John Mueller (2007), has become more important than ethical aspects of research itself, involving the indoctrination of ideology (especially directed at junior scholars). An evolving bureaucracy is demanding more resources and hard money, produces delays in doing research, promotes non-controversial topics and methods in research, advocates self-censorship, and brings about an 'adversarial campus climate and ruination of careers' (Mueller, 2007). Research-ethics committees can even curtail so-called low-risk projects: 'Yet we were dismayed,' exclaim Debbie S. Dougherty and Michael W. Kramer, 'and surprised by the IRB's tendency to deviate from this narrow mission of protecting human subjects, with the result that it can become a significant barrier to conducting even low-risk projects' (Dougherty and Kramer, 2005). The research-ethics system is beset by its own contradictions that do not appear to diminish the system's impact on desultory researchers.

Researchers, ethics administrators, and members of research-ethics committees have all noted the contradictions inherent in the system. Ironically, as universities are increasingly seeing research as a force that will move the university forward, research-ethics review now curtails or changes meaningful research (Grayson and Myles, 2005). One may ask whether a system that apparently routinely does not approve research proposals discourages researchers from securing research grants?

As strange as it may seem, social researchers themselves, too, are embracing constraints on knowledge production (Kevin Haggerty, Fieldnotes: 425). One philosopher describes research ethics as parasitic, saying that it depends on research (Michael Yeo, Fieldnotes: 158). Some ethics administrators note the struggle to differentiate between law and ethics, or between protecting research participants and the university (Interviews E13-M and E15-S). In this context, Malcolm M. Feeley (2007:

765) argues that IRBs want to 'preempt speculative harms.' And does a higher ethical standard mean more paper work (Fieldnotes: 70)?[6] Too, there are always doubts among those who must adjudicate the ethicality of research proposals about whether to pick apart a proposal or let things go through (Interview E13-M). My interviews and ethnographic research show other contradictions: Why do smaller universities have larger REBs? How are research-ethics committees making use of participatory-action and feminist research to weaken social research in general?[7] Why do some research-ethics committees link methodology and ethical research, while others do not? Finally, there is an extreme example of a contradiction: Does the ethics committee ask a researcher who does autobiographical work to sign his/her own consent form (Interview E12-M)? *The Seduction of Ethics* intends to explore other contradictions in the course of this research, but the previous examples demonstrate the unique place of research-ethics committees vis-à-vis research.

Ignorance and Scholarship

What necessitates an ethnographic study of research-ethics review is the profound absence of systematic research on research-ethics committees themselves.[8] Researchers, by contrast, are habitual writers of their own research predicaments,[9] but there is an enduring silence about these experiences from the perspective of research-ethics committees. The world of research-ethics review in universities is shrouded in mystery. The following conveys a typical experience of a student (who is now the chair of an REB):

> When I was doing my [graduate research] and I did it here at [University X], approaching the REB was a frightening experience. I got back a nasty letter from the REB. I thought, 'Oh my God, I'm never going to be able to do my research,' and it was with the guidance of my supervisor that I managed to get it through the REB. But they were this big, mysterious group that met that I had no idea who they were, and I certainly didn't want to seek them out. (Interview C09-B)

The identity of IRB members is largely unknown (NCA, 2005: 208) and Katz reports that IRB membership is often kept confidential, administrators resist attempts to put names of members on their websites, and that the processes of research-ethics review is normally closed from outside oversight (Katz, 2007: 800). Mark Wilson, a frequent commentator on medical ethics, reports that meetings are held in secret (Wilson, personal communication to author, 13 November 2003),[10] even though, '[t]he more open a committee, the more positive the relationships' (Fitzgerald, 2004: 37).[11] There are no financial figures to detail all the resources used by IRBs, including space, office equipment, paid and volunteer staff, and so on (Mueller, 2007: 822). Even though HREC (Human Research Ethics Committees in Australia) use the confidentiality argument, a lack of accountability and transparency (Fitzgerald, 2004: 35) maintains a veil of secrecy, similar to ethics committees in other countries. What is more, research proposals are handled discreetly; IRBs hold intimate knowledge about faculty and students (Katz, 2007: 800). REB members tend to produce anonymous ethics reviews of applications (E12-M).

The mysteries of ethics committees extend to their interactions with researchers. IRBs shield from public view their communications with researchers, according to Katz (2007: 800). They normally offer no explanations for the differential treatments of projects and researchers. For example, the National Communications Association (NCA) asks why communications scholars are treated differently than psychologists? Why are some procedures acceptable at one time but not another (NCA, 2005: 208)? The NCA also wonders why 'some seemingly more controversial studies (e.g., people's personal sexual communication) [are] treated more leniently than relatively mundane scholarship' (NCA, 2005: 208)? One communications researcher was told by the IRB coordinator: 'If you're going to survey real people about real communication behaviors, be prepared to undergo the same review a biomedical study would receive' (NCA, 2005: 219).

In terms of developing local policies or useful insights, because meetings are closed, IRBs rarely, if ever, solicit input from researchers about policy issues, including the application form (Hamilton, 2002: 192). Katz touches upon another point where consultation between the IRB and researchers might be useful: he learned that IRBs never invited researchers to make available the choice whether non-funded research should be included in the review process – in fact, such research does not have to be, according to national ethics codes (Katz, 2007: 806). We also learn that members with considerable research experience in one of a university's biggest departments were not asked to serve on the ethics committee despite their repeated requests (NCA, 2005: 208). And when ethics committees do open themselves to observation, whether to researchers or others, they require the guest to sign a confidentiality agreement (S46-B in Fieldnotes: 927; S10 in Fieldnotes: 1223, 1316; C09-B in Fieldnotes: 401). The motive for some is to get the researcher 'hooked' to serve on the REB (S35-B in Fieldnotes: 1136). A point of irritation for researchers is that staff members in ethics offices who are gatekeepers have no research experience (NCA, 2005: 208). According to Mueller (2007: 820), '[T]he research-ethics industry seems especially blind to its own faults, and continues to blame the researchers.'

REB members usually do not publish their experiences or reflections. To be sure, an article by Kate Connolly, a qualitative researcher, and Adela Reid, a staff member, (2007) sheds some light, but in the article they are more prescriptive than analytical: they describe two case studies to suggest how their REB at Concordia University could facilitate, rather than hinder, research. Kristine Fitch, an ethnographer and IRB chair at University of Iowa, published an account in a newsletter called 'IRB Advisor' that social science investigators may find surprisingly sympathetic to their concerns. A recent series of interviews with IRB experts in that newsletter, for example, suggested the experts believe that federal regulations are often over-interpreted by local IRBs (Fitch, 2005: 275). Ivor Pritchard (2001a, 2001b, 2002), a member of the United States Office of Human Protection, has made some valuable contributions to the discussion.

However, IRB members themselves are reluctant to become subjects of research (De Vries, 2004: 282). De Vries documents the experience of M. Casper and his researchers in *The Making of the Unborn Patient* (1998) as they faced 'the delays and stonewalling . . . in their attempts to get IRB approval of research on IRBs' (De Vries, 2003: 13n42). Debbie Dougherty and Michael Kramer (2005: 185) revealed the following obstacles they encountered when attempting to write a narrative about an IRB: 'In the email we mentioned that the narratives [in a journal] would be about IRBs. Suddenly, our project went from one of little concern to our IRB to one that needed approval, possibly from the whole board. Apparently there was greater risk to human subjects in writing narratives for publication about IRBs than in writing them on other topics.' My own research for *The Seduction of Ethics* tried to enlist fifteen REBs for participant observation. Only five responded favourably: some denied the request, and many more did not reply. Of those who denied my request, one REB chair 'considered its work not open' (Interview C11-M), while another member of the same REB was not willing for me to attend just one REB meeting, but would settle for my attending six meetings to avoid any misinterpretations (Interview E12-M). Our profound ignorance (and the lack of visibility) of the workings of ethics committees leaves no doubt about its effectiveness in enhancing its power, says Hamilton (2002: 200), who has drawn on Foucault (1980b) for this particular observation.

Any researcher studying ethics committees will be faced with three other methodological challenges. The first speaks to the diversity of ethics committees and research projects under the purview of these committees. Can one legitimately draw conclusions about ethics committees, in general, while relying on data from even a random sample of ethics committees? On what basis should one draw a stratified sample? What about drawing generalizations from a case study of one ethics committee (Stark, 2007: 792)? The wide differences among research projects and even the temperaments of researchers might make any comparative study of ethics a futile exercise. Second, as Laura Stark (2007: 783) mentions, the prevailing discussion is about whether we should look at an ethics committee as a body or as a group of individual members, but certainly not as 'some amorphous bureaucracy' (NCA, 2005: 225)?[12]

Third, every researcher encounters the problem of provocative stories (Stark, 2007: 783). Inevitably, when academics hear of my research, they tell stories, some personal and some they heard from 'a colleague.' These stories (such as the ones I heard) can inadvertently shape the direction of one's research. Some stories turn out to be urban legends having no basis in reality, even though they might be frequently repeated. So there is always the need to 'get the story straight,' preferably from someone who has actually undergone the experience. Before labelling such stories as urban myths, one notes, however, that these troublesome issues are raised so frequently and repeatedly; they are not idiosyncratic (Feeley, 2007: 766).

Similar to researchers, ethics committees also promulgate 'provocative stories,' especially regarding controversial studies such as *Darkness in El Dorado* (a critique of Napoleon Chagnon's work among the Yanomamö in Venezuela), Kennewick Man (ownership of a prehistoric skeleton, 1990s), Laud Humphreys' *Tearoom Trade* (1970), to mention a few. Fitzgerald lists six controversial social science 'clouds' and another eleven involving medical/psychology studies (Fitzgerald, 2005: 319, table 1). Occasionally, ethics committees and staff publicly solicit on various LISTSERVs more horror stories where social science research has gone bad without proper ethics review. Last year, there was a call by members of an ethics LISTSERV for 'war stories' (Fieldnotes: 1105), but none were offered or came to light. It is the 'controversy machine' that drives the ethics-review process, according to Donald Chalmers and Philip Pettit (1998), which then redefines the relationship between ethics committees and researchers. Interestingly, the harms of some social research escape the purview of ethics committees. It was Irene Glasser (1988) who raised the harmful impact of the term 'culture of poverty' coined by Oscar Lewis from his research (1966) on poor populations in Mexico, Puerto Rico, and New York. Policymakers, researchers, and even the general public now use this term to frame their understanding of the lives of poor people. One could say that the term has led them to blame the poor for their own intractable situation.

The Scholarship on the Metabolism of Research-Ethics Review[13]

Few researchers, even those critical of the current research-ethics review process, have spoken about the transformations occurring in the social sciences as a result of this process, let alone their homogenization and pauperization. Rachel Hurdley (2010) is one of the very few who has systematically looked at these changes in terms of her own research plans on 'the corridors of power.'

The scholarship on the metabolism of research-ethics review nurtures the perception that the worlds of ethics committees and researchers constitute two different realms. As noted earlier, the world of ethics committees hides behind a shroud of mystery that hovers over their proceedings. Ongoing scholarship reinforces, rather than erodes, the distinctions between these two realms. Staff and members of ethics committees are not likely to commit to publishing critical, scholarly, or analytical accounts of their work, thus maintaining the opaqueness of their world. Still, scholarship, from the perspective of researchers and policymakers, is growing, but it is sometimes not located in easily accessible venues. No month goes by without another article on the topic. Charlotte Baarts (2009) recently added her voice in a piece that examines the political context of research-ethics review. Lisa Wynn of Macquarie University, Australia, is conducting an online survey of the experience of ethnographers with research-ethics oversight.[14] But the voices of ethics administrators are notably missing. Even among scholars who have busied themselves with exploring various aspects of the work of ethics committees, there is the widely held belief that there is virtually no research available on the topic. The Illinois College of Law (ICL, 2006: 17) recently declared: 'In fact, examination reveals that virtually no scientific evidence is brought to bear on any aspect of the debate about how IRBs function.' Similarly Dixon-Woods et al. (2007: 2) proclaim that ethics committees are 'surprisingly neglected by sociologists as an object of study. Much of the commentary has come from health researchers, traditionally in the form of complaints about bureaucracy, delay, and stifling of research.'

My personal, ongoing bibliography's annotation of the interactions between ethics committees and researchers, from the earliest days of such research to the end of 2008, has 462 entries. These works pertain to many fields: sociology, anthropology, political science, oral history, management, education, ESL, quality-assurance studies, geography, English, psychology, journalism, law, and organizational research. The entries include a swathe of articles and books dealing with polemics (usually negative), analytical observations about research ethics, policy-oriented pieces, some empirical works, a number of experiential narratives, and conceptual pieces and commentaries. The batch also includes non-analytical works that unquestionably accept research-ethics review as a given. Slightly more than half of the entries speak to the negative impact of ethics committees on research. My bibliography also includes twenty-six empirical studies. Interestingly, twelve of these studies found that ethics review interfered with research. A special niche are the twenty-eight entries that relate the personal experiences of researchers with ethics committees, either as the major thrust of the article or as a minor component of a larger discussion about their research project. At least twenty-one of these personal experiences offer a deleterious description of the researchers' interactions with ethics committees.

There is a rise of special issues of journals devoted to ethics review and the relevant scholarly society that publishes the journals. For example, the *Canadian Social Work Review* (2006) carried a 'Forum on Ethics.' The editor of the *Journal of Applied Communication Research* (2005) asked communications scholars to contribute to a special issue on ethics review to classify their narratives as positive or negative, or as advice or resistance, but they could also address multiple categories. Based on these classifications, there were 17 positive, 36 negative, 19 advice, and 9 resistance narratives. The majority of the narratives were not favourably disposed towards their experience with ethics review and even some of the positively inclined narratives did not exclude negative aspects to their experience (Dougherty and Kramer, 2005). Management research also has a number of articles on REBs and researchers, amounting to at least eight such studies (Bell and Bryman, 2007: 75–7).

It is fair to say that the vast majority of other published works speak negatively about the ethics-review experience. Complaints have come from academic bodies, such as the American Association of University Professors (AAUP, 2001), the Canadian Sociology and Anthropology Association (Pool, 1998), and the American Sociological Association (Levine, 2001). Judith Taylor and Matthew Patterson (2010) conducted interviews with sociologists from twenty-one PhD-granting programs in Canada and found that for many an ethics review 'marks the end of an era of unfettered (and superior) intellectual pursuit in sociology.'

While academic bodies articulate their complaints with the intent of hopefully modifying ethics regimes, others are unreservedly polemical (e.g., Shea, 2000). A cursory glance at the medical literature reveals that complaints come as easily from medical researchers as they do from social researchers, emphasizing that the review process is too slow (NCA, 2005: 222). Only a few voices offer an alternative interpretation of the ethics-review process. Adam Hedgecoe of the United Kingdom (Hedgecoe, 2008: 874) is one of those voices who claims that sociological discussions on the topic

> have tended to misrepresent what RECs do and how they treat qualitative research, and as a result have distorted understandings about how REC review impacts on the research relationship. Most importantly, they have over-emphasized the difference between sociologists and other, mainly biomedical, researchers in an attempt to distance sociological research from the need for ethics review.

Hedgecoe's observations bring to us the need to explore the main criticisms of researchers towards ethics review, while at the same time bringing in the voices of those most closely affiliated with review, namely chairs of ethics committees, their staff, and administrators. Chapter 2 intends to do just that.

Throughout *The Seduction of Ethics* I will make links to specific concepts and theories that can shed light on our findings – after all, one must work on the inductive premise that theory must fit data, not the other way around. At this moment, however, it is sufficient to give a bird's-eye view of the conceptual scheme upon which I draw.

Conceptual Scheme

Long before I came across Michel Foucault's term *seduction into simulation*, I had thought that the ethics-review process was a matter of seduction, pulling the ethics bureaucracy *and* the researchers into its arms. The process of submitting to adjudication about the ethicality of a research project and rendering an ethics judgment about a project – *believing that the process replicates decisions about genuine ethics* – is a simulation. It is not about authentic ethics. 'Lack of visibility, as Foucault (1980b) would suggest, enhances the effectiveness of power' (Hamilton, 2002: 200). Hamilton offers a very useful tool in understanding the position of ethics committees vis-à-vis researchers:

> As Foucault (1980b) ... point[s] out, the power/knowledge nexus has lived consequences that can be seen in social processes, institutional practices, and personal experiences, the roots of which can be traced to historical constructs that are ultimately deployed daily in our collective and individual lives ... Employing Foucault's position that discourse *constitutes* organizations, and the value he and others place on ordinary texts, i.e., the written products of ordinary, local, day-to-day existence of regular people doing regular things, the data for this study, as described, is predominately these forms of texts. In this manner, one would find Foucauldian analyses and resistance readings of various documents produced within the system, including government reports, local application forms, and documents designed to provide guidance to compliance. (Hamilton, 2002: 42)

Another tool that benefits our analysis originates in the works of Erving Goffman. Letters from ethics committees to researchers, for example, are front stage; they 'display' due process, care, thoroughness, thoughtfulness of the REC, and stylized language. These letters (or other communications) can 'also serve,' following Dixon-Woods et al. (2007: 7), 'to deflect challenges about the pains taken by the committee, and to give a single, consistent, apparently rational account of the considerations of the committee.' Goffman (1961) calls these a form of 'institutional display.' Even though, according to Dixon-Woods and his co-authors, 'many letters' are 'poorly punctuated, or rude, ... they couch their discourse in a manner that is a display of their authority' (Dixon-Woods et al., 2007: 7–8).

The position of researchers, however, has to be understood from both a Foucauldian and a Goffmanian perspective. First, the discourse of ethics committees entails normalization, whereby the researcher 'becomes an object of control, coercion, examination, judgment, and intervention' (Foucault, 2003: 254). Normalization can be characterized as a mode of observation, ordering, intervention, hierarchy, exclusion, and control that simultaneously homogenizes and individualizes its target populations by taking charge of individual behaviour through forms of subtle authority (see also Foucault, 1984). Second, Goffman's *Asylum* (1961) sheds light on the interactional dynamics between REBs and researchers. We can speak of the underlife of an institution when all the members adumbrated by the attention of REBs 'severally and collectively sustain' secondary adjustments (199). In the case of REBS, secondary adjustment refers to any habitual arrangement by which a researcher employs 'unauthorized' means to get around the REBs' assumptions as to what the researcher should do. While some researchers embrace the social entity of REBs too warmly and wholeheartedly (also known as primary adjustment), some do not embrace it enough.

The Seduction of Ethics points to the many strategies researchers use to handle the demands of REBs, from total avoidance to full compliance, and all intermediate points of adjustment. Rather than seeing secondary adjustments as norm-violating behaviour, we can see these adjustments as a normal and fair response to a social context that drives researchers to re-evaluate the ethical dimensions of their own research.

Thus, both ethics committees and researchers constitute an 'organization' in the sense that Berger and Luckmann (1966) intend it to mean, namely, that reality is constituted by the participants, i.e., meaning in the world of participants is a reality that leads to Foucault's (1972) position that discourse constitutes organization. 'This would suggest,' according to Hamilton (2002: 237), 'that researchers have more power to deconstruct the IRB process, in the literal sense, than they may presume they have. The process is constituted . . . through discourse (and certainly the IRB system relies on written texts). Therefore, regulators cannot "really" accomplish the process without the researchers' cooperation; that is, researchers have to play along (and research participants, too) in order to make the regulation process work.' Goffman's invention of the concept of primary frameworks (1974: 21–39) is very useful in this regard. The application of such a framework, according to Goffman,

> is seen by those who apply it as not depending on or harking back to some prior or 'original' interpretation; indeed a primary framework is one that is seen rendering what would otherwise be a meaningless aspect of the scene into something that is meaningful. (21)

The process of research-ethics review is precisely a primary framework that can be transformed or altered, and analysed the way experience is organized for individuals because the ethics-review system can be seen 'as a system of entities, postulates, and rules' (Goffman, 1974: 21), and it 'allows its user to locate, perceive, identify, and label a seemingly infinite number of concrete occurrences defined in its terms' (21). Frames may be created through discourse, and are at least mostly invisible to the participants themselves in the day-to-day life-world, even if they were not always so; that is, frames are learned. So when they were first being learned, they were more visible, perhaps.

Research Methods

The Seduction of Ethics is not a strictly qualitative-research study. While it does rely on qualitative research as its core, the book also invokes historical and international-comparative data, as well as other techniques of gathering data. I refer the reader to appendix A for a detailed overview of the methods I used in this research. As mentioned earlier, I employed participant observation involving my attendance at five research-ethics committees in Canada and at conferences and symposia on ethics in research. Over the five-year period of research, I attended twelve such conferences. I formally interviewed thirty-one people – researchers, chairs of REBs, other members of REBs, staff members in the ethics or research offices, and senior-level administrators.

Textual analyses took several paths. First, I compared the texts of both earlier and current policies at one university, noting tone and emendations. Second, I took advantage of my three-year stint as the Sociology Book Review Editor of the *Canadian Review of Sociology and Anthropology* (now *Canadian Review of Sociology*) to examine the 200 books that crossed my desk in terms of references to research-ethics review boards and correlations with the chosen methods of research.

Outline of *The Seduction of Ethics*

The Seduction of Ethics is an ethnography that spells out the social and cultural milieu of research-ethics review and describes the conditions and particularities of its rise in the research world (chapters 1 to 3). Chapter 4 provides a benchmark of the kinds of social research that were not unconventional before the rise of research-ethics review. The next five chapters (5 to 9) constitute an ethnographic portrait of ethics committees in universities; i.e., their structure and composition, their cosmologies (in other words their perspectives and beliefs), their procedural routines, their decision-making at meetings, and their communications to researchers reflecting their idiosyncratic and inconsistent world.

Chapters 10 and 11 are about the researchers themselves and their perceptions, relationships, and activities vis-à-vis ethics committees. Chapters 12 and 13 reflect the subtitle of the book, namely, the transformation of the social sciences through the research-ethics review process, whereby some methods are waning, while others are increasingly being favoured through this process. Chapter 14 links all of the elements of the research-ethics review process to larger structures, a system of 'vertical ethics' that in many respects works like a franchise system, albeit quite imperfectly. Conceiving the thrust of this chapter in another way, I see ethics in a political framework. The final chapter (15) summarizes both the homogenization of research methods and the pauperization of the social sciences brought about by research-ethics review.

While *The Seduction of Ethics* takes a critical stance of the research-ethics review process, it should be borne in mind that it *cannot* advocate the discontinuance of policies on ethics in research. Ethics policies are here to stay. The point is that the current framing and implementation of these policies are, on the whole, inappropriate for the social sciences. When such policies become appropriate, they will be an essential guide for social researchers as they traverse the tundra of research, guiding them through the dwarf shrubs, sedges, mosses, lichens, and marshes that biomedical researchers can normally ignore. Some of the best social research takes on a nomadic form, not a careful movement from hypothesis to hypothesis.

2   An Archeology of Research-Ethics Review

Conventional wisdom places the beginnings of the research-ethics review at the Nuremberg Trials of 1946–7, born out of the use of Nazi medical experiments based on involuntary consent of their 'participants,' physical and mental suffering, and expectation of death through the experiments.[1] The Nuremberg narrative offers us a continuing linear history of the development of ethics review primarily through the establishment of the World Medical Association's Declaration of Helsinki in 1964 (and subsequent emendations). The review of social science research would be next in line to follow the same 'high' ethical procedures as the medical sciences. *The Belmont Report* of 1979 (National Commission for the Protection of Human Subjects of Biomedical and Behavioral Research) is thus considered to be the first document to integrate ethical principles common to all the sciences, including the social sciences. *The Belmont Report*, as the story goes, became the basis of Institutional Review Boards in the United States. They became the first university-wide bodies to preview all research, including social research, for ethical vetting. Historical raconteurs, as can be expected, streamline the historical narrative. It is a narrative, some argue (e.g., Dingwall, 2008) that misshapes or distorts the meaning of events.

The intent of this chapter is not to offer a detailed revisionist account of how the current practice of research-ethics review came to pass. While cognizant of plausible alternative explanations, the chapter has two interrelated purposes; namely, to explain the rise of research-ethics review in the larger cultural and social contexts, with a brief nod to alternative accounts, and to offer a glimpse of national developments, notably in Canada, the United States, the United Kingdom, and Australia. I have chosen these countries because much of my data are derived from the North American experience and, to a lesser extent, from these other countries. Moreover, as the principal anglophone countries push-ing forward on ethics review, they are watchful of each other's develop-ments and progress.

Robert Dingwall describes the history of research-ethics review as a 'creation myth' (Dingwall, 2008). Drawing on Hazelgrove's 2002 histor-ical work, Dingwall argues that the ethical principles that accompanied the Nuremberg Trials were not an accepted ethical practice. They had to be 'hastily invented by the US prosecutors, in collaboration with the American Medical Association, in order to sustain the charges against the Nazi doctors' (Dingwall, 2008: 2). After the Second World War and before 1960, medical researchers worked in an ethical vacuum and the Nuremberg Code was marginalized until Henry Beecher and others revealed questionable ethical practices in 1966. Efforts to de-marginalize the Nuremberg Code relate to efforts to legitimize

> the interests served by the institutionalisation of ethical regulation. It points to the breakdown of the established professional mechanisms of peer control with the massive expansion of biomedical research after World War II and sees regulation as one of the ways in which traditional elites tried to retain their power and influence. It considers the so-called 'rights revolution' of the 1960s, especially in the US, where the establi-shed social order faced a crisis of legitimation in the face of demands from historically underrepresented or excluded groups like women, people with disabilities, or members of minority ethnic communities. Patients and experimental subjects were located among these oppressed classes and ethical regulation was seen as a strategy for legitimising biomedical science in the face of these demands. (Dingwall, 2008: 2)

But when did ethics guidelines for social research enter the picture? At first, many professional societies had ethical guidelines that were not enforceable (Truman, 2003: 3). Nor were researchers regularly rep-rimanded, except by extreme social pressure. However, in due course, a variety of cultural and social factors prevailed to make formal ethics review an inevitable outcome of those factors.

Outside the Ethics Regime: What Drives the System of Ethics Review?

There are four broad cultural and social factors around the world, but particularly in the anglophone world, that stimulated the develop-ment of the research-ethics review system. These factors remain, even though the peculiarities of specific historical circumstances, political demands, and policy issues differ from country to country. The larger factors include the societal trend to (1) see human beings as vulnerable, in need of protection and privacy; (2) see science as a dubious enterprise occasionally marked by scandals and disasters (from which the public needs protection); (3) allegedly experience fear and insecurity, needing the imposition of legislated codes of research practice, in other words, a moral panic; and (4) have the need for accountability and societal discipline to be achieved through surveillance, or a panopticon. I now turn to each of these cultural and social elements.

Seeing Human Beings as Vulnerable, in Need of Protection

The contemporary life of the individual is surrounded by ironies that give power and strength but also take them away in a greater measure than they were given. Technologies provide an abundance of opportunities for communication and power, but they also offer the means for others to nestle the individual in a web of dependence. Corporate entrepreneurialism puts out a wealth of consumer goods whose range and diversity would astonish the denizens of half a century ago, but still this entrepreneurialism jockeys for vertical integration and monopolies that can stifle even the most ardent advocate of free choice. The democratic political machinery is premised on the casting of one's vote every few years, but is undermined by its undoing wrought by lobbyists and by vested interests. There is increased privacy, yet loss of privacy. Catherine Scott re-animates Mary Douglas' argument that

> the shift over the course of the twentieth century from a society characterised primarily by a hierarchical 'cultural project' to a competitive individualist one has left individuals increasingly anxious about their own positions, and seriously undermined trust. This explains the apparent paradox that a putatively more individualistic society should also be characterised by increasing rather than diminishing regulation. (Scott, 2004: 2)

This cultural crisis, according to Stuart Derbyshire (2006: 45), 'sees subjects as fragile and science as a dubious enterprise [that] is much more likely to look upon previously standard scientific procedures as unethical.' Dramatic examples of research in the past, such as Kotarba's 1979 study of intimacy in public jail visiting and the 1995 study by Rim on online pornography (Thomas, 2002: 2) nurture the perspective that human research subjects are fragile. Similarly, examples of disasters in medical research at various universities, such as Johns Hopkins (Thomas, 2002: 3, 4), especially in the late 1990s, made U.S. officials look more carefully at research on campus, creating a national panic at universities (Katz, 2007: 799). Even though, according to John Mueller (2007: 812), most of the abuses of research in the past were conducted by government and involved medical research, they provided sufficient 'scare tactics' to warrant whole scale research-ethics review.

Seeing Science as a Dubious Enterprise

Derbyshire, along with many other observers, notes that there is an 'increasingly strong view of science as a malign force in the world and a belief that no risk, however small, should be accepted in the pursuit of further knowledge' (Derbyshire, 2006: 44). Scott had already, a few years earlier, argued that '[a]ttacks on teachers and scholars tapped into a deep vein of anti-intellectualism long existent in the culture' (Scott, 2004: 11). Popular images of mad scientists who were 'the people who brought you Hiroshima' fuelled anti-intellectualism. 'Academic researchers,' Scott continues, are 'holders of arcane knowledge and wielders of power and authority . . . [and] thus . . . under suspicion of harbouring dangerous and self serving motives' (Scott, 2004: 105). The oversight process, according to Power who wrote the influential *The Audit Explosion* (1994: 3), 'concerns a qualitative shift: the spread of a distinct mentality of administrative control, a pervasive logic which has a life over and above specific practices. One crucial aspect of this is that many more individuals and organisations are coming to think of themselves as subjects of audit.'

It is no easy task to either catalogue or characterize ethical mishaps in the social sciences. The telling of these mishaps occurs in a universe of discourse. For example, the three-decade-old debate by anthropologists to 'remap their cultural and intellectual terrain' (Robin, 2004: 4) challenged the validity of anthropology to deliver 'scientific truth,' led many to question older anthropological work and to use that work to reconfigure a new ethics for a new anthropology. One notes, among others, Derek Freeman's challenge (1983) and debunking of Margaret Mead's classic work on Samoan culture (1928), which Freeman believed was based more on Mead's own distortions of a few austere facts. In the aftermath, there were numerous critics of Freeman and defenders of Mead (Robin, 2004: 124). Another realm of discourse involves the complicity of government to use anthropologists to serve nefarious government intentions, whether it was under the cover of the Society for the Investigation of Human Ecology in the late 1950s to research the lives of Hungarian refugees (Israel and Hay, 2006: 4) or, currently (in 2010) the U.S. Army's Human Terrain System Proof of Concept Program that combines scholarly research and military information-gathering in Iraq and Afghanistan (Institutional Review Blog, 25 December 2009). It is ironic that those working in this military project are not censured because they are deemed to be working outside the IRB system.

An earlier social research project known as Operation Camelot was clandestinely undertaken by sociologists on behalf of the CIA in Chile in the 1960s. It stands out as a case of a government trying to 'predict and influence politically significant aspects of social change' in Latin America (Homan, 1991: 27–8), leading to widespread condemnation in sociology (Horowitz, 1967), but no penalties were exacted.

A further realm of discourse about ethical mishaps in social research is largely confined to informal discussions and sometimes visceral reactions in academic conferences. In this connection, the work of Laud Humphreys on homosexual behaviour surfaces as a prime example. Alvin Gouldner's reaction to the perceived ethical breaching embodied in Humphreys' *Tearoom Trade* was to deliver a punch to Humphreys' nose, although others thought that Humphreys had publicly mocked Gouldner.[2] These discussions and reactions, however, do invade the next realm, namely, the world of research-ethics review and constitute the bulk of warnings about how social research can experience ethical mishaps.

Cultivated by a Moral Panic[3]

There has been an explosion of interest in 'ethics.' In Canada alone, in 1999, there were 5,000 ethics conferences, as opposed to 100 in 1994 (Curtis, 1999: D1). Similarly, there has been a staggering rise in the number of ethicists, ethics companies, and ethics policies in business, administration, sports, and science. According to Jenefer Curtis, it is the decline of religion and the rise of 'intense individualism' that have created a moral vacuum that 'ethics' is now trying to fill. In the process, however, the word 'ethics' has become 'perverted' (Curtis, 1999: D1). Citing Tom Hurka of the Department of Philosophy at the University of Calgary, she points out that because there is not much public trust, institutions put in place a code – cut and dried rules – instead of training people to have good judgment (cited by Curtis, 1999: D4).

Under such circumstances, one wonders whether the parallel rise of research-ethics review might not be a case of a *moral panic*. Coined by Stanley Cohen (1972), a 'moral panic is a societal response to beliefs about a threat from moral deviants' (Victor, 1998: 542) that exaggerates their threats. A moral panic is indicated by hostility and sudden eruption of measured concern that is shared by a significant segment of the population, with disproportional claims about the potential harm moral deviants are able to cause (Goode and Ben-Yahuda, 1994). Within the context of *The Seduction of Ethics*, moral panic occurs throughout the research-ethics review that so heavily relies on the deductive model of research as normative, proclaiming the rest as non-normative. Moral panics involve exaggeration of harm and risk, orchestration of the panic by elites or powerful special-interest groups, the construction of imaginary deviants, and reliance on diagnostic instruments. According to Scott (2004), the twentieth century

> saw a profound change to the model of persons and the relationships between them commonly accepted in the West ... The abandonment of traditional value systems and codes of behaviour that accompanied this change have been major sources of the fear and risk aversion that have 'gripped' Western cultures. One response to this fear and insecurity has been the imposition of legislated codes of practice designed to protect us from each other.

Needing a Panopticon as a Form of Accountability

In uncertain spaces, too, agents are seeking new forms of surveillance of both researchers and what they do (Cheek, 2007: 1053). By picking on a politically weak group (academics), security, media, and corporate interests can 'range unchecked' (Dingwall, 2008: 6). The process is, according to Malcolm M. Feeley (2007: 765), 'spawning an immense bureaucratic apparatus that is poised to consider the remotest risk. In an increasingly risk-averse environment,' he further states, 'IRBs employing an instrumentalist cost-benefit analysis regularly withhold approval or require significant research modifications in order to pre-empt speculative harms.' According to Lesley Conn, '[A]udits as tools of governance are essentially political technologies in the Foucauldian sense, deceptively concealing the economy of power that is at work through them' (Conn, 2008: 502).

What is more, the effect of the ethics-review panopticon means that the space occupied by qualitative research has become 'uncertain, fragmented, and precarious' (Cheek, 2007: 1057). Qualitative research provides a systematic approach to research that diverges radically from the biomedical approach. It relies on induction and making sense of data by relying on emergent research designs. Rather than trying to fit data analysis into a preconceived theoretical framework or using data to (dis) prove hypotheses, qualitative research is best done when theoretical ideas fit into the data.[4] Moreover, the purpose of qualitative research is to find ways to portray the perspective of research participants. The qualitative researcher aims at depth and richness of portraying that world.

Through ethics review, however, medical research is now able to contest and colonize that space (see, e.g., Cheek, 2007: 1057). We have already noted in the previous chapter that medical researchers are entering narrative studies and, according to researchers in the fine arts, are beginning to define the ethical parameters of fine arts, as the research-ethics regime is being rewritten with a heavy dollop of biomedical representation. Qualitative research is succumbing to the heightened value placed on interdisciplinary research: the unique facets of qualitative research (and indeed of other research techniques like doing interviews, participant observation) are being levelled by those who are not trained in these areas, but are willing to adopt, nay adapt, them to other qualitative research.

Inside the System: Institutionalization of Research-Ethics Review[5]

Research-ethics review is in a dynamic state of development, like a steadily larger-growing lake gradually being filled by many rivers. While many incumbents in universities take this development for granted, its unintended consequences flow in all directions. Christine Halse and Anne Honey (2007: 338) are close to the mark when they claim that the

> discourse of ethical research evolved imperceptibly over time. Through a thousand minute accretions, it gathered intensity and coagulated with other discourses until it became so ingrained in the fabric of institutional life that it seems almost impossible to untangle it or think of its not being, even if we might desire otherwise.

Extending beyond the template of paper or electronic forms, one finds disciplinary struggles, certified ethicists, ethics conferences, training workshops, professional literature, scholarly journals, research programs, local networks, and national and international associations focused on research ethics (see Halse and Honey, 2007: 340).

It is beyond the scope of this ethnography to render a full description of these accretions, from the origins of research-ethics review to the present, although these developments do touch on particular parts of the ethnography. I trust that it is sufficient to give a general overview of how some of the national research-ethics regimes became established before moving on, in the remainder of *The Seduction of Ethics*, to render an ethnographic analysis of relations between ethics-review committees and researchers.

The current ethics regime came as a surprise to social researchers. Traditionally, in North America, academic social research was not well funded. In 1952, for example, 96 per cent of federally funded research in the social sciences was for the United States military, but only 10 per cent of all social research was publicly funded. According to Mueller (2007: 814), 90 per cent of social science was not funded at all. The idea that an ethics review system was necessary to make social research accountable is a misrepresentation 'of the history of social science research [which] seem[s] ideologically motivated, and serve[s] only to create a fictional need for IRB controls' (Mueller, 2007: 814). For example, even now, despite the high pressure to secure external research grants, 80 per cent of the research at the University of Chicago and reviewed by the university's social science IRB 'are personally funded, privately funded, or unfunded' (Shweder, 2006; see also Mueller, 2007: 814n19).

When the latent effects of medical experiments of the 1950s and 1960s became manifest – often twenty or thirty years later – and with the subsequent rise of lawsuits, the public and government became acutely aware of the ethical implications of medical research and, indeed, of all research. First, through professional societies, and then more vigorously through the state, ethical guidelines became explicit.

Bolstered by legal enforcement, formal ethics review assumed legitimacy that has spread across North America to other settings, such as, indeed, to the Third World where researchers are more likely to abandon traditional moral principles in favour of the ethics codes in which they were trained in Western society (Charbonneau, 1984: 21). Similarly, social research on Canada's North must undergo a process of ethics review that seems more appropriate for the hard sciences than the social sciences. For the stated purpose of protecting Inuit culture from researchers, the northern granting bodies rely on a Western model of ethics review, reinforcing the very research approach that is being rejected. The setting up of such non-Western review bodies[6] echoes the Western, deductive template. Structurally, these policies have produced a dislocation of the social-science research, and the qualitative-research enterprise in particular.

Canada[7]

During the early years of this evolution of ethical normalizing, the Canada Council (in 1978 it became the Social Sciences and Humanities Research Council of Canada) constituted the Group of Ethics in 1976, a set of policies that Canada's three granting agencies eventually implemented as a policy on scientific integrity in 1978. Although we can point to some of the general cultural and social forces that paved the way for these early policies (that include what was going on in the United States in mid-1970s), there were two specific events in Canada that pushed this need.

Until the mid-1990s, universities did their own screening and monitoring of research ethics, but something more definite than guidelines was needed (Rolleston, 2008). First, the so-called Fabrikant affair[8] in 1992 at Concordia University and, second, the opening phase of research on reproductive technologies and genetic research in 1987 (that were not adequately covered) led to the development of the ethics regime familiar to us now. These events led to the Tri-Council Working Group (1996)[9] on Guidelines for Research with Human Subjects and the statement on 'Integrity in Research and Scholarship' on 16 November 1994. Only seven social scientists were part of the 137 scholars and others who submitted suggestions for emendations. The Group involved the Medical Research Council of Canada (MRC) (now called the Canadian Institutes of Health Research), the Natural Science and Engineering Council of Canada, and the Social Sciences and Humanities Research Council of Canada which began the process of drafting in 1998 the *Tri-Council Policy Statement on Ethics Involving Human Subjects* (the *TCPS*). The MRC had decided to expand its range of activities beyond biomedical research. In 2001, this document became part of the 'Memorandum of Understanding' signed by all of Canada's over seventy universities and university colleges, obligating them to follow the recipe of the *TCPS* in guaranteeing that all research pass ethical muster in order for universities to continue receiving grants for research involving humans.[10] From the first instance, the *TCPS* harboured problems from the perspective of social-science researchers.[11]

When the three funding agencies created the Interagency Advisory Panel on Research Ethics (PRE) in 2001, changing the *TCPS* was uppermost in the minds of its founding members. Soon, PRE established standing and ad-hoc committees to further these changes. One of the working groups was the Social Sciences and Humanities Working Committee on Ethics that, since its establishment in early 2003, produced six relevant reports outlining the gaps and discrepancies of the *TCPS* with regard to social-science and humanities research (SSHWC, 2004, 2007, 2008a, 2008b, 2008c, 2008d). The work of this and other committees allowed PRE to redraft the *TCPS*, preparing it for public consultations in 2009. It is significant to note that the draft of the 'new *TCPS*' now (in 2010) includes a chapter on qualitative and ethnographic research.

The first public meeting at the Canadian Congress of the Humanities and Social Sciences in 2002 at the University of Toronto was sponsored by the Interagency Advisory Panel on Research Ethics – the newly created trustee of the *TCPS*. It was a standing-room only meeting with social and humanities researchers, reflecting the intensely adverse reaction to the new policy, involving approximately 150 researchers. However, as each year progressed, these gatherings have become smaller so that at the 2005 Congress held at the University of Waterloo, only thirteen attended; towards the end of that meeting three remained in the room, besides the presenters (Fieldnotes: 201). Emotions were becalmed. Or were they? *The Seduction of Ethics* documents the ways researchers have devised ways to adapt their research to the requirements of the *TCPS*. The central argument of *The Seduction of Ethics* is that these adaptations not only involve modifying research strategies, but also the personal initiatives of researchers that resist the new ethics regime. In the end, the social sciences have become impoverished because a number of these adaptations follow the biomedical model of research. The ethics-review committees, too, have changed their mandate to adumbrate these changes, whether in research, in-course research projects, in-classroom research, or even evaluation research.

The United States

Numerous are the studies in the United States that have publicly prompted the need for ethics review. What prompted this need in particular was Henry Beecher's 1966 revelation of twenty-two cases of unethical experimental research (Gunsalus, 2003b: 1).[12] David R. Rothman's book, *Strangers at the Bedside* (1991) provides a further analysis of these studies, many of which involve human experimentation. The most disturbing, according to Rothman, was the Tuskegee research by the U.S. Public Health Service from the mid-1930s to the early 1970s. The research involved the study of secondary syphilis in a group of Black men whose was withheld because the researchers wanted to examine the long-term effect of syphilis (Rothman, 1991: 182).[13] Along the same lines, researchers at the Willowbrook State School for the Retarded infected its residents with hepatitis. This study was part of a long list of experiments that violated every possible tenet of human decency. Zachary Schrag (2009a: 21) points out that 1965 represents the first step in regulating research, when a New Jersey congressman had a personal crusade vis-à-vis 'a number of invasion-of-privacy matters.'

Stanley Milgram's experiment (1963) on obedience, which involved the administration of fake shocks to a 'subject' (who was an accomplice in the experiment) by an unwary participant, intensified the debate about ethics in research (see, for example, Baumrind, 1964).

In 1974, the National Health Act set forth requirements for establishing Institutional Review Boards that led to the creation of the National Commission for the Protection of Human Subjects of Biomedical and Behavioral Research (Hamilton, 2005: 109) even though there were warnings from within the Department of Health, Education, and Welfare that the regulations might be inappropriate for the social sciences (Schrag, 2009a). In this context, authorities conceived of the new idea of 'expedited review' in 1978 to mitigate the rules against social sciences (Schrag, 2009a). In 1979, the authors of *The Belmont Report* (named after the hotel where the policy conference was held) emphasized respect for persons (especially those with diminished 'autonomy'), the obligation not only to avoid harm but also to maximize benefits, and for research to be just (i.e., people receiving benefits should bear the burden of research). With the publication of the 1979 draft regulations, the most vocal opponent was Ithiel de Sola Pool, a political scientist who claimed that the regulations constituted an attack on free speech and the concept of the university (Schrag, 2009a). The sentiments around that attack still reverberate in the United States scholarly community, especially among philosophers and professors of law.

The United States ethics regime entered a new phase. Between 1980 and 1983, a presidential commission was charged with the task of pushing these ideas into a code on ethics for researchers, during which time, the Department of Health and Human Services gave final approval in 1981 to what would become codified as 'Federal Policy for the Protection of Human Subjects,' or DHHS 45 CFR 46

(Hamilton, 2005: 103–4) (known as the 'Common Rule'). At the outset, the Department of Health, Education, and Welfare did consider the unique aspects of social research, but was not mindful in consistently promoting those aspects (Schrag, 2009a). Hence, social research would fall under the purview of the 'Common Rule,' originally designed to watch over medical-research ethics. By the late 1980s, education research was no longer exempt, mostly due to the rise of qualitative and ethnographic research. Annette Hemmings was one of the few observers who noted that these developments 'caused ethnographic and qualitative education researchers to reconsider their ethical frameworks' (Hemmings, 2006: 13).

By 1991, seventeen federal agencies (twenty in 2005) had adopted the 'Common Rule' and the Federal Policy for the Protection of Human Subjects (Hamilton, 2005: 109). It has become the operational document for all IRBs (Hamilton, 2005: 197). This arrangement tied federal research funding to the ethics approval of all university research involving human subjects. There are currently 3,000–5,000 IRBs in operation (Hamilton, 2005: 116).[14]

However, all is not well on the research-ethics front. In 2006, the National Conference on Alternative IRB Models (Hauck, 2008: 1) advocated the waiving of signed release and fewer restrictions in, for example, online research (NCA, 2005: 224). Moreover, according to some, both the rise of a 'vast "licensing authority"' as well as the regulatory expansion to include non-funded research threatened scholars (Feeley, 2007: 764). As Gunsalus argues, there is a huge distance that has grown between the 'original regulatory meaning of "minimal risk" [as in *The Belmont Report*] and its present applications' (Gunsalus, 2003a: 3). 'For almost three decades following the creation of the IRB system,' argues Richard Shweder, 'almost all academic institutions voluntarily renounced their legal right to apply the federal regulations only to federally funded research projects' with the brave exception of Harvard, Yale, Princeton, University of California at Berkeley, and the University of Michigan (Shweder, 2006: 6). There are indeed no legal requirements that would stretch the IRB process 'beyond federally funded projects' (Shweder, 2006: 8).

Canada vs. the United States: Differences

The development of research-ethics review is quite different in the United States than it is in Canada, owing primarily to political and legal circumstances. In Canada, the instigations towards ethics review came mainly from the activities of the MRC that wanted to extend its research into other areas, such as genetic research. In the United States, medical experiments that had placed the lives of research subjects in danger stimulated ethics review (Stark, 2007: 780; Thomas, 2002: 3). There are other, no less important differences.

To explain the dynamic nature of change in research-ethics review, one must first contextualize it in terms of the broader political contexts of both countries. Both the United States and Canada are liberal democracies, emphasizing individualism, the right to privacy, and the importance of free and informed consent, among others (McDonald and Meslin, 2003: 77). Despite such an important similarity, their national political and policy contexts differ greatly.

First, the United States' national ethics codes (National Commission for the Protection of Human Subjects, 1979) constitute a regulatory system, as opposed to a system of guidance in Canada (McDonald and Meslin, 2003). In the former, a legal system shrouds its research-ethics oversight regulations; whereas in Canada, the *TCPS* clearly advocates itself as a policy document, rather than a legal entity.[15]

Second, the Canadian experience of formulating national research-ethics standards is much younger than the United States' standards, which assumed a greater degree of control than is the case in Canada. As John Johnson and David Altheide explain:

> The animus for the IRBs, after all, was the federal government, in 1971, specifically the Department of Health, Education, and Welfare. Their published 'guidelines' for research became binding for research funded by the federal agencies . . . IRB control over research ethics is now so firmly established, for example, that our recent search of the NEXIS information base shows that topics related to social science ethics are rarely mentioned apart from IRBs. The IRBs, then, essentially own, operate, and control the discourse on social science and research ethics. Indeed, what we now think of as 'ethics' has been modified and transformed by its associations with institutional control. University-based researchers and scholars no longer plausibly claim independence from their state patrons and sponsors. (Johnson and Altheide 2002: 61)

Third, the Canadian research-ethics experience is made more complex by virtue of the difficulties arising from federal–provincial relations (McDonald and Meslin, 2003: 77). Caught in this web of relations is research funding in Canada that flows principally from federal and provincial coffers. These diffuse sources create many more legislative stakeholders than is the case in the United States, leading to the reliance on consultation to exercise changes in the *TCPS* and other ethics guidelines. The existence of two distinct legal traditions in Canada, that is, civil law and common law (McDonald and Meslin, 2003: 77), perpetuates this complexity.

Fourth, another context that sets Canada apart from the United States' research-ethics regulatory system is its specific parliamentary democracy that allows control of debate and issues at the ministerial level. According to McDonald and Meslin (2003: 77), it is relatively easier to 'bury contentious issues and manage information flows in a way that would be regarded as exceptionally secretive in the U.S.' As a consequence, there is a higher benchmark needed in Canada to justify action and change; such (political) justification, if it is to have staying power, comes in the form of widespread public consultation and engagement. Along these lines, too, one can argue that contentious research-ethics issues are less likely to emerge than in the United States where public and political figures are more likely to engage in 'serious, often acrimonious debate at all levels of national government' (McDonald and Meslin, 2003: 70).

Fifth, there are several other features that distinguish the Canadian framework from its American counterpart. There are subtle organizational differences. While REBs in Canada do seem to exercise autonomous authority over the research-ethics review process, there is considerable reliance on the Secretariat on Research Ethics to provide interpretation to the community of researchers, research administrators, and REBs. When new interpretations are sought (there are about twenty-five each year), the Secretariat turns to the Interagency Advisory Panel of Research Ethics to consider the wording and intent of such interpretations. The Panel consists of members who come from diverse backgrounds. In the United States, there is no such federal mechanism; researchers must turn to their own IRBs for interpretations that vary greatly among universities. This is where the difference between regulatory and guideline approaches (McDonald and Meslin, 2003: 79) seems large. IRBs in the United States exercise virtually exclusive control over the process as local, regulatory bodies acting on behalf of federal agencies. REBs in Canada seem to defer more naturally to the federal agencies for advice and insight, like co-trustees of the ethics guidelines. Federal–provincial guidelines also heighten the difference as compared to the United States.

A sixth distinction relates to the kind of discourse and audience each set of national ethics codes must consider. In Canada, public consultation is a pre-eminent feature of any contemplated change to the guidelines, making it harder for special-interest groups to assert themselves. The American experience suggests that the process of bringing about change in the national ethics codes is more contingent upon individual professional and scholarly groups' assertions as to why and what changes are necessary. Recent events surrounding efforts to exempt oral-history research from research-ethics review in the United States, involving huge disparities in the interpretations, are a case in point.

The Americanization of the Canadian research-ethics regime is something that even American scholars are concerned about. For example, Hauck (2008: 2) worries about what will happen if 'the flawed American system is diffused' in Canada. The process of diffusion seems to be going forward despite the significant differences in character between the Canadian and United States systems. For one, much medical research in Canada is contingent upon proportionally more lucrative research grants emanating from the United States. As a consequence, Canadian medical researchers are agitating to have Canadian ethics committees certified by the American Office of Human Research Protections (OHRP). The National Cancer Institute of Canada, the Children's Oncology Group, and the Radiation Treatment Oncology Group, all located in Canadian centres, follow the OHRP regulations and require REBs to be compliant. Since most REBs have decided to be consistent across all clinical trials, they consistently apply these regulations.[16] The annual FOCUS – Forum for Research Ethics Boards (REBs)/Institutional Review Boards (IRBs) in Canada and the United States – meetings bring together American and Canadian ethics administrators.[17] The Society of Research Administrators (SRA) International Annual Meetings always provide a common ground for administrators, including in the area of research-ethics review (and the invitations also go out to the Canadian Association of Research Ethics Boards). The 2006 annual meeting in Quebec City, for example, saw only the distribution of United States ethics-review materials by the United States Office of Research Integrity (Morier, 2006). FOCUS alternates its meetings between the two countries, but its themes are thus driven by issues that interest Americans more than Canadians.[18]

However, there are other processes at work that are silently undermining the Canadian spirit of research-ethics review. For example, a Canadian researcher who attended an information session of the

Interagency Advisory Panel on Research Ethics at the 2002 Qualitative Analysis Conference in Hamilton (Ontario) later conveyed his worry to the panellists that Canada would not follow the American example by issuing ethics certificates instead of concentrating on education, which would be the Canadian spirit of 'doing ethics' (Fieldnotes: 700). A member of a private Canadian REB expressed his deep concern that Canada's ethics regime is increasingly being accountable to American ethics agencies, whereas they should be accountable to the Canadian public. He was referring in particular to a 'determination letter' a Canadian REB in Vancouver had received from the United States OHRP (R107, Fieldnotes: 1140).

Canadian LISTSERVs regularly rely on United States practices, seeing if they can be applied to the Canadian system. The United States National Human Research Protections Advisory Committee often spearheads ethics issues (for example, in April 2002) that only later influence Canadian Research Ethics Boards in broadening the ethics wings, whether with respect to research experiences in the classrooms and courses, public use of data sets, or student research (Fieldnotes: 357).

An REB chair at a mid-sized university said that such American influences have something to do with the *Zeitgeist*, such as accountability and avoidance of litigation, creating 'an intellectual paranoia that overrides common-sense' (C13-M, Fieldnotes: 50), a belief that is shared by a veteran researcher (Interview R045-B, Fieldnotes: 147). The same chair mentioned that at a major Canadian national ethics meeting in 2005, the medical sciences not only dominated the proceedings, but that the meeting also fervently welcomed the comments by the representatives by the United States Office of Human Research Protections speaking in favour of standardization and harmonization of the ethics codes. It is also clear that there is a dividing line among REBs in Canada: some are eager to share horror stories from south of the border (such as human pesticide dosing approved by the Environmental Protection Agency for research purposes) (C14-M, Fieldnotes: 1151), while others do not relate to those stories.

The United Kingdom[19]

As there are differences between Canada and the United States, so, too, the origins of the United Kingdom's ethics regime varies in some essential aspects. The initial impetus came in the late 1960s from the Royal College of Physicians to set up Regional Ethics Committees

(RECs). By 1972, over 70 per cent of hospitals had set up ethics committees (Hedgecoe, 2009: 332). However, it was the National Health Services that eventually took the lead in setting up RECs in the United Kingdom. Interestingly, as Hedgecoe frames it, '[t]he origins of ethical peer review lie not in the knee-jerk reaction to policymakers and bureaucrats to some research scandal, but in the realms of professional social control' (Hedgecoe, 2009: 333). Maurice Pappworth's writings (1962, 1967) drew attention to a number of ethical breaches, but it was a letter from the United States Surgeon General that prompted the establishment of RECs: the situation was that a form of ethical commitment had to be made if funding were to be forthcoming from the United States. It was not until 1975, however, that a Medical Research Council document first mentioned humanities and social research (Dingwall, 2008: 4). It took another sixteen years, in 1991, for the Department of Health to issue the ruling that no NHS body should support research without the approval of a local ethics committee (Derbyshire, 2006: 35; Dingwall, 2008: 4). In 2000, the Central Office for Research Ethics Committees was established to 'maintain an overview of the operation of the research ethics system in England' (Derbyshire, 2006: 35).

The publication of the *Research Governance Framework for Health and Social Care* by the Department of Health, first in 2001 and followed by a second edition in 2005 (Bell and Bryman, 2007: 65), institutionalized 'ethical decision making to a greater extent than has formerly been the case.' In 2006, the Economic and Social Research Council announced a new 'Research Ethics Framework' for social science research, which offered greater flexibility, but universities did not take advantage of this flexibility and are therefore maintaining a system like that in the United States (Dingwall, 2008: 4). The ethics structure will now be more onerous (Bell and Bryman, 2007: 65).

Today, COREC (the Central Office for Research Ethics Committees) coordinates REC activities. COREC is an organization whose aims are to develop and implement operating procedures and standards for RECs that are consistent across the United Kingdom. Governance arrangements for RECs define the remit and accountability of RECs, and give guidance on membership and the process of ethical review. Standard operating procedures were introduced in 2004, mainly to meet the obligations of the EU Directive. Under the Central Office for Research Ethics Committees, 'RECs are obliged to register each application they consider onto COREC's Research Ethics Database (RED)' (Dixon-Woods et al., 2007: 2). However, it appears that university RECs are far less bureaucratic and more flexible than those operating in the NHS system (Richardson and McMullan, 2007: 1126).

Most recently, the Economic and Social Research Council decided to see how an ethical framework can be developed for social science. According to Israel and Hay (2006), the new framework also demands that research be done honestly and be of high quality.

Australia

As in the three countries mentioned above, Australia's ethics codes were written in the early 1990s in the context of medical research under the aegis of the National Health and Medical Research Council (NHMRC) (Israel, 2005; see also Fieldnotes: 657–9). Without consultation or negotiation, Australia extended these codes to include social research, despite considerable complaints from the social scientists. Social scientists were again not consulted when NHMRC produced, in 1999, a new national statement, the *National Statement on Ethical Conduct in Research Involving Humans*, to cover all research (Halse and Honey, 2007: 340). Soon, the NHMRC insisted that all universities establish local Human Research Ethics Committees (HRECs) to oversee research.

As Mark Israel (2005) comments, the HRECs have taken an 'increasingly interventionist stance,' akin to 'ethics creep.' Their chief weakness was the 'uncritical application of principles, informed consent, harms and benefits, and relationships' between the researcher and research participants. Remedy seemed to be on the way when the Australian Health Ethics Committee invited, in 2004, the Australian Research Council and the Australian Vice-Chancellors Committee to create a working party to review and revise the national statement. Following Canada's example, the principles behind the group include transparency, community engagement, and consultation. In 2004, the working party produced a report based on the experiences of Australian criminologists that also reflected the concerns of social scientists. This document drew heavily on the findings in other countries about the shortcomings of ethics committees vis-à-vis social research. In 2007, Australia published its 'National Statement on Ethical Conduct in Human Research' (Commonwealth of Australia, 2007).

More than using only one method of research (such as focus groups) ethnographic research on any topic requires a wider cognition of all the elements that might feed into the ethnographic moment. In the case of my study of ethics committees–researchers relations, it is apparent, from chapter 1, that the research-ethics system is beset by its own contradictions. These contradictions do not appear to diminish the system's impact on researchers. We also note that there is a profound absence of systematic research on research-ethics committees themselves and that such research presents methodological challenges. What is clear, however, is that under the research-ethics regimes, the social sciences are being transformed, and even pauperized, by the force of homogeneity of methods sought by ethics committees ... and researchers themselves.

Chapter 3 shifts to another background canvas that is relevant for our study. That canvas consists of several strands. Some claim that ethics codes offer an inappropriate model for social science research, while others say that research ethics is strangling legitimate social research. We also find in that background canvas the belief that ethics review curtails academic freedom and that ethics committees have become bureaucracies, thereby exercising a hegemonic influence of the ethics-review system. Ethics committees have developed an idealized version of their work that results in particular claims making, namely, that they ought to be trusted to be guardians of ethics in research.

The present chapter explored some of the forces from which the research-ethics review system has sprung. These forces entail the larger cultural and social forces and trends that see human beings as vulnerable and in need of protection and privacy. These forces see science as a dubious enterprise occasionally marked by scandals and disasters (from which the public needs protection), and allegedly experience fear and insecurity, needing the imposition of legislated codes of research practice, in other words, a moral panic. These forces also have the need for accountability and societal discipline to be achieved through surveillance, or a panopticon. It is only within such larger cultural and social forces, filled with a thousand minute accretions, that we can understand the origins and thrust of national ethics regimes. In Canada, the United States, the United Kingdom, and Australia, the forces that impelled those societies to establish research-ethics regimes were worries about biomedical research whose theatre of operation now extends to social research. Some remedies are on hand, but are they too late to remedy the homogenization and pauperization of social science research?

3 The Criticisms of Research-Ethics Review

The previous chapter on the archaeology of research-ethics regimes hinted at the problematic aspects of those regimes as they pertain to the social sciences. Those problematic aspects are not specious.[1] Chapter 3 outlines the thrust of these criticisms and the way the research-ethics world attempts to transcend them. It is my intention to demonstrate that the criticisms that result from those problems are based on the perception, or fear, of researchers that the ethics-review process harbours inevitablechanges in the way social scientists conduct their research. These changes primarily touch the fundamental methods (rather than the ethical dimensions per se) employed by social researchers that, in turn, will bring in their wake a significant transformation of the social sciences themselves.

The cacophony of complaints by researchers centres around five issues. Given the diversity of researchers and the local contexts of ethics committees, each issue has a different intensity from the other ones depending on who has the problem. Each issue is not only a flashpoint but also provides the vital contexts that define the interactions between ethics committees and researchers. The context of these criticisms would be incomplete without including the perspectives of people associated with ethics committees. As mentioned in chapter 1, however, there are virtually no published materials conveying the perspectives of committees. Thus, this chapter relies extensively on interview materials, chats, public presentations, emails, and LISTSERV threads to bring these perspectives to the fore. It also delves deeply into what scholars have thought about these issues, often conveying their own or someone else's experiences. I ought to mention that Adam Hedgecoe (2008), Ivor A. Pritchard (2002), Kristine L. Fitch (2005), and Kate Connolly and Adela Reid (2007) have assiduously studied many of these criticisms and issues and have found a variety of helpful ways that social researchers and ethics committees can address them.

The next five sections convey the perspectives of eight REB chairs, five staffers, two administrators, and four members of ethics committees in three small universities, six medium-sized universities, and two large universities.

Does the Ethics Regime Offer an Inappropriate Model for Social Science Research?

From the earliest days of national research-ethics regimes, social researchers have been vocal about the prevalence of the biomedical paradigm vested in the creation of those regimes. The regimes follow the 'sovereignty of traditional [scientific] paradigm' (Silva, 2008: 325; see also Tilley and Gormley, 2007: 369; Kellner, 2002; Tolich and Fitzgerald, 2006; SSHWC, 2004; AAUP, 2001). Social researchers commonly accept the perception that IRBs 'inappropriately view social science research through perceptual lenses and policies shaped by experimental biomedical research' (NCA, 2005: 219).[2] Susan Boser (2007: 1060) avers that 'the framework typically used by an IRB for monitoring research ethics is predicated on post-positivist epistemological assumptions of a distanced objectivist research stance.'

Although ethics committees are sometimes confused by claims that this paradigm is inappropriate for social research, researchers themselves entertain no doubts about its irrelevance and the problems it creates for social research:

- nonsensical when applied to social research (Hamilton, 2005: 173)
- ill-fitting and irrelevant (Hamilton, 2002: 187)
- trained incompetence [of committee members] (Bosk and De Vries, 2004: 10)
- more than bothersome, galling, or benignly unsettling (Halse and Honey, 2007: 342)
- rigid (Richardson and McMullan, 2007: 1127)
- an exercise in creative distortion (Conn, 2008: 503)

The full implications of the biomedical paradigm, according to Koro-Ljungberg et al. (2007: 1076), means that 'IRBs embrace specific interpretations of, first, what science is or should be and, second, what ethical codes or behaviors should lead to acceptable scientific practices.' Ethics committees now directly link methods to what constitutes ethical research (that explains the decline or rising support of some methods) and thus evaluating applications entails assessing both the methodology and the ethical framework. Linda Eyre (2007: 91) suggests that the biomedical model is 'problematic for feminist researchers,' especially in light of the inadequacy of positivist research 'to explain the oppression of women and bring about social change.' The impact extends into whether the position of research participants will improve in addition to 'seriously hamper[ing] social research' (Mäkelä, 2006: 6). Jonathan Church, Linda Shopes, and Margaret A. Blanchard (2002) provide a telling example of how ethics committees had trouble understanding the social research conducted by one of Church's students. He reports that one IRB member held on to the belief that upcoming social researchers are in the same position as a first-year medical student who is performing surgery: 'I [Jonathan Church] confronted the IRB member who had so thoroughly dissuaded the student and told him what types of research were permitted on other campuses. The response: "Jon, would you let a first-year medical student perform surgery?"'

One REB chair took the position that the biomedical model might not work for social researchers. In answering a criminologist, he averred:

> Maybe, just maybe, REBs and investigators together are doing a great job ... If your issue specifically is that models are being carried over from biomedical to social science inappropriately, then you may well be right. (C14-M, Fieldnotes: 1005)

Is Research Ethics Strangling Legitimate Research?

The obstacles researchers face in pursuing research have caught the attention of Sharon Begley of *The Wall Street Journal* (Begley, 2002),who writes that 'IRBs ... are cracking down on social sciences, where the risk to volunteers amounts to hardly more than bruised feelings ... Surely we can protect people in medical trials without strangling legitimate social-science research.' But the 'cracking down' American scholars endure is also a familiar experience for clinical researchers in the United Kingdom, where the number of applications to RECs fell in 2003–2004 by around 40 per cent and where researchers are reporting problems that ethics review may be impeding, delaying, and sometimes distorting research (Richardson and McMullan, 2007: 1119). Student research is also undergoing a 'chilling effect' (Church, Shopes, and Blanchard, 2002). Ann Hamilton's empirical study offers this perspective:

> The system as it presents itself at the [Ohio University] IRB appears often-times to stifle rather than facilitate the pursuit of knowledge (academic inquiry, at least), but the hegemonic (positivistic) discourse also promotes 'thinking-in-a-box-ism' in a place where that kind of non-thinking should be discouraged, rather than prescribed. (Hamilton, 2002: 234)

David Calvey (2008: 908), who wrote about his experiences with an ethics committee, has found that the regulatory forces of committees, 'can deter, fetter and discourage creative covert research. What these ethics codes articulate is ultimately a species of both protectionism and privileging.'

Some staff and members of ethics committees agree with these assessments, while others strongly disagree. A researcher 'always had misgivings about ethics review' and that was the reason why he wanted to become chair of the REB so that he could mitigate, to some extent, the challenges for researchers (Chat C28-M, Fieldnotes: 145).

Still others thought that preventing legitimate research would not be an issue. As one staff member puts it, 'The perception is that REBs are difficult, but REB members are researchers' (Interview A12-B). A presenter, an ethics administrator at one of Canada's three federal research agencies, announced at the 2005 annual conference of the Canadian Association of Research Ethics Boards that 'researchers should never say that ethics is a barrier' (Presentation, E4, 6 June 2005, Fieldnotes: 163). A chair of an REB (who is a researcher himself) shared on a LISTSERV that he 'frequently finds [himself] saying to the REB, "Our job is not to stop people doing research, but to help them do it better" ... [and] REBs and researchers have to come out of their trenches and listen to each other and decide ... how their mutual goals can be achieved' (C14-M, Fieldnotes: 402, 1005, and 1238). A chair of another REB (C09-B, Fieldnotes: 401) concurs:

> We should be doing everything we can to educate everyone ... on what good research looks like ... I think that changing the culture to be one of helpfulness rather than fear/gatekeeping ...

The director of an ethics office at a medium-sized university admits that there are situations 'where REBs have gone overboard or been overly restrictive . . . [I]t is possible that the very uncertainty or fluidity of some SS&H [social science and humanities] methodologies introduces an element of concern which prompts a more conservative approach by REB's [sic] and hence the friction that arises' (S30-M, Fieldnotes: 960). A reviewer of an early draft of *The Seduction of Ethics* felt compelled to draw attention to

> the ultimate irony, as far as I'm concerned: universities are not required to submit their own research for ethics approval as long as it is described as administrative. Hence, real amateurs can be sending out meaningless questionnaires to students while I (and we can assume I know what I'm doing) must subject myself to ethics review.

An ethics officer at one university says that she 'never acts as a gate-keeper,' while encouraging students and faculty to send in applications for commentary before going to the REB so that 'I can alert them to ways they can satisfy the needs of the REB without compromising their research goals' (S13-M, Fieldnotes: 1245). One chair of an REB at a large university took the initiative in promoting ethnographic research by inviting researchers to illuminate the REB members about that form of research (Interview C09-B).

Does Ethics Review Curtail Academic Freedom?

Initially, the notion that an ethics review curtails academic freedom garnered much attention, and it still does in some quarters of the academic community. In the United States, the issue takes form as a constitutional one; in Canada and other anglophone countries, it takes the shape of academic freedom (Sikes, 2008: 248). In any case, many researchers believe that ethics committees violate researchers' rights (Stark, 2007: 777; Dingwall, 2008: 7; Hamburger, 2005 and 2007; Gunsalus, 2003a: 2; Hamilton, 2005: 251; Rasmussen, 2009) and induce censorship (Lindgren, Murashko, and Ford, 2007). In a survey conducted in the spring of 2000 (AAUP, 2001: 246), some researchers 'worried that the regulatory structure could improperly restrain freedom of inquiry and the pursuit of knowledge, and others claimed that it had done so already' (Hamilton, 2002: 241).

Ivor Pritchard (2002: 5), however, takes issue with ideas regarding academic freedom: he argues that (a) the government is not required to provide support for anyone's exercise of the right to do research or speak freely about it, and (b) researchers do not have the right to demand the cooperation of others, or compel people (including students) to air their opinions. 'If investigators want to move into research territory where the participation of research subjects is sought,' says Pritchard, 'they must provide a justification for impinging on the lives of others in their quest for knowledge.' Such elegant arguments do little, however, to dissipate the gut reaction of researchers that research-ethics review touches too close to the bone of academic freedom. Can social researchers mount a legal challenge to Pritchard's arguments?

As several observers have noted, 'the costs and uncertainties of litigation have thus far deterred professional associations in the social sciences and the humanities from pursuing a legal challenge' (Dingwall, 2008: 8; see also Gunsalus, 2003a, 2003b; ICL, 2006; Koro-Ljungberg et al., 2007). According to Rachel Aldred (2008: 899), 'market mechanisms have undermined the traditional supports of academic independence and professionalism.' She also argues that academic freedom is not a unified whole, but is contested among junior and senior scholars. For senior scholars, academic freedom is a – hard-won issue; junior scholars are unable to push academic freedom to the same extent given the place in their career, often being without tenure or unlikely to ever get it. For that reason, academic freedom has become less of an issue than it was in the past.

One side of the academic freedom debate involves the 'deprofessionalization' of academics (Bell and Bryman, 2007: 66) whereby professional societies have lost the autonomy of establishing, maintaining, and controlling the parameters of their discipline, including ethics codes. In this context, the use of the term 'best practices' touted in ethics codes involves a deskilling and a nonintellectual approach to scholarly research that allegedly transcends disciplinary peculiarities (Deborah K. van den Hoonaard, personal communication).

All in all, according to Yvonna S. Lincoln and William G. Tierney (2004), [b]etween Federal imperatives for how research projects should be designed, and IRB scrutiny and disapproval of non-conventional forms of inquiry, academic freedom is undergoing radical challenge. The threats to the academy of the stark politicization of research and its methods will no doubt pose the gravest threat to researchers and academic freedom in the past half-century. (10)

As an officer of a major United States ethics organization commented on a LISTSERV in 2004, it falls on the IRB 'to trust but verify' the researcher's compliance (A12, Fieldnotes: 987). A director of an ethics office found that 'problems with [research] participants do not arise from evil intent, [but] more from inexperience, pressures to get research done. The REB helps researchers look at research through a different lens' (S30-M, Fieldnotes: 959).

REB members and staff also spoke of how they do *not* want researchers to see them; what they fear most is being regarded as an 'intellectual gestapo' who stops research. They also do not want to be seen as 'Big Brother' (Interview E15-S). A member of still another REB prefers to see his REB as 'supportive rather than accusatory,' and what he fears the most is 'being too harsh, [but] also being challenged' (Interview E27-S). The chair at a large university wants to convey the image 'she doesn't have two heads' and that she 'will talk to anyone' (Interview C05-B).

Are Ethics Committees Bureaucracies?

Although not a primary issue for researchers, the alleged evolving bureaucracy of ethics regimes provides additional fodder for criticism that can be used to dismiss the need for ethics review of their research. The intense workload alone (to be described later) necessitates a bureaucracy that is destined to streamline, prioritize, and centralize routines. The system of 'vertical ethics' (see chapter 14) that holds each level of review to a higher assessment level demands careful scrutiny and safeguarding of the paper trail sometimes referred to as the 'blizzard of paperwork,' but the review process might get in the way of its primary mission: the protection of research participants (ICL:, 2006: 4; Dougherty and Kramer, 2005: 184). The blizzard of paperwork falls back on the researcher. A United Kingdom survey reveals that 8 per cent of 130 social scientists believe there was 'unnecessary duplication of information required' and 11 per cent of respondents claim that research-ethics review left too little time to complete their research (Richardson and McMullan, 2007: 1123). Ethics committees are aware of this irony (Lincoln and Tierney, 2004: 228).

Based on these factors alone, it is clear that power inevitably comes to rest in ethics committees and their staff. These 'entanglements of power' (Halse and Honey, 2007: 336) mean that the bureaucracy not only seeks to avoid legal liability (NCA, 2005: 208; Hemmings, 2006: 13), a fact that even members of ethics committees acknowledge is a 'problem' but also are sometimes not inclined to consult with researchers. Ann Hamilton (2002: 101) noted that her IRB chair at University of

Oklahoma, proudly declared that they had revised administrative rules without input from more than a few people. Increasingly, other scholars are noting that 'too much oversight presents its own problems' as a consequence of bureaucracy (Schrag, 2009b: 1).

Ethics committees' call for more material and human resources reflects the evolution of an 'overwhelmingly expansive' bureaucracy (Katz, 2007: 799), although there is a tendency towards centralizing ethics-review functions. Instead of having multiple small ethics committees, universities are eliminating these so that there is only one ethics committee for the whole campus. An example of this can be found at the University of Illinois at Urbana-Champaign, where thirteen IRBs were replaced with one (Fieldnotes: 543). John Mueller (2007), a long-standing critic of the current ethics-review system, reiterates a commonly held position of researchers:

> Confronted with criticisms, IRB advocates often indicate that they could do a better job if they just had more resources. Where do those come from? They have to be reallocated from some other campus enterprise, so that, for example, the English department would lose faculty positions, psychology classes would get even larger, and so forth – all to get more money to keep doing something that we have no evidence is needed or effective? (820)

Mueller and others noted that in response to alleged problems at Virginia Commonwealth University, 'the result was a 450 per cent increase in IRB administrative personnel (2 to 9), a 250 per cent increase in IRB membership (20 to 50), and a 1875 per cent increase in the budget (from US \$40,000 to US \$750,000)' (Mueller, 2007: 820). Mueller (2007) also contends that the call for more resources entails 'jobs, jobs, jobs' and that an accreditation scheme would create more jobs (820–1).

Local bureaucracies, some believe, mirror the ethics regime at the national level. In Canada, there are at least thirty-one bodies embedded in the process;[3] in the United States, in 2002, there were at least four panels, groups, and committees concerned with regulations for the social sciences, including the National Human Research Protection Advisory Committee (which advises the Office of Human Research Protections) (Shopes, 2002: 7) and the OPRR.[4] Part of the problem is the growing tendency for ethics agencies to go beyond their mandate. For example, the OPRR maintained a list of IRBs despite the fact that the organization 'had no legal reason to keep such a list; they have no jurisdiction unless federal funds are involved' (Hamilton, 2002: 197).

Despite the rather narrow definition of research articulated in ethics codes, ethics committees are easily inclined to include new 'research' activities under their purview such as in-classroom student work, quality assessment, autobiographies, ethnographies, pedagogical exercises, and the work of student interns in their temporary places of employ. To be sure, not all ethics committees advance in a homogeneous fashion in all areas. However, as the definitional frontiers expand, so do the use of templates into which researchers, instructors, and students must pour specific research and teaching activities. Interestingly, Ann Hamilton (2002: 220) notes that '[e]ven regulators themselves indicate that if "template fever" runs too high, the template may add symptoms (demonstrating, incidentally, that regulators can admit that even templates have points of diminishing returns) . . . '

A compliance officer frankly admits that 'administrative fumbles, especially major ones, is an incredibly important part of improving the system, but is not adequate justification for eliminating the system altogether' (S16-M, Fieldnotes: 956).

According to an experienced ethics officer at a major Ontario hospital, medical researchers are also frustrated and under tremendous pressure to negotiate 'the research [ethics] labyrinth,' that is 'daunting and time-consuming;' that is, there is no one place to get all information, and many researchers feel they must 'beg' for money from research agencies 'who all want something different.' 'Is it any wonder that they are frustrated and or irritated when they hit the REB phase?' (S08, Fieldnotes: 1202). Another ethics staffer admits that information 'the "form" is seen by researchers as obstructionist, that the REB is asking about the research, and why it takes so long, exclaiming, "just get me through this!"' (Interview S46-S).

Frequently, my interviews with people associated with ethics committees also reveal a profound awareness of how they could be seen by researchers:

– not interested in mono-mania or power trip, or nit-picking (Interview C11-M)
– hates being the ethics police, [would] much rather be a facilitator (Interview C30-M)
– spending too much time on irrelevant details (Interview E15-S)

There might also be practical constraints on ethics committees that determine how many details they can watch or follow in any research. An REB chair said that no one can decide on all the details, such as 'authorship, trust, appropriate credit, legal issues, et cetera, et cetera' (Interview C25-M).

In a focus group with some members of an REB at a small university, one person admits that there is some justification for researchers 'to see us as bureaucratic overkill; most research projects are minimal risk and guidelines [were] designed for more serious stuff' (Focus Group REB1-S). The chair of an REB believes she is 'not suffering from a terminal case of ethics chill' (Interview C05-B), and the same chair says that the 'REB must see itself as research services, no place for control freaks.' Significantly, she draws a comparison with IRBs: in Canada, 'researchers need to take control of REBs, don't give in to bureaucrats (like they do in the United States).' A staff member, however, expresses her disappointment when she sees applications where researchers have 'given no time or thought to ethical issues or to the application; bureaucracy sometimes has a point ... most people are really good about it though' (Interview S47-M). Interestingly, only one interview participant, an administrator at a small university, sees the REB role as not only protecting research subjects but also the university (Interview A11-S).

Does Ethics Review Develop and Maintain the Hegemony of Ethics Committees?

'Hegemony,' in the words of Alvesson and Deetz (1996: 201), 'is a process of infiltrating common sense (after having devalued it in the hegemonic discourse of science, as mentioned) and becoming part of the way we construct reality, the way we view the world, understand ourselves, experience needs, or get certified.' Chairs are fully aware of the power they can exercise over researchers:

> So then people know that we're not ... here trying to criticize, that people are judging them ... I think people are probably prone to see us that way. It's the whole authority thing. *Yes, it scares people.* Yah, well, I have a lot of power. [Interview participant's emphasis] (Interview C03-M)

Some of the harsher critics of ethics committees state that their role is a part of the Western hegemony where surveillance, control, limiting critiques, and debates are *de rigeur* (see, for example, Lewis, 2008: 685). Ann Hamilton (2005: 170) notes the extent to which multiple interests coalesce in the existence of ethics committees: legal, commercial, and political interests. Michael Burawoy's American Sociological

Association's Presidential Address was a call to action for resisting the hegemony of ethics committees. Ethics committees are the public face of universities, especially when research has gone off the rails and falls under public scrutiny. It is the desire to stay out of the public's eye that motivates the hegemony of ethics committees. For them, it is better to err on the side of caution and scrutinize all research applications. The scrutiny involves standardized forms and routine application procedures (which chapter 7 explores in greater detail).

Standardized forms and posted rules create the necessary compliance. 'The simulation' of research ethics, according to Hamilton (2002: 190), 'is comprised of the mundane story of compliance' and 'as such this reification becomes the reality rather than life processes.' As a consequence, researchers experience ethics review as a real, concrete, physical thing, something that is 'obvious,' 'unquestionable,' and 'self-evident.' Hamilton (2002: 240) reminds us of Deetz's statement (1995: 136), 'To the extent that a person uses [a] codified form, he or she implicitly consents to the values and processes by which it was formed. The potential interest-laden value debate is thus suppressed in the face of the neutral and natural.'

Hamilton states that the ethics application process (2002: 186–7), '(even for minimal risk, non-treatment studies) has become "normal," even when many parts of it are considered unreasonable (and even impossible) for some kinds of studies.' Thus, both the regulators and researchers now maintain the hegemony of ethics review. In this light, she continues, 'the rules and procedures are not questioned by many participants, who (hegemonically) accept the idea that rules and regulations in general work to intended effect and/or are unavoidable' (83–4). Other processes flow into these channels of normalization. For example, the National Association of IRB Managers has offered the IRB Management Certification Examination, indicating the development of tools to standardize the thinking, and subsequent certification, of IRB members themselves (see NAIM, 2001; also Southwick and Monastersky, 2001; and Southwick, 2002). The availability of 'dummy' standardized forms has become a more frequent phenomenon, as seen in the case of City University of New York, where prescribed forms are available for applications, namely the 'Information Sheet,' 'Sample Consent Form,' 'Request for Amendments or Modifications for Approved Protocol,' 'Adverse Event Report Form,' 'Subject Information Confidentiality Agreement' for all non-CUNY personnel working on CUNY-related research, 'Unanticipated Adverse Event and Unanticipated Problem

Report Form,' 'Continuing Review Application,' and, at long last, the 'Final Report Form' (http://web.gc.cuny.edu/rup/human subjects. html#Forms).

During a focus group discussion, one of the ethics staff indicated that the source of fear, even 'hostility, suspicion, and resentment' on the part of researchers is the REB's veto power and the fact that this power does not originate in the researcher's discipline (Focus Group REB1-S). An administrator, like many others, believes that 'education' allows researchers to move around the resistance.

For some ethics staff, it is always a question of nurturing or punishing researchers: 'I am trying to be either the patient mother or the punishing mother. However, I stopped being the punishing mother' (Interview S46-S). In this light, ethics staff act as guides through the ethics tundra, either patiently showing the path of rescue or 'punishing' researchers when they stray from the imagined ethics path. If we acknowledge the existence of the two social worlds of researchers and ethics committees, there is an ongoing discussion within each of these worlds on how to approach the other. Two REB chairs at a large university summed up this sentiment: 'researchers have to learn how to approach the REB' (Interview C09-B) – a sentiment shared by researchers but flowing in the opposite direction. The next section outlines some of the initiatives by REBs and researchers to bridge the two worlds and transcend the criticisms.

Attempts to Negotiate the Two Worlds and Transcend the Criticisms: The Perspectives of Ethics Committees

The Seduction of Ethics provides an extended discussion in later chapters about the interactional order between REBs and researchers – the principal theme of the book – but for now, this section presents *idealized* perspectives of REBs on how they can improve such interactions and what will detract from such interactions.

While researchers tend to idealize their descriptions of their relationships to research participants in in-depth interview settings, ethics committees tend to eschew such idealized notions, but point out that such idealizations do constitute a perspective whose goals are worth striving for. The two REB chairs I interviewed together talk about the prevailing climate of mutual respect that governs their relationship with researchers (Interview C10-B). Some staffers attribute the climate of respect to the fact that the REB 'works well because of its wide representation'

(Interview S47-M), a perspective echoed by the chair of that same REB (in a separate interview), saying 'the place of an REB at a small university[5] is more interdisciplinary where every department is represented.' She further avers that 'our job is not to stand in the way of research: the REB visits departments, and departments have representatives on the board . . . anthropologists and [the] REB chair resolve problems by a friendly chat' (Interview C30-M).

The utopian key to such a climate of trust includes the fact that a 'researcher can talk to any REB member and the REB tries to alleviate fears by being open' (Interview C11-M). At a small university, the REB chair nurtures the same principle of communication and 'is eager to communicate with researchers, does not want to be adversarial, wants to be diplomatic when critiquing. At a small college,' she argues, there are 'informal, discussions in the hallway,' although she finds that informal meetings in hallways increase the pressure on REBs which can result in too many expectations on the part of researchers (Interview C12-S). A senior administrator confirms that 'because it's a small university, there's a lot of talking back and forth to clarify the language' (Interview A11-S). In such a setting, 'to get compliance, you need staff sympathetic to researchers whom researchers are free to call upon if a situation arises' (Interview C05-B).

My interviews with chairs, staff, and administrators in seven universities reveal a consistent pattern of how they practically bridge the two worlds. The top priority of the initiatives is having representatives of the REB or the ethics staff holding in-depth discussions with researchers and/or departments, especially to sort out problems with student research (Interview C12-S). A member of the REB at the same (small) university (Interview E15-S) prefers 'meeting regularly with researchers, likes to have them there, at the meeting to discuss their applications.' Other members of the same REB visit department meetings monthly to 'educate them, allowing for informal chats with researchers, but not discussing what's on any [specific] application forms.' Some REBs, however, hesitate to discuss specific problems with the 'bad' proposals, saying that it is 'important for REB members to show others how to do it [fill in an application form], build skills . . . to clarify things before proposal gets submitted' (Interview E25-S). A similar spirit animates an REB at another small university (S6). In light of researchers 'seeing [the REB] as an obstacle, the REB has started talk to researchers and especially new graduate students, on the basis of a difficult decision.' The same REB spoke with the psychology department, to see if the department 'still trusted their services.' The REB also thought it would be 'best not to wait to receive applications, but better to set up a session in advance to discuss these things' (Focus Group REB1-S). One REB holds the belief that 'what accounts for researchers' acceptance of REB role are information sessions for faculty,' and working with researchers 'to come up with ideas about ethics of classroom research' (Interview A11-S). One illustration of the interventionist nature of an REB was described by a researcher (Interview R118-M) who reported that after a student had written his brief document about the ethical dimensions of his research, an REB member had a discussion with him, and this would be reported back to the REB.

The chair of one REB explicitly stated that the two worlds can be bridged by trying to develop policies that are 'not bureaucratic' (Interview C30-M). In this vein, a staff member (Interview S47-M) found that creating departmental committees 'has really helped everything,' including sending out a survey to faculty about wording on an REB form, and holding several workshops a year on variety of topics. At this university, there appears to be a lot of cooperation between the staff members and the REB chair in setting up all of these arrangements.

The REBs at some universities, such as M8, go the extra mile in providing 'collective feedback to the researcher, [while making sure the] REB [does] not sit on applications for six weeks.' Unusually, the REB also had a researcher come in to talk about autobiographical research and it commissioned a background paper as well (Interview E12-M). We also know that a political science professor came to the REB to explain about research on political figures (Interview E13-M) – a significant step, given the contemporary resistance by political scientists to ethics review. The issue of whether or not political scientists need ethics approval to research 'public figures' (which technically falls outside of needing such review according to the *TCPS*) lies at the base of this resistance by political scientists. At the same university, the REB chair goes to professors' offices and 'figure[s] out any thorny issues, triaging in public administration, which gets applications in very good shape' (Interview C11-M). An REB at a large university invited researchers to become part of the decision-making process after having sent a letter of apology to researchers and students for having overlooked certain essential things, in the hopes that the researchers will do all that is necessary to make their research 'pass' the next time around (Interview C10-B).

We must realize that the above observations made by REBs (and the one that is to follow in the next section, 'Interactions that distract from cooperation') as to what they see as beneficial in bridging the gap between the two worlds is a perspective that comes from REBs alone. We would expect that some researchers might share some of those perspectives, but as later data will show, researchers have an entirely different conception of what might work, including one that promotes the eradication of the review process itself.

Even within the limited perspectives of the REBs, one must acknowledge that their suggestions and insights do have a practical, even very practical, use when operating within the research-ethics review system.

Two of the four REBs who offered their perspectives on these distractions offered some practical approaches. One said that the REB cannot delay an REB meeting for a month when a researcher submits an application (Interview C07-S); another offered a suggestion (that I can personally relate to) that the REB should not ask questions about participant observation in public settings (Interview E15-S). Of the two remaining REBs, one made the point that looking at the methodology of an application was not something that researchers want: 'some researchers say, "stay out of that crap – just tell us what's ethical, don't go into methods"' (Interview C11-M). The other REB does not recall ever meeting with researchers (Interview E25-S). I hope to show that 'truth' in ethics, as promulgated by the world of ethics committees, is something, according to Michel Foucault, that can 'be understood as a system of ordered procedures for the production, regulation, distribution, circulation and operation of statements' (Foucault 1980a: 133). While Foucault demonstrated his 'games of truth' around the politics of knowledge and the researcher's identity, it is not a far stretch to think that the same 'game' is played out within the research-ethics review system, backed up by formal ethics codes, a bureaucracy, salaried staff, deeply involved volunteers, and a mandate to approve or reject research applications. With each new application, ethics committees and their representatives assemble and reassemble 'truth' in ethics. In a sense, it is an 'ensemble of procedures' that produce 'truth' (see Gauthier, 1988: 15, cited by Peters, 2004). In some cases, the assemblers (i.e., ethics committees) of games of truth need not even have to offer an explanation of how they have arrived at that truth. The REB at a large prairie university told a student straight out that she could not study plants as used in the Aboriginal community. Although the student asked for a reason, no reason was given, and she was not allowed to present her case (Interview R007-M).

At the local level (as well as the national), participants in research-ethics review processes, 'strategically' enter 'into such games' and play them to best advantage,' and, following Peters, 'various institutional contexts (research associations, conferences, journals, training regimes) thus constitute "games of truth"' (Peters, 2004: 57). *The Seduction of Ethics* will have many opportunities to demonstrate how these 'games of truth' are explicated within the context of research-ethics regimes.

The cursory look at the data presented so far has already made it apparent that the size of the university plays a significant role in the extent to which the two worlds can be bridged. The setting in small universities provides a pervasive sense of community that allows the walls of the two worlds to become porous. One wonders whether the 'games of truth' played out in such settings are something that are shared by both the world of ethics committees and the researchers. Not infrequently, the researchers I have interviewed in smaller universities recall their ethics-review experiences in larger universities where they obtained their PhDs. One member of an ethics committee who is still active as a researcher (E12-M) describes the differences between large and smaller universities: at the large university, REB members see their work as a burden, a bureaucracy where 'no replies' are common. The large university makes a point of owning the intellectual property rights of its researchers, while the smaller university does not. At the smaller university, the REB is very approachable, 'wonderful with researchers, without the power trip, and ... never had an angry researcher come to an REB meeting. Collegial, not bureaucratic.' One is almost inclined to argue that new researchers are better off in smaller universities where 'games of truth' are more widely shared and encouraged.

Before entering into a discussion about the ethnographic data in *The Seduction of Ethics,* the next chapter presents, in general, the social scientists' take on ethical principles. More specifically, it also presents three case studies of social research as examples of classic representations of such research to demonstrate that this conventionally ethical research would have a hard time fitting in with contemporary ethics codes.

4 What Is the Normative Ethics Framework for Social Researchers?

I have thus far taken into account elements of the research-ethics review process that fall outside social research *itself*. It is clear that researchers and members of the ethics-review system hold the view that the ethics regime offers an inappropriate model for social science research, that the regime can sometimes appear to strangle legitimate research, that ethics review might curtail academic freedom, that ethics committees have become bureaucracies, and that the hegemonic influence of the ethics-review system advocates the normalization of ethics (but from the perspective of that system).

What is vitally missing from the discussion so far are the normative conceptions about the kinds of research to which social researchers adhere. What is needed is an inside perspective as to what constitutes good, ethical social research. This chapter's two tasks consider the social science conception of the human 'subject' and 'data,' and present three conventional social research models that speak to the well-worn predicates of research in the ethics pantheon, such as consent, autonomy, confidentiality, vulnerability, to name a few. The decision to choose these three model studies rests on the premise that they include conventional social research ('The World of the Congenitally Deaf-Blind' by David Goode [1979]), research lacking confidentiality and anonymity (*Sidewalk* by Mitchell Duneier [1999]), and covert research (*Making Gray Gold: Narratives of Nursing Home Care* by Tim Diamond [1992]). The scholarly world holds these studies in very high regard. The aim in outlining these studies is to demonstrate the ethicality of these researches, despite their variance from normative ethics as promoted by the research-ethics regime. In other words, what is the normative ethics framework from the perspective of this research?

And what can we learn from this research that would help all of us to improve the research we do under the current ethics regime? I urge the reader to consider these works independent of my own judgment.

The 'Subject' in International and National Research-Ethics Codes[1]

Protecting 'subjects' is the claimed central purpose in all international and national research-ethics codes. The World Health Organization, in its *Operational Guidelines for Ethics Committees that Review Biomedical Research* (2000), clearly states that '[c]ompliance with these guidelines helps to ensure that the dignity, rights, safety, and well-being of research participants are promoted and that the results of the investigations are credible.' It furthermore claims that a 'cardinal principle of research involving human participants is "respect for the dignity of persons."' Canada's *Tri-Council Policy Statement on Ethical Conduct for Research Involving Humans* highlights the collaborative nature between researchers and human subjects which, 'entails an active involvement by research subjects, and ensures both that their interests are central to the project or study, and that they will not be treated simply as objects' (Medical Research Council, Natural Sciences and Engineering Research Council, and the Social Sciences and Humanities Research Council, 1998: i.7; hereafter MRC et al.). *The Ethical Guidelines for Social Science Research in Health* of India (Indian National Committee for Ethics in Social Science Research in Health, 2000) elucidates four principles underlying research ethics. One of them is the principle of non-malfeasance: 'Research must not cause harm to the participants in particular and to people in general.' There are, of course, such principles in other codes throughout the world.

Concern about experiments on humans[2] have penetrated national research-ethics codes and have subsequently shaped ethics codes that also govern social research, not just biomedical research. The protest of social researchers against the application of such codes to their research has been well documented, although rarely taken heed of (for example, W. van den Hoonaard, 2002). Structurally, these policies have produced, and continue to produce a dislocation of the research enterprise in the social sciences.

Currently standing at the cusp of governments' internationalizing research-ethics codes, we can already discern a number of features that stand to leave a mark on the future of research in the world. First, as alluded to above (and in chapter 3), the formal research-ethics codes are so extensively based on biomedical research that they have disenfranchised many other forms of research, or at least made it more problematic for those who wish to pass ethics review. At the same time, these disenfranchised researchers have become restive.

Florence Kellner (2002: 27) avers that the implementation of these ethics codes 'may bring ethics pertaining to natural science even closer to us than it had been' before the new policy came into effect. The 'gold standard' for ethics review might, in fact, be tainted because of its blind eye to the reality of other forms of research, such as inductive and qualitative research. The Canadian *Tri-Council Policy Statement on the Ethical Conduct for Research Involving Humans* (*TCPS*) contains 476 paragraphs, of which only four are devoted to 'natural observation' research, with three of those paragraphs stated as cautionary notes. Moreover, the word 'subject' is favoured in this and other codes over 'research participant,' a term that finds more resonance among qualitative researchers because the term 'subject' has a pejorative connotation for these qualitative researchers.[3] For while it is true that one occupies the position of 'researcher,' there is a far greater sense of collaboration with interviewees than is customary in, for example, survey research. The latter part of this chapter gives three illustrations of how this works out in social-research field settings.

National research-ethics codes extend to judging the adequacy of the research design itself. They speak of the importance of maintaining a 'common standard' of research and scrutinizing applications on the basis of various levels of harm that might be inflicted on research subjects. These codes speak of research 'protocols,' a term that makes eminent sense to biomedical researchers, but is quite unfamiliar among social researchers who use a more emergent-research design.

While hypothesis testing is familiar to biomedical and other researchers, the idea of emergent research paradigms is wholly absent from national research ethics codes. Such ethical areas as publication, which are crucial to social researchers, are entirely ignored. While biomedical researchers are more likely to receive anonymized data,[4] social researchers remain familiar with the identity of those whom they have interviewed or observed. As a consequence, ideas about anonymity, confidentiality, and privacy take on a different colour for social scientists.

As for the dilemma of defining the human 'subject,' I would like to present a number of models of 'subject.' Indeed, one might raise the question, What is a 'subject'? It is a question that significantly defines the kind of research one is pursuing. Figure 4.1 provides one idea as to what research 'subjects' can look like.

Some would argue that the crash-test dummy does not represent a 'living human subject,' in the words of a number of ethics codes and, therefore, any research on crash-test dummies would not require ethics review. The dummies are, in fact, inorganic objects in every sense of the word. But are they? Countless are the number of lives affected by the selection of particular crash-test dummies, including death if the 'wrong' ones have been tested. The 'pregnant' crash-test dummy in figure 4.1 acknowledges its reality as a proxy human. There are no known places in the world where research on proxy humans would have to go through ethics review.

The use of archival papers, as represented by the second item on the left in figure 4.1 (as a 'static form of dust'), is another example of a research subject, albeit not used as such in any North American setting. However, enough about archival papers has been said to allow them as human 'subjects' for research purposes as is the case in France.[5] Who is to say that the living descendants of those collections are not affected by archival searches? Ironically, historical papers may shape the future and may invoke research-ethics review as 'static forms of dust.'

The most commonly accepted view of the 'human subject' is the perception that it is an organic entity. Little needs to be said about this orientation as common as it is. A heightened sense of individualism is one consequence of this view of the 'human subject.' The relevance of autonomy and independence of the *individual* research participant is salient from this perspective, and it is this perspective that dominates the discourse on ethics in research.

The next frame, the research participant as a social being, points to the social nature of the human being. It was George Herbert Mead (1964) who linked the 'discovery of society,' with the child's discovery of the self. There is, therefore, very little that is 'personal data' in the individual. The term 'personal data,' from the perspective of sociologists, functions more as a heuristic and functional device than one based on social reality. From the perspective of sociologists, much is assumed under this social nature, ranging from body postures and mental outlooks, to social interaction in, for example, a card game (including people's receptivity to being photographed by a sociologist). Even illnesses and sickness fall into a moral hierarchy, entirely constructed by society, shaping their treatment or research (Charmaz, 1999). The sufferings of children on account of an illness beyond their control are accorded a

Figure 4.1. 'What is the human subject?'

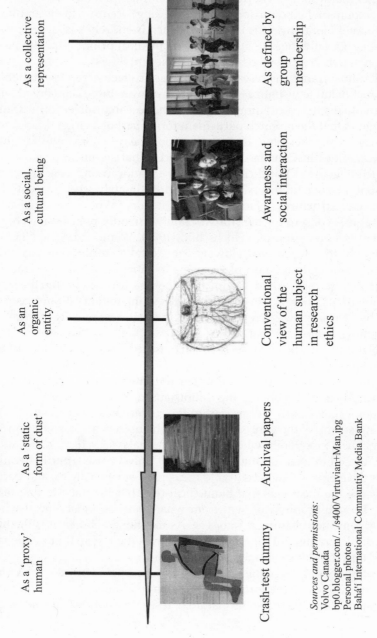

As a 'proxy' human

As a 'static form of dust'

As an organic entity

As a social, cultural being

As a collective representation

Crash-test dummy

Archival papers

Conventional view of the human subject in research ethics

Awareness and social interaction

As defined by group membership

Sources and permissions:
Volvo Canada
bp0.blogger.com/.../s400/Virtuvian+Man.jpg
Personal photos
Bahá'í International Community Media Bank

higher moral status, whereas adults who bring upon themselves illness on account of their own doings (e.g., smoking) occupy a lower status on the moral hierarchy. This hierarchy, which is entirely socially derived, shapes not only the self, but also the biomedical priorities proffered to the research, treatment, or cure of the relevant illness.

The final frame, the research subject as a 'collective representation' is more difficult to visualize for those of us who are more acquainted with individualism as a running concept of the research subject. This frame suggests that the research participant forms part of a larger whole, and perceives him/herself in that manner, too. The case of many Aboriginal communities in Canada comes to mind. What significance must one attach to getting ethical clearance from a leader to undertake research among his/her followers? Who should, ultimately, give consent? Do corporate structures fall into the same category? Who, in the final analysis, gives consent for the study of family-friendly policies at a corporation (see, for example, Hochschild, 1997). Would it be the CEO on behalf of the employees? However, the 'total institution' (a sociological concept to designate a place where its inhabitants (inmates, mental patients, etc.) are provided with all of their basic needs within the institution) does not fall into this frame. These inhabitants do not, as part of their world view, surrender their individuality to the larger whole. If anything, some fight that view.

Naturally, the boundaries between these differing conceptions of the human subject are blurry. For example, is a patient's medical record an archival artifact or does it fall under the category of 'organic entity'? Does research involving the Munchausen-by-proxy syndrome fall under 'organic entity,' or as part of the subject as a 'social being'? The point is simple: the concept that research subjects are organic entities might be a moot point when it comes to social research.

We need to focus on the concept of the 'subject' itself, partly because it is the element that is central to the core of ethics policies, and partly because the meanings that biomedical researchers attach to that term can be significantly different from what social scientists mean when they come across human 'subjects.' As mentioned earlier, it is the biomedical paradigm of the 'subject' that drives the research-ethics debate and that confounds social researchers.

International and national ethics codes resonate with the following as core values of the human 'subject': individuality, autonomy, independence, and the 'personal' nature of research information. *The Ethical*

Guidelines for Social Science Research in Health (2000) of India highlights this individuality:

> Research involving participation of individual(s) must not only respect, but also protect the autonomy, the rights and the dignity of participants. The participation of individual(s) must be voluntary and based on informed consent. (Section II, iv)

Autonomy and independence are concepts that align themselves well with the idea of individuality. The most recent Australian draft document contains only two mentions of autonomy, including this one:

> It centrally involves recognising that each human being has a value in himself or herself, and that this value must govern all interaction between humans. Such respect includes recognising the value of human autonomy—the capacity to determine one's own life and make one's own decisions. (Australia, 2006: 13)

Canada's *TCPS* mentions 'autonomy,' 'autonomous,' or 'independence' (as related to research subjects) at least four times (MRC et al., 1998). The Council for International Organizations of Medical Sciences refers five times to the concept of autonomy in its revised/updated *International Ethical Guidelines for Biomedical Research Involving Human Subjects* (2002). Even more numerous references to 'autonomy' can be found in *The Belmont Report* (1979) of the United States which lists at least nine such references. For example:

> Respect for persons incorporates at least two ethical convictions: first, that individuals should be treated as autonomous agents, and second, that persons with diminished autonomy are entitled to protection. (National Commission for the Protection of Human Subjects of Biomedical and Behavioral Research, 1979: B.1)

It is an important philosophical premise to see individual human beings as primarily 'autonomous' entities. Such a premise conjures the view of a human being without relation to others. Such an extreme reduction of humans ignores the relevance and importance of wider social relations in which every decision and every consideration by a single person carries the baggage of previous experience, culture, and history. Human subjects, of course, do have numerous instances of individuality and specific attributes, such as age, height, reactions to pain and pleasure, responses to treatment and clinical trials, but even then, there is so much invested in culture and society that it is impossible to claim that a human subject is autonomous, let alone the social circumstances in which trials are administered by another human being. There is no escape from social relations.[6]

It is a logical step to regard any data emanating from the 'autonomous' human subject as 'personal.' Research ethics codes thus privilege the idea of 'personal data' that then must be anonymized and protected. We have no disagreement with the fact that data must be protected. However, we are concerned that such narrow perceptions of human subjects as 'autonomous,' rendering 'personal' data do not provide any avenues for conducting advanced qualitative research.

Advanced qualitative research works on a different premise than conventional biomedical research. The research is inductive; that is, clues about the nature and direction of the research are usually driven by the research participant, not the researcher. Second, the sort of data that qualitative researchers seek is social-context based (while in biomedical science 'controls' are used to factor out social context). The data generated by participant observation, in-depth interviews, focus groups, conversations, chats, etc., are related to cultural and social facts. Qualitative researchers do not pursue 'personal' data as an end in themselves; rather, they see their data as 'social,' for their analytic framework is a social one, not driven by personal information.

This conception of the non-autonomous human subject and the analysis of data as social concepts challenge conventional views of research. The qualitative researcher enters into the social world of the individual and describes that world as a social activity that has meanings that emerge through the interaction of that individual with others. What is significant for the qualitative researcher is not so much the 'individual,' as his/her thoughts, attitudes, activities, identities that are all lodged in social relations. An exclusive focus on the 'person' would be quite meaningless for a qualitative researcher. It is the *social* world 'within' that individual that is analytically significant. Qualitative researchers only come to 'personal data' tangentially, and even then 'personal' data are social scripts for the human subject, the researcher, and those who read the findings.

Here is one example of 'personal' data as 'social.' In her study on older widowers, Deborah van den Hoonaard (2004) held in-depth interviews to learn about the meanings that the men attach to having become widowed. Her analysis of the interviews is suffused with social, not personal data: the manner in which the men answered her questions, the data pertaining to the interaction between her and each man, and how the men explain their own personal experiences. All of these aspects would have remained below the analytical periscope if she had regarded the data she obtained as purely 'personal.' Instead, she could only make meaning out of the data when she related to the social world of what it is like being an older, widowed man where there are few masculine models available. Even aggregating personal data would not have helped her: she had to find themes that correlated with wider, social scripts about masculinity, and about meanings the men attach to being without work and without women.

A new paradigm of the research 'subject' is essential in this process. It is vital that concepts of 'autonomy,' 'independence,' and 'self-reliance' be abandoned as an inadequate cornerstone of research-ethics policies. If, however, biomedical researchers have difficulty abandoning the older concept of the research subject, it is time to permit social scientists to take on the concepts that are vitally relevant to their research. In other words, the outdated biomedical definition of the research subject should be discarded in favour of a social concept of what it means to be human.

Bursting the Contemporary Ethics Bubble: Three Case Studies[7]

The following three cases are each radically different in their research settings: the study by David Goode (1979) focuses on the world of the congenitally deaf-blind; Mitchell Duneier's overt work (1999) on homeless bookstall vendors in New York City lacks the anonymity usually accorded to research participants; Timothy Diamond's classic work (1992) on Chicago-area, for-profit nursing homes represents covert research. In Goode's case, he dealt with a world marked sharply by intellectual and mental differences. Duneier, over a protracted length of time, faced differences of race, class, and occupation. Diamond's research had to grapple with a system in which humans lost their dignity. What unites all three studies was the great length these three scholars took to establish relationships with their research participants. As will become clear, each researcher had to 'burst out of his bubble' to create such a relationship and produce insightful, admirable, and important scholarship.

Method to the Madness

Howard Schwartz and Jerry Jacobs, in their comprehensive volume *Qualitative Sociology: A Method to the Madness* (1979: 279), make a point about background assumptions that enter into all interactions that define relations. These assumptions can include anticipatory socialization and discovering the 'generalized other' when you learn to see yourself in the light of the expectations of others and adjust your behaviour accordingly (369).[8] Any 'successful' relationship relies, ideally speaking, on a common stock of knowledge shared by the researcher and research participant. But what happens when such a common stock of knowledge is absent? What is a researcher to do? *Qualitative Sociology: A Method to the Madness* includes a case study that exemplifies the great lengths to which a researcher, David Goode, had to go to discover the hidden world of a deaf-blind nine-year-old girl, Christina.

Over thirty years ago, David Goode (1979: 381–93) conducted a year-and-a-half long ethnography in a hospital for congenitally deaf-blind, mentally retarded (children with rubella syndrome). He was motivated to see the interaction of the congenitally deaf-blind with normally seeing-hearing persons. To that end, he focused on 'Christina' and spent a number of daily cycles with her, sharing daily routines with her, using naturalistic observation. His long and steady involvement with her life allowed Goode to arrive at an understanding unavailable to biomedical practitioners and researchers who would normally spend relatively little time with her during medical examinations.

Christina was born with a severe syndrome of multi-handicaps (the rubella syndrome). The after-effects included bilateral cataracts, congenital heart disease, deafness, clinical microcephaly, central nervous system damage, abnormal behaviour patterns, and severe developmental delays. Goode writes that '[at the age of five] Chris was diagnosed as legally blind, legally deaf, and mentally retarded and was placed in a state hospital for the retarded' (1979: 382).

Christina occupied her own world in a manner that did not touch the symbolism of the world of 'normals.' As a consequence, Goode as a researcher, striving to understand her world, had to enter it on an intersubjective level. Despite his attempts at imitating her deaf-blind state with the use of earplugs and blindfolds, he realized that he was still guided by his own world view; his experience with earplugs and blindfolds was still explainable by his own life. Goode lived in his own 'bubble' that had to be burst if he were to enter Christina's world. He needed a more radical approach – one in which he would willingly suspend his belief in the 'normal' world as the point of departure. The seer-hearer culture's version of Christina's world could not become the dominant explanatory perspective. In other words, it was not a question of reshuffling her behaviour into different categories; it became a matter of allowing Christina to organize her activities. Here is an example of such an activity:

> Chris maneuvered me in such a way that she was lying on my lap face up and had me place my hand over her face. By holding my hand she eventually maneuvered it in such a way that my palm was on her mouth and my index finger was on her right ('good') eye. She then indicated to me that she wanted me to tap on her eyelid, by picking my finger up and letting it fall on her eye repeatedly, smiling and laughing when I voluntarily took over this work as my own. (She has also 'shown me,' by moving my body, that she wanted me to speak in her ear and flick my fingers across her good eye.) While I tapped Chris's eye, she licked and sniffed my palm occasionally and softly hummed seemingly melodic sounds. *We did this* for about ten or fifteen minutes. (Goode, 1979: 388; emphasis in original)

What distinguished Goode's understanding of this activity from what the staff saw, was that Goode interpreted the activity, not as 'play' (as the staff did), but as purposeful and relevant to Christina's making sense of her world.

Other activities followed that Goode fully cooperated with, often resulting in peaks of excitement. It was only after he surrendered his 'remedial stance' (1979: 389), for example, trying to make Christina listen to sound in the 'right' way, was he able to see her treatment of light, sound, and tactile stimulation as a rational and 'even intelligent' quality. In 'listening' to a beat, Goode continues,

> Chris was providing her otherwise impoverished perceptual field with a richness her eyes and ears could not give her. She accomplished this by the use of her available and intact bodily resources – her good eye, her nose, her muscles, and her skeletal frame, which provided for the possibility of making such movements. I was, and still am, struck by a certain inventiveness in this activity. (390)

In the context of the mental institution, the staff based their thinking of Christina's behaviour on a set of 'fault-finding' procedures, whereas from Christina's imputed perspective, her behaviour was rational and purposeful, although 'self-seeking, hedonistic, and amoral' in her inter-actions (Goode, 1979: 392). By the time she was nine, the staff regarded her behaviour as 'infantile,' but she was no infant and 'had lived long enough to have gained some sophistication in achieving her pleasure-seeking activities' (Goode, 1979: 392).

The following two cases represent a different kind of blindness, but no less powerful in its impact. It is the blindness that the researcher has when attempting to understand a social world quite unlike his or her own.

Sidewalk

Mitchell Duneier's Sidewalk (1999) features photos of twenty-eight peo-ple at the front of the book. Except for very few, minor, instances, there is no attempt to cover the identity of the people featured in this ethnog-raphy; real names were used, too, in addition to the actual photos.[9] It is a study of the social structure of sidewalk life in New York City, and of the corner of the Avenue of the Americas and Greenwich Avenue in particular – an area of three city blocks. The radical divide between Duneier's social world (Jew, white, university professor) and that of the men who were selling books or magazines on the street (Black, home-less) could not have been more striking. In Duneier's own words:

> I begin by looking at the lives of the poor (mainly) black men who work and/ or live on the sidewalks of an upper-middle-class neighborhood . . . maga-zine vendors like Ishmael Walker are without a home; the police throw their merchandise, vending tables, clothes, and family photos in the back of a garbage truck when they leave the block to relieve themselves. (9)

Duneier's urban ethnography constantly reminds the reader of the vul-nerability of the sellers in the face of authorities. It also relates their seemingly personal challenges to wider social structures. As such, his questions become pertinent:

> How do these persons live in a moral order? How do they have the inge-nuity to do so in the face of exclusion and stigmatization on the basis of race and class? How does the way they do so affront the sensibilities of the working and middle classes? How do their acts intersect with a city's mechanisms to regulate its public spaces? (9)

Their world was quite unfamiliar to Duneier who had to dissociate their 'indecency' from their personal attributes and find a logical connection to the ways of the wider world:

> How can we comprehend types of behavior such as sidewalk sleeping, urinating in public, selling stolen goods, and entangling passersby in unwanted conversations? ... How can we understand the processes that lead many people to regard those who engage in such acts as 'indecent'? How do the quantity and quality of their 'indecency' make them different from conventional passersby? (10)

Despite the disparate worlds of Duneier and that of the street vendors, the vendors responded with approval to Duneier's open method of research. His first-hand observations took four years; he held twenty interviews and drafted the services of a professional photographer of urban life, Ovie Carter,[10] an African American. His field method also involved the intense use of a tape recorder, usually kept in a milk crate under a vending table. The recorder picked up all kinds of voices. Duneier got even permission to quote almost all the people who were being taped without their knowledge. In case of the police officers who were being recorded without their knowing it, Mitch used false names when using their words. In all other instances, he used real names (13).

Duneier gained entry as a browser and customer at Hakim Hasan's table in 1992. Hakim became a key participant in the project and introduced Duneier to other vendors:

> Once in the network, contacts and introductions took place across the various spheres. Eventually, I worked as a general assistant (watching vendors' merchandise while they went on errands, buying up merchandise offered in their absence, assisting on scavenging missions through trash and recycling bins, and 'going for coffee.' Then I worked full-time as a magazine vendor and scavenger during the summer of 1996, again for three days a week during the summer of 1997 and during part of the fall of 1997. I also made daily visits to the blocks during the summer of 1998, often for hours at a time, and worked full-time as a vendor for two weeks in March 1999, when my research came to an end.
> ...
> I was myself eventually treated by them as a fixture of the blocks, occasionally referred to as a 'scholar' or 'professor,' which is my occupation. My designation was Mitch. This seemed to have a variety of changing

meanings, including: a naïve white man who could himself be exploited for 'loans' of small change and dollar bills; a Jew who was going to make a lot of money off the stories of people working the streets; a white writer who was trying to 'state the truth about what was going on.' (11–12)

Some on the street volunteered to 'manage' the taping by themselves when Duneier was out of town. The vendors interviewed each other before giving the tape back to Duneier. Hasan wrote the afterword for the book in which he points to the basis of the relationship:

> How could I prevent him from appropriating me as mere data, from not giving me a voice in how the material in his book would be selected and depicted? How does a subject take part in an ethnographic study in which he has very little faith and survive as something more than a subject and less than an author? . . . The idea of race as a lived experience could not be avoided; at the same time, if I made the mistake of denying Mitch *his* humanity on the basis of race, without giving him a fair chance, there would have been no way for me to know whether he could write about my life accurately . . . Mitch did not react to what I had to say with the cool, clinical detachment I had imagined to be the sociologist's stock in trade. *He listened attentively. I came to respect his sensitivity, and soon I trusted him to write about my life.* (Hasan, 'Afterword,' 1999: 321–2; emphasis added)

Duneier then invited Hasan to teach an undergraduate seminar with him. It was ten weeks long and included nineteen students whom they selected together. After the seminar, and based on questions from students, Duneier rewrote the book.

When Duneier began studying the magazine vendors (not the book vendors), the fact that he was writing a book didn't concern them. What they wanted to know was how much money they could get out of him. Hasan underscored the fundamental principles of a good relationship between Duneier and him:

> Mitch eventually learned how to say no to requests for money from seemingly desperate people. *He established goodwill through his seriousness of purpose and sincerity as a sociologist* . . . In the end, any sociologist who simply believes that time spent in the field qualifies him as 'one of the boys' is not only sadly mistaken but in grave trouble . . . He [Mitch] never pretended to be anything other than he was: *a human being and sociologist attempting to understand the meaning of our lives.* (Hasan, 'Afterword,' 1999: 325–6; emphasis added)

The relationship between Duneier and the research participants is deeply rooted in everyday understandings of how many human relationships operate in general. For example, Duneier (1999: 336) claims that '[f]ieldwork can be a morally ambiguous enterprise ... The question for me is how to show respect for the people I write about, given the impossibility of complete sincerity at every moment (in research as in life).' Fieldwork, according to Duneier, is like life: 'We may *feel* fully trusted and accepted by colleagues and "friends," but full acceptance is difficult to measure by objective standards and a rarity in any case. If we cannot expect such acceptance in our everyday lives, it is probably unrealistic to make it the standard for successful fieldwork' (338).

Reaching beyond conventional postmodern research approaches, Hasan claims that Duneier was a departure from the 'scholar-knows-best' paradigm. The idea of 'the subject's voice' is merely a 'romanticized idea.' Significantly, Hasan adds the observation that the 'radical willingness of the social scientist to listen is quite another' (Hasan, 'Afteword,' 1999: 327). Listening to the 'subject's voice' can have an ironic twist especially when a researcher aims at submitting the research participant to the researcher's reading the text straight out of the draft of the book, hoping to solicit approval and perhaps some changes, even minor ones. In this regard, Duneier (1999) had a profound realization:

> ... the effort to be respectful by showing the text to the person in it sometimes turns out not to seem very respectful at all. In this case, I end up insisting that the individual listen to me, and imposing my agenda on someone who seemed annoyed by my efforts. (348)

Making Gray Gold

While *Sidewalk* represents a form of scholarship and research liberated from the shackles of anonymity and confidentiality, Timothy Diamond's book, *Making Gray Gold: Narratives of Nursing Home Care* (1992), serves as an example of how to conduct covert research, involving intricate relationships with all those with whom Diamond came into contact.

Diamond worked in three different nursing homes in Chicago for three to four months each. Unable to overtly access for-profit nursing homes, he obtained the certificate of nursing assistant using that as a basis to access the nursing homes. He went to school for six months in 1982, two evenings a week and all day Saturday. Among the lessons he and his fellow students struggled most to comprehend during the training was how to 'overcome the fears, embarrassment, and nausea through building the work into a relational context' (Diamond, 1992: 217). Several chance encounters with exhausted and complaining nursing assistants in a local coffee shop had aroused his curiosity about life and work in nursing homes. Diamond (1992) describes his research strategy as follows:

> I would surreptitiously take notes on scraps of paper, in the bathroom or otherwise out of sight, jotting down what someone had said or done. Off duty I assembled the notes and began to search for patterns in them. The basic data are these observations and conversations, the actual words of people reproduced to the best of my ability from the field notes. (6–7)

During the interview for the job, Diamond resolved not to lie, but he 'was not particularly eager to announce the whole purpose of my project, preferring the strategy of one step at a time' (36). As his research moved along, the circumstances of the nursing homes forced him to conduct undercover research (8). However, he was the only white person on staff at least at that level and, as such, his presence would evoke questions. As he confesses, 'In this atmosphere [of poorly-paid work and tension], since the workers had viewed me with some suspicion in the first place, it became increasingly impossible for me to reveal to management that I hoped to write about my experiences' (48). He told some co-workers and some residents about his writing, but never the administrators (50). The suspiciousness of the climate and divisions of power between management and staff prevented him from disclosing his work. 'Eventually,' Diamond confesses, 'I disclosed to some residents that I hoped to write about nursing-home life,' at which point they proceeded to give him advice (51, 54). His scribbling notes during his work shifts led co-workers to ask the question, 'What are you doing, Tim, writing a book?' He came up with a reply, fearing a rejection, but his disclosure resulted in people saying, 'Hey, good luck . . . ' The nursing assistants even said that he should not forget to put this or that item in his fieldnotes (21–2).

Diamond's account is rather significant in the annals of social research. His research is demonstrably highly ethical and shows authentic relationships with nursing staff and the residents in the nursing home.[11] Part of that authenticity stems from his admission that he came into the nursing home with many preconceptions of which, through his interactions with the research participants, he was able to let go. No doubt, his attitude towards learning and his eagerness to learn played into his interactions. These genuine relationships permitted him to see his own prejudices and stereotypical views of nursing homes. In his own words, these were the stereotypes that initially prevented him from conducting ethical research:

- 'Eventually, the very concepts of job and wage versus unemployment and poverty that I had brought with me began to break down.' (44–5)
- 'Full-time work meant earning less than the cost of subsistence; it did not alleviate poverty . . . You can't get by on just one job, unless you worked long shifts, part-time moonlighting, double-shifts.' (48)
- 'Among the many insults that nursing assistants absorb as they perform these skills, I came to think of none more naive than to enquire why they don't just get another job.' (46)
- 'Before starting this research I had been under the impression that nearly all people in nursing homes were bedridden . . . Many were free to walk around and even left the building, but were penniless and mistaken as vagrants. Some even begged and bartered things outside when their allowance started to run out.' (63)
- 'What sometimes initially appeared as crazy behavior emerged over time as rational, desperate attempts to guard what was slipping away' [e.g., possessions were constantly being 'lost']. (68)
- 'I clung for a while to the notion that residence in a nursing home must at least be better than living on the streets . . . ' (69)
- The place of families in nursing homes: popular conception that families have abandoned them – but not true. (70)
- The lives in nursing homes were lives of passivity: the charts recorded their lives in terms of sickness and diagnoses. The receiving end, 'acted upon rather than acting.' (84)
- His perception of silence in the nursing home broke down: 'Not only did people in the day room have a lot to say to the nursing staff, but quiet friendships bloomed throughout the room.' (100)

By abandoning these preconceived ideas through his relationships and by having a listening and observant attitude (rather than using interviews) – in other words, by bursting out of his own bubble – his original question 'What can we do for them?' transformed into 'What is their life like?'

The first portion of this chapter highlighted the significant differences of the concept of 'subject' and 'data' that pervade the social sciences and that vary so greatly from their conceptions in national ethics codes. The three case studies on relationships between researcher and research participants underscore these variances and represent extremely varied social settings and approaches. Their selection allows us to offer a stronger basis when speaking about what unites them in developing our understanding of such relationships and normative ethics from the perspective of social researchers. There are four elements that stand out.

First, the researchers in all three cases surrendered the 'remedial' attitude. In David Goode's study of Christina, the deaf-blind nine-year old, we learned that he has eschewed the medical attitude of remedying her physical and social attributes. In the second study, Duneier was not vexed by the thought that he ought to 'fix' things for the homeless men and women selling books or magazines. Similarly, Diamond's work was far removed from the immediate urgency of remedying the organization of for-profit nursing homes.

Second, each of the three researchers came to realize that the 'how' question was more relevant than the 'why' question. Social researchers tend to gravitate to the 'how' questions in any case because they apprise them about the social processes that created the social setting in the first place. 'Why' questions would only generate explanations of 'motives,' a vocabulary of motives, which are always subject to change and interpretation as one moves through life and social circumstances.

Third, by entering into an authentic relationship with research participants, the researchers were able to dispel their prejudices and stereotypical perspectives of the social setting. The relationship liberated force-fed data; the data now were free to reflect the social setting more accurately.

Fourth, each of the three researchers actively 'burst the bubble' that distanced them from research participants. They stepped out of their own immediate cultural and social worlds and were ready to adopt, or at least experience, the world of their research participants.

Each of these four elements was shaped by (and also shaped) the relationships the researcher had with research participants. We see that relationships that allowed the development of these elements also permitted a sharper, more authentic gathering of data. The data never replaced the relationship; the relationship stood at the core of these exemplary cases of research.

The previous three chapters were necessary precursors to the rest of *The Seduction of Ethics*. They dealt with the taken-for-granted discourse about the research-ethics review process, namely, its archaeology, the criticisms that have been levelled against it, and the common stock of ethical practice that social researchers see as normative in their field. Purposely, I chose a wide range of research practices: first, one-to-one interactions between a researcher and a research participant; second, a setting that eschewed anonymity; and, third, a setting that involved covert research. Collectively, the three chapters reveal the discourse surrounding ethics review and position the approach that social researchers take. We now turn to the ethnographic portions of the book, the prime purpose of my study. The next five chapters focus on the world of ethics committees, to be followed by two chapters analysing the doings of researchers in that world of ethics review.

5 Structure and Composition of Research-Ethics Committees

The previous chapter presented three social-research activities that underscored some approaches which, as one can see, met ethical criteria but might be considered impossible to undertake under current research-ethics regimes, despite the fact that all three researchers provided a respectful and dignified relationship to their research participants – indeed one of the formal goals of research-ethics review. These three cases – which give sharp contrasts to what is not possible in research today – already illustrate the powerful role that the ethics-review system can play in determining (in)appropriate research methods. This chapter approaches the world of research-ethics review from the perspective of its local structure and composition as contingent realities that explain why some research methods in the social sciences are beleaguered or favoured. The subsequent chapters (6 to 9) also deal with other facets of research-ethics committees that account for the decline or rise in research methods.

Ethics Committees as Part of the University

Ethics committees represent an anomaly in the university. They have the power of veto, but have no comparable resources; they are appointed by universities and yet they are autonomous; they deal with research, but membership is not confined to researchers. Operating in such a framework, a chair of an ethics committee believes that the REB 'need[s] a big personality' to deal with the university at large (Interview C05-B). Some claim that REBs are 'little kingdoms' (Interview C10-B). A member of an ethics committee simply declared that the REB is a bureaucracy, with a gap between administrators and researchers. 'To protect their asses,' says the same member, 'dirt work comes down to the REB from

Ottawa ... the more bureaucratic you become, the more you are mis-understood' (Interview E15-S). Of twelve Canadian REBs, two chairs reported to the VP (Academic), three to the VP (Research), two to no one, and five to 'other' (Ellard and Dobson, 2007).

Costs of Maintaining the Ethics System

It is fascinating to consider the direct costs of maintaining not only the Canadian research-ethics regime but also those of the three other countries I often refer to, namely, the United States, the United Kingdom, and Australia. I extrapolated my findings from my own estimates of costs related to operating the Canadian ethics regime.[1] The research-ethics review regime costs at least $35.33 million (or, on the average, $113,100 for each of the 300 REBs) when we exclude the costs of the Interagency Advisory Panel and Secretariat on Research Ethics (see endnote 1 for this chapter, which explains how I arrived at these figures). When one considers there are seventy-six university-based REBs in Canada (some universities have more than one REB), all Canadian universities must aggregately lay out about $8.5 million each year. These are immense costs, but, as many observers (R013-S, Fieldnotes: 543) have noted, there is no way of knowing whether the regulations are achieving their purpose. Given these 'investments,' it stands to reason that one needs to take an in-depth look at an 'indus-try' that occupies such a large budget.

With such estimates in hand, we can now consider the annual direct costs of maintaining ethics regimes in the three other countries. United States research institutions maintain 3,000 to 5,000 IRBs (Hamilton, 2002: 116, citing several sources), the United Kingdom has 150 (Hedgecoe, 2008: 875), and Australia has 220 (Israel, 2004: 9). These numbers include ethics committees devoted to all research involving humans, such as in hospitals, universities, and a few other research settings. No doubt, there are some structural and other differences among ethics committees and my estimates suggests that the four countries (Canada, United States, United Kingdom, Australia) have an ethics 'industry' worth $432 million – a powerful body of vested interests allied with evaluating the ethics of research.

The Size of Ethics Committees

The size of ethics committees varies across a broad spectrum. We already noted that smaller universities tend to have larger memberships in their eagerness to have a wide representation of their academic 'community.' Larger universities have smaller memberships, perhaps compounded by the fact that they also are in process of centralizing the ethics-review system, eliminating ethics committees specializing in particular disciplines. The forces of accountability and demands from federal research-ethics regimes insist that local ethics committees be more wary of their own practices . . . just in case. For example, the University of Illinois has one IRB replacing thirteen, due to budgetary cutbacks and fear of litigation (R013-S, Fieldnotes: 543). Similarly, Simon Fraser University has chosen to have one REB rather than many smaller ones (Fieldnotes: 652).

John H. Ellard and Keith S. Dobson (2007), Canadian researchers at the University of Calgary, report that the average membership of Canadian REBs is 9.83 members, but is higher in Ontario, namely, 11.67, although one of the universities I visited has 27 members on the board. This board, where every academic department is represented, cannot imagine the workload that would have to be carried if there were 'just six or seven members' (S47-M). Another REB has 20 to 25 members, but six members come from the Faculty of Education because 30 per cent of applications are from that Faculty (C11-M). In the United States, in their 2001 study of eighty-seven IRBs, Raymond De Vries and Carl Forsberg (2002: 203) found that the average size was thirteen members; they also report that an earlier study in 1978 indicated fourteen members as average.

Whether in Canada or the United States, there are as many rationales for dividing up the system of ethics committees as there are committees, producing sometimes a bewildering array of possibilities. A professor of nursing doing social research on health must submit her application to a biomedical REB (university B6), but the same kind of researcher at another university must submit the application to a non-medical REB (university M3). A social researcher at another university will have to be content with submitting his/her application to a biomedical REB, while still another university will have set up an ethics committee just for the social sciences. The permutations are endless. Some universities foster departmental committees that must vet applications before they go on to the university ethics committee. At some universities, there might indeed be a departmental committee, but researchers are not required to pass their application through it, only as a matter of courtesy, rather than as a requirement.

There are universities that do not divide up ethics committees according to disciplines or even have one integrated ethics committee; rather, they arrange ethics committees by type of invasiveness in the lives of research participants implied in the research (S49-B, Fieldnotes: 1379).

Membership

The composition of members on ethics committees in all four countries shows remarkable similarities. Table 5.1 covers data from Canada's six big universities, ten medium-sized ones, and eight small universities. In the United States, among eighty-seven surveyed university and hospital IRBs, 32 per cent of members are physicians, 24 per cent behavioural scientists (mostly psychologists), and fewer than 10 per cent are medical researchers. The medical side constitutes 46 per cent of members. And among 1,161 IRB members, one finds only twenty professional ethicists (De Vries and Forsberg, 2002: 205–6).

As is evident in table 5.1, psychologists constitute the largest representation on REBs (16.6 per cent). Although the proportion of community members is equally high as that of psychologists, their impact on REBs is far less; community members are not chairs of REBs, while it is more likely for psychologists to be so. Among the six big universities, one-third of the REBs are chaired by psychologists; for medium-sized universities, half are headed by psychologists; in small universities, one-fourth are chaired by psychologists. A sociologist and his colleague inform us of the following:

> One possible short-term [solution] is to make the IRB more interdisciplinary. Currently, it is dominated by psychologists who are deeply wedded to experimental research design . . . It has been a key problem for us. (R114, Fieldnotes: 378)

Membership on an ethics committee might be a problematic one from the perspective of the committees themselves. An ethics committee normally desires to have a wide representation from across the campus – in fact, ethics codes often mandate a wide representation – but might be stymied in its desire because there is no equal desire or availability from all disciplines to serve on ethics committees. Serving on a committee absorbs an enormous amount of time and energy, perhaps leaving

Table 5.1   Memberships in 24 Canadian Research Ethics Boards, by Disciplines (in Number and Percentage), 2008

	Number	Percentage
Psychology	38	16.6
Professional[a]	35	15.3
Social Science (excluding Psychologists)[b]	33	14.4
Philosophy, Law, and Religious Studies	24	10.5
Business and Economics	22	9.6
Science and Engineering[c]	16	7
Health Sciences[d]	12	5.2
Humanities and Performing Arts[e]	11	4.8
Community Member[f]	38	16.6
Totals	229	100

[a]Education, kinesiology, journalism, library science, social work, nutrition.
[b]Includes anthropology, sociology, criminology, political science, geography, communication and culture, tourism, indigenous studies, and applied human sciences.
[c]Includes science, mathematics, environmental health and safety, biology, mechanical engineering, agricultural science, forestry, computer science, and civil engineering.
[d]Nursing, epidemiology, dentistry, medicine, pharmaceutical sciences.
[e]Theatre, linguistics, English literature, history, modern languages, classics, and French literature.
[f]Also includes student representatives (n=4).
Source: Canada, Fieldnotes: 1398–407.

too little for research. There is also a steady rotation of ethics-committee members (Feeley, 2007: 769). A new chair laments the departure of the previous chair:

> We lost [the previous chair] which was a big loss to the committee and we've had a number of other changes so that I think the committee may be this year a little closer to the Tri-Council [TCPS] in terms of a positivist orientation than we probably were earlier and so I kind of keep reminding people of [names of previous chair's] good direction as we were getting started. (Interview C03-M)

Faculty members on IRBs serve a short time (two to three years) without any proper preparation, and one can see that they are 'not prepared to suffer criticism in light of career sacrifices' (Katz, 2007: 800). These two elements – voluntary membership and rotation – leads, according to Malcolm Feeley (2007: 769), to self-selection, 'self-appointed protectors of ethics gravitate to and remain on these committees (and their permanent staffs) while others quickly come and go.' Researchers (such as R136-M, Fieldnotes: 482; and R015-M, Fieldnotes: 653) have noted the lack of broad expertise on these committees. The membership of an REB at a mid-sized university (M7) includes a food-bank person, a police officer, a social worker, and the former chancellor.

One interview participant, a former ethics-committee member, served on the REB for two years, but resigned. He did not want to be 'a gatekeeper' (Interview R002-M). One of the interview participants said that he was already interested in ethics when he was asked to serve, but he has never done research (Interview E13-M). Still others join ethics committees for selfless reasons. A fresh PhD graduate was motivated to serve on the ethics committee of his new university since he had a terrible experience with an REB (as student) at one of Canada's major West Coast universities (Interview E15-S). Another researcher said he got a call from the VP academic, who said flattering things, although, as he points out, 'I was the fiftieth person on his list' (Interview E25-S). Another researcher sees herself as sharing responsibilities in a university, without a particular role except that she could contribute on account of her good training in the health sciences (Interview E25-S).

However, there are efforts to have a wider representation of researchers on ethics committees, although some ethics committees tried to match the representation with where most of the applications come from, such as criminology because of its large number of students (Interview C12-S). A researcher from a major Canadian university said that he 'got on the REB for seeing the two solitudes and wanting to help' (C14-M, Fieldnotes: 1238). Other ethics-committee members who are researchers echo similar sentiments. For example, an active biologist's research interests (that involved working with Aboriginal people) evolved into an interest in ethics, but she also became interested in inadequacies of policies, hoping to contribute to changes (Interview E12-M). Another researcher got into ethics via his work on Aboriginal map-making (E15-S). A medical sociologist became interested in ethics through his interest in research methods and having served on a student-ethics committee (Interview E27-S).

The Illinois College of Law reported that IRB staff at one major university drew up a list of twenty experienced senior faculty thought 'to be especially suitable for appointments as IRB chair but could find no one willing to serve.' It also reported that '[e]ven among the entire IRB memberships there are virtually no full professors' (ICL, 2006: 11). Laura Stark (2007: 784) indicates a similar finding. The 'inadequate representation on IRBs,' according to Koro-Ljungberg et al. (2007: 1086), 'further normalize[s] IRB reviews.' Cary Nelson (2004: 212) claims that IRBs 'have not a clue about the culture of history or anthropology' and that, '[i]n 2002, the Illinois IRB included not one humanities faculty member; a year later an anthropologist was added.' Others have also noted this singular lack of research experience on IRBs. For example, Ivor Pritchard (2002: 8) refers to the 'Bell Report' (Bell et al., 1998) that says that 21 per cent of researchers reported that bias or lack of expertise by the IRB was a problem. A Canadian researcher sees the problem with having an ethics expert on REB: 'He's usually a philosopher, but a philosopher has no research experience' (Interview R118-M). The chair of another REB rhetorically asks, 'Would a philosopher/ethicist on the REB just muddy the waters?' (Interview C25-M). An REB chair believes that the REB is mistaken if it believes it needs a lawyer (Interview C09-B). In some respects, she is quite right, for the *TCPS* (Section B2, Article 1.3, subsection b) dictates that 'for biomedical research, at least one member is knowledgeable in the relevant law; this is advisable but not mandatory for other areas of research.'

Significantly, Kristine Fitch observed the following when she was appointed to her IRB:

> Appointing me rather than a quantitative social scientist was an attempt by the administration to reach out to those in the research community whose practices and procedures were the furthest removed from the biomedical side. They were well aware of the biomedical bias in human-subjects regulations; their goal from the start was to incorporate the perspective and research experience of an ethnographic researcher into the changeover from department-based review to centralized review. (Fitch, 2005: 271)

'The dynamics of IRB interaction with many social science researchers – applied and otherwise – are an agonizing problem at too many academic institutions' says Fitch. She elaborates:

> At Iowa, the keening threnody [wailing] has reached epic levels, predictably, at moments of significant change in the system. One of those changes was a shift from four separate review committees, in which unfunded research (i.e., most of the social and behavioral side) was reviewed at the departmental level, to only two centralized review committees: biomedical and social/behavioral science . . . (270)

According to an administrator, it is now easier to recruit faculty members, especially the young ones who already have familiarity with the REB experience as they are 'much less resistant to process' (Interview A11-S).

Given the alleged paucity of active researchers on ethics committees, it is easy to see why Pritchard states that IRBs are seen as 'testy creatures' (Pritchard, 2002: 7). A chair of a Canadian REB who spoke about the 'two solitudes' admits, 'Frankly, it is appalling that it has even got this bad, perceived or otherwise' (C14-M, Fieldnotes: 1246). One REB chair admits that in her opinion, the REB is 'not flexible enough, and [it's] not just a question about how many men and women are on the REB, but about [diversely open] perspectives' (Interview C03-M). At one university, there is an exceptional difference: except for two, all members on the REB are researchers (Interview C30-M). One chair only wants researchers on the REB (Interview C05-B). However, the chair of another REB poses an interesting issue and says that a university's reputation is at stake if only experts get to decide on ethics applications (Interview C25-M).

Solutions

Solutions to problems of membership are not easy to come by. A prominent researcher who is deeply interested in the problem of ethics committees mentions the importance of 'not turning a numerical over-representation on REBs into a methodological over-representation' (Interview R015-M). One researcher (who has faithfully served on both local ethics committees and national bodies dealing with ethics) mentioned how the Council of Graduate Departments of Psychology thought that the best arrangement involved having 50 per cent of IRBs as non-researchers, but the problem of getting the public to meetings would slow down the process (R013-S, Fieldnotes: 542). For others, the solution can be found in smaller universities where the research is 'less intense,' where 'researchers are happier with the REB,' and where there is no 'multiplier effect that the bigger universities have.' Less variety makes the situation also easier to deal with at a small university (Interview E15-S).

Interestingly, structural solutions are hard to come by, but, as the next section shows, chairs of ethics committees can make a critical difference in bridging the world of ethics review and that of the researchers. The comments of an REB chair reaffirmed the importance of the staff in the ethics office to maintain good relationships with researchers: 'I had a very good board and I had a very good, you know, person in terms of the associate director in charge of ethics in research services who's now retired, but we have a good personal relationship from her' (Interview C05-B). The human dimension remains a critical factor and that factor is perhaps best expressed when there is a sense of community, most visible in small universities.

Role of Chair and Staff

As mentioned in the earlier section, chairs and staff are a vital link between the ethics committee and the researchers. However, at times, says Ann Hamilton (2002: 101), 'the IRB system seems remarkably closed,' with IRB chairs overhauling, for example, an application system without consulting researchers.[2] Typically, the appointment of REB members is for three years, but some REB members serve for a much longer period (Ellard and Dobson, 2007). The change of a chair can often result in a drastic change in the direction of the ethics committee, from one that interprets the ethics codes in a literal sense to one that approaches the codes in a more liberal manner. Equally typical, the movement from liberal to literal interpretations happens, too. To alleviate these sharp regime departures, one REB has developed a policy about how prospective chairs learn the ropes: they first act as vice-chair (Interview C12-S). It is surprising that 60 per cent of administrators in the United States report that the IRB chair has no ethical expertise (De Vries and Forsberg, 2002: 209). At one university, the chair of an ethics committee became so proficient in ethics that she called herself the 'Ethics Queen,'[3] while at the departmental level of another university, the head of its ethics committee called himself the 'Ethics Czar' (Fieldnotes: 153).

It is also apparent that chairs of ethics committees and staff members play the critical role in the adjudication of ethics approval for research. It is only they who handle many of the proposals through a process of 'expedited review,' which in most cases is the vast majority of applications (rather than going to the 'full' board). Typically, according to one REB chair, the chair is the only member who reads all applications, in addition to the coordinator of the ethics office. The chair is also responsible for the writing of the initial review and for the letter that goes out to the researcher. The chair is also responsible for the follow-up correspondence that includes reviewing the revised 'protocols' (C19-S, Fieldnotes: 1229-30; S16-M, Fieldnotes: 953).

Disciplinary Representation

The disciplines 'represented' by REB chairs in Canada (2008) that deal with the social sciences and humanities[4] reveal an important source of frustration for social scientists, especially because chairs play a central role in the adjudication of research proposals and set the general tone of the REB decision-making process (see table 5.2). What is notable is the proportionally larger number of psychologists, ranging from 17 to 35.3 per cent of chairs across all three types of universities (small, medium, and large). One researcher at a mid-sized university remembers that every chair of his REB had been a psychologist over the past twenty-three years (R136-M, Fieldnotes: 482). They are usually experimental psychologists who speak to outdated institutional beliefs about psychology's touting individualism and individualistic approaches to research participants (Fieldnotes: 67).

The second-largest group represented are from fields that are neither social science nor medical, such as business, education, geography, and home economics. They constitute roughly 17 per cent of the REB chairs.

Medical researchers (nursing, health sciences, biology) constitute the third largest representation, namely, from 8.3 to 17.6 per cent of all chairs. Oddly enough, social science researchers (that includes anthropology and economics), are the fourth largest group, from 5.9 to 25 per cent of chairs. Chairs in the fields of the humanities (philosophy, ethicists, religious studies) are the fifth largest group to be chairs, from 6.3 to 11.8 per cent.

But what about the representative dispersion of all of these fields according to the size of the university? Whatever the size of the university, psychologists garner the highest proportion of chairs. Given the central role of chairs, one can see how the biomedical model of research is so much more easily promoted than, let us say, inductive research.[5] Only the large universities have REBs with the same high proportion of social scientists as psychologists acting as chairs.

However, in the small and medium-sized universities, chairs with a social science background (other than psychologists) rank fourth – a rather surprising low rank given that these are social science and humanities REBs! Chairs with a humanities background occupy the

Table 5.2   Social Science REB Chairs by Discipline and University Size, Canada, 2008

Discipline	Small	Medium	Large	Average
Psychology	8 (17.0%)	6 (35.3%)	3 (25%)	17 (22.4%)
Other social science[a]	3 (6.3%)	1 (5.9%)	3 (25%)	7 (9.2%)
Humanities[b]	3 (6.3%)	2 (11.8%)	1 (8.3%)	6 (7.9%)
Other non-medical[c]	8 (17.0%)	0 (0.0%)	2 (16.7%)	10 (13.2%)
Medical[d]	5 (10.6%)	3 (17.6)	1 (8.3%)	9 (11.8%)
From outside campus	0 (0.0%)	0 (0.0%)	1 (8.3%)	1 (1.3%)
Not available	20 (42.6%)	5 (29.4%)	1 (8.3%)	26 (34.2%)
Totals	47 (100%)	17 (100.0%)	12 (100%)	76 (100.0%)

[a]Includes anthropology and economics.
[b]Philosophy, ethicists, religious studies.
[c]Business, education, geography, home economics.
[d]Nursing, health sciences, biology.
Sources: (1) Statistics regarding number of applications: Research Offices/Services in related universities. (2) Size of university: SSHRC Report, 'Research Capacity' (29 October 2001, unpublished); Fieldnotes: 140.

fourth (or in one case the third) rank as chairs. Chairs with a medical background still feature quite strongly in this configuration, ranging from second to fourth position. Again, a surprise. Another surprise is the large proportion of university websites devoted to REBs that do *not* contain the names of their chairs.

For the small universities, this absence applies to almost 43 per cent of websites, 29 per cent for medium-sized universities, and 8 per cent of the big universities. These discrepancies are probably due more to a lack of resources in small universities to maintain websites than for any other reason. In Canada, in 2003, 47 per cent of chairs of seventeen social science REBs were psychologists, 11.8 per cent were chemists, 11.8 per cent were kinesiologists, and 5.9 per cent each were historians, professors of education, nutritionists, and philosophers (Fieldnotes: 1383–4). Note that there were no social scientists on this list. Chemistry professors come next to psychologists as heads of REBs, that is, nearly 12 per cent. When I interviewed a chemist who is also a member of such an REB about this seeming anomaly, he said he was not surprised. For him, chemistry departments in the university must politically defend themselves because the university sees them as offering only 'service courses' and are therefore occupying many administrative positions at the university, including being chairs of REBs (E07-S, Fieldnotes: 144).

Although chairs can wield such power, it is curious to note that being a chair does not necessarily mean he/she has a PhD (Interview C03-M), has tenure, is a researcher, or has conducted research with human subjects. These conditions are not anomalies and can create a significant disruption between the ethics world and that of the researchers. Just last year, a mid-sized university (M14) appointed a professor of a technical field to head its REB, although he had no experience conducting research involving humans.

The staff of ethics offices are, next to the chair, vital in the functioning of ethics committees. Usually they serve as ex-officio members at meetings of ethics committees. They labour under a tremendous workload (to be discussed later), have no research experience, and many still do not have expertise in ethics. According to De Vries and Forsberg (2002: 208), nearly 75 per cent of administrators surveyed report that 20 per cent or fewer of them have any ethical expertise. When this finding is combined with the fact that very few administrators have any ongoing research experience, we can see why researchers find the situation intolerable. In the past few years, there has been a noticeable increase of professionals trained in ethics, but their acquaintance with various research techniques and approaches is still inadequate.[6]

No doubt, staff members take over much of the paperwork from the chair so that the chair can concentrate on what is more important. As one chair put it, 'To get compliance, you need staff sympathetic to researchers whom researchers are free to call upon if a situation arises' (Interview C05-B). A staff member also handles the REB-approved proposal subject to changes (Interview A11-S). A member of an ethics committee points out that the staff person would direct queries to the chair or other REB members (Interview E27-S). In some cases, the Office of Research Services has been almost completely taken over by ethics staff (Interview R002-M). Some staff worked originally in 'research services,' until the *TCPS* came along, and they moved over to doing ethics-review work (Interview A11-S). It is not unusual to find staff who have stayed at their post since the *TCPS* came into effect in January 2001. One staff member emphasizes her role as someone who 'is at the front of the issue of not releasing funds until REB has approved them' (Interview S46-S). Usually, the staff's work also extends to visiting departments and researchers to acquaint them with the research-ethics review process (Interview S47-M; Interview E15-S). There seems little, however, in the matter of research ethics that gets conveyed; it is normally about application forms.

The work of the ethics committee suffers when there is a change of staff. It is not unusual that 'a change of staff caused a file to be overlooked and the research application went back and forth: ethics review couldn't be secured without funding, but funding was not forthcoming without ethics review' (Interview C10-B). In the course of my research across Canada, I have very seldom heard of any complaints from REBs or chairs about staff. Almost to the person, there is praise for their indispensable work in relating to both the ethics committee and researchers at large. One chair describes the staff member as a 'wonderful coordinator who takes care of things' (Interview C11-M). Another one characterizes her as a 'good staff assistant' (Interview C12-S). Their presence at national ethics gatherings imbues the meetings with a keen interest and enthusiasm in ethics. One staff person describes her work as 'satisfying' and 'rewarding' (Interview S44-B).

Community Members

With constantly shifting and rotating memberships, along with the ongoing centralizing processes of ethics committees, it is difficult to even pin down a one-time 'photo' of community members, who are referred to as 'community volunteers' or 'external members.' Some membership lists reveal the occupation of these members. Others simply state organizational affiliation, while still others only mention their professional expertise. In a 2004 website survey of twenty-four REBs across Canada, conducted by an undergraduate student[7] on my behalf (Fieldnotes: 1398–407), the student found thirty-three community members, but twenty-three had no other identifying information except a name. For those with identifying information, we found three lawyers, two public-health officials, two ethicists, and one each as teacher, naturopathic doctor, and someone who worked for the Canadian Forestry Service. Ellard and Dobson surveyed twelve REBs: eleven reported having one or more lay members; seven had lawyers (Ellard and Dobson, 2007).[8] The age of community members apparently is increasing, according to the observations of a community member herself (Presentation by E09-B, 7 May 2005, CAREB Meeting, Fieldnotes: 166) who attends ethics committee meetings at a large Canadian university. At least publicly, chairs of REBs believe it is good to have a community member (Interview C12-S).

The purpose of community members on ethics committees is not very clear. In theory, they are meant to bring 'community attitudes' to the table, but their presence, according to the Illinois College of Law, 'constrained the social sciences in the past towards the propriety of the subject investigated' (ICL, 2006: 15). A community member who made a presentation at the 2005 Annual Meeting of CAREB (Canadian Association of Research Ethics Boards), asked the question about the definition of 'community member' and asked if he should take the perspective of the community or the research participant (Presentation by E11-B, 7 May 2005, CAREB Meeting, Fieldnotes: 166). He eventually decided that he would take the perspective of the research participant, asking himself, for example, whether he would understand the consent form or whether he would allow his daughter to participate in such a study. He also noted that, based on his own experience, 'women community members try to figure out the research participant, while men community members follow their own voice.'

A survey undertaken by the Canadian Sociology and Anthropology Association reveals a common attitude by researchers that 'ethicists and lawyers are not a better judge of community interests than researchers' (Muzzin, 2002; Fieldnotes: 568). Moreover, anthropologists at a special session on ethics in research at the May 2002 CASCA annual gathering mentioned that lawyers and community members of REBs have 'a naive perspective about academic research' (Fieldnotes: 322). A thesis by Colin Newman,[9] a graduate student at Acadia University, reported a study by J. Porter (1987) that found that 60 per cent of community members on REBs judged the research merit of proposals; 34 per cent did not (Newman, 2004: 8). One can imagine how hard it is to demand more of community members who work as volunteers and are seldom reimbursed even for their travel and other minor expenses. As one administrator put it, 'It is hard to come by a community member because we don't pay them' (Interview A11-S).

In 2005, the Standing Committee on Education of the Interagency Advisory Panel on Research conducted a focus group about the role of community members in REBs (Standing Committee on Education, 2007). The committee found that many community members had a prior link with the REB either through a current or former REB member who was a (close) friend or former community member. The reasons for accepting an invitation to become a member of the REB varied. Some believed that they would learn about research and research ethics, some had time available, or some wanted to 'give back to the system' because they or family or friends had benefited as participants in research. Others wanted to learn more about the institutional structure. Regarding their mandate on the REB, community members believed that their role was to ensure that the 'community members' voice[s were] heard and their experiences [were] recognized and understood.' They enjoyed their work on the REB and held a 'positive view of their role and contributions.' They held the view that they brought 'pragmatism and humility to the ethics review process.' Community members also believed that they could 'help ensure that the research [was] of the highest possible quality.' Their concerns related to the role they played in 'assessing the quality and the content of the information letters or brochures and the consent forms written by researchers for participants,' that is, the length, type of language, and content, which are neither 'too technical, nor simplified to the point of losing accuracy.' It is significant to note, however, that very few community members, according to this Report by the Standing Committee on Education, had the 'background, training and experiences of community members in research ethics' to allow them to make substantial contributions to the REB. Like other new REB members, 'few community members were provided with a formal orientation program' and, if they receive a binder with a copy of the *TCPS*, there were 'no opportunities for discussion about the materials or for mentoring by another REB member. In reality, community members learned on the job' (Standing Committee on Education, 2007).

Whatever their contributions to the debate around the table, ethics committees marginalize community members. According to Anne Hamilton (2002: 167), these members are

> sort of a dual token minority, a 'non' ... this situation has served to marginalize the non-affiliated, non-scientific person, making the member a distinct minority-on-purpose. It seems reasonable to believe this 'non' person might be hesitant on most occasions to articulate concerns, and on the rare occasion when s/he might, might actually say something irrelevant (or that seems irrelevant to other, i.e., affiliated, scientific IRB members), or be focussed on an issue outside the purview of the IRB (and over time, stop contributing or questioning altogether).

When master's student Halle Showalter studied the IRB decision-making process at a major children's hospital on the West Coast in the United States, she observed that every IRB member had a plaque in front of him / her that identified her / his name and title except for community members whose plaques only read 'Community Member.' The biomedical researchers on the IRB ignored their comments that carried no weight in the discussion of applications (Showalter, 2005). Showalter's findings shadow those of Hamilton who also observes:

> This is not to imply these members are in a general way incompetent, but they, by categorical admission, are less apt to know what *is* relevant, i.e., within the purview of the board. Therefore, having the regulation in place has produced little if any effect. It is another cumbersome yet meaningless activity (with the exception of obligating [the] nons to attend meetings). The ambiguity in the rule provides opportunity to negate the effects of the rule requiring non-affiliated, non-scientific representation on IRBs. (Hamilton, 2002: 167; emphasis in original)

More than a few of my interview participants observed that community members 'are supposed to be trained like anyone else' (Interview C09-B).

Jurisdictional Power and Independence

In all important aspects, ethics committees are autonomous within universities, and this means that they are 'procedurally answerable to no one' (Nelson, 2004: 214). Debbie S. Dougherty and Michael W. Kramer (2005a: 186–7) speak of the irony of 'no-one assigned to oversee the IRB,' that 'gives the IRB an unbridled ability to monitor and expand its oversight of research without anyone assigned to reining it in when it goes astray.' Appointments are made by a vice-presidential officer or a university senate and, save for exceptional cases, they are left alone when REB members carry on with their work (Interview A11-S). The term 'board,' which is used in both Canada and the United States, carried greater authoritative weight than 'committee.'[10] According to *Webster's Seventh New Collegiate Dictionary* (1965: 93), a board refers to 'a group of persons having managerial, supervisory, or investigatory powers.' However, there are considerable, practical differences in the way boards exercise their power.

Some ethics committees actively promote goodwill among researchers to ease the work of the committees, while others find themselves at the other end of the spectrum, aloof and remote. In any case, whatever social distance exists between the ethics committees and the researchers, it does not take away their autonomous nature, at least at the local level. To maintain independence, a research officer had to give up REB membership as his membership would have contradicted the *TCPS*

(Interview C12-S). Chapter 14 will refer the reader to 'vertical ethics' that makes ethics committees beholden to other authorities, including editors of peer-reviewed journals, in a procedural sense. However, in terms of decisions regarding the ethicality of specific research, the ethics committees are technically autonomous. Of twelve Canadian ethics committees, two chairs report to the VP (Academic), three to VP (Research), two to no one, and five to 'other' (Ellard and Dobson, 2007).

There are other agencies that have jurisdictional power and independence, like ethics-review committees. The critical difference, however, is that the proceedings of the other agencies are publicly available. The results of court trials become public knowledge. Formal inquiries about police brutality, for example, also fall into the public domain. No ethics-review committee has made its consultations and decisions a matter of public record. As we shall note in a later chapter, even the membership composition of ethics committees is often unknown or not published. In the end, this lack of public knowledge about what goes on inside the chambers of ethics-review committees reinforces their authority and power. More significantly, this lack of public knowledge lays the foundation for idiosyncratic and inconsistent behaviours and decisions by ethics-review committees – a topic to which I shall return in chapter 9.

Workload

The lack of resources and the vast increase in the number of applications are the two defining aspects of the workload of ethics committees and their staff.[11] They believe that these aspects undermine the very mission of their mandate. In other ways, however, they inadvertently dictate more narrowly the kinds of research or research strategies to be undertaken by researchers. There are also other unexpected results of the heavy workload and pressure of time that ethics committees and their staff face.

Numerous are the observations that there is a 'glaring need' of resources for the ethics office to do its work properly (for example, De Vries and Forsberg, 2002: 213). One chair puts it this way: 'The university wants to be with the big boys, push into doing more research with pressure on workload. There is a night-and-day change in the research culture' (Interview C11-M). One member of an ethics committee describes the paperwork as 'phenomenal' (Interview E15-S) and describes the work as 'tedious,' but then adds, 'never boring!' The chair of another

REB exclaims that universities do not support REBs (Interview C05-B) and, says a member of an ethics committee, while the university 'recognizes the heavy workload of [the] REB, [it] gives members only two lighter committees' (Interview E27-S). An administrator states that the REB 'can only do so much!' (Interview A11-S). The chair of an REB at a small university finds that the huge workload affects recruitment of members to REB (Interview C12-S). The workload at one university has become so intense that a chair of an ethics committee suggested that a separate research-ethics office has to be created rather than remain nested in the Office of Research Administration, to prevent the workload absorption of the latter by the former (C14-M, Fieldnotes: 1248). Academic departments, although wanting to review their own work, do not want their own ethics committee because it is too much work. A psychology department is 'overwhelmed by many students needing ethics review of their research' (Interview C12-S). Other universities, too, have trouble dealing with the large volume of applications from students. One member of an ethics committee admitted that 'some of the research that psychologists do doesn't turn my crank, but reviewing them does!' The actual process of vetting them is never boring, he admits (Interview E15-S).

An empirical researcher of the IRB process in the United States claims that research applications have 'tripled over the past 20 years [1982–2002]' (Hamilton, 2002: 282). Even in small universities, the number of applications has increased rapidly (C26-S, Fieldnotes: 1199). A Canadian university can expect to assess eight to 900 applications a year, depending on the size of the university. Even small universities can expect to handle 60 applications a year, with a minimum of staff (probably with just one staff member) meaning that there are 3–4 applications at each meeting (Interview E15-S). A large university, with an REB of 27 people, considers 6–8 applications each month (B3). Each REB member in a mid-sized university reads a maximum of 18–20 applications per year, but on the whole, the REB must handle 65–70 applications per month, which is a 'hectic schedule' (Interview C11-M).

Appendix B (which lists Canadian REBs with the known number of applications) shows that the large universities handle between 777 and 900 applications per year, medium-sized universities receive between 200 and 800 applications (with many well below 500), and small universities normally handle between 8 and 124 applications (one exception saw a small university receive as many as 250). The number of applications in each university is dictated by how REBs define research, whether pedagogical research exercises in courses are included, and the types of academic departments present. Researchers come to the REB even when quality assurance studies indicate journals might require an ethics certificate and this increases the workload (S46-S). Some IRBs, according to De Vries and Forsberg (2002: 210) had a hard time figuring out how many studies were currently active.

To that end, universities as the ethics community claims, need to devote many resources. At the University of Iowa, for example, the Human Subjects Office 'employs 9.5 FTE [full-time employees] to review approximately 1,100 new studies a year, 300 of which are in social and behavioural science. There are five IRB chairs, four of whom are faculty who are paid for their service and one who is a full-time staff member' (Fitch, 2005: 275).

Frequency of Meetings

The yearly routines of work for REBs mean that they meet anywhere from ten to twelve times (S17, Fieldnotes: 234; E15-S).[12] One suspects that the frequency of meetings does not vary greatly among countries. For example, Parker et al. (2005) explain that an Australian medical REB meets monthly for two to three-and-a-half hours. At a small Canadian university, the REB meets three to four-and-a-half hours each month (Interview C12-S). One member of an REB spends four to six hours each week working on application forms (Interview E15-S). A chair in a small university spends twenty hours per week, fifty-two weeks per year (Interview C26-S, Fieldnotes: 1200). In a survey, De Vries and Forsberg (2002: 209–11) learned that an IRB meets, on the average, fourteen times a year. Meetings last two hours and fifteen minutes, and each IRB is responsible for 408 studies. In a study of Canadian ethics committees, Ellard and Dobson (2007) learned that of the twelve surveyed REBs, each REB typically met once a month, but one reported six meetings per year, another seven per year, and one only met once a year.

It is clear, though, that work on the ethics committee interrupts a faculty member's other work, which often continues after one goes home (C12-S). An REB chair admits that reviewing proposals is very time consuming; he gave up on empirical research for honours theses and it also became impossible to do graduate research proposals (R013-S, Fieldnotes: 542). A chair at a large university explains,

I spend a minimum of four hours a week and it's more like six, going over protocols with the associate director of the support staff. That's just all going through the files. (Interview C05-B)

Another REB chair explains that

you always feel like you are running around trying to bite your tail, because it's not only the volume of work that so constant. I mean it's just at a high level and just doesn't slacken off right through the entire twelve months. Secondly, you are trying to honour the genuine educative function of REBs. Third, you are trying to keep up with a lot of new *TCPS* revisions and more conversations and all the rest of it. Fourth, you are trying to keep up with the heretofore undiscovered ethical aspects of emerging methodologies and so forth. So the whole parcel is a full-time job. It's a hugely intensive job. (Interview C11-M)

The same chair added thoughtfully:

So there is a lot of reading and a lot of conversations because as you know there is a lag time between the writing of the notice of review for the researcher and the time when the researcher actually takes care of what our concerns are. So there is an approval period as well. So, I mean, you've moved on two, three weeks into a whole different batch and then you are always looking backwards at the folks who are just getting the work done now, and then you are ready to review it again to see that they've met the conditions. Then you issue the certificate of approval. (C11-M)

This chair, too, thought it was important to acknowledge the hard work of members and made a point of treating these members (and himself) to a nice dinner. It was not clear to me whether these dinners were paid for with the university's money.

Given the formidable workload challenges facing ethics committee staff, it is not surprising that, according to De Vries and Forsberg (2002: 213), 'the existing structure of IRBs inclines researchers and research institutions to put their interests before the interests of the subjects of research.' In the foreseeable future, the workload is more likely to increase than not as research gets defined more broadly (Interview C30-M). So, too, will 'higher' ethics standards mean more paper work (Fieldnotes: 70) and recent changes in the *TCPS* will demand more work from REBs (C26-S, Fieldnotes: 1199).

Strategies

As a consequence, the work overload and lack of resources lead to 'inappropriate' shortcuts, 'reflexes rather than reflection' (Pritchard, 2002: 7). There is also universal agreement among the people I interviewed about the difficulty of taking a 'sober look' at applications (Interview C09-B). The chair of an REB at a mid-sized university says that 'no clear voices are heard or that applications get any careful voting.' He asks, 'Do REB members vote yes, because everyone else does? Things get rushed through. [There is a] lack of knowledge about the application. [Moreover, would the number of applications] prevent us from getting at the real issues' (Interview C25-M)? Significantly, says another chair, 'the workload now prevents REB from learning things together.' One cannot go through all the files (Interview C03-M).

The workload also prevents ethics committees from engaging in any deeper reflection and wider discussions about policy. The chair of a large university says that the load of work prevents her from looking at interpretations by the Panel on Research Ethics (Interview C05-B). A member of an ethics committee confesses that he is far too busy to really carefully read documents that come from PRE (Interview E15-S):

> ... stuff comes down the pipe, I'll be honest with you, I've got stuff from the *TCPS* I've scanned through. I haven't read it. Most of us are busy. Academic life places a lot of demands on you – you can't read everything that comes in front of you ... at this university especially where ... most faculty are told [by the university] to try and teach seven courses ... We don't have TAs here so our teaching roles are full and some of us like myself are on two, three, four different committees and you want a home life too. So, I'll be honest with you ... this stuff, quite frankly, is tedious. There's no way that I can see this REB submitting any thirty-page document [and] when we are doing policy revisions I took it upon myself to revise the student policy ... I spent the better part of a week just on that and that's like a four-page document and the paper work is phenomenal. So, I'll be perfectly honest with you: I've got the *TCPS*. Some of it I've glanced through ... I don't have the time.

The above problem of workload, which specifically refers to documents and consultations coming from the federal research-ethics regime, has enormous implications for the issue of 'vertical ethics' that I approach in chapter 9. As a consequence, some chairs feel they do not have a lot of time to advocate changes: 'I am busy keeping things moving, not much [time] for anything else' (Interview C03-M).

In light of this work pressure, it stands to reason that REB and ethics staff are adopting strategies to relieve themselves of the workload. Some of these strategies also bring relief to researchers (such as when applications cannot be carefully scrutinized) but also a measure of frustration to the ethics staff who believe they are not doing the work they are supposed to be doing. One of these strategies involves classifying the review of research applications as 'expedited.'

More and more applications are being considered for 'expedited review' (Fieldnotes: 1542), but there are two sides of this issue. For some, expedited review does not make for less administrative work (S30-M, Fieldnotes: 1524), while others who have not immersed themselves in the day-to-day handling of applications believe that it *will* lessen the paperwork (R112-M, Fieldnotes: 342). A report by Hirtle and Weisbaum (2004) shows that, by scaling down the assessment of risk by REBs (which would trigger an expedited review), paperwork will be reduced. A chair mentioned an interesting case that involved an REB who was not able to get back to the researcher very quickly because of his/her workload and was prompted by the researcher to give an answer. On account of this delay, the REB decided the application would go through an expedited review, especially because the project was the same one that had been submitted the previous year (Interview C12-S). As a member of an ethics office mentioned, one needs discipline to keep the applications on track (Fieldnotes: 66).

It is clear, though, that the bulk of the work falls on the shoulders of staff and that members of ethics committees partake in that work outside of the formal meetings. A reviewer of a draft of *The Seduction of Ethics* makes the point that, 'less than five percent of applications are ever examined, discussed, or decided on by the full board or in a meeting' (Reviewer A, 30 November 2009). The situation implies that researchers must pitch their proposals to staff and board members outside of the meetings. It is a situation that can make the application process more complex . . . or easier, depending on the individual experience, training, and knowledge of the staff and board members.

Other strategies, born out of the need to get around workload, also have an impact on research. One ethics office decided to approve projects until some end date rather than asking for annual applications for review (E20-B, Fieldnotes: 1216). Another office asks researchers just to submit modifications instead of resubmitting the whole application

(S16-M, Fieldnotes: 953). Some REBs have stopped trying to monitor research (Interview C11-M; Interview C12-S). One chair tries to group projects with similarities to overcome workload in departments (Interview C12-S). Still another chair is aiming towards redistributing the workload by having a larger REB so that not all applications are seen by the same people (Interview C30-M); a similar effort is guiding the work of another REB (Interview E15-S), namely, to double up the REB. Still others are hoping to make better use of summers to continue their review work (Interview E15-S). Reducing the number of application forms from nine to one or two is another technique (Interview S47-M).

In summary, ethics committees do not occupy an enviable position. There are few, if any, countervailing forces that deal with the high administrative burdens and costs of well-functioning ethics committees and staff who face a heavy workload as they carry out their duties. To that end, ethics committees develop strategies to make do and to reduce their workloads. Their needs are glaring. Such pressures are bound to influence their relations with researchers. Other pressures are derived from the internal dimensions of ethics work: the lack of training in, or the grounded familiarity with, social research by ethics staff. In this chapter, I also discussed the problematic aspects of community members on ethics committees as well as the structural aspects of ethics committees that play a significant role in shaping research on campuses: the dominant position that psychologists, medical researchers, and those whose research does not involve humans hold as chairs can be very influential forces. The disciplinary representation on committees is poor, but not for want of trying. What also weighs in is the fact that there is no formal oversight of ethics committees. Moreover, the lack of public knowledge about their decisions (unlike judgments in the court system which are generally open to public) creates uncertainty among researchers.

I now turn to presenting the moral cosmologies of the research-ethics review, followed by an in-depth look at procedural routines, the meetings themselves of ethics committees, and finally, at how idiosyncratic and inconsistent that world really is.

6 The Moral Cosmology
of the Ethics-Review World

Moral cosmology (a system of beliefs) is integral to any study of a social world, including that of ethics committees and staff. In our context it will be important to explore not only the perceptions and beliefs that chairs, members, and staff of ethicscommittees have about themselves but also the beliefs they have about researchers and research participants. It is the ethics-review world that drives these perceptions and beliefs, a sort of 'emotion work' (Hochschild, 1983: 17–18), feelings that staff and members of ethics committees feel obliged to create, nurture, and sustain while being part of the ethics-review process.

About Themselves

What especially emerged from an analysis of the in-depth interviews are six defining perspectives that chairs, members, and staff of ethics-review committees are committed to. They nurture a positive self-image and believe in the goodness of rules, but recognize that the review process is onerous and challenging. On the 'darker' side, they also maintain a negative self-image, are haunted by 'shades of the past' (i.e., research that went wrong ethically), and believe that there are barriers between their world and that of the researchers.

It is no surprise that members of ethics committees and their staff see their work in a positive light. They are part of a critical link in the university system. There is a 'strong ethos of volunteerism' that is 'compelling,' and as a result, 'the members occupied a "moral space"' (Parker, James, and Barrett, 2005: 16). Because of the diversity of the committee, members have to speak in lay terms to each other and one chair said that many members on his committee 'enjoy the interdisciplinary nature of REB work' (Interview C03-M). A member of the ethics community praised her REB as 'very competent and thoughtful' (Interview E12-M). Interviews with chairs, members of ethics committees, and staff reveal the following attributes of their work:

- doing socially valuable work on REB (Interview C05-B)
- very pleased with REB team, happy to see good work done (Interview C10-B)
- proud that her REB is very cutting edge (across the country) (Interview E12-M)
- thrilled and excited to be part of the REB, unlike any other REB (Interview E12-M)

The annual conferences of the National Council on Ethical Human Research (NCEHR) in mid-February and the Canadian Association of Research Ethics Boards (CAREB) in early May are highly supportive in maintaining the value of ethics office staff and, therefore, their enthusiasm for their work. Their agendas and presentations proclaim the supreme validity of ethics codes, seldom punctured by counternarratives.[1] If there are reports of difficulties, they are seen as procedural, not substantive, but they underscore the important role of ethics staff to solve all of these problems. The community of ethics reviewers is, after all, vindicated by a recent self-rating survey in Canada that tells us that 91 per cent of REB chairs, 64 per cent of REB members, and 100 per cent of REB administrators have either 'excellent' or 'good' knowledge of ethics (McCambridge and Owen, 2007).[2] The corresponding figure for researchers in the same study stands at 88 per cent. Naturally, one may ask what is understood by ethics: ethics-review procedures, ethics codes, ethics in research, applied ethics, or ethics in general? Perhaps the understanding applies a little to each, in uneven proportions. The self-rating of efficiency by REBs (1 being extremely well, 5 being extremely poorly) indicates a rather high level of satisfaction with Western and Prairie universities (1.67), in Ontario (2.67), Quebec (2.33), and in the East (1.33).

The positive self-image of members of the ethics-review community rests on the belief that the rules that guide the ethics-review process are inherently good. The chair of a small university REB (Interview C12-S) expresses a deeply felt sentiment when she says that committees 'want to be seen doing their mandate,' while a member of an ethics committee at another small university (Interview E25-S) affirmed that we 'must be careful not to be in the way of people, but if something is not right, we should be in the way. That's the point.' Committees are, after all, according to a member of an ethics committee at the same university as the above-mentioned chair, 'doing a job that not a lot of people want to do, living with the consequences of decisions,' and, this person adds, 'we do help researchers think more clearly' (Interview E15-S).

Their devotion to the goodness of regulation and rules reminds one of Ann Hamilton's discussion in which she avers that regulators seek a lack of ambiguity that is 'consistent with Weber's observations about the goals of bureaucracy' and which, furthermore, reinforced the idea that people prefer the simplicity that rules bring (Hamilton, 2002: 241).

Despite the espousing of a positive self-image and the attachment to their mandate, members of the ethics community underscore the onerous and challenging nature of research-ethics review. One report found that ethics committees find the review of proposals 'tedious' (NCA, 2005: 225), in addition to these comments regarding their work:

– onerous and often unnecessary (De Vries and Forsberg, 2002: 199)
– nobody likes going through bureaucracy (Interview C30-M)
– administrivia detract from sound ethical analysis (C14-M, Fieldnotes: 1191)
– I spend every waking moment reading applications (Interview C11-M)
– spending too much time on irrelevant details (Interview E15-S)

A member of an ethics committee always tried 'to get the REB focused on what's really important,' such as ethics breaches beyond minimal risk, minimal intervention in qualitative research proposals, and not wanting to destabilize the process (Focus Group REB E15-S).

On a moral plane, observers have noted that IRB 'staffs and members can also be corrupted by the ideals of justice and advocacy that energizes them' (Nelson, 2004: 209). A theologian who was a keynote speaker at the 2005 CAREB meeting noted that the base problem of ethics involves 'self-aggrandizement, individualism, and power' (Presentation R035, 6 May 2005, CAREB Annual Meeting, Fieldnotes: 163). Still, some chairs exhibit a good deal of modesty when they acknowledge, like the researcher, that 'someone else needs to look over her stuff in case she has missed something' (Interview C30-M).

A permanent challenge for all ethics committees concerns the institutional context of research at university (Interview E12-M) that can undermine the work of ethics committees. Professional jealousies, vengeance, and competition exacerbate these challenges, causing participants to wonder more cynically than ever before about the efficacy of the research-ethics review process.

I have already noted the differential treatment by ethics committees of novice and veteran researchers. Janice McKendrick (2006) observed that, in her experience, REBs abide by a hierarchical assessment as to who should receive a more expedient assessment. Lesley Conn (2008: 508) reported that when the REB learned that a researcher held many grants, including a large one, her application was suddenly no longer a burden! Upon reading an early draft of *The Seduction of Ethics*, one researcher at a mid-sized university informed me that it is the opposite in her case, and that having many grants actually worked against her. She said that 'it almost seems like they want to prove to me that I am nothing special just because I am well-funded.' Similarly, a report by the Canadian Sociology and Anthropology Association (CSAA-CIRS) contained the remark of a researcher who claimed that 'hospital REBs find anything done by insiders to be more ethical; outsiders are held to a higher standard' (Muzzin, 2002, Fieldnotes: 56E8). The chair of an ethics committee proffers the vision that the decision to approve research 'depends on the status of the researcher, veteran or newcomer, or from what university' the researcher hails from (Interview C25-M).

One might infer that the ethics-review process threatens collegiality and heightens conflict (Nelson and McPherson, 2004), especially when vendettas are also a part of these challenges. A member of an ethics committee (Interview E12-M) described how a student was not allowed to do non-public domain research. There were political reasons behind the decision preventing her from doing the research and the question was whether the REB's goal was to impress upon a recalcitrant department the importance of getting an ethics review or to inflict a form of punishment. A senior administrator has also had a personal reaction to her research. The REB used this case to push an REB member to moderate her view about facilitating research. 'A real heartbreak for all,' says a member of an ethics committee in hindsight. Another example involves an REB's desire to create obstacles for a very promising, relatively young and highly acclaimed researcher. Members of the REB were jealous of that researcher's accomplishments (Fieldnotes: 1862). The seduction of ethics provides the power. Even grant committees not affiliated with any research-ethics committees, according to a reader of an early draft of this book, are now routinely not satisfied with merely looking at methods or scope, but find in ethics a new power.

David Wright's experiences (2004) constitute an egregious example of misuse of power and privilege by an IRB. He was charged with 'bad research practices' for writing about a student without having obtained prior consent and for 'unethical behavior' 'for failing to report that student for the crime that he had alleged to have committed.' What surprised Wright was that he, in fact, had not conducted 'research' at all. He wrote a personal essay as part of a creative, non-fiction narrative about a complex of societal and personal observations 'dealing with race, class, and pedagogy.' In that essay, his 'experience with the student prompts the reflection and drives the narrative.' Wright does admit that he 'did not seek out the student's prior written consent.' At the time of the class in question, however, he had no idea that he would write about it. Still, Wright 'had in fact gone to great lengths to protect him and his identity – which is the motive for requiring consent' (Wright, 2004: 204). After a remarkably lengthy process involving the IRB, the editors of a prestigious literary magazine, and senior university administration, he was finally absolved of his ethics misdemeanour.

According to Kate Holland, these 'ethics surges' (rather than 'ethics drift') also position researchers as the source of ethical problems and reviewers as having the unique responsibility and power to keep these problems from arising, which could result in refusals to approve research that poses any difficult questions (Holland, 2007: 905, based on Chalmers and Pettit, 1998). To enforce moral behaviour, the ethics regime is centralizing its system of control (ICL, 2006: 6). Centralization puts distance between the researcher and his / her research, between the researcher and the ethics committee, and between the ethics-review process and moral conduct. Catherine Scott (2004: 11) makes it clear that scholars understand the implications behind the demands – that they are either 'incompetent or malicious . . . [this] explains the outrage that attends the activities of ethics committees.' As committees become more fully aware of their discrepant behaviour, it is a matter of time (at least for some committees) before they reflect on their own conduct and seize on the understanding of their negative self-image, which is apparent to so many researchers but veiled from the eyes of the committees themselves.

Despite the positive self-image and their ability to weather onerous challenges, members of the ethics community find themselves in a quandary coupled with apologetic behaviour. Here are some extracts from the interviews and from the correspondence I received from members of the ethics-review community:

- I am apologizing more and more to students regarding the REB. (R50-M, Fieldnotes: 706)
- I always had misgivings about ethics review. (Chat C28-M, Fieldnotes: 145)
- I hate being told by NCEHR that I am a 'non' [not a medical REB] and hate being called a 'behavioural' et cetera committee. (Interview C03-M)
- Here is what I fear the most: being too harsh, but also being challenged. (Interview E27-S)

Leaving aside the debate about 'why procedures developed in response to medical scandals should apply to social scientists' (Aldred, 2008: 889), the early years of the establishment of ethics committees saw members of the ethics community using remembrances or evocations of earlier social research violating ethical norms justifying regulatory mechanisms. Today, the predilection to use this earlier social research as a red flag is gone. The regulation of research through ethics review is now an accepted fact (Derbyshire, 2006: 44).

Members of the ethics-review community deny there are fundamental barriers between their world and that of the researchers. In doing so, they affirm their positive qualities and claim they are 'not malicious and rigid' (Bach, 2005: 262). After all, others say, all you need to do is look at the REB and realize that there are members who are researchers. A report echoes this same sentiment: 'We ought to be seen as a group of individual faculty members, not some amorphous bureaucracy' (NCA, 2005: 225). The interviews and chats in the course of my research reveal the same tone:

- My job is not to stop people doing research, but to help them do better . . . I want to change to being helpful, rather than creating gatekeeping and fear. (C09-B, Fieldnotes: 401–2)
- REBs are listening now more to researchers. (Interview C09-B)
- I see my role not as a hurdle, but as having educative function. (Interview C11-M)
- I don't want to be another layer of difficulty. (Interview C30-M)
- I don't want to be seen as Big Brother. (Interview E15-S)
- We are meta-cognitive as enablers of research. (Interview C11-M)

Among members of the ethics community, there is also the belief that barriers can be done away with, not only through personal initiatives facilitating change in the REB but also by including an active ingredient of cooperation. One chair reinforces this sentiment when he says that research ethics has to be 'a collaborative affair' (C14-M, Fieldnotes: 1238), while an ethics-committee member at a small university wants 'to minimize [her] interventions' (Interview E15-S). Being supportive of researchers, 'rather than accusatory' is another way that the barrier can be overcome (Interview E27-S). One administrator (Interview A11-S) prides herself for having developed 'a real goal of reaching out to researchers, especially with the Institute [mentions a research-oriented group]' (Interview C30-M). Some exhibit a positive approach to researchers, such as 'it's fun knowing [about] all the research that's going on [around] campus . . . [it's] one of the perks' (Interview E12-M).

Naturally, as previous chapters have shown, the barriers between members of the ethics community and researchers can cause considerable grief. Yet, in some universities, there is an element of surprise on the part of the ethics community when they hear of troubles elsewhere. A chair shared with me his 'surprise to hear of complaints on other campuses' and said he found that what researchers say about ethics review in national gatherings 'does not correspond' to his experience (Interview C30-M). Still, problems in overcoming the barrier, such as administrative fumbles, are 'not enough to get rid of the system' (S16-M, Fieldnotes: 956). A staff member sympathizes with researchers and admits 'there is some justification for researchers to see us as bureaucratic overkill; most research projects are minimal risk and guidelines were designed for more serious stuff' (Focus Group REB1-S). Ironically, Maureen Fitzgerald, an Australian researcher, notes that ethics '[c]ommittees advocate to be closed, giving them an identity, [and] providing a unified front' (Fitzgerald, 2004: 43). That identity is intended to make the committee cohere. That coherence can prove to be useful in bridging the gap . . . or maintaining it, as the next section shows.

About Researchers

Apart from trying to understand what chairs, members, and staff of ethics committees believe and say about themselves, it is crucial to know what they believe about researchers. No doubt, it is also important to know what researchers claim that ethics committees believe about researchers. We should also consider those beliefs that mitigate a moral agency as well as those beliefs and practices about helping researchers.

One needs to distinguish between what ethics committees themselves say they believe about researchers and what researchers claim ethics committees believe about researchers. There has been a gradual shift over the past few years in the belief of research being more a 'privilege' than a 'right' which has slipped into the mindset of the ethics-review community. It is this mindset, often unconscious, that frames the perspectives, beliefs, and practices towards researchers and that constitutes a radical departure from the usual givens of academic life. Richard Shweder (2006: 20) faithfully attended a social and behavioural sciences IRB training session at the University of Chicago, where he learned from the IRB staff that '[c]onducting research is a privilege and NOT a right.' To someone outside the university or not versed in the ethos of research, this 'categorical slogan' could well make eminent sense. However, the idea behind it 'flies in the face of the University's own mission about research.' Significantly, according to Shweder, the 'entire tradition of academic freedom . . . is simply set aside.' Sentiments about research as a privilege produce an entirely different approach than thoughts about research as a right. One can muster an attack against privileges, but not against rights.

There is a common belief among members of ethics committees that 'many researchers and academic departments don't read ethics stuff, like the *TCPS*' (Interview E15-S) and that 'researchers ignore information on our website' (Interview C05-B). The researchers, moreover, 'don't have time to think of broader issues' (Interview C09-B). In fact, the troubles started at the very inception of ethics policies at universities, and when the new policy came to university senate, 'some voted against it, there was hostility, suspicion, resentment regarding REB's veto power not coming from one's discipline' (Focus Group REB1-S). One staff member (Interview S46-S) believes that researchers see the application form as 'obstructionist,' namely, that the REB is asking information about the research, for example, 'why does it take so long?' and leading the researcher to lament, 'Just get me through this!' The same staff member believes that 'a lot of researchers can't wait for ethics approval' because there is not enough time in their research schedule. So the researchers' main question becomes, 'How quickly can I get approval? I already have a student working on the research.'

Members of ethics committees base these assumptions on their own experiences, but these are assumptions that might apply to merely a few researchers, all told. Still, these beliefs will lead ethics-committee members to believe that 'it's not good enough just to assume that researchers will fix problems' (Interview E25-S). A chair claims that 'researchers have fears, they don't understand the chair's methodology' (Interview C30-M). If a researcher proves to live up to these expectations, and especially 'when a researcher pisses her off,' the chair brings the case to the full REB (Interview C05-B). However, there is the prevailing belief among members of ethics committees that they should be 'cautious about researchers; don't give them grief; they might fight back' (Interview E25-S). The same ethics-committee member said that her REB is 'afraid of a meltdown' with the researcher; 'the researcher may get back at the REB; the researcher may give grief back.' Indeed, she says, 'the REB is more fearful of researcher than vice versa.'

Thus, while IRBs in the U.S., according to Gunsalus (2003a: 3) are defensive about the concerns of researchers, some IRBs still maintain review procedures and decision-making patterns that are 'opaque in their logic and arbitrary in appearance' (Fitch, 2005: 271). Ascan Koerner's own research on ethics committees denotes not only antagonistic and protagonistic actions of ethics committees but also negative perceptions and positive perceptions of committees (Koerner, 2005: 231). What triggers many ethics committees is what they call the 'trust me approach' adopted by researchers. An ethics-committee member 'resents when she sees a poor proposal from an experienced researcher who says "trust me"' (Interview E25-S). This approach is unlikely to be persuasive to the ethics committee, 'operating as it does from assumptions of hierarchical power relations' (Boser, 2007: 1066). A chair's comments suggest that a researcher's insistence that he/she is a 'good person' means that the researcher is trying to assume power:

> I go crazy with people who say 'I'm a good person. Nothing I do is at all wrong.' I mean, if you think automatically that you are a good person and everything that you do is right, then you're never going to be able to see if there is anything controversial about what you do . . . so that's, you know, it's really the power thing.

And:

> I am concerned about that, and I think what people are bounded by is their own timidity and their own need to feel like they're good people rather than by the research ethics boards.

Also:

> It seems odd that you would have problems with our [REB staff] who
> are service-oriented people, who want to help other people and they
> have a very hard time seeing that getting out of the I-am-a-good-person
> thing, 'but I am doing this work because it is socially valuable work'
> and if you're asking me about it then you are casting aspersions on me.
> (Interview C05-B)

A member of an ethics organization (A12) encouraged IRBs to 'trust
but verify' – a phrase taken from the cold war. These approaches pave
the way for increased surveillance and governmental and institutional
control (Lincoln and Cannella, 2004: 7). One study summed up the
IRB's beliefs about the researcher in this manner: 'The researcher is not
trusted' (ICL, 2006: 6). Despite these varying beliefs about each other's
self-proclaimed qualifications, researchers, according to an administrator of one of Canada's federal funding agencies, 'should never say
that ethics is a barrier' (Presentation E04, 6 May 2005, CAREB Annual
Meeting, Fieldnotes: 163).

Betsy Bach, studying narratives in the ethics world, shows that IRBs
perceive researchers to be 'lazy, unwilling to adapt to institutional
requirements, or uneducated about the research process' (Bach, 2005:
260). Lesley Conn still feels 'disheartened' about the 'the strenuous and
generally unpleasant review process' that betrays the 'cynical nature of
the committee [that] presumes that a researcher is guilty of unethical conduct unless she can prove otherwise' (Conn, 2008: 508). One also learns
that ethics-committee members believe that social science researchers
submit 'unclear, hastily prepared proposals that don't adequately
assess risk' (Sieber and Baluyot, 1992, cited by Newman, 2004: 9).
Researchers offer 'poorly prepared applications' (Interview C05-B).
Ethics committees see researchers as cavalier (Church, Shopes, and
Blanchard, 2002). Ethics staff perceive the lack of preparation as a personal
disappointment when they 'see applications where researchers have
given no time or thought to ethical issues or to the application . . . [but]
most people are really good about it though' (Interview S47-M).

Stuart Derbyshire (2006: 37, 48) has discovered 'increasingly suspicious and mistrustful attitudes towards social science researchers' and
'an assumption of guilt and dishonesty on the part of researchers.' John
Mueller (2007: 825) also claims that 'researchers are demonized and
infantilized' by ethics committees. In this light, some committees refer

to particular researchers as having been 'problems' and speak of '*that researcher*' within the confines of their meetings. Maureen Fitzgerald, a researcher who has closely observed such meetings, learned that members invoke these cases 'by a codeword only known to members' (Fitzgerald, 2005: 327). When in another committee one speaks of the 'nurse's study,' this obscure reference is enough to recall to the minds of the committee members the related problems of the application (Hedgecoe, 2008: 879).

'A sort of disciplinary cross talk occurs,' say Church, Shopes, and Blanchard (2002: 4), while 'the ethnographer thinks that he or she has been scrupulously honest in presenting a research project with minimal risk ... the IRB member senses a flawed and incomplete research design that may put individuals at risk. The IRB member concludes that more information is needed at a full review.' IRBs carry such beliefs to the next step, according to Ann Hamilton (2002: 189), convinced that 'researchers must be carefully monitored ... i.e., the idea that researchers can't be trusted and must be closely and constantly supervised, spoon-fed via "templates," and monitored via the institution of paperwork processes (see Brainard, 2001, Sept. 28, for an alarming example).' The personal knowledge that committee members have of the applicant, such as by saying that they 'knew' him/her, or at least heard of him/her, allows them 'to match it with the file and [get] a straightforward passage,' especially if the researcher continued in the same area of research. Consistency is key and it was 'reasonable' (Parker, James, Barrett, 2005: 22). It should also be noted that an ethics committee believes it is 'not vital to know something about the researcher' (Interview E25-S). What is more, ethics committees greatly exaggerate the power of social researchers, especially ethnographers; the power normally remains vested in the research participant to accept or reject participation in the research (Fieldnotes: 322).

Beliefs That Mitigate Moral Agency

The practices of ethics committees that frame beliefs about researchers undercut the very notion of creating a moral agency by researchers. As Koro-Ljungberg et al. claim (2007: 1080), '[T]he university governance and protocol structure [involving ethics committees] ... work against the very idea that researchers and research participants are supposed to constitute themselves as "moral subjects of their own actions"' (citing Foucault, 1984: 352). For example, there is an account about a PhD student's going 'through ethics' and realizing that she should invite the REB member to speak to one of her classes: 'Sure,' said the REB member, 'I'd be happy to, but we try to do that in our qualitative research courses. For some reason, the students in your department just *aren't getting it*' (Johnson, 2008: 223; emphasis added). To underscore this relationship, we have already referred to ethics committees now vetting research and 'proposing the silliest things' (S31-M, Fieldnotes: 959).

Tellingly, John Mueller makes these observations:

> Although posturing themselves as creating respect for ethical research, IRBs have in reality created an adversarial relationship between researchers and IRB reviewers. Instead of increasing attention to ethical principles among researchers, the IRB's obsession with forms and process has produced a pragmatic minimalist response: Researchers learn to play the game, and in the process they self-censor their research proposals. (Mueller, 2007: 822)

In addition, Mueller (2007: 833) claims that he sees no evidence that 'federal regulators and campus zealots are willing to see themselves as even part of the problem; therefore, they will continue to blame researchers.' This perspective was exemplified when an ethics committee realized there is a serious contrast between new and veteran researchers (new researchers already think along the lines of ethics review), 'the veteran researchers now have to answer to an internal review' (Interview C09-B).

It is interesting to note the use of the term 'ethics,' when, in fact, it refers to the 'ethics-review process.' On that basis, the claims or beliefs by ethics administrators can be easily misconstrued as if the researcher is 'unethical.' For example, one administrator says, 'you have a real problem when the supervisor *doesn't understand ethics*' (Interview A11-S; interview participant's emphasis). Another ethics administrator notes that the 'REB is watching over profs who do research on students' (Interview C12-S). The implied mistrust takes the reader back to the previous section. A staff member notes reassuringly that 'a gap still exists: not malice, just lack of knowledge' (Focus Group REB1-S). Much of how ethics committees relate to researchers is based on their presumed lack of knowledge about 'ethics,' such as 'trying to get researchers a sense of what's proper treatment of people and what's dangerous' (Interview C05-B). It is not surprising that a staff member is 'trying to be either the patient mother or the punishing mother' (Interview S46-S).

These assertions and interactions stand in the way of what is most important: the need to create 'morally-active individuals' (Richardson and McMullan, 2007: 1128). Ironically, if researchers aimed at treating research participants in the same manner as ethics committees treat researchers, there is no question that that research would 'pass ethics.' According to a chair, the respect that ethics committees have for researchers is as important as the researcher's respect for research participants (Interview C03-M).

While the next two chapters convey in practical terms the means by which ethics committees convey their beliefs, namely through the creation of application forms and the drafting of letters to researchers, conveying to them the news that the research has been approved and whether it is subject to heavy or light modifications, or has been rejected outright, this section conveys the overall approach of ethics committees in light of their beliefs about researchers and in terms of the moral agency spoken about in the immediately preceding section.

Catherine Scott (2004: 11) articulates the view in the minds of ethics committees that 'researchers do not understand, leading to offers to help the researchers understand their sins of omission or commission.' A chair says, 'Junior faculty and students are a dream to work with unless poisoned by senior faculty.' Some of those sins pertain to grammar and syntax that account for 90 per cent of applications to a medical ethics committee. The committee returns them, according to an ethicist who had conducted research on this very topic (E02/R27, Fieldnotes: 142). However, researchers await such help with trepidation, as Cary Nelson informs us:

> . . . the persons in power declare, 'We are your friends. We want to work with you.' And in every instance, the person hearing the message wholly or partly discounts it. It does not matter whether this anxiety is well founded, because it is a predictable product of the power differential inherent in the system. (Nelson, 2004: 216)

The approach taken by the IRB of the University of Iowa is echoed by other ethics committees: 'We make a real effort to do this with a light hand, recognizing that there is nothing so galling as to hear that your *pet project* sounds like a waste of time' (Fitch, 2005: 274; emphasis added). Still, there is a dismissive tone with this 'light hand' and 'your *pet project*.' One might also read the same dismissive tone or a backhanded compliment when a member of an ethics committee said that the 'researcher's heart is in the right place,' but worries about action research and the role of knowledge as research gets carried out (Interview E13-M). Still, we also learn that the chair of another ethics committee 'tries to be gentle with researchers about suggesting methodology' (Interview C09-B).

The weight of power still rests with the ethics committee, often the object of complaints that it considers itself the only one qualified to make judgments about risk (e.g., R136-M, Fieldnotes: 1661) because as ethics committees extend their expertise about assessing risks, they engage in 'ethics creep.' In reply to a complaint about ethics drift from a critical researcher, a chair of a medical REB said,

> if you don't think ethics review by an REB improves the quality and rigour of research then either that is a sad commentary on the ethics reviews you are familiar with or that you are so cynical about ethics review, that you might want to consider another line of work. If 'ethics creep' means improving the quality of research, then so be it – but I and my REB members will run, not creep, with researchers towards that ethics 'imperialism' – even if some timid folks go bald as we dash by! (C031, Fieldnotes: 1660).

Adam Hedgecoe sees the difference between researchers (in this case, sociologists) and ethics committees as incongruent. He argues that,

> [a]t the heart of sociologists' claims of the 'difference' of their research, and hence the inappropriateness of ethics review, is ethnography, where the problem revolves around committees' requests that informed consent be sought, and that such committees require applicants to be able to list all the possible risks and harms that might arise, an apparent impossibility given ethnography's inherent 'flexibility.' (Hedgecoe, 2008: 880)

About Research Participants

The safety and protection of research participants stand ideologically at the centre of ethics codes. But do ethics-review procedures protect research participants? How paramount are the interests of research participants? Do ethics committees have the right 'pitch' in understanding research participants? Are consent forms insulting and paternalistic? Does the research-ethics review process take away the moral agency of research participants? And are ethics committees' notions of vulnerability a far stretch?

Given the centrality of all ethics regimes to protect research subjects or research participants, it comes as a surprise that there are virtually no studies about research-ethics review and research participants. Embedded in many ethnographic studies are in vivo reports about the relationship between researchers and research participants (see, for example, Wax and Cassell, 1981; Wax 1982), but it is only very recently that such relationships have been scrutinized with the view of learning more about the impact of research-ethics review on research participants. Whether one refers to these older studies or the newer ones, social researchers are more likely to argue that 'research reciprocity' is a more illustrious goal than merely establishing the 'forms' by which informed consent is achieved. The latter brings in its wake numerous unforeseen practical problems.

The other problems that informed consent forms bring include the under- and over-pitching of consent forms (i.e., forms treat research participants as either ignorant or forms are far too complex for anyone to understand). The principle of informed consent has also proven to be insultingly paternalistic in its understanding of the world of research participants. The principle does not bestow moral agency on the participants.[3] The following paragraphs raise these and other issues.

It was only in the past few years that SSHWC commissioned two of its members, Michelle McGinn of Brock University and Ted Palys of Simon Fraser University, to undertake such a study. Kakali Bhattacharya (2007) conducted her own in-depth study of the consent form and process, with a particular reference to a research participant who has entered her life personally. What are the fluctuating boundaries? What is the framework on which stands her relationship to the research participant – a friendship? a sisterhood? a mentorship? Should she consider or ignore any observations made before the friendship took hold? In a highly reflexive study, Wiles et al. (2006: 286) and Crow et al. (2006) studied how academics use consent in their research. Their observations also included the interesting reaction of academics to the use of consent forms: formal consent forms alienated these two sets of academic researchers from their fellow academics. Another study, at the initiative of the Interagency Advisory Panel on Research Ethics and presented at the 2005 CAREB meeting in Toronto, emphasized the importance of ongoing consent and that researched populations are diverse and consent should embody that diversity (Hirtle, Letendre, and Lormeau, 2004; Fieldnotes: 164). One researcher pinpoints the needs, problems, and ethics of working with research participants in this manner:

> What did they [the research participants] think? So this is a kind of a discourse analysis. Different discourse from the ethics staff, the committee members, the researchers, the participants, just to see what are the differences. I think that would be a big difference, [involving] varied research findings, participants' opinions, their opinions on ethical issues, whether or not they think we should have the review or not, or what issues should have to be approved before they conduct research. (Interview R002-M)

Canada's draft proposal for a new *TCPS* reflects a new discourse about informed consent. It now recognizes that

> [r]especting autonomy means giving due deference to a person's judgement and ensuring that they are free to choose without interference. Autonomy is not exercised in isolation but is influenced by a person's *various connections to family, to community, and to cultural, social, linguistic, religious and other groups.* Likewise, a person's decisions can have an impact on any of these. (PRE, 2008: 4; emphasis added)

It further states that the requirement to acquire consent

> ... reflects the commitment that participation in research, including participation through the use of one's data ... should be a matter of choice and that, to be meaningful, the choice must be informed. An informed choice is one that is based on as complete an understanding as is reasonably possible of the purpose of the research, what it entails, and its risks and potential benefits, both to the participant and to others. (PRE, 2008: 5)

A useful and insightful study about consent in research involved prenatal HIV tests and treatments. Dale Dematteo (2002: 74), a graduate student in the Department of Public Health Science at the University of Toronto, asked women what 'informed consent' meant. The research participants did not know and thought it means to give your permission to be tested or your right to be told before being tested. However, no women identified the three essential components of informed consent, namely 'potential benefits, potential risks, alternatives to all treatments or procedures offered or prescribed to patients.'

In recent years, there has been a rising concern among ethics committees about the unequal dynamics of relationships of power between the researcher and the research participant (for example, Seifert, 2005: 7–9). In general, ethics committees assume that the researcher operates with 'power' over the research participants. In that world view, according to Susan Boser (2007: 1063), the risk of harm (by the researcher) figures prominently and 'all responsibility, and power, is held by the researcher ... with a limited view of the potential for human agency among participants in the study.' However, every researcher in the social sciences who conducts field research knows full well that the power imbalance, in fact, favours the research participant (see, for example, Bell and Bryman, 2007: 68). Still, ethics committees are dedicated to the belief that power imbalance 'favours' the researcher, but with some sad consequences for research. Boser reports a PhD-level action-research project undertaken by Feroz (2006) in which an IRB did not allow a particular stakeholder group to participate. It saw 'as the potential for this group to experience harm in that the lead researcher held a position of greater relative structural power within an organization.' However, this groups saw their 'inability to participate in research and decisions that affected them' as threatening, resulting 'in negative consequences to the research group as a whole, consequences that were unanticipated by the IRB' (Boser, 2007: 1065).

Several studies have shown that ethics-review procedures not only do *not* protect research participants but also actually harm, or favour the researcher and the research institution instead. Humphreys, Trafton, and Wagner (2003), in an economic study of the costs of multi-site research-ethics review worth $56,000 (16.8 per cent of research budget), discovered that these extensive IRB procedures had no discernible impact on the protection of human subjects. 'The essential procedures of the study,' they claim, 'never changed substantially, despite exchanges of over 15,000 pages of material among the nine sites' (77). Ann Hamilton's research on the subject asks, 'What are IRBs "really" doing for the benefit of human subjects of qualitative and survey [research]?' Her experience suggests that

> local IRBs convolute the process for researchers, infringe on their rights to conduct free inquiry, and contaminate the natural world. Further, IRBs are not offering 'protections' to human subjects of these treatments, mostly because none are needed. (Hamilton, 2002: 251)

As an illustration of harming research participants, albeit in a medical study, Lindgren, Murashko, and Ford (2007: 403) noted the IRB regime's potential for 'slowing down or deterring studies that may lead to positive medical, scientific, and intellectual developments.' In thirty-one interviews and focus groups with researchers regarding consent while working with vulnerable populations, Crow et al. (2006) described both 'optimistic' or 'pessimistic' scenarios (i.e., no conflict between doing ethical research and getting fine data, or doing ethical research undermining getting good data). There was a correlation between ethics and getting good data.

Many others have noted the worrying fact that the 'existing structure of IRBs inclines researchers and research institutions to put their interests before the interests of the subjects of research' (De Vries and Forsberg, 2002: 213), a viewpoint shared by another researcher (R015-M, Fieldnotes: 979) who is an active observer and participant in the research-ethics community. A member of an ethics committee (Interview E13-M) had noted a contrary perspective: the interests of research participants are very much paramount. What further undermines the value of the ethics-review mandated consent process is that the interests of research participants are not paramount – a subject to which we now turn.

If the interests of research participants were paramount, it would be important to see if they have the same understanding as implied by the researcher. Although hardly a researched topic, it is already clear that the research participant will have different understandings of what is to take place (see, for example, Wiles, et al., 2006: 295; Bell and Bryman, 2007: 67). Some years ago, I was engaged in a study about what parents with asthmatic children do when they need to rush the child to the emergency room of a nearby hospital. We researchers became convinced that the mothers thought their abilities as parents were being tested, while we were in fact interested in the social process that attend such decisions and steps. It is perhaps for this reason that a member of an ethics committee (Interview E13-M) said in an interview that counsellors' doing focus group research with at-risk youth are not likely to help these youth. Wiles et al. (2006: 295) would agree that in the case of relatively powerless groups, 'informed consent *procedures* have limited ability to impact meaningfully on participants' decisions around participation' (emphasis in original).

Using terms or words demanded by ethics committees can also mean that the research participants' interests are not paramount. One researcher (Interview R173-M) had to remain faithful to a disciplinary concept of leisure, as opposed to how women activists defined that concept, a definition that was at odds with what the researcher was asked to use by her supervisor and affirmed by the REB. The women were deeply offended by this change in the definition, which made the research more difficult. Kate Holland (2007: 898) had the same experience when she used terms in a study on mental illness that did not resonate with IRB's conception, but did with the research participants. In the same study, the IRB prohibited her from identifying herself to a research participant as someone with mental illness, a revelation that would have facilitated the interview. The researcher thought that the prohibition was akin to deception (903).

On a larger scale, research participants did not respond to a particular research design that was specified by the Local Ethics Committee (Truman, 2003: 5). It also became harder to study business and government elites when the mandated ethics-review form had to be used (Bell and Bryman, 2007: 68). The story of a linguist's having preliterate people sign a consent form has become so ubiquitous that one wonders about its veracity, although it is widely cited (see, for example, Dingwall, 2008: 5, citing an AAUP, 2000 study; Sieber, Plattner, and Rubin, 2002: 1). More worrisome was an ethics committee's insistence on giving copies of consent forms to victims of abuse. The use of these forms dramatically increased the danger to these women (NCA, 2005: 204). As Nelson indicates, 'consent forms can create the anxiety they are designed to ameliorate' (Nelson, 2004: 215) – a point of view Ann Hamilton agrees with when she says that 'the protection procedures become a greater discomfort to human subjects than the actual treatment' and that 'the regulatory requirements may take more time than the research itself' (Hamilton, 2005: 200).

One IRB required the exclusion of teachers and students who did not sign the consent forms. As a result, 'researchers were barred from documenting the words and deeds of excluded individuals' (Hemmings, 2006: 14). The consequence of such exclusion may seem quite normal to ethics committees, but only seems to cause bafflement on the part of researchers. One anthropologist (R023-M, Fieldnotes: 141) who studied immigrants in Canada said to me that a research participant resisted the consent letter – she was offended by the clause that she could withdraw from the interview.

The veil between the world of ethics committees and that of the researcher is fiercely maintained by such puzzling decisions. The requirements mandated by the ethics committee with regard to research participants are borne out of a lack of understanding about the world of research participants. As a consequence, the interests of research participants are not paramount, despite claims to the contrary.

So far removed from the world of research participants, especially those living in a vulnerable context, ethics committees may either under- or overestimate what the research participants need to know about the research. For example, a study about women prisoners concluded that it was *hard to know whether they understood* to what they consented. It concluded that research participants are ignorant about what they are consenting to (Truman, 2003: 6). More typically, though, the length and the amount of paper work needed for research participants to follow the informed consent process can be too long or too complex. Richardson and McMullan (2007: 1125), for example, found the information sheets too long and complex, and noted that informants have stopped reading them. Crow et al. (2006: 90) concluded that consent sheets are a barrier to research participants who are now confronted with 'a whole load of paperwork.' In another instance, concerning the death of a research participant at Johns Hopkins University, regulators indicate that the use of a complex form may have contributed to the problems related to the death of a volunteer; the informed consent form 'appeared to include complex language that would not be understandable to all subjects' (Hamilton, 2002: 221). In any case, according to Hamilton, 'the "instructions" are impossible (or nearly so) to follow, i.e., to include all the required information produces a document longer than the recommended length, found in the same set of instructions' (222). It is not unusual for consent forms to be rewritten by ethics committees because respondents might 'include some illiterate or marginally educated individuals,' but, as one scholar noted, 'the rewritten draft was far more convoluted' (NCA, 2005: 220).

While it is difficult to approach the world of research participants in a suitable and relevant fashion, this problem pales in comparison to the insultingly paternalistic beliefs about those participants.

Countless are the researchers forced to comply with consent forms which contain 'overly detailed, insultingly paternalistic informed consent procedures' (Sieber, Plattner, and Rubin, 2002: 4). Crow et al. (2006: 91) found such forms patronizing (e.g., asking the question, 'Do you understand this?'). Amy Flowers who studied phone-sex workers ('fantasy agents') wrote,

The premise that individuals are somehow damaged by exposure to offensive or controversial ideas is contrary to the goals of research, knowledge, and education. This protectionism presumes a paternalism every bit as strong as the one that dictated that subjects be protected from knowing anything about the research. This newer paternalism simply protects the subjects from insights about themselves. (Flowers, 1998: 21)

A researcher (Interview R173-M), the same one whom I reported was studying women activists, mentioned how the women she interviewed 'were deeply insulted' by her mandated use of consent forms that had to be signed. She was considered a part of the problem the women were fighting against.

Paternalistic practices emerged out of the medical context, where the idea of 'beneficence' implies paternalism, that 'only medical researchers would know what's good for you' (Presentation by theologian Alastair Campbell, Canadian Bioethics Society, 30 October 2004, Fieldnotes: 161). One researcher (R015-M, Fieldnotes: 973) concurs that the view of research participants by REBs can be seen as 'condescending or/and offensive.' A community member (E10-B, Fieldnotes: 161) on an REB shared that perspective, saying that the tone of the consent form is 'condescending and patronizing.'

Trust relationships are one of the most prominent components in field research. Robert Dingwall learned that a UK researcher received approval from management to study a large Asian factory, but when LEC required him to get ethics consent, the management at the factory was 'grossly offended' by the implied lack of trust and disrespect in the Anglo-Saxon consent process (Dingwall, 2008: 6). Another researcher, Lesley Conn, had a successful round of research investigating intersex surgery in a hospital, side by side with her medical colleagues. However, when she had to secure written consent for her study, two research participants withdrew, and 'one doctor avoided eye contact and would never acknowledge researcher as a person.' She pointed out that the forms made the medical doctors feel that their position as experts who were in control was challenged. As a consequence, she found the 'relationships were inadequate, tense, less congenial' (Conn, 2008: 508). 'Long consent forms,' other researchers inform us, 'that spell out every possible risk... can only serve to scare subjects... and further erode trust in the process' (Derbyshire, 2006: 49; Sieber, Plattner, and Rubin, 2002: 3).

The use of a signed form of consent could break a personal, friendly bond.[4] Other interviewees will regard the use of forms as a disloyal act on the part of the researcher. This dilemma occurs even though one is known as a researcher, a fact that is stated in advance of any research project. This vexing problem was brought to my attention recently by a graduate student who is conducting fieldwork in Nunavut. She had obtained ethics approval from her department, and her proposal was passed by the Nunavut Council on Research. Both groups insisted she use consent forms that 'seemed to ferment the stereotype of a researcher from outside as self-centred' (Anonymous, personal communication to author, 1999). In addition to having a signed consent form and a mission statement, the student had to repeat the process for the interpreter, who also had to be provided with an 'Interpreter Confidentiality' form. Each sheet was not only drawn up in two languages, but copies were made for all parties involved, including research agencies – a total of twenty-two sheets of paper had to be available and signed before the interview could begin. In the words of the researcher:

> The woman looked at all of the papers, looked at the consent form, and refused to sign it, stating that her daughter had told her not to sign anything. I had to respect that . . . I wondered just how different the interview might have gone had I not felt the need to be so formal with her. When I left she refused to even keep the (unsigned) participant consent form . . .
>
> Every other interview started with a confusing first five minutes and the interviewees would say, 'whatever,' whenever she would explain why she had all of these forms. The researcher concluded that the 'consent forms were obtrusive and established an atmosphere of formality and mistrust.' (Anonymous, 1999, Fieldnotes: 345–6)

Finally, there are puzzled reactions by research participants. Hamilton (2005: 18) found that 'participants may be puzzled about why they are being asked to sign such a [consent] form . . . It seems foolish to ask people to sign a form that says they are being interviewed.' A scholar contributing to a special issue of the National Communications Association tells his readers that 'inmates in a study got upset: they didn't see how he needed their approval to interview them: after all, the warden and they already approved' (NCA, 2005: 228).

There is no question that the wholesale application of ethics review to social (and medical) research has tested the traditional approaches to research participants. A researcher-cum-journalist concluded that IRBs are guaranteeing rights to participants who did not think they had them (R137, Fieldnotes: 733). It is hard to predict if this emphasis on rights will lead to a 'rights' movement among research participants.

However, we already know that research on Aboriginal peoples must take the notion of rights as articulated by the ethics-review system into account. As strange as it may seem, the articulation of rights by ethics committees on behalf of research participants has not led to an empowerment of those participants. On the contrary, it has been diminished.

Numerous are the studies involving research participants where there is a visible absence of the participants' knowing the economic differences between population and researcher. Flicker et al. (2007), for example, noted that no ethics-review forms asked about economic differences in community based participatory research. This situation 'further disempowers individuals and communities by suggesting their time, energy, and resources may be of little worth, and they should participate simply because they have been invited' (Flicker et al., 2007: 6). The review system, according to Carole Truman (2003: 4), 'exacerbates' the distance between researcher and research participant so that the latter have no way of deciding what is (un)ethical. Koro-Ljungberg et al. (2007: 1084) reaffirm Truman's observation that the consent form 'precludes a more participatory process of consent' with research participants. Taking it a step further, research participants 'can feel threatened,' which 'makes them feel more reticent' (Crow et al., 2006: 90).

An interesting issue touches on the human rights of research participants. Do consent forms that formally require a signature prevent individuals from participating in the research if they do not wish to sign such a form, but do wish to participate in the research (Alderson, 1999:60; Truman, 2003: 6)? On the other side of the human rights issue, some research participants are 'not always free to give consent' (Tilley and Gormley, 2007: 372) because of institutional insistence that everyone cooperate with the research. In other settings, research participants are not allowed to exercise their free consent to participate in research and are forbidden to participate (373–5).

Vulnerability. This is a simple idea but it is also fraught with implications for any research participant. It is a concept that reinforces the lack of comprehension that ethics committees have of the world of the research participant. There is a profound sentiment and belief that research participants are vulnerable and fragile (Derbyshire, 2006: 36). These attitudes fall in line with the overall cultural sentimentality about the essential weakness of people. 'Certainly,' as Catherine Scott (2004: 4) claims, 'the implicit model, or beliefs about actual or potential research participants that underlie the activities of university ethics committees is one of profound vulnerability.' For example, any study that involves grieving, sadness, or sudden loss (to name a few) triggers a heavy response from the ethics committee. Betsy Bach (2005: 264) reported that an IRB demanded a psychologist be available for the debriefing of participants in online research that asked individuals to recall memorable moments surrounding the death of a family member.

By the same token, researchers are finding it difficult to research groups whose members are in vulnerable contexts,[5] 'because we make doing research with them so difficult' (Crow et al., 2006: 88). In this context, Graham Crow et al. (2006) warned about researching youth gangs and had concluded that 'you could never do this kind of research anymore' because parental consent worked against the interests of children in settings where 'most of the parents don't know they're in gangs and if they did the young person in question could actually run a risk of abuse or certainly alienation from the family' (89). In the course of receiving ethics approval, research devolves to protecting those who are discharging their duties regarding people in vulnerable contacts, such as parole officers, youth workers, and so on (Katz, 2007: 804). However, the protection against research works both for the people in vulnerable contexts and for their supervisors and organizations, whether these be cigarette companies, businesses, or university administrations (Feeley, 2007: 769) – none of whom like to be portrayed in an unflattering light. Would the ethics committees I studied warrant such protection?

Despite the imagined dangers imputed to research participants by ethics committees, the consent form is crafted in such a manner that it is the research participants who carry the burden of risk, not the researcher or the university. As Stuart Derbyshire (2006: 49) notes, 'consent is becoming less of a vehicle to inform [and protect] research subjects ... and more of a means by which the risk of experimental and therapeutic practice can be offset from the investigator and the institution and onto the subject. ... ' Still, the ethics committee firmly believes that dangers abound for research participants once they become involved with research. Tellingly, Derbyshire continues, 'these [alleged] dangers include not only the diminishment of science but the diminishment of those who volunteer for scientific investigation' (47).

It is not possible to enumerate all the risks imagined by ethics committees. Typically there is a lack of clarity about the conditions under which lack of anonymity represents a genuine risk to participant privacy, even for those who are volunteers (NCA, 2005: 211). One REB proclaims that participation in focus groups runs risks (S16-M, Fieldnotes: 1303), while another REB makes no distinction between the risks to athletes and the risks to non-athletes, even though the musculature of the two groups are quite different (R013-S, Fieldnotes: 158), or between children who have undergone many medical interventions and children who are unfamiliar with medical interventions. Sometimes, too, it is the researcher who might run the risk, as is exemplified by Amy Flowers' study of phone-sex workers (1998: 22). She was called upon by her IRB to protect her research participants, who themselves were tattooed or pierced, gay or transsexual 'hard core.' She writes that it 'was the researcher who would be more "shocked, offended or traumatized" by them who were so open and honest about sexual issues.'

In summary, this chapter considered the web of moral cosmologies (or systems of beliefs) that surrounds the work of ethics committees. Some of these moral cosmologies involve the perceptions and beliefs that ethics committees have about themselves, affecting their positive and negative self-image, beliefs about the goodness of rules they interpret, their perceptions that the review process is both onerous and challenging, beliefs about the 'sins' of past research, and beliefs about the barrier (both imaginary and real) between their world and that of the researchers.

When exploring the perspectives, beliefs, and related practices about researchers, I resorted to learning more about what ethics committees believe about researchers, and what researchers claim ethics committees believe about researchers. I concluded that those beliefs mitigate a moral agency on the part of researchers.

The constellation of beliefs should always include the world of the research participant. To that end, *The Seduction of Ethics* asked a number of questions: 'Do ethics-review procedures protect research participants?' and 'How paramount are the interests of research participants?' This chapter also explored the extent to which ethics committees under- and overreach the understanding of research participants. In this context, we noted that consent forms constitute insults and paternalism, depriving research participants of their moral agency. Finally, I looked at the idea of vulnerability which seems to permeate all considerations of the world of the research participant.

The next two chapters consider the crux of the ethics-review process: namely, the nature of application forms and the deliberations that take place within the meetings of ethics committees, including the missives that communicate their decision to the researcher.

7   Procedural Routines: The Application Form and the Consent Form

Administrative routines occupy a key role in the research-ethics galaxy. These routines, however, act as a wall between the world of research-ethics committees and researchers from diverse, non-medical research traditions. The routines consist of developing application forms to be used by researchers and formulating standardized consent forms. These routines involve written texts and create a discursive regime that often works against the expression of diverse research approaches. Michel Foucault, among others, sees this discursive regime as an inevitable expression of power. For him, the 'problem of the "discursive regime"' deals with 'the effects of power peculiar to the play of statements' (Rabinow, 1984: 55). Put in another way, Dorothy Smith (1986) speaks of institutional ethnography whereby texts define the relations of ruling. One could argue that these textual routines attempt to canalize the diversity of research approaches into a coherent whole, at least from the perspective of research-ethics staff.

This chapter discusses the size and the extent of application forms, 'checklists,' and the obvious and not-so-obvious functions of application forms. Alongside the application forms, the development of the consent form itself occupies a central part of the administrative routines of ethics committees. The chapter examines the history, length, and nature of the consent form. The consent form also has ritualistic and fetishistic aspects that ethics committees feel obliged to follow. Still, there is room for negotiation about the nature of the consent form, especially in light of its odd place in qualitative and anthropological research. Finally, the chapter presents cases where the consent form flummoxes social research.

The Application Form

The application form stands at the heart of administrative routines in the galaxy of research-ethics review. In Foucault's terms, it is an 'event' (Rabinow, 1984: 56). Foucault, in a conversation with Paul Rabinow (1984), argues that the event 'sets the geneology of relations of force, strategic developments, and tactics' of the issuing agent of power (56). The event, Foucault further claims, sustains the institutional power through the text itself and it 'traverses and produces things, it . . . produces discourse' (61).

The application form sets the stage for an ethics committee and a researcher to start a 'discussion' about the ethical dimensions of a specific research project. However, it is not the researchers but the ethics committee that sets the content and language of the application form. The discourse generated by the application form is the alpha and omega of all subsequent ways and canalizes the interactions between the ethics-review committee and the researcher. Borrowing a phrase from Foucault, the application form shows a 'radical deafness' to the animus of social researchers (Rabinow, 1984: 53).[1] In the same vein, another observer of the research-ethics world speaks about the 'blind and deaf, ethical superiority of the biomedical community [which] has contributed but negatively to the "other two [research] councils"' of the *TCPS* (R099, Fieldnotes: 548).

Often, though, before a researcher can submit an application form, he/she must undergo online training which can produce desperate feelings on the part of the researcher:

> I come to you practically in tears. Last fall, our college created a new IRB which appears to be determined to bury us in paperwork and hoop-jumping. Previously, our student projects were usually approved within 1–2 days but now it takes 2–3 weeks and several drafts of the application. Now, our IRB informs us that all of us must go through an online training (1 hour for students and 2–3 hours for faculty!) from an outside provider (citiprogram.org) in order to be 'certified' or we can't even submit IRB protocols. (R178, Fieldnotes: 1875)

Length and Extent of Application Forms

Application forms are ubiquitous; to my knowledge, there is no university that does not use forms.[2] In Canada, of twelve surveyed REBs, nine used a standardized application form and two allowed electronic submissions; only two used standardized review forms for REB members (Ellard and Dobson, 2007). As the United Kingdom Department of Health (Ad Hoc Advisory Committee, 2005: 6) has noted, many researchers "expressed frequently and very strongly about the difficulties encountered with obtaining permission to conduct research." Standard Operating Procedures, including strict timelines, have been imposed, virtually eliminating variations in application procedures.' Carole Truman cites the guidelines issued by the South Cumbria Research Ethics Committee:

> [The Ethics Committee] receives many applications and has developed a form of application which enables it to deal expeditiously with new applications. It is not, therefore, prepared to receive applications on any other form than that which is made available to potential applicants. (Truman, 2003: 5)

The IRB at Oklahoma University, for example, insists that researchers submit eleven copies of the form (Hamilton, 2002: 174–88). Ethics committees have a virtual free hand in drawing up their application form. Because national guidelines often describe themselves as 'minimal standards,' local ethics committees believe that their own guidelines should be more 'rigorous,' and they see this rigour as more 'virtuous.' Such rigour normally involves more paperwork (Hamilton, 2005: 195).

Ethics committees go to great lengths to draft application forms. A staff member once said that she and her ethics committees have revised the application form four to five times, and that the process is of an ongoing nature (Interview S47-M). Very seldom do ethics staff seek the opinions of faculty in developing the form – only one university (M) that does has come to my attention during my six years of research on the topic. Given the substantial resistance to the content and language of the application form, which researchers see as 'obstructionist' (Interview S46-S), it is easy to understand that researchers might be reluctant to participate in such an exercise. Researchers hesitate to construct a device that grants them no freedom in pursuing their own research. The 'pathologies of an [sic] censorship regime' (Feeley, 2007: 771) affects both ethics-review committees and researchers, leading both sides to undertake activities unthinkable in everyday life. Ethics committees are more inclined to refute some of the insights (even if they are sound) and comments made by researchers, such as the case of a sociologist at a college in Massachusetts:

> ... we sent a short letter to the IRB outlining our problems. The chair of the IRB then asked us to elaborate our concerns in writing, something we did not want to do given the time constraints at the end of the semester. However, the alternative appeared worse to us. The IRB suggested that if we did not have the time to produce a written document, we could come to a planned meeting and verbally articulate our concerns. Given the hostility of some of the IRB members to our challenges, we worried that such a dialogue would become too personalized and ultimately counter-productive. Thus, we elaborated our concern in writing with suggested reforms.
>
> The memo wound up being five pages long, single-spaced. It was difficult to write because of our frustration with the IRB and desire to make the memo as professional as possible. It was also difficult to produce because we were critiquing the very foundational logic of the committee ... In it we suggested that the IRB was overstepping its mission, inappropriately imposing a biomedical model on sociological research, creating an imbalance between risk and reward (i.e., perceived risk), and questioned the organizational composition of the committee (i.e., too many psychologists!) ... We requested that the organizational structure of the committee be altered to have equal representation among the social sciences, develop ethical guidelines appropriate to sociological research, develop a working definition of perceived risk, and not make methodological and literature review criticism contingent upon approving an application unless it clearly demonstrates harm to the participants. As you can imagine, this document did make some of the members of the IRB defensive, and I imagine my colleague and I are not the most popular among some of the psychologists at XX College. However, much to our surprise the IRB agreed to undergo a process of structural reform! We received a written response from the chair that – in some ways – attempted to refute each of our critiques. This was not terribly surprising. Although we attempted to be as professional and understanding to the position of the IRB members, we did offer a sweeping critique. What is important to us is that they agreed to change the organizational composition of the committee to equally represent members of the social sciences. They also agreed that there is biomedical bias in ruling on the ethical soundness of research projects! As a retort, they did suggest that most of the delays were from poorly designed student research projects. We disagree, but the important thing is that we have begun the process of reform.

> Frankly, we were shocked by the response. Given our past history with
> the IRB, we thought they would be far more resistant to reform. When we
> first heard about their willingness to undergo reform, we both stood there
> with our mouths wide open! (R114, Fieldnotes: 374)

Nevertheless, research-ethics administrators go to great lengths to develop 'better' application forms by scanning the websites of other universities (Interview C12-S). Similarly, we learn that an ethics staff member (Interview E15-S) uses 'a standard form, drawing on those used at other universities.' The same university (S19) hopes that the Canadian Interagency Advisory Panel on Research Ethics will put out 'a standard form.' This university is now developing a flow chart, and is making use of templates for consent forms. At another university, 'the same form must be completed regardless of type of research' (Hamilton, 2002: 78). The situation at a mid-sized Canadian university (M-14) insists that an expedited review of a research proposal requires the same format as full applications (S30-M, Fieldnotes: 1522). At a large Canadian university, the REB chair reserves for him/herself the right to send class research projects out for full review, even when involving mostly low-risk research (S37-B, Fieldnotes:1177). Ann Hamilton notes that whether or not the research ought to be exempt, the amount of documentation required is the same (Hamilton, 2005: 198). Koro-Ljungberg et al. relate the following experience, underscoring this insistent drive towards standardization:

> An example of such lack of researcher's autonomy is the practice by IRB
> officers to advise the researcher to follow exemplary protocols *word for
> word* to guarantee expedited and unproblematic approval of research
> protocol. Recently, when one of the authors of this article became a new
> member in a research institution, he or she was advised by tenured faculty
> members to meet and greet the 'gatekeeper' at the local IRB office. During
> this visit, an IRB officer showed him or her the university's preferred pro-
> tocol with pre-existing sentences, gave him or her a copy, and advised the
> researcher to follow it *word for word* – simply 'plug in' the words descri-
> bing his or her current study. In this way, the officer explained, researchers
> can guarantee positive and expedited review. (Koro-Ljungberg et al., 2007:
> 1083; emphasis added)

A researcher who is unable or unwilling to address this discourse runs the risk of delaying his or her application, and application forms do spell out that every aspect of the application form must be addressed. As Ann Hamilton (2002: 175) has learned, the textually embedded warnings by ethics committees constitute 'another managerial suggestion that resistance is futile.'

The troublesome aspect about ethics committees using forms from other universities is that they do not sit down first to establish the parameters of what constitutes ethical research before borrowing or plagiarizing forms developed in other venues. The drive towards the standardization of application forms also means that researchers with diverse, non-biomedical research approaches will find it increasingly difficult to present their research plans within the confines of highly standardized application forms. The use of a standardized ethics application form simply excludes and is not relevant for some forms of research, such as community-building participatory research (CBPR), because all forms requested a scientific rationale, none asked about involving the community in defining the research problem, and there were no questions about building capacities in the community (Flicker et al., 2007).

The worst aspect, according to Ann Hamilton, implicates the standardized form as a means of producing 'forced self-aggrandizement' among ethics administrators. In this respect,

> [e]ven regulators themselves indicate that if 'template fever' runs too high, the template may add symptoms (demonstrating, incidentally, that regulators can admit that even templates have points of diminishing returns) rather than operating as a cure for a sick system. (Hamilton, 2002: 220)

Of all the elements related to application forms, the 'checklist' and 'consent form' generate the most debate on the part of both ethics administrators and researchers.

The 'Checklist'

If the application form constitutes the heart of administrative routines in the ethics-review world, the 'checklist' constitutes the artery of the application form. The checklist is a template that channels the researcher's key points in an application along a path of ethical dimensions spelled out by the ethics committee. As stated earlier in this chapter, it is not uncommon that ethics committees borrow templates from each other. The checklist simplifies the application as a whole and alerts the ethics committee to the salient points that must be covered by a researcher.

Attitudes towards the usefulness of the checklist vary across research-ethics administrators and researchers. Some oppose the checklist's use, others reluctantly accept it, while still others endorse its use. It is clear that such diverse opinions prevent either the downright acceptance of the checklist or complete opposition to its use. Although typically only chairs of ethics committees use a checklist, the application form itself contains a checklist, functioning as an abbreviated, complementary application form. It ensures that all grounds are covered. When, for example, only the chair of an ethics committee uses a checklist, the list reveals much about the perspective of the chair. As an illustration, the chair of an REB at a mid-sized university developed a checklist containing twenty-nine major items, with another twenty sub-items, for a total of forty-nine items that he checks when an application starts the journey through research-ethics review. We note that only 37 per cent of all items touch on ethical issues, and 12 per cent involve procedural ones. The remaining 51 per cent are concerned with identifying the names of researchers, sponsors, and so on (Fieldnotes: 1871–2).

The chair of an REB in a mid-sized Canadian university frowns on developing a checklist (Interview C03-M). A researcher, formerly the REB chair at the same university, did not want to develop a checklist, but 'wanted researchers to think, to solve problems in the context of ethics' (Interview R118-M). A similar opinion prevails at another mid-sized university that does not give 'much credence' to checklists (Interview C11-M). Kakali Bhattacharya (2007: 1107) sees them as reducing the IRB guidelines.

Ed Gabrielle at Rutgers University maintains that 'the ethics mission follows the form, rather than vice versa;' and that it is 'easy to create checklists – they make us comfortable' (Notes on Presentations, CAREB, 6 May 2005, Fieldnotes: 163). Ethics administrators and researchers each derive their own reasons for using the checklist. For administrators, the checklist provides a helpful reminder of the 'completeness' of the application. Researchers can also regard the checklist as a reminder. However, in the case of many researchers, the checklist reminds them of the ethical dimensions left *out* of the equation of their research. The narrow requisite of answering either 'yes' or 'no' or having to offer a very brief explanation of their research allows the researcher to formally comply with the demands of the ethics committee without seriously revealing additional aspects of their research. For example, when presented with the question whether the researcher intends to conduct interviews, he/

she can unhesitatingly offer a 'yes,' without having to indicate that, for many qualitative researchers, taking fieldnotes before, during, and after the interview is *de rigeur*. Gaps on the ethics checklist provide a measure of safety, allowing the researcher to engage in some additional forms of research that ethics committees do not strictly know about.

Finally, both ethics administrators and researchers can appreciate the use of the checklist. One researcher commented that 'students were a bit resentful; students resented extra pieces of work and wanted a checklist instead' (Interview R118-M). One administrator, whose REB developed the checklist with the help of the *TCPS*, found the checklist 'useful even if N/A is indicated' (Interview A11-S). REBs do rely on checklists, more so than on the full description of the research project (Comments on a Presentation, Department of Justice, Ottawa, 30 October 2003, Fieldnotes: 67). A sessional instructor in a small university who wants to do research finds the checklist quite useful in outlining what the ethical dimensions of her research would entail (Anonymous, 2006). However, that sessional's perspective is rather singular, and no other researcher I have met seems to share her particular viewpoint.

Checklists and application forms serve several functions, both overt and covert. They do not merely keep chairs and researchers on track. They instill in researchers the 'proper' understanding of what ethics in research means. It is impossible to deviate from the path laid out by the checklist and the application form. However, when REBs sometimes add items to checklists, it is difficult to know which checklist ultimately prevails. Researchers fear the negative presence of absence when it comes to such checklists.

Overt and Covert Functions

Application forms constitute a complex set of routines. From the applicant's side, according to Dixon-Woods, the routine can include a submission of a prescribed set of documentation, including an electronic application form, protocol, participant information sheets and consent forms, any data collection instruments (e.g., questionnaires, diary cards, interview schedules), evidence of prior scientific peer review, and curricula vitae (Dixon-Woods et al., 2007: 8). Some applications are somewhat less complex. (Chapters 10 and 11 touch on the approaches researchers use for filling out the application form for research-ethics reviews.) Researchers with prior experiences with the form have learned to minimize their explanations, to make 'benign fabrications' in their application (such as those dealing with the start and end dates of the research), and creating 'strategic ambiguity' (i.e., taking advantage of the ethics committee's lack of familiarity with particular research techniques).

Ethics staff appreciate the researchers' anxieties. One member of an ethics committee at a small university made a point of saying that 'only when a researcher has gone through the REB several times, will he or she know how to fill out the form' (Interview E27-S). A staff member in an ethics office believes they can resolve the researcher's anxiety by stating more clearly what the REB expects of the researcher. 'The researcher just does not want to guess what the REB wants: "just tell me that you expect the data to be kept for three years, et cetera"' (Interview S47-M). It is not just the uncertainty about the forms that bedevil researchers but also the lack of knowledge on the part of ethics committee members. Bravo, Dubois, and Paquet (2004: 5), for example, point out that 35 per cent of IRB members did not know anything about legal requirements for getting consent to study incapacitated adults (and 45 per cent of researchers did not know this either).

The command, 'Please explain,' that normally appears several times on the application form conjures up a great deal of uncertainty. Researchers find this an awkward statement because they do not possess the 'universal skeleton key' (Foucault's term) that would open up the meanings implicit in that command (Rabinow, 1984: 61). Saying too little in answer to this command leaves the researcher open to being asked to explain yet another detail; similarly, saying 'too much' invites the ethics committee to seek further clarification.

The application form is the flash point of all the worries researchers have about the research-ethics review process, and yet it is only the first step in what might become a route filled with unexpected twists and turns. As a veteran researcher – a psychologist – noted:

> Many REBs are quite tough on follow-up aspects of studies where the researcher (usually because of some new questions that have arisen from the data) want[s] to go back and get consent from subjects again for a new aspect. Some REBs (but not all) insist that you simply start over again. (R013-S, Fieldnotes: 581)

The significance with which ethics administrators endow the application form finds fulfillment in several corners of the research-ethics review world. A workshop in Western Canada on ethics and social research, hosted in Edmonton, Alberta, by the National Council for Ethical Human Research (NCEHR) on 22 February 2004, devoted two and a half hours to the minutiae of filling out application forms, but allocated merely one half hour to discussing ethics in social research (Notes on Presentations, Fieldnotes: 151–2).

Another corner of the ethics galaxy touches university 'ethics' courses. Increasingly, universities feel compelled to set up a course on 'ethics' with the overt intention of indicating to students (and to the university) how important ethics is in their research.[3] As one chair of an ethics committee indicated to me, such a course would benefit from students filling out an application form for ethics review. He concludes that, 'as such, the requirement for ethics review is educational on a broad range of topics' (C16-M, Fieldnotes: 551). Usually, it is the research-ethics office staff that offer parts of such courses (S01-M, Fieldnotes: 550). One sad, inadvertent result of the focus on research-ethics application is the suspension of critical thought either about the purpose of application forms or about ethics in research. Properly filling out the form supersedes the importance of discussing ethics in research.

The Consent Form

The consent form appears under a variety of guises: as a form signed by the research participant and the researcher, as a form signed exclusively by the research participant, and as a form (usually called an 'information sheet') signed only by the researcher. Typically, the struggle between the ethics-review committee and the researcher involves (1) whether the ethics committee requires a written consent (and it usually does), (2) the textual content of the written consent form, and (3) the requirement to have the research participant sign the consent form.

History, Sizes, and Nature of the Consent Form

Using signed consent forms, and even information sheets was a rare occurrence in anthropological and sociological fieldwork before the advent of ethics committees. If the relationship between the research participants and the researcher were to be based on personal trust, both sides of the party would see the use of signed consent form as a serious violation of that trust.[4] Anthropologists trace the first use of a written consent form to 1957, when Leonard Waltz allegedly used it in his research (CASCA, May 2002, Fieldnotes: 321).[5] The range of applications for the consent form are not only quite wide but also can change from situation to situation. For example, an ethics committee at a small university (Interview REB1-S) had earlier insisted that a written consent form be used for research involving telephone interviews; that requirement no longer stands. There are also large variations with respect to the length of written consent forms. In the social sciences, a form can be barely one page in length, while in the medical sciences, it can be as long as ten pages.[6] However, there are still variations within the social sciences. One researcher in a faculty of education at a medium-sized university uses a three-and-a-half-page form (R050-M, Fieldnotes: 711). In a recent report, the Illinois College of Law reports consent forms running twenty pages or more (ICL, 2006: 11).

Ethics-review committees have come to expect that a consent form needs to inform research subjects what the objectives and data collection strategies are (in short, they need to know what they are getting into), any procedural change during the research, the contingency of what happens with the chance discovery of the unexpected (e.g., abuse), and guarantees of anonymity and confidentiality. The main interest of ethics-review committees is in researchers gaining voluntary participation and consent (Interview C03-M). Ethics-review committees are inclined to include additional safeguards in the consent form, such as informing a research participant that a witness will be included during the research itself (such as in a study of gun owners or young drug users conducted by Mark Israel in 2005). In a number of cases, ethics-review committees also expect someone other than the researcher to witness the research participant's signing the consent form!

It is rather common for ethics committees to advance the idea of a template for consent forms.[7] The Canadian Institutes of Health Research advocated the 'Protocol and Consent Template' in 2005. A small Canadian university wants to see consistent consent forms – a template – to make sure that every caveat is included (Interview E15-S). Another small university has nine samples of consent letters. However, these do not reflect the needs of qualitative researchers and committee members admit that their samples follow the medical model of research as outlined in Canada's *TCPS* (Interview REB1-S). The social science researcher can already recognize the inherent problematic nature of these written and signed consent forms. For ethics committees, the required use of consent forms is equivalent to getting informed consent. From that perspective, there is no difference between the form and the consent.

Ritualism and Fetishism

Many critical commentaries about the use of consent forms point to their ritualistic and fetishistic aspects (Calvey, 2008: 907, citing Sin, 2005; R177, Fieldnotes: 289). At Brown University, the ritualism of putting equitable measures in place (i.e., not excluding any population) for research on how the public views animals requires the recruitment and signatures of women and minorities, and warns about including prisoners, fetuses, pregnant women, and individuals with diminished capacity (even though this research was exempted from review) (Brown University Memorandum, 18 October 2004, Fieldnotes: 1325). A session at the 2002 CASCA annual meeting in Windsor highlighted the concerns of anthropologists that there is an overemphasis on consent and confidentiality in such forms (CASCA session, 3 May 2002, Fieldnotes: 321). One researcher was required to get signed consent forms even though her research involved rather informal chats with faculty for an in-house study (Interview E12-M). Another researcher (Interview R003-M) managed to get a small grant from an NGO to test visiting habits to a website. Only visitor data would be collected; no identities would be available, let alone revealed (most websites have this feature), but he had to convince the REB that it was okay not to get signed consent forms. A young researcher who was conducting a participant observation study of a group of older activist women gathered at their convention had to bring consent forms to the gathering that all who attended had to sign, without exception (Interview R173-M). One sociologist (R095) at Indiana University had to get consent to 'study my own life' and had to include this statement in his last IRB renewal:

> In signing this Amendment Form, I hereby grant myself consent to utilize all of my own past, present, and future writings, drawings, and other of my own personal records and creative products for the purpose of research and publishing purposes. I understand that since this is an overtly autobiographical study and my identity as the author will be publicly knowable, I will be identifiable in all published accounts. (R095, Fieldnotes: 797)

Some of the reactions of members of the LISTSERV where this item was posted included (SSSITalk LISTSERV, Fieldnotes: 797):

- I have this flashback to the 'Blazing Saddles' scene where Sheriff Cleavon Little holds his own gun to his head and 'arrests' himself to escape the lynch mob.
- Sad, but funny.
- Silly . . . Crazy stuff, ain't it?

To get around the fetishism of having the signature of research participants, one researcher studying juvenile auto thieves decided to have them sign false names, rather than real ones (R092-B, Fieldnotes: 479). In the case of Amy Flowers' research on phone-sex workers, *The Fantasy Factory* (1998), she wrote in a LISTSERV posting:

First, I had already been working as a phone sex operator, and wished to use my notes from those experiences as post hoc participant observation. This was eventually disallowed to protect the privacy of my anonymous co-workers, as well as my clientele, also anonymous. Second, I interviewed operators who responded to an advertisement I ran in the local free paper. The only time I asked for an interviewee's real name was in signing the consent form, and the only hesitation/moment of distrust I encountered during the interviews was around the signing of the consent form. I found that I had to explain in the telephone conversation arranging the interview that this would be required, as some operators wished to speak only on the condition of complete anonymity. Thus, there had to be consent to consent, which was more difficult to get than consent to be interviewed. A few signed using their phone-sex monikers, so that I ended up with a handful of consent forms signed 'cum-monger' and 'snow-white.' Not exactly what the board had in mind, but it seemed to work! (SSSITalk LISTSERV, Fieldnotes: 386)

The fetishism thus extends to research participants who read the consent forms. One researcher (Interview R024-M) mentions that the reaction to the consent form varies, some read it word by word, others skim it. It is the reaction to that piece of paper that counts, rather than a need to understand the content of the consent form. In a telling case, one researcher at a mid-sized university describes her experience with her REB whose members demanded that her research participants to see her questions beforehand, even though this requirement altered the data and spontaneity of the interview (R143-M, Fieldnotes: 574). The fetishism with consent extends to survey research, where a political scientist required written consent for the commercial mailing list for a survey (Dingwall, 2008: 5, citing AAUP, 2000 study). A researcher experienced a 'consent-to-get-consent' process whereby she was required to get signed consent forms *before* sending a survey form to participants (ICL, 2006: 4). Similarly, in another instance, an IRB required a researcher to get written consent in a voting survey by a political scientist before mailing the survey. The people had already agreed to participate (Sieber, Plattner, and Rubin, 2002: 1).[8]

The arms of consent reach into quite unexpected places, even including images that are publicly available. An IRB attempted to deny a master's student her diploma because she did not obtain prior approval to request copies of generally available printed material (Dingwall, 2008: 6, citing AAUP, 2000 study). A researcher (the same one who was required by her ethics committee to get signed consent from everyone in an observational study of a gathering) was told by her REB that she must have personal consent from everyone who appeared in public photos, such as those found in newspapers (Interview R173-M).

The University of Illinois at Urbana-Champaign IRB insists on a signed consent form from the student's relative to be interviewed (even if it is his/her mother) to be on file (Nelson, 2004: 215). The fetishism with consent can produce unwarranted fears, such as in the case of an IRB's mandating the inclusion of a consent section in the call for narratives, even before research participants were recruited and the research had started. Dougherty and Kramer (2005: 186) found that the IRB approval process made the call 'more negative and critical than intended.'

Here is an account of a nurse and sociologist who has taken on the task of interviewing people in home care situations:

> I gave each of them [caregiver and the older person] a copy of the consent form and asked them to review it and then I would answer whatever questions they had. Both Mrs McK [caregiver] and George [older person] read it carefully (took time).
>
> George says that he has a question for me about the form . . . He looks at me rather thoughtfully and asks, 'What difference will it make whether I sign it or not?' Thinking he might be having second thoughts about my being there for the study, I reminded him that he could ask me to leave his home if he didn't want to participate. 'No, you don't understand my question,' he replies. 'Will you do anything differently here this morning

if I sign the form than if I don't sign it?' I can see that he is not concerned about my being there but seems to be questioning the need for his signature. I've just driven for forty-five to fifty minutes to be at this home. If he's not objecting to my being there and knows why I am there, would I actually have to leave if he doesn't sign? These thoughts are racing through my head. While I'm thinking about this, George leans over and signs the consent. I still have another form for George to sign, the consent for the follow-up interview with the family caregiver. (R065-S, Fieldnotes: 570-1)[9]

Ethics Committees and Researchers' Negotiating the Consent Form

Given the widely divergent opinions between ethics committees and researchers about the use or the nature of consent forms, it comes as no surprise that committees are constantly refining consent forms over and over (ICL, 2006: 11). Ann Hamilton, one of the few scholars conducting empirical research on the workings of ethics committees, noted that 'IRB members become copy editors to the potential detriment of more significant issues' (Hamilton, 2005: 197). Among many such instances, changes usually involve the wording, such as changing 'you have been selected' to 'you are invited,' or to remove all bolding (Hemmings, 2006: 16).

Paradoxically, ethics committees and researchers negotiate the content of a consent form, only to agree on the original submitted by the researcher. For example, one researcher commented that a consent form came back with eleven major changes, 'but in the end it was virtually identical to previous one, except for minor wording and title changes' (NCA, 2005: 207). In some instances, an REB would push for the use of a consent form only to give up on that idea if a researcher (in this case a student) persisted (R041-M, Fieldnotes: 621). Betsy Bach (2005: 263) notes that a researcher prepared an easy-to-read consent form for factory workers, only to have it rejected because the IRB assumed workers were illiterate. The IRB then provided its own form, written in academese, defeating the purpose of the original, plainly written form.

To resist an ethics committee takes a persistent and persuasive talent. A PhD student (R175-M, Fieldnotes: 1855) wanted to study boys and girls from age six and up, only to be rebuffed by her REB – widely known as an orthodox committee – who insisted that she was not allowed to study anyone younger than twelve. The iterations occurred over a one-year period, and after the student pointed out to the REB some of its own inconsistent advice, the board relented. Still, the student 'lost' one year of her studies. There are very few cases showing such sacrifice and commitment. It reminds one of Kierkegaard's essay on the practice of complaining about an academic grade (Kierkegaard, 1966).

The negotiating process may leave some researchers with unsettling results. For example, the chair of an REB wanted the researcher to let observed families and patients know they should modify conversation when observed by the researcher (Interview C10-B). Another ethics committee had ordered that the consent form needed to have a legal clause because the researcher was interviewing old women who are sometimes involved in illegal activities (Interview R173-M). The REB in a small university rejected a researcher's application three times, demanded major changes regarding privacy because it involved potentially 'politically sensitive stuff' (Interview E15-S).

Not infrequently, ethics committees would only approve consent forms when particular words or phrases were deleted, changed, or added. A psychologist (Notes on Presentations, R176-M, Fieldnotes: 158) was asked by a journal, a surrogate for the university ethics committee, to remove the question 'Are you thinking about suicide?' from his study. Some of the suggestions border on the politically correct such as when an ethics committee asked the researcher to change 'safe sex' to 'safer sex' (NCA, 2005: 225). Another IRB wanted to add 'rape' to the consent form because victims of rape 'need to know' they are victims of rape (NCA, 2005: 208–9).

Lest the reader believe that the consent form only deals with gathering data, we turn to a sociologist whose ethics committee believes that the consent also extends to research participants approving the write-up of data (R124-M, Fieldnotes: 803). Increasingly, some ethics committees are now requiring researchers to have their interview transcripts approved by research participants. The irony is not lost when we realize that after research participants have already surrendered so much of their time to the interview(s), they are now required to go over the transcriptions. This is a topic to which we shall return in a later chapter.

Still, other researchers have creatively circumvented strict rulings of ethics committees, while maintaining the ethical nature of getting consent, as seen in the case of a scholar doing research among anorexic young women:

The concern was not with the legitimacy of the arguments we presented [to the ethics committee] but with the financial threat of a litigious parent or caregiver. With no option but to acquiesce on this count, we circumvented the restrictions imposed by our [ethics] committees by using a different form of consent involving 'ongoing consensual decision-making' . . . before, during, and after the interviews so that participants had repeated opportunities to withdraw or to qualify consent. This strategy could not guarantee the knowability of informed consent or obviate unseen power relations, but it offered a greater degree of empowerment by providing girls with multiple opportunities to qualify and negotiate their involvement in the research. (Halse and Honey, 2005: 2152)

The Place of the Consent Form in Social and Qualitative Research

As can be inferred from the above, the consent form, whether or not it is *signed* by the research participant, figures prominently in the world of research-ethics review. Readers accustomed to biomedical research might be puzzled by the resistance of many social researchers, especially qualitative researchers, to the use of the *signed* consent form. No doubt, REBs whose membership or chair consists of people whose vision of science follows hypothesis-driven, deductive research, will be equally puzzled and impatient with the approach taken by qualitative researchers.

We hear of a sociology PhD student who does a participant-observation study of gun owners and his university's REB requirement that he get a signed consent form from all owners of guns (Chat R031-M, Fieldnotes: 719). As mentioned earlier, we remember a researcher who was required to get the signature of everyone at a gathering of older, activist women while she was doing a participant-observation study of the group (Interview R173-M). Ironically, all the women at the gathering protested this requirement because they believed it overstepped the boundaries of surveillance. As well, they had invited the researcher to study them, but the signed consent form was, they felt, insulting and pushed beyond the boundaries of courtesy. The researcher was not able to use any of her data, not even making to make a notation about the protests from the women. In another case in New Brunswick, a researcher struggled with an REB who insisted that a detailed consent form be used, even though Grade 9 is the average level of education attained in that province (Interview R173-M). Another researcher lost her struggle with her IRB after she proposed an alternate route to informed consent 'because the Cherokee tribe she was studying took exception to signing documents. A half-hour later, the door [of the IRB chamber] opened and she left crying' (Johnson, 2008: 216). At another university, a PhD student literally shed tears in a colleague's office when she heard that her own supervisor insisted on her using signed consent forms, anticipating that the REB would reject her application if it carried a statement about not using the signed consent form (Chat R062-M, Fieldnotes: 144). Her research involved hearing-impaired children with whom she already had worked for many years earlier.

The consent form, whether 'signed' or not, puts qualitative researchers in a quandary, as the Social Sciences and Humanities Research Ethics Special Working Committee Report, 'Qualitative Research: A Chapter for Inclusion in the TCPS,' underscores:

> [a] dynamic, negotiated and with an ongoing free and informed consent process: Entry into a particular setting for research purposes sometimes requires negotiation with the to-be-studied population; the process sometimes cannot be ascertained in advance of the research in part because the relevant contexts within which the research occurs evolve over time . . . Indeed, the emergent nature of many qualitative studies makes the achievement of rapport with participants and feelings of interpersonal trust crucial to the generation of dependable data, which often would only be undermined by more legalistic approaches and notions of consent as 'contract.' Indeed, research often becomes a collaborative process negotiated between the research participant(s) and the researcher. All this fits well with an inductive and emergent strategy that sees considerable time spent initially simply figuring out what the research will be about, and what questions are considered by both parties to be the important or interesting ones to ask. (SSHWC, 2008d: 4, 6; emphasis in original)

The last sentence in this quote bears upon the issue of informed consent. How can a research participant be truly informed of the intent of the research if the researcher him/herself is still unclear after having embarked on the research?

For many social researchers, 'informed consent is a non-starter' (Nelson and McPherson, 2004). Anthropologists gathered at the May 2002 CASCA meeting collectively expressed their horror at the required use of consent forms (Fieldnotes: 321). The chair at mid-sized Canadian university says that because 'more than one-half of research at her university is qualitative research; i.e., involving diverse populations, signed consent forms are not an option; there are also few research participants involved in very intensive research'

(Presentation at a Seminar by C30-M, Fieldnotes: 168). Even at another mid-sized university, one that particularly studied Aboriginal peoples, the use of signed consent forms is still required (Comments made at a Presentation at M4, Fieldnotes: 259). It comes as no surprise that an enumeration of these and similar cases yielded 'a paranoia' among social researchers (Couch-Stone Symposium, Fieldnotes: 353). Lynne Roberts and David Indermaur (2003) provide detailed explanations regarding why consent forms are not applicable in social research, especially in criminological research.

Cases Where the Consent Form Flummoxes Social Research

The recruitment of research participants is closely allied to the issue of the ethics committee demanding that consent forms ought to be used. Without a consent form being prepared in advance, the researcher is not allowed to recruit participants. These barriers flummox social research. Let us look at a few documented examples of such distortions in research, which often actually lead to abandonment of research.

Robert Dingwall (2008: 6) reports that a graduate student was not allowed to study victims of medical accidents because the sample was not recruited through the records of National Health Service in the United Kingdom. In another study, Annette Hemmings (2007: 14) states that doctoral students wanted to do holistic school ethnographies involving observations in multiple classrooms and interviews with several teachers and students, but were 'so daunted by the need to obtain written consent from every person, that they curtailed their research to one classroom.' In the United States, we learn through Jack Katz (2007: 803) that the University of California-San Francisco IRB 'blocked [an observational] study that would have examined compliance by bathhouses with public health regulations,' after demanding that the researcher seek verbal consent from bathhouse managers. One of the most highly respected scholars on ethics in research, Joan Sieber, relates the story of a routine classroom exercise for pedagogical purposes (where students were asked to make judgments and discuss their reasons). The consent included 'the proviso that students may choose not to participate' and 'warns about non-existent risks.' No data were collected; no research was done (Sieber, Plattner, and Rubin, 2002: 2). We learn from Crow et al. that

> the requirement of parental consent made some projects unfeasible, as in the case of one interviewee's PhD student who had contacted young

gay men through clubs but was required by an ethics committee to gain their parents' consent for them to be interviewed, as a result of which 'he actually couldn't do that research.' (Crow et al., 2006: 89)

In other cases, research is not abandoned where researchers were obliged to use consent forms, but significant distortions of research results may have occurred as a result. Paul Grayson (2004) speaks of his 2003 survey of students, where he found that legal wording of the cover letter in surveys affected the response rates. If the cover letter was impersonal, the response rate would be considerably lower than if the cover letter was friendly and personal. The higher the response rate the greater the probability that the sample represented the population. York University and Dalhousie University REBs approved the more ideal (friendly, personal) cover letters, while the University of British Columbia and McGill University had a more legally stringent one. The response rate, respectively, was 43 per cent and 38 per cent for the friendly letters, but 33 per cent and 20 per cent for the legalistically worded letters. We note again the same researcher who studied older women activists but was required to leave the interview when they refused to sign the consent form (Interview R173-M). She had been hoping to interview fifty women, but ended up with only seventeen, partly due to the requirement of the consent form.

Lesley Conn's experience (2008: 505) with her research on medical doctors in a hospital demonstrates that gaining signed consent from research participants not only had a detrimental effect on her research but also soured previously friendly and open interactions with them. The medical doctors enjoyed their participation in her research project, but were very offended when she asked them to sign the consent forms required by her ethics committee. The latter felt such a requirement was a departure from the research she initially described to them. It also fundamentally changed their status vis-à-vis one another. She became the 'expert' when they had to sign forms, and they resented it.

Her experience is echoed many times over in other research settings involving professional elites. In a presentation at the 2004 'Canadian Qualitatives,' held at Carleton University in Ottawa, Robert Campbell described his interest in doing research on scientists and science education. When he submitted his proposal to the equivalent of an REB, he received a reply saying that he should 'not bother scientists with his research – that they were too busy – and that he should study some other group' (Fieldnotes: 157). Similarly, a sociology student at one of the universities in Toronto described her difficulties getting her research through ethics review because she was planning to interview individuals in the Ministry of Finance and 'those folks are too busy to be participants in her research' (Chat R22-B, Fieldnotes: 141).

The requirement of the signed consent form even paralyzes veteran researchers, who are now worried about students: will they, or will they not, require a signed consent form when undertaking an interview as part of a class project (R146-S, Fieldnotes: 326)?

Evaluation research presents an interesting dilemma of its own. If a researcher discovers that the evaluation holds promise as a potential research publication, the ethics committees require the researcher to get consent from the previous participants (Interview A11-S). What about collecting data at an invited ethics workshop? The organizers of the workshop told Maureen Fitzgerald that she would not be able to collect data. Ironically, the organizers did not seek the consent of the participants to produce that decision (Tolich and Fitzgerald, 2006).

Our discussion would be remiss if we did not discuss the use of consent forms in relation to research participants. We have already alluded to some instances above, but the following are additional extracts that have come to my attention during the past few years.

In one study, participants argued with a researcher about having a legal clause in the consent form (Interview R173-M). In yet another study (by an anthropologist), research participants (refugees in Canada) resisted the consent letter that contained a statement that the participants had the right to withdraw from the study (Chat R23, Fieldnotes: 141). In a graduate research project, a researcher (R173-M) explained her experience with birders who did not want to sign the consent form. When asked, one said to her: 'I invited you into our home, [and] made you a meal. Why would I have to sign a form?'

In summary, the routinization of procedures seems to make bureaucratic sense. The routinization typically involves standardized application forms, 'checklists,' and informed consent forms. They can attain a ritualistic and fetishistic character. Ethics staff see these standardized forms as 'educational' tools – something to teach social researchers about ethics. The forms acquire a highly valued place in the research-ethics review system. They have a dark side, however, and can be flashpoints of contention. Despite their 'educational' character, the forms produce a guessing game (e.g., what does 'Please explain' refer to?). Ethics staff do not seem to seek the advice or opinions of researchers with respect to developing the forms. The forms convey the message that 'all resistance is futile.' Indeed, researchers are not in a position to resist the routinization of the ethics-review process. Instead, some researchers try to circumvent the rules that stand at the base of standardized procedures – a topic which we shall return to in chapter 10. In the meantime, the next chapter brings us to the inner chambers of research-ethics review committees. It focuses on how ethics committees arrive at decisions, dispose of applications, determine the category of review (such as whether an application should be 'expedited'), and how multifaceted all these processes actually are.

8 The Meeting: Making Agendas and Decisions

This chapter is devoted to data I gathered while conducting participant observation at four ethics committee meetings. The first section concerns the agenda of the meeting of the ethics-review committee itself. It became quite apparent (to me) that the agenda constitutes, in fact, two agendas. The official agenda contains, for the most part, decisions and issues related to the applications. However, there is an unofficial agenda that revolves around administravia where some of the topics focus on attendance, problems due to lack of staff and resources, and relations between professors and students and between the faculty and the ethics-review committee, among other things. The second section delves into the paradigms of thought that shape the conversation about ethics. More than anything else, what guides such conversations are disciplinary and individual perspectives rather than reliance on guidelines found in national ethics policies. The third section raises the question about how members of committees go about making decisions in meetings about ethics in research. This section identifies several facets of this process, a number of which are grounded in the members' unfamiliarity with ethics policies themselves.

Before doing fieldwork among REBs, I asked eight REBs to approve my conducting a participant observation study of their meetings. Of this group, five REBs accepted my invitation to be part of this observational research,[1] which took place between January and March 2006. Sadly, as I had misplaced my fieldnotes of one setting, I was unable to report on the workings of that REB. This misfortune became a latter-day blessing as none of the four REBs reported in my study will know whether or not the report pertains to them, further promoting anonymity. Beaverdam U is a small university,[2] Moosegate U is a mid-sized university, Nanook

U is a large university, and Bear Mountain U is another small university. As a rule, the smaller the university, proportionally fewer the faculty who submit proposals to the REB. On a per-capita, annual basis, the REBs at the two small universities (Bear Mountain U and Beaverdam U) have comparatively similar workloads; a proposal comes to the REB from 2.4 and 2.3 faculty members, respectively. For every 1.7 faculty at Moosegate, there is one proposal that comes to the REB. Nanook, the largest, has, on the average, nearly every faculty member producing a proposal. These annual figures are not absolutely correct because some proposals come from students and some come from faculty who submit more than one proposal. However, they do indicate the comparative workload for each REB.

Small universities were, with one exception, far more welcoming to this research than mid-sized or large universities. This openness seems to correlate with small-sized universities having a perception of themselves as relatively open communities of researchers. As there are many pressures placed on the shoulders of REBs, I felt that my request for being allowed to take fieldnotes in their meetings would entail considerable effort and time on their part. To acknowledge this sacrifice, I offered to give a public presentation on ethics, which three universities accepted. The talks were entitled 'Is it Possible to Teach Ethics in Research?' All the talks were well attended, with an audience of faculty, staff, and students, ranging in number from twenty to fifty. As a rule, I did not interview researchers at these universities.

I wish to underscore the limitations of my observational research during the REB meetings. First, my research did not capture all the decisions related to ethics review. Especially in the case of expedited review, it is usually the chair (and sometimes involving a few other REB members) who makes decisions to approve the application or to suggest changes to the researcher. Second, the small number of REBs who responded to my invitation does not allow me to make overarching statements about meetings of REBs in general; in any case, as noted elsewhere in *The Seduction of Ethics*, the diversity among REBs would make it difficult to extrapolate findings that might apply to all REBs. Third, the topics of discussions at REB meetings greatly vary during the year. April and May, for example, is a time when researchers submit applications once they received funding from the Social Sciences and Humanities Research Council. The start of a new term brings in applications based on student research, and so on. The arrival of newly appointed REB members sets the stage for presumably deeper discussions about ethics. Moreover, without attending meetings of the same REB year-round, it is hard to fully understand the back story of decisions made by REBs. Finally, my attempts in this chapter to hide the gender of the REB chairs to protect their identity profoundly undermine, I believe, the finely woven distinctions in how women and men who are acting as chairs conduct meetings. Such resulting blandness of analysis is a price that one must pay to retain anonymity.

To allow me to prepare for the meetings, I asked each REB whether they would share any minutes or application files with me. Moosegate provided me (with the approval of researchers) the files of seven cases while Bear Mountain shared its ongoing list of cases during the past year. None allowed me to keep copies of the minutes of their meetings. Some REBs meet once a month while others meet more frequently. As mentioned earlier, the meetings do not represent the totality of the decision-making process of ethics review. In cases of expedited review, for example, it is the chair that usually makes a decision outside of the REB meetings.

In all instances, the chair of the REB introduced me at the outset to those attending the REB meeting. The shortest meeting was one-hour long (Beaverdam U). Moosegate U took two hours for its deliberations, while the meeting at Bear Mountain U took two and a half hours. The longest meeting took three and one-quarter hours (Nanook U). There appears to be no correlation between the size of the university and the duration of the REB meetings. Nanook included a refreshment break, as did Bear Mountain, where they called it 'a bathroom stop.' Two REBs provided refreshments at the outset: coffee, tea, juice, and cookies.

Stepping into a meeting room that was named 'Chancellor's Room' or 'Public Affairs Room' gave the occasion an air of authority, reinforced by the room's decor. One room had a wall of portraits of former chancellors; in another, the REB members had cards with their names printed on them reserving their spots at the meeting table (I, too, got a card but my name had been written, not printed). In one case, the chair was dressed in more upscale fashion than when I had seen him/her a day earlier. Individuals' rising to get their coffee or tea and doughnut undercut the formality of the meeting. Typically, after settling in, each member would sit silently, reading the minutes or files placed in front of them.

Attendance and Membership

We see a close correlation between attendance and membership. On one hand, large REBs may consist of systematic representation of all academic units in a university (which are usually small), but may suffer from lower attendance rates in light of the challenge of organizing a meeting time that is suitable to all members. On the other hand, one tends to find big universities with a smaller REB membership. Moreover, it might not be possible to achieve a balanced proportion of disciplinary representation – a key issue in adjudicating fairly the applications that come before the REB. In appointing members to the REB, the university must count on a certain degree of voluntary enthusiasm of potential members to guarantee their full participation in REB meetings. Thus, the size of the REB, the availability of time of members, and the challenges of achieving disciplinary representation or balance all feed into the nature of attendance and membership.

Beaverdam U has a small board of about half a dozen members with a participation rate of 83 per cent. Moosegate U (a mid-sized university) has twenty to thirty members on the REB (one from each university department), but 55 per cent attended. The small-sized Bear Mountain U has a board of under a dozen members, with 56 per cent attending the meeting. Nanook U, a large university, also has a board of under a dozen members, of which 75 per cent attended. In addition, a future member was attending for orientation purposes as well as a researcher whom the REB had asked to attend for the purpose of being 'disciplined.'

Low rates of attendance can shape the discussion on ethics at the REB meeting in unanticipated ways. Flagging attendance at REB meetings is a deep concern at each of the four REBs I observed. This concern can emerge several times during a meeting. It is usually the chair who raises this issue. The chair at Nanook U (which had 75 per cent attendance at the meeting I observed) spoke of a 'high priority to have a bigger REB.' The chair had already invited a prospective new member to the meeting. When the new member asked if there were qualifications to be an REB member, the chair said, 'Not really; we are looking for people who are interested and people we can get along with.' When the discussion turned to faculty/departmental representation on the REB, the chair and members clearly believed that while a 'broader representation' is important, they couldn't be choosey. As the chair said, 'We can't afford to be choosey. I don't care about what fields. People are not partisan, anyway.' Along those lines, the chair mentioned the importance of 'having enthusiastic members, which is more [important] than the requirement of disciplines.' The chair also mentioned that 'a personality conflict ... could stand in the way ... We need people who are practical and problem-solving.' Janice McKendrick, a graduate student who has deeply reflected on the nature of REBs, noted that because there are no set criteria in universities for selecting REB members, members are handpicked for like-minded views – and this is a flawed process (Fieldnotes: 520). In short, it is personal characteristics or personality rather than being knowledgeable, or even 'representing' a discipline, that make an individual a 'good' candidate for serving on an REB.

There is another fact that guides the selection of new members: it is highly important to recruit someone from the very disciplines the REB is 'having problems with.' This discussion points to two practical criteria, namely, enthusiasm and representation of a problematic discipline.

The concern with disciplinary representation runs deep in every REB. Worries about membership were expressed at the meeting of the Beaverdam U REB even though its attendance is the highest among the four REBs I studied (83 per cent). When the minutes of a previous meeting had to be approved, however, there was no one among the general membership who had been at that meeting who could approve the minutes – the previous meeting had been attended by only 17 per cent and all those who happened to be at that meeting were now absent from this meeting. No one seemed too surprised at this anomaly.

Moosegate U, a mid-sized university, is also concerned by the issue of membership and the fact that 'representatives' from the community are often absent.[3] Sometimes they do not have a quorum – they have a membership of between twenty and thirty. In fact, of the thirty meetings held between March 2002 and January 2005, eleven were short of the quorum. And if they do meet a numerical quorum, the REB is still bound by the stipulation that a quorum should consist of twelve people, including two *representatives of the community.* But what happens if the community representatives are absent from the meeting? To get around this problem, the REB decided to approve applications if they posed only 'minimal risk' to research participants. One REB member suggested that 'maybe we should make the REB membership smaller' – that is the opposite of what was suggested at Nanook U. In trying to solve the problem of community representatives at Moosegate, the discussion went as follows:

MEMBER A: Maybe the community representatives don't understand the importance of their attendance. Maybe they can be reminded.

CHAIR: We need to have them here.

MEMBER B: If people don't attend, poll them by email. Community members have jobs during the day.

MEMBER C: I'm against polling by email.
CHAIR: Any other ideas?

No new ideas were forthcoming about community representation (or even about recruiting new members for the following year). The chair started the brief discussion with the comment, 'Anyone who wants to be REB chair? Please feel free. I have no attachments.' One member did not know when his term was up and the administrative secretary responded, 'It's on the Web.' The same member then recalled that departing REB members were sent a thank-you letter. No need even to look it up on the Web. But at Nanook U there were ongoing discussions about the challenge of finding new members in general: should they look in under-represented departments or mainly seek anyone as long as they could be enthusiastic about the work at the REB? Regardless of disciplinary background, there was one concern that pervaded the thoughts of Nanook U, namely, to find someone 'who is willing to serve.' These concerns are perennial, it seems, and discussions are inconclusive. Some members agreed that such decisions should be left in the hands of the administrative assistant, while the chair continued to insist, 'We should settle this now.'

Even such small-sized, liberal arts universities such as Bear Mountain U (56 per cent attendance) deeply worry about the issue of membership. In consulting about their new 'Policy Manual,' the REB members struggled with the alleged notion from the *TCPS* that some members should come from 'scientific' areas. Interestingly, these REB members are ill-informed about one of the requirements for REB membership that is actually in the *TCPS* that 'at least two members have broad expertise in the methods or in the areas of research that are covered by the REB' (*TCPS*, B.2., Article 1.3.a). There is no mention of 'scientific' areas in the *TCPS* (it becomes evident later that REB members are generally poorly informed about the *TCPS* text). Still, despite this misunderstanding, such an imagined requirement can raise eyebrows in a liberal arts university. One member suggested, 'We should make membership less stringent ... What is "scientific versus non-scientific"? We may not get "scientists."' The chair agreed with this problem and said, 'What concerns me is that we are driven by the [what the] *TCPS* [says] regarding membership requirements.'

The above discussion about membership leads one to consider to what extent such discussions form part of the agenda. Officially, they do not form any part of the agenda. But they do form a part of the spontaneous discussion. Thus, the career of the agenda consists of both the formally set agenda points and the informally set agenda points of discussion.

The Career of the Agenda

The formally set agenda of the meeting does not usually square with the actual proceedings ('informal agenda'). What percolates through the informal agenda are issues that have been visited over an extended period of time. The issue of participation and membership has been noted above, but there are also discussions about outstanding administrative procedures that press themselves upon administrative staff, questions about how files are kept ('digital?' 'hard copy?'), and, out of the blue, questions about ethics. Each REB places its own stamp on the order of the informal agenda. A researcher would be challenged in comparing the agenda of even these four REBs. One needs to say, in advance however, that the REB meetings are not chaotic operations.

Table 8.1 provides an overview of the agenda of each of the four REBs. One can examine the career of the agenda in terms of the actual topics discussed, some of which appear on the official agenda, some of which seem to arise spontaneously in the conversation or consultation, that is, that are unrelated to the official topic. The shaded areas in table 8.1 indicate the spontaneous sharing of these sorts of ideas. Moreover, one can derive the extent to which the topics concern ethics, whether specifically related to a case under consideration, or ethics in general. Finally, when we match the utterances with individuals from specific disciplines, we are able to trace the distinctive contributions that disciplinary 'representatives' who are members of REBs tend to make to the consultation. This last point is important because it shows the challenge of addressing ethical issues in research outside one's disciplinary paradigm.

At the outset, I claim some shortcomings in the presentation of my data. Every REB member, indeed every REB as a whole, carries forward particular ideas based on earlier experiences. What seems spontaneous to an observer like myself may well be part of a larger matrix of ideas through which an application may be adjudicated. Still, these spontaneous expressions of insight might offer us clues as to what matters in the minds of REB members. Moreover, some of the applications are vetted in advance of a meeting, in which case the chair or the relevant REB member is simply giving an update. In other words, we are stripping the agenda of

Table 8.1   Overview of the Agenda among the Four Studied REBs

Beaverdam U (1 hr.)	Moosegate U (2 hrs.)	Bear U (2½ hrs.)	Nanook U (3½ hrs.)
Approval of minutes	Introductions	Approval of minutes	Introductions
Case 1	Quorum issue	Cases: General report	Online student evaluation
	Cases 1–3: report Quorum issue	Case 1	Case 1: "screw up" Disc. on how little supervisors know about the work of their students
'Down the road?'	Chair's report	Policy Manual – membership – capitalizations in text	Soc. Sci. REB Problems with a department
Case 2	Attendance at REB meetings	*Bathroom stop*	Minutes
Case 3	Status of community representatives		Report from sub-committees on several faculties
Internet studies	Student Reps.	Report from a research committee	Staffing problems and hiring
	Workshop announcement	Keeping track of student researchers	Case 2
Report from a committee (unrelated to ethics review)	PRE doc of privacy and confidentiality – public figure? – subject-centred perspective	Case 2: presenting student research to REB	NCEHR conference
An admin. routine	Discussion re *TCPS* – *TCPS* not good as code – shouldn't want to be too codified – *TCPS* too complex, use of common-sense	Comparing REB with one at larger university	Report on U.S. conference on academic freedom
	U.S. policies: illegal to do research on illegal immigrants	Case 3: storing of data REB annual report	PRE report New members

(Continued)

Table 8.1   *Continued*

Beaverdam U (1 hr.)	Moosegate U (2 hrs.)	Bear U (2½ hrs.)	Nanook U (3½ hrs.)
Approval of minutes	Introductions	Approval of minutes	Introductions
	Omit ref. to child abuse in consent forms	Case 4	Other REB's using this REB
	Next year's membership	Processes and forms	
	Reports from departments	Good natured comments about my (WCvdH) research	1st report on various cases
	Research by undergraduates	PRE proportionate review document	−anyone can send letter to REB −disc. on ethics vs. scholarly integrity −student/supervisor relation
	Meeting schedule	University survey verification form	*Break* (used to discuss admin. matters, e.g., next meeting, moving into new office)
		CAREB meeting	2nd report on various cases
			3rd report on various cases
			Discussion about walking into a researcher's office asking questions and becoming complicit in the research

Note: The shaded portions refer to spontaneous topics of discussion that are not listed on the official agenda.

its official items of discussion, leaving us with a remnant of spontaneous contributions that, in turn, allows us to tap into another current of issues and concerns. It ought to be mentioned that research-ethics reviews also occur outside the REB meetings, such as in the case of expedited reviews which are generally handled by the REB chair. It is not unusual to find that the majority of applications involve expedited reviews.

Beaverdam U, the small university with a high REB attendance of 83 per cent, has four topics on the agenda, although three others enter into the discussion spontaneously. Approval of the minutes appears as the first item, followed by three applications and a report from a committee (unrelated to research-ethics review). Between the first and second application, an REB member wonders about the implications of a decision for future research. Between the third application and a report from the aforementioned committee, another REB member points to the rising field of Internet studies and the potential ethical dimensions of such research. The topic that guides the closing of the meeting deals with in-house administrative matters.

Moosegate U, a mid-sized university (which has 55 per cent attendance), has seven topics on the official agenda, in addition to the nine that seem to appear spontaneously. This REB has the largest membership of the four I studied (20–30), which might explain such a proportionally large number of spontaneous contributions. The official agenda includes formal introductions by each person, the chair's report on three applications, another report by the chair, an announcement about a workshop on ethics at the university, a discussion of the Interagency Advisory Panel on Research Ethics' (PRE) document on privacy and confidentiality (that generates some questions about confidentiality, who public figures are, and the matter of the subject-centred perspective), next year's membership, reports from a variety of departments, and arrangements for the next meeting. Among the spontaneous topics, the issue of what constitutes a quorum comes up twice, along with the problems of (low) attendance, the role of community representatives and students, a variety of thoughts about the *TCPS*, the illegality of doing research in the United States on illegal immigrants, and research by undergraduates. The question of mentioning limits of confidentiality on consent forms related to a researcher reporting child abuse was also raised. The chair said that he/she does not recommend mentioning limits of confidentiality related to child abuse or illegal activity on consent forms for research projects that are entirely unrelated (such as studies involving simple arithmetic or memory for word lists), in which such participant information is extremely unlikely to be disclosed. For projects in which such information could possibly arise, such cautions on the consent form were deemed necessary.

The career of the formal agenda at Bear Mountain U (a small university with 56 per cent attendance at the REB meeting) holds quite firm. The REB approves the minutes of an earlier meeting, it alternates topics on its agenda by examining four cases (applications), it discusses a report from the Research Advisory Committee, considers its annual report, looks at its own processes and forms, handles the proportionate review document of the Interagency Advisory Panel on Research Ethics (PRE), considers a university survey verification form, and, finally, speaks about the possibility of members going to the meetings of the Canadian Association of Research Ethics Boards (CAREB) in May 2006. There are only two spontaneous contributions to the discussion: when REB members wonder how an instructor can keep track of so many students who are doing research, and when they compare themselves (favourably) with an REB at a much larger university.

Nanook U (the large university with 75 per cent REB attendance) has twelve topics on the official agenda, but eight more topics emerge spontaneously, unrelated to the previous topic. The REB handles five applications, some new, some old, sprinkled throughout the whole meeting. Approval of the minutes falls halfway down the agenda. We find reports from subcommittees from half a dozen faculties, as well as an appeal for some REB members to go to the forthcoming NCEHR conference (in early April 2010, members of the NCEHR LISTSERV received word that NCEHR had run into funding problems and that it could no longer keep its staff and undertake its activities). A report from PRE and the issue of new members also appears on the agenda. Interspersed among the official agenda items are discussions about the new online student evaluations, about how little supervisors know about their students' research, the failing of a smaller REB in another faculty, the usual, typical problems with an academic department, staffing problems and hiring staff for the ethics office, an informal report on a conference on academic freedom in the U.S., the thought that anyone can send a letter to the REB, a discussion about ethics versus scholarly integrity, and student – supervisor relationships. Finally, REB members express the worry that, if they walk into a researcher's office (to discuss ethical issues about the research), they may inadvertently side with the researcher when the application comes to the REB. This sentiment is not unusual. Laura Stark noted that IRB members see the involvement of the principal investigator in ethics review as 'contaminants' (Stark, 2007: 784). Maureen Fitzgerald (a researcher who conducted participant observation in ethics committees in Australia) saw a committee that also 'discouraged a member to seek clarification with the researcher about questions raised by the committee – the chair discouraged it in particular. All contact with the researcher had to be in writing, leaving a paper trail' (Fitzgerald, 2005: 327). During the break, while members are munching their cookies, there is some discussion about administrative routines, such as the next meeting and moving into a new office.

All four meetings experienced joking as a way of releasing tension. This experience is similar to what Maureen Fitzgerald has found (Fitzgerald, 2004: 43). With long meetings, she noted that members became fatigued and needed a break; some meetings could last six to seven hours (even though none of the meetings I attended lasted that long); she also remarked that each application is not given the same amount of time (Fitzgerald, 2005: 330). Amidst periods of 'slow and deliberate scrutiny and debate,' there are periods with 'short bursts of accelerated activity where applications are reviewed with great swiftness' (Fitzgerald, 2005: 330). As we shall see below, discussions are sometimes not directly related to the applications. There are cues (e.g., looking at a watch) and comments by someone to 'move faster' (Fitzgerald, 2005: 330–1) that determine the career of an agenda. As Fitzgerald noted in her own study, that 'when [the] committee thinks it's moving too fast, there is a sense that it's not doing its job. Under time pressure, however, issues can be dealt with "out of session" by chair, staff, or a particular committee member' (Fitzgerald, 2005: 331).

As Fitzgerald found, each meeting has its own rhythm. Although the four REBs in our study handled no more than six applications during a single meeting, Fitzgerald noted that typically a meeting ranged from three to four up to 200 applications requiring a full review, with thirty to forty of those being reviewed for the first time. Other committees would review seventy applications at one meeting. While the break is seen as a reward, there is a 'fear that committee members are perhaps not doing their job with sufficient rigor' and thus the periods of greatest scrutiny and discussion occur at the very beginning, shortly before the end of the session, and just before and after the break. The last one or two of the applications do not involve much scrutiny; 'members' heads are already somewhere else, and some issues are moved out of session' (Fitzgerald, 2005: 331–2).

Ethics committee members usually review applications in the order in which the ethics officer receives them. When a researcher arrives earlier or later than scheduled, however, the applications follow a different order. Moreover, applications that needed longer discussions are moved to the beginning or end of the meeting (Fitzgerald, 2005: 332). (I found that such applications tended to be moved outside of the meeting, to be resolved by the chair, often with the help of the administrative assistant.) Significantly, according to Fitzgerald, it is not the quality of the application that often determines its fate, 'but where it stacks up with other applications during a meeting,' that is, after a difficult case or in a period when things went swiftly. She also discovered that 'in instituting a new rule, members would have considered a particular difficult case, only to apply it to the next case, regardless of the dissimilarity, just to be "consistent"' (Fitzgerald, 2005: 333–4). She also found that 'the shifts in attention are provoked by a moral panic about not carrying out their moral duty as members of the committee' (Fitzgerald, 2005: 333).

Spontaneous Offerings of Insights

When we cull the official agenda items from the REB deliberations, we are left with a large number of spontaneous offerings of insights, comments, and questions. Table 8.2 summarizes these findings.

In descending order of frequency, the REBs offered a variety of spontaneous insights that, strictly speaking, were not part of the official agenda. The most frequently raised issues pertain to attendance at meetings and meeting the quorum, and researcher/professor–student relations. There were discussions about the interactions between researchers and the REB, along with informal contributions to the discussion that compared the REB favourably to other REBs, in addition to administrative matters and staffing problems.

As I indicated earlier in this chapter, the topic that has garnered the most spontaneous comments relates to (low) attendance at meetings and meeting the quorum requirements. Moosegate U is, in particular, worried by this issue (remember, only 55 per cent of members attend and 'representatives' from the community were often absent).[4] At Nanook U there are discussions about the challenge of finding new members: should they be found in under-represented departments or should the REB simply seek anyone who is enthusiastic about the work at the REB?

The next-most frequent spontaneous topic is related to researcher/professor–student relations. At Beaverdam U several REB members expressed the opinion that 'maybe it's not a good idea to collect academic information from the students who want to be researched.' That opinion led to others' weighing in about researching students in general. 'What,' one member asks, 'if it's part of the requirements of a course?' At Bear Mountain U, some REB members were puzzled by

Table 8.2   Spontaneous Offerings of Insights Based on Observational Study of Four REBs, 2006

Topics	Beaverdam U	Moosegate U	Bear Mountain U	Nanook U	Total
Attendance, quora	✔	✔✔✔✔		✔	6
Researcher/ professor–student relations	✔		✔	✔✔	4
Interactions with students, faculty		✔		✔✔✔	4
Compare itself favourably with other REBs in the U.S.		✔	✔	✔	3
Major ethical topics (e.g., integrity), TCPS		✔		✔	2
Administrative matters, staffing problems	✔			✔	2
Specific decision re: consent form		✔			1
Other*	✔			✔✔	3

*'Other' includes discussions about future fields of research and conferences, and more germane topics about the university.

how an instructor can keep track of thirty-five students doing research. It is unclear whether the REB thought it would more practical to have thirty-five students in a class doing the same assignment or whether they thought there was an attempt by an instructor to overwhelm the REB with potentially thirty-five applications. At Nanook U, there was general discussion about how little supervisors know about their students' work or the research they are doing. One REB member added that this could be 'putting students in danger . . .'

General interactions between students and researchers, as well as the interactions between the researchers and the REB itself, constitute the third largest source of spontaneous comments.[5] As a researcher myself, I found these comments rather revealing, but not surprising. Bear Mountain U refers to its most challenging cases by the name of the researcher: 'Here's the [Martin (a pseudonym)] file – go read this!' Several minutes later in the same meeting, the administrative assistant widens the space between her thumb and index finger and says to me, '[Macdonald (another pseudonym)] has a file "this" thick on just one thing.'[6] In other ethics committees, one finds a similar practice, namely, reference to a particular case by the name of the person associated with a similar, troublesome issue (Maureen Fitzgerald, email to author, 9 July 2004, Fieldnotes: 382).

Research-ethics committees get particularly piqued when they receive applications from researchers who ask the committees to 'trust them.' Maureen Fitzgerald quotes this pejorative phrase uttered by an ethics-committee member: 'Oh yeah, another one of these: "Trust me. I'm a researcher"' (Fitzgerald, 2005: 331).[7] She found that the ethics-review process is based on the assumption that researchers in general are not 'trustworthy' and that is 'why their work has to be scrutinized and audited' (Maureen Fitzgerald, email to author, 9 July 2004, Fieldnotes: 382).

At Nanook U, the REB had called in a supervisor regarding a case that the REB had 'screwed up.'[8] Although this agenda item was part of the official proceedings, it was revealing to see how the researcher/supervisor related to the REB to whose meeting he was summoned. Here are the extracts from my fieldnotes from that meeting:

(Before the supervisor came in – he was waiting in the hallway – some REB members raised these questions:)

MEMBER A: Is there a timetable of these events? *(Going through the report)* I see that the student waited for a year to get approval and worked for six to eight months on the research. The student [and supervisor] had written an angry letter to the REB, and that attitude came through in the letter.

REB CHAIR: Yes. The student was foolish enough to put his 'attitude' on paper.

MEMBER B: I have a few questions. *(He had written four of them on a yellow pad)* Does the consent apply to the student's stated protocol [i.e., written] or to the one he used? Did the student start his research without telling his supervisor or his committee? The student is a police officer himself and, of all people, he should have understood the importance of process. I'd like to see his dossier with time line. I understand that the delay was due to an REB mix up ...

MEMBER C: It's a question of whether it is research misconduct or [whether it] is about a disciplinary problem?

REB CHAIR: There is no procedure in place at [Nanook U] to handle these screw-ups.

MEMBER A: The letter is offensive, but the question is whether there is real harm done.[9] The topic was a bit sensitive, but not overly so ...

REB CHAIR: I don't want the REB to be the big stick. *(In anticipation of calling the supervisor in, she then formally introduces everyone, not just for my benefit but also for the observer, i.e., the prospective member of the REB, it seems. She then went to the door and called the student's supervisor in.)*
(As soon as the supervisor sat down, he said, 'Don't kill me!' That got a good laugh)

STUDENT'S SUPERVISOR: *(The supervisor admitted to the blame:)* I should have pursued the issue more vigorously. While the student was in [name of town] and waiting for ethics consent, I told him to start the research and get oral consent for now . . . *(He admits his pet peeve: ethics comes from medicine, psychology, and anthropology)* Years ago, I was interviewing people from [a major governmental agency]. The consent form was a big issue. The people whom one is researching are not familiar with ethics procedure, and it took me forty minutes to explain this procedure. *(He then told the REB the nature of the research of the student)*

MEMBER A: Is there anything in the research that would be harmful?

STUDENT'S SUPERVISOR: Not at all.

MEMBER B: But the student used a different format.

STUDENT'S SUPERVISOR: I used different methods when I was a student. The student had a form which he read out to the participants.

MEMBER C: He would have read out the information to the participant, subject?

STUDENT'S SUPERVISOR: Yes.

MEMBER C: I have no difficulty with that.

MEMBER D: There is the problem of oral consent, but the consent is not complete, not fully informed. Are you sure there is full consent?

STUDENT'S SUPERVISOR: Absolutely! One is not talking to children. They are adults. The people are very intelligent. They understand. It's the context, the social context that one must take into account. The problem of consent arose out of a different research culture. My student did not ask for private information. There can be all kinds of research. By producing a written consent form, people get lawyerly.

MEMBER E: *(Laughs, as many others do at this comment, pointing to an REB member who is a lawyer)*

What is notable is the interaction between the student's supervisor and the REB. His first intervention ('Don't kill me!'), although humorous, was a symbolic and exaggerated plea for mercy (although part of the mistake was a lower-level REB's not keeping in touch with the student). His admission ('I admit I dropped the ball') was an effective use of performative language. Regardless of who was at fault, an admission of alleged guilt goes a long way.

The REB had also taken note of the student's letter as being 'offensive' and as being an 'angry letter to the REB,' an attitude that 'came through in the letter.' There are no indications that the REB might have sympathized with the student's situation. In the final upshot, the REB did grant ethics approval to the student's completed research although the REB did not utter the term 'retroactively.'

Meeting face to face with an ethics committee can cause anyone to be very nervous, especially an upcoming PhD student whose application is up for review, as Tara Starr Johnson shows:

> I attempted to adopt a professional, inquisitive mien as I looked around the room of mostly White faces. Although there wasn't a clear hierarchy implied by the layout of the room, one white-haired, aquiline-featured man wearing a white lab coat and stethoscope radiated the markings of authority. (Johnson, 2008: 215)

What entrapped, the student, however, was not the 'markings of hierarchical authority,' but something more complex. She sums up her experiences as a 'betrayal narrative' (Johnson, 2008: 225):

> What had at first seemed like a betrayal was in fact much more complex. I had been caught in a you're-either-with-me-or-against-me binary, which was hypocritical given my supposed post-structural theoretical stance. I revel in shades of gray, but I had unfairly and self-righteously fixed these professors' locations in black and white. If I ever am in a position like theirs, I cannot now say unequivocally that I will vocally champion qualitative research when it may well be in my students' and the discipline's best interest for me to lay low and practice subversive resistance. (229)

Whether one is a professor or a student, it is easier not to revel 'in shades of gray,' but to be forthright about the errors of one's way, whether factual or not. She learned a valuable lesson:

> And who knows what work they [IRB members] did for me behind the scenes? Silence or the appearance of cooperation can be a form of resistance . . . ; sometimes subversively negotiating around obstacles is more effective than directly confronting them. If the goal was to get my application approved, then their means of doing so – initially going along

with their IRB colleagues and then helping me get it right for the next round – may well have been the best strategy. (Johnson, 2008: 226)

As part of the spontaneous discussions, at least three of the REBs compared themselves favourably to other REBs, including those on the same campus. At Moosegate U, an REB member talks about the United States, averring that 'the proposed law there makes it illegal to do research on illegal immigrants.' What generated this spontaneous comment was the REB chair's announcement that he/she has researchers take out references to having to report child abuse and illegal activities from the consent forms, because this reference makes the research participant think that the research is about something else.

An REB member at Bear Mountain U assured me during the meeting that 'researchers coming from [name of a large university on the West Coast] find our REB more friendly.' Interestingly, later in the meeting, the REB chair offered to pull together the forms the REB is developing, as he/she would like to do them properly. He/she was 'planning to use forms from the Ottawa REB and UBC REB.' An REB member offered to give his ideas to the chair about the forms, but he 'doesn't like the forms from the Ottawa REB.'

Several elements during the discussion at the REB of Nanook U referred to the inadequate performance of a lower-level REB at the same university. One was in 'a mess,' another one had created an 'ethics chill,' and another one had a big 'backlog' of cases.

These findings point to an important obstacle to research, namely, the multi-centred research proposal. It is seldom noted (if ever), but one wonders whether the need to go through multiple REBs might suggest that each REB does not trust the ethics decision-making process of the other REB(s) (Interview E13-M). A chair of one of the REBs at Nanook U commented that 'each REB looks at an application as if it is new, even though it has gone through other REBs (for multi-site research).' This latter approach speaks to the very issue of not trusting other REBs to make the right decision.

Aside from the predictable administrative items slated on the official agenda of REBs (such as the problem with quorums), there were several instances where individuals on the REB offered questions about administrative routines. An initial reading of these questions suggests that REB members might not be well acquainted with the daily routines of business at the ethics office. At Beaverdam U, for example, an REB member had to ask whether files were kept in hard-copy or digitalized formats.

At Nanook U, the chair's reporting on staffing problems underscored the imminent move by the administrative assistant. Problems are compounded because there is no new person in sight, and there were 'boxes [in the ethics office] which had not been filed for three years.' As there are no other opportunities for 'venting,' an REB chair may well see the REB meetings as the only legitimate venue to vent his/her frustrations with the lack of resources and the slow pace of change, for example.

The next section explores a number of contingencies that mark the decision-making process in ethics committees. The first contingency is about disciplinary perspectives and how they shape the conversation about ethics and the second is about how individual perspectives shape the conversation about ethics. The second discussion has a striking absence of ethical principles.

Paradigms and Perspectives That Shape the Conversation about Ethics

At Moosegate U, there were only one or two spontaneous reflections about ethics, one of them involving the *TCPS*. One REB member declares it as 'a general statement . . . general principles of *TCPS* are good, but as a code it's not good. It shouldn't be too codified.' Another one says, 'The *TCPS* is complex, but we need to use common-sense. I'm not sure whether I'm on top of things. It is important not to make things complex.' Another chimes in, 'Laws can be turned inside out by those with evil interest.'

At Nanook U, the chair reported on a conference on academic freedom and heard the usual academic freedom-versus-ethics debate. He/she confidently declares, 'This issue has been solved. Ethics is here to stay.'

Common sense would have us see REBs as repositories of knowledge of ethics in research. In this light, one would expect REBs to be engaged in extended or broader discussions of ethical principles, or at least involved in establishing foundational guidelines for their subsequent decisions about applications. I found the opposite: virtually no time was dedicated to such discussions. It would be uncharitable to conclude that REBs are not interested in these foundational principles of ethics (that would surely make their later decisions more coherent). The staff at ethics offices, as well as the chair, have already thought about and prioritized the ethical issues – albeit more routine ones – that apparently govern decisions about applications. What may be more at play is what Dawne Clarke calls the 'tyranny of the immediate' as a governing concept in her study about professors' failed attempts at writing (Clarke, 2005), whereby urgent, daily requirements demand immediate attention and intrude on any long-term activity or intentions. Indeed, the need to process up to five or six files during a meeting, along with the need to dispense with administrative matters fills up so much time that no luxuries of introspection are left.

The discussion of ethics in all four REBs follows the disciplinary interests of those individuals who contribute to the discussion. Potentially, the REB has at its disposal the opportunity to raise any issues it wishes about ethics. In the end, though, the REB members, individually, raise a limited number of topics. If one compares any consideration of ethics to a pie in which each slice offers a different fruit, it is clear to see how individuals decide to cut it on the basis of which one or two slices will satisfy their disciplinary tastes.

Disciplinary Paradigms

Across the four observed REB meetings, some twenty-six topics about ethics surfaced during the discussions. These are topics that have the potential of spilling beyond the application under consideration (such as 'consent'). The 'representatives' from the Faculty of Education would raise issues related to research in the classroom. Someone from nursing was more likely to be concerned about not mixing interviews with therapy, whether harm can come from research, and whether the research involves sensitive topics. One member had several disciplinary interests that she called upon to further her work on a new REB. She recalls how in the previous REB she was the only one with qualitative research experience and she felt obliged to 'contribute in that way' (Interview E27-S). The same person acknowledged that recruiting vulnerable people for research was her particular interest and she would pay attention to that in the proposals being submitted. Her other interest grew out of working with illiterate individuals, and she expressed a heightened interest in consent forms, especially when researching children and immigrants.

A psychologist was more inclined to query about the consent procedures than any other topic, while a student representative involved herself in questions related to 'taking care of students' and professor – student relations. Interestingly, the representative from geography was concerned about data storage. There are, no doubt, anomalies in this pattern. For example, a computer science representative queried what constitutes 'research,' and the lawyer on the REB was interested in methodology. Personal interests were at the base of these anomalies. My interviews with the chairs and members of other REBs confirmed my initial findings about the disciplinary bent of ethical issues raised during the REB meetings. A member of an ethics committee admitted that she pushes for consideration of community-based projects drawing from her own PhD work (Interview E12-M). Another member, whose training is in counselling, said that he focuses more on the interview, making sure that it should not be seen as therapy (Interview E12-M). Another REB member (at the same university) sees his main contribution to discussions on the ethics committee as raising the 'big issues,' namely, confidentiality, sharing information, and client – counsellor relationships. He notes, among other things, that he is not so interested in the 'administrative aspects' of research, that is, in 'getting permission and how to store data, step-by-step stuff.' Instead, he confesses, 'I look at people's emotional stability' (Interview E13-M). Tellingly, a member of another ethics committee, found that 'making ethical decisions are all over the map [at REB meetings], where people rely heavily on [their] own backgrounds, e.g., philosophy, nursing, et cetera. Can't avoid that' (Interview E15-S).

Individual Perspectives

However, there are also individual (rather than disciplinary) factors to consider and the important role they play in the career of the meeting. Any individual member of an ethics committee can play a preemptive role, provided that he/she is vocal. An interview participant told me that the meetings she attends are very quiet, but 'there is one person who has read everything and who tells the rest what to look for' (Interview S47-M). A member of an ethics committee (Interview E12-M) wants to see 'more precision' in the applications. Damon Parker and his co-authors found that medical specialists on such committees 'adopted the attitude and language of generalists, and subsumed this within their lay habitus' and relied on 'persuasive rhetoric of self-effacement, such as "I'm not an expert in this area, but I wonder if...," or "I'm not sure if this is relevant, but..."' to get their point across (Parker, James, and Barrett, 2005: 19). Indeed, as Maureen Fitzgerald found in her participant-observation of several ethics committees, the influence of one member can be quite critical, so much so that one individual was responsible for a committee to have 'a standing policy that all transcripts had to be returned to participants; this was standard and a "good" practice' (Fitzgerald, 2005: 327).[10] Such 'self-assignment' of roles is not uncommon among members in an ethics committee.

A second defining aspect of individual opinion that gets absorbed into discussions on ethics relates to what can be defined as 'reasonable,' not unlike in clinical-practice meetings about patients, where common understandings are subjectively built up (Bloor, 2002: 181). Without training in philosophy or ethics, it seems impossible to build a system of ethical guidelines. Without such training, members of ethics committees rely on 'being reasonable.' However, the idea of 'reasonableness' varies within each ethics committee and among ethics committees, creating inconsistencies, for example, deciding who is a 'public official'? (Feeley, 2007: 770). Parker and his co-authors (2005: 18) found that 'reasonable' is the word that cropped up consistently when he examined ethics committees (Parker et al., 2005: 18). 'Reasonableness,' according to Parker, tacitly invoked core cultural family values (Parker et al., 2005: 20) and the 'practical logic of reasonableness also carried force because it tapped into and was reinforced by core cultural values concerned with fairness and care, as well as fundamental social norms of reciprocity and exchange' (Parker, James, and Barrett, 2005: 25). However, throughout this process, one chair still wonders where the 'use of collective judgment (to make ethical decisions) may not be always be right.' He/she further asks, 'Is the democratic way of deciding on applications the best way, that is, through collective wisdom of the REB?' (Interview C25-M).

All in all, the application of ethical principles in discussions within the ethics committees is seriously compromised by the members themselves feeling more at home discussing professional (rather than ethical) matters, the propensity to weigh in with disciplinary and individual viewpoints, and the appeal to what sounds 'reasonable.'

As we shall note below, ethics committee members struggle with major gaps in their knowledge of ethics guidelines. Moreover, members fall into what one could call 'private zones' of ethics reflection. One explains, 'I try to take a practical approach, rather than a "rule-generating" one' (S13-M, Fieldnotes: 1245). A researcher at a major Canadian university, rhetorically asks, 'Isn't research ethics just common sense?' (R108-B). A staff member of an REB confesses that her REB is 'second-guessing their [social workers'] way of doing things' (S22-M, Fieldnotes: 1130).

Implications of the Role of Disciplinary Paradigms
and Individual Perspectives

There are several implications of the fact that the discussion in ethics-committee meetings relies so much on either disciplinary perspectives or individual participation. First, the absence or presence of particular members determines the flow of the discussion of ethics in a substantial manner. The absence of one person means that his/her perspective will be missing from the evolving and collective thought of the REB during any given meeting. If a discipline is habitually absent from the meetings, some ethical questions might never be raised. When meetings of the REB are consistently attended by some (vocal) members (and not others), it means that their perspectives will become the ruling ethics paradigm for that meeting.

Second, there will seldom be an opportunity to consider the full panoply of ethical issues. Who knows what kinds of ethical issues truly reside in the minds of those disciplines never represented at the table?

Third, given such fluctuations of ethics paradigms, it is left for the chair of the REB to establish the wider ethics principles that guide the discussions of any given application. Indeed, as the National Communication Association pointed out, the changing interpretations of standards depend on who chairs (NCA, 2005: 211). As Maureen Fitzgerald notes, '[S]ome people are more likely to evoke change than others, but the chair can evoke major change' (Fitzgerald, 2005: 334).

Fourth, there is the curious problem on REBs where the rule of subjective opinions of REB members gets in the way of academic freedom.[11] When subjective opinions gain dominance in assessing research applications, all too often the REB forgets that the researcher has the right to pursue particular topics or use his/her own research strategies. The idea of academic freedom takes a distant seat when the subjective opinions of REB members hold sway.

Under these circumstances, it is difficult to develop a consistent ethics paradigm from REB to REB, from the previous chair to a newly appointed chair, and even, to some extent, from meeting to meeting of the same REB (unless the same members attend each meeting). One can go further and claim that 'shifting priorities [are] based largely on IRB membership' (Bach, 2005: 262), both within a given meeting or between meetings, especially if attendance is poor or low. Still, in an interview setting, some chairs of ethics committees are likely to present a rosy picture of what transpires in their committees with respect to discussing ethical issues in general. One says that going through all applications together is a 'learning process' (Interview C03-M), while another (Interview C30-M) vows there are 'general discussions' that 'allow the REB to apply ideas to specific applications.' A more realistic approach, as one REB has done, is to create a subcommittee in a faculty than can come up with ethical and political insights about a particular research approach (such as autobiography) (Interview E12-M).

Making Decisions without Principles

In the absence of discussions about ethics, the ethics committees' labyrinth of decision-making takes on several forms, namely, making discretionary judgments, desiring to 'protect' the research participant, being unfamiliar with national ethics policies, relying on distancing mechanisms, working like manuscript editors, being attuned to the location of the ethics committee, and being jealous and engaging in vendettas.

Making Discretionary Judgments

Scholars have already noted the tendency by ethics committees not to discuss overarching ethical principles. Damon Parker and colleagues (2005: 18), for example, found that members 'did not normally discuss the relative merits of applications with overt reference to these principles' and that 'autonomy, beneficence and justice were not deployed as working models for decision-making.' M.E. Dixon-Woods and co-authors found that ethics-review committees are 'sites of discretionary judgement: there is no single "right" answer to (most) ethical issues . . .' (Dixon-Woods et al., 2007: 4). In his study of Australian ethics committees, Mark Israel, found that if ethical principles do enter the discussion, there is an 'uncritical application of principles associated with bioethics, confidentiality, informed consent, harms and benefits, and relationships' (Israel, 2005: 30). Still, as one interview participant mentioned (Interview E12-M), she ranks her ethics review 'in light of what other REB members write about any particular application' rather than against a set of ethics principles. Another participant (Interview E13-M) said that he/she 'sees ethics not in terms of principles, but as emerging concepts, constructing as we go.' In a focus group I held with members of an REB at Bear Mountain U, the participants admitted that 'discussions about ethics are comparatively rare,' that 'we don't have time to consider more general discussions on ethics,' and that 'we have not had a general discussion about the *TCPS*.' The lack of depth in such discussions has led one member of an REB to declare that she finds her work on the REB 'boring' (Chat E03-M, Fieldnotes: 141).

Desiring to 'Protect' the Research Participant

When I asked a member of an ethics committee what guided his/her conversation about research applications, he/she said 'protecting research participants.' In the same breath, without any prompting on my part, he/she admitted that he/she has not yet thought about 'protecting academic freedom.' For some (e.g., Interview E13-M), academic freedom is not on the table. Despite the prominence of academic freedom (and responsibilities) in the introductions of both the 1998 *TCPS* and the draft of *TCPS.2*, at least one chair (Moosegate U) does not believe that academic freedom is an appropriate topic for REB discussion:

> Academic freedom is related to the issues we choose to investigate, not the specific methods by which we obtain our knowledge. Our particular committee has the explicit goal of helping faculty and students conduct their desired research within ethical limits, so if we think a *TCPS* principle hasn't been considered, we attempt to suggest other ways to achieve their research goals, rather than just denying approval.

When I, the interviewer, did raise some issues of larger ethical import, the interview participant would typically say, 'I haven't thought of that... I have to keep my eye on that...' There are many who, like Linda Eyre at the University of New Brunswick, believe that the *TCPS* cannot address the ethical questions of concern to feminist researchers (and to research participants), because 'it smooths them over and avoids careful ethical reflection' (Eyre, 2007: 100). Ivor Pritchard of the United States Office for Human Research Protections notes that IRBs have to 'twist projects' either into the 'Common Rule' (which seventeen different federal agencies have agreed to use), or twist the 'Rule' into the project. When ethics committees go 'by the rules,' they 'see things in black and white, yes or no.' However, perceptions of risk and perceived conflict among ethical principles involve compromises that 'are truly arbitrary,' although they all implicate the research participant (Pritchard, 2002: 8).

Sometimes, there are particular sections in the *TCPS* that spark criticisms. A member of the REB at Beaverdam U finds parts of the *TCPS* 'scary,' especially insisting that women be included in (social) research and pregnant women in particular. She mentions that 'it is not easy to find all participants in the right place.'[12] The chair of an REB at a mid-sized university found it puzzling that a researcher had to justify her choice of gender in her study of women's employment (Interview C03-M). Feminist researchers, such as Marika Morris of the Canadian Research Institute for the Advancement of Women (CRIAW), found it puzzling to see the two subsections adjoined in Section Six of the *TCPS*, 'Research Involving Women' and 'Research Involving Those Who are Incompetent to Consent for Themselves.' From the perspective of social research (rather than medical research), the assumption of connecting women to those who cannot consent for themselves is deeply insulting (Notes on Presentations, Congress of the Social Sciences and the Humanities, Halifax, 3 June 2003, Fieldnotes: 151). For some, like Patrick O'Neill, a psychologist, the dictum in the *TCPS* that research should 'involve the smallest number of human subjects...' (Section C, 'Guiding Ethical Principles') does not resonate at all with social research (Presentations, UNB Psychology Department, 21 May 1004, Fieldnotes: 158).

Being Unfamiliar with National Ethics Policies

It is troubling that my fieldnotes on the four REBs confirm what I have learned from the data I have gathered from interviews, other notes, and what scholars have said in general about ethics-committee members' knowledge of federal policies: they are unfamiliar with them or have too little familiarity. For those who are familiar, they are critical of the policies. Finally, some see federal policies as quite flexible which, in the case of defining what 'research' is, might be problematic. We now turn to each of these points.

Interviews at Beaverdam U revealed a vast gap in the REB members' knowledge of the *TCPS*. Some of their comments:

[I] have read the whole TCPS, but [it] was some time ago; I refer to it once in a while. Can't remember the details of paragraphs that pertain to naturalistic observation [despite the fact that I am a qualitative researcher].

I see *TCPS* as the Bible. I can't remember the first section, but remember the two sections on informed consent which I see as relevant for my university.

An administrator at Beaverdam U told me that 'a lot of people don't read the first part of the *TCPS*, but it's about protecting unsuspecting individuals, not putting up barriers to research.' In at least one other interview, these sentiments were echoed when an REB member said, 'Frankly, I just glance through the *TCPS*. I don't have time' (Interview E15-S). There is also a lack of knowledge about recent attempts to change ethics policies at the national level. Two chairs at Nanook U, for example, do not know what happened to the *Giving Voice to the Spectrum Document* [SSHWC, 2004] that has been flowing through the REB system. An REB member at a small university informed me that he 'just scans the consultation documents [from PRE],' and that there is 'not enough time' to do any more (Interview E15-S). New REB members have no or little time to learn formally about the *TCPS*. For example, one REB member (Interview E15-S) said that his/her new colleagues receive no formal instructions to read TCPS or even to do the *TCPS* tutorial (that is available online). The chair at Moosegate U claims that he/she reads 'PRE stuff' and NCEHR materials and talks to other universities, but 'mostly it's internal conversation.'

It might be a feeling of discomfort with these policies that feed into REB members' lack of knowledge because there is a reluctance to learn about policies that one disagrees with at the start. Still, there are those who believe that although some criticism of *TCPS* is justified, the *TCPS* does allow for flexibility.[13] A presentation by Tim Seifert (2005), who was the chair of the Interdisciplinary Committee on Ethics in Human Research at Memorial University of Newfoundland, contains major, well-thought out criticisms of the *TCPS*, but he also believes that the *TCPS* 'may be envisioned within a spirit of collegiality and education' (13). The REB chair at Moosegate U claims that,although 'the code is biomedical, it is adaptable' for the social sciences. 'Fortunately,' says another chair, 'there is room in the *TCPS* for interpretation' (Interview C03-M). Ivor Pritchard also notes that the 'Common Rule' can be quite inflexible in some areas, but flexible in others (Pritchard, 2002: 8–10). Marie Hirtle and Karen Weisbaum, 'Virtual Scholars' for PRE, noted at a conference that there are many discrepancies in the *TCPS* (Presentations, CAREB Conference, 6 May 2005, Fieldnotes: 165). A member of an REB says that 'there are always grey and greyer areas' and that the 'PRE and guidelines are not very precise' (Interview E12-M). The chair at Nanook U relativizes the guidelines, averring that the *TCPS* should be read as 'may,' not 'must.' He/she also believes that her/his university's own guidelines are 'bad.' In any case, according to another interview participant, 'the *TCPS* should encourage each of the disciplines to have debates within themselves about ethics' to solve some of the contradictions and discrepancies (Interview R118-M).

Relying on Distancing Mechanisms

Moreover, ethics committees are increasingly relying on guideline documents rather than actual research to tell them about research. While some relativize the federal ethics guidelines, policymakers and members of ethics committees use 'distancing mechanisms.' One could describe distancing mechanisms as the use of documents instead of 'real' research to define the element that ethics committees must deal with (Hamilton, 2002: 142–3). Without relying on immediate knowledge of real research (such as actually having someone who knows about research), ethics-committee members use documents instead which 'distance' the member from knowing about the research and making relevant decisions about that research. To that end, and further to Ann Hamilton (2002: 118), Regulators and administrators particularly are 'seduced by the goodness of the (stated purpose for) rules to create the paper process' and to believe such a document can be meaningful.

These distancing mechanisms (i.e., reliance on documents) lead REB chairs to have different interpretations of 'research.' Moreover, as a researcher on the topic of research-ethics review found (Email, Fieldnotes: 411), 'there was little agreement regarding how to best distinguish projects which needed review from those that did not.' Even after he/she presented specific instances of cases, 'there was still no agreement among the experts which could be used for consistent decision making regarding whether to submit a project for review.' Although inconsistent decision-making is the hallmark of the REB process, there is one consistency – as noted in a focus group of REB members at Bear Mountain U – and that is, namely, that REBs will side with a safe interpretation. We shall return to this theme in a later chapter as it deeply affects the kinds of research that ethics committees inadvertently block or promote.

Working Like Manuscript Editors

The lack of an in-depth discussion on ethics (to concentrate on, for example, only immediate needs of an application) is something that scholars have observed in general. Dr Timothy Christie (Personal communication, 9 June 2005), a philosopher and ethicist, found in his research on hospital REBs that when an ethics committee is interdisciplinary, there is a tendency for those who are not acquainted with the discipline of the applicant to be eager to 'contribute' to the consideration of an application by recommending grammatical or textual changes. In fact, in Dr Christie's experience, some 90 per cent of all initial applications are turned back first time around because of these reasons alone. Jeffrey Brainard (2000: A30) in *The Chronicle of Higher Education* noted that ethics committee members 'operated more like manuscript editors than researchers.' Jack Katz (2007: 800) underscores this penchant by ethics-review committee members to correct applications and suggests that they have a discomfort 'doing ethics,' and that 'their need to correct formal imperfections in applications denotes their comfort in doing professional stuff, and perhaps discomfort doing ethics stuff.' One REB chair states:

> It is possible that an applicant doesn't adequately communicate their procedure in their application due to poor writing, so that reviewers might need to request clarification, but this is very different than denying ethical approval.

A less charitable viewpoint about the eagerness of members of ethics committees to each advance their own opinions about the application has some seeing REB members as having 'a pissing contest' over who can offer the most suggestions about grammar, spelling, and syntax (Fieldnotes: 141).

Being Attuned to the Location of the Ethics Committee

The geography, or more accurately the location, of an REB can also shape the discussion of proposals. For example, the chair of an REB told me that because his/her university is located in a building near a First Nations community, it tends to think more deeply about ethics and researching Native populations (Interview C25-M). A similar perspective was shared by another chair (Interview C30-M). In the same vein, a PhD student's study on women in a factory was greatly facilitated because her medical REB already had an institutional connection with the Workplace Safety and Insurance Board. She learned that women had more brain cancer than in other parts of the same factory; she then went through the medical REB where her research was quickly approved (Interview R024-M).

A number of scholars have pointed out the relevance of the geographical locations of ethics committees in adjudicating proposals. For example, Brigham Young University in Salt Lake City blocked research on attitudes of homosexual Mormons towards their church, but it was approved by Idaho State University (Katz, 2007: 801). Similarly, one wonders whether a university REB situated in the same city as major federal agencies or corporate headquarters might not approach applications of research sponsored by them in a more expeditious manner, in contrast to an REB's lacking either such expertise or funding links. Parker and his co-authors (2005) discuss the relationship between Research Ethics Committees (RECs) and pharmaceutical companies: a small pharmaceutical company is more likely at the cutting edge of innovation, in phase one trials, with little money, and an adverse decision by the REC has major consequences for the pharmaceutical company on the stock exchange. A big pharmaceutical company, in contrast, is usually involved in the more expensive phase two and three trials, has a lot of money, and is more equipped to answer questions from RECs, following 'a liturgical order' whereby questions are followed by answers in a preordained sequence, like two heavenly choirs. As a result, the fiscal pressures made relations between RECs and the small pharmaceutical companies less consistent, less predictable, and more pressured (Parker, James, and Barrett, 2005: 23).

Being Jealous and Engaging in Vendettas

Both through interviews and documented experiences, it is clear that decisions in some ethics committees are guided by jealousies and sometimes even vendettas. One of my fieldnotes contains a reference to a brilliant young scholar whose ethics committee has been a constant source of opposition to her research. A senior scholar confirms the junior scholar's difficulties with the REB whose members are jealous of her accomplishments (Fieldnotes: 11 November 2008). These stories are hard to come by except when they are volunteered by friends or sympathetic colleagues of the offended researcher. Few like to sing the tune of sour grapes when an ethics committee turns away an application or when they put near-impossible demands in place. However, there are hints, usually not detailed ones that, according to the head of a major non-profit research centre in Ontario, show that an 'ethics review is seen as an affront or a challenge to the researcher's ability, [and a] punitive, demeaning exercise' (Fieldnotes: 1297).

David Wright (2004: 203) mentions that his troubles originated in an academic vendetta. His ethics committee charged him with 'bad research practices' for writing about a student without having obtained prior consent and for 'unethical behavior' 'for failing to report that student for the crime that he had [been] alleged to have committed.' He is quite puzzled about these allegations because he wrote a personal essay, a piece of a creative non-fiction narrative about a complex of societal and personal observations dealing with race, class, and pedagogy. The immediate effect was a prohibition directed against his publishing his essay in a literary journal. In Wright's words,

> In the essay, my experience with the student prompts the reflection and drives the narrative. It is true that I did not seek out the student's prior written consent. At the time of the class in question, I had no idea I would write about it nor, had I known, did I suspect that I would need his consent to do so. However, I had in fact gone to great lengths to protect him and his identity – which is the motive for requiring consent. (Wright, 2004: 204)

This participant-observation exercise of four REBs has left us with a number of facets. We now need to understand the homogenization of research methods and the pauperization of the social sciences through research-ethics review. We found the tendency of REB members' was to follow the dictates of their own disciplines and subjective, individual thoughts when contemplating the ethical dimensions of research applications. Reflections about research ethics flowed out of their own disciplines and individual interests rather than out of the exigencies that might have emerged from the applications. It also became clear that each REB member chose self-assigned roles during the decision-making process (such as one watched for grammar, another for accuracy, and still another for adequacy of consent). With uneven attendance at REB meetings, it also meant that the flow of discussions would vary on who was present or absent, and therefore an REB would never be able to consider all angles in a given ethics issue.

The crux of REB meetings should rely on familiarity with ethics policies. The 'tyranny of the immediate' took away any luxury of time that the REB might have had to delve judiciously and thoughtfully into those policies. REB members accepted, uncritically, the biomedical model, inherent in those policies. Members of the REB seemed very unfamiliar with the policies or just would have passing or cursory acquaintance of them. Similarly, there was a lack of knowledge about particular research approaches. The members relied on 'distancing mechanisms' to inform themselves about these approaches, that is, secondary knowledge rather than personal knowledge. Taken together, all of these facets – with REB members looking at applications from their own disciplinary and personal interests; the inability to sustain an on-going vision of the larger ethics picture (due also to varying attendance at meetings); and relying on distancing mechanisms – of the decision-making process in REBs sowed the seeds of increasing homogeneity and impoverishment of the social-scientific methods. The self-proclaimed sole focus by REB members to 'protect' research participants undermined, too, a holistic perspective of research. Broken down into its constituent parts, research became a humpty-dumpty, a broken research project that it is impossible to reassemble. The richness and variety of particular research methods (and even of the social science itself) is becoming a thing of the past.

While the previous chapter explored the preliminary aspects of submitting a research proposal to the ethics committee, and this chapter examined the decision-making processes, the following chapter presents findings related to the final stage of the ethics review process, namely, returning the proposal to the researcher, which expresses widely divergent interpretations of ethics guidelines. The basis of communication with researchers can involve idiosyncratic and inconsistent decisions, often inexplicable ones. Chapters 5 to 9 conclude the inside view of ethics committees.

9 An Idiosyncratic and Inconsistent World: Communications between REBs and Researchers

The previous chapters have suggested that there are a large variety of factors that lead to ethics committees' making idiosyncratic and inconsistent decisions, such as uneven attendance at meetings, the interjection by committee members of disciplinary paradigms and individual perspectives (i.e., private reflections about ethics), discretionary judgments, the attitude of what is 'reasonable,' varying desires about what it means to protect research participants, unfamiliarity with ethics policies, the use of distancing mechanisms, the tendency for committee members to work as manuscript editors, and the influence of jealousies and, sometimes, vendettas. All of these elements contribute to a destabilizing process in making decisions about applications. What adds to the instability is the absence of making public the decisions of ethics-review-committees, quite unlike the courts where trials and decisions are given regular public airing. The public's lack of knowledge of what transpires inside ethics-review committees contributes to having only a piecemeal knowledge of decisions about the ethical dimensions of research. Such a lack of knowledge also puts ethics-review committees in a position of making idiosyncratic and inconsistent decisions.

This chapter takes a more focused perspective and examines the problem of the interpretation of ethics policies as an important factor in making the research-ethics world an idiosyncratic and inconsistent one. As an illustration of this world, the chapter looks at how these idiosyncratic and inconsistent features come alive in letters from ethics committees to researchers. It first gives some illustrations of those inconsistencies and then examines more closely five cases of communication between ethics-review committees and researchers. In particular, the chapter looks at the content and language of those communications. Finally, the chapter lodges the communications from REBs in the larger context of the ethics regimes in universities.

The layers of misinterpretation, gaps of knowledge, and private zones of ethics reflection are made even more opaque by disagreements as to what should or should not be reviewed. Should research on translation software be subject to ethics review (9 June 2005, Fieldnotes: 1161)? Should a class project that has students' reviewing social workers and then discussing their findings later in class be subject to review (13 January 2005, Fieldnotes: 722)? Should an Aboriginal research project be approved only if it goes through the band council, rather than through a traditional group of elders (University M6, Fieldnotes: 230)?

There are other inconsistent perspectives of ruling about ethics reviews. For example, a puzzling outcome of a decision involves the case of two researchers who submitted identical proposals to the same REB, where the research included interviews and observations in a school setting: one was exempted, while the other was not (Koro-Ljungberg et al., 2007: 1086). In another example, the chair of an REB learned of her REB's objections to member checking. 'The researcher,' it decided, 'must not be a ghost writer' (Interview C05-B).[1] In another instance, bizarre requirements can pervade research completed many years ago. A supervisor (Interview R002-M) had a student who had graduated three to four years earlier and was only later asked to fill out ethics-review forms, which he/she had to do within four days. He/she was also asked for data-release forms and was required to go back to research participants to secure the accuracy of the student's transcripts.

In the end, there are no guarantees that a project will be approved, rejected, or modified, even retroactively. As Halse and Honey (2005) so eloquently state:

> ... research ethics is deeply embedded and implicated in the social context. Factors like project timelines, the requirements of funding bodies, the local practices of different ethics committees, personal relationships in the research setting and with ethics officers and committees, and ethics committees' anxiety about litigation all play a potent, if sometimes mute, role in decisions about ethics. Researchers are embodied in the ethical process: meeting and negotiating with ethics officers and others in the research setting; refining the research design to address ethical issues; writing and rewriting ethics applications; and wrestling with decisions that kindle an array of intersecting emotions, including discomfort, anxiety, relief, anticipation, optimism, and hope. The practice of decontextualizing and

disembodying ethics occludes the investments researchers bring to 'getting through' the ethics process and the role these processes can play in privileging particular voices and eroding the relationship between participants and researchers. (2156)

The data gathered through participant-observation illustrate the findings and commentaries offered by members of other ethics committees (in Canada and the United States), scholars, and by my interview participants outside of the four REBs that I observed. Depending on one's own perspective, the decision-making process is either idiosyncratic or inconsistent (or both).

Interpretation as the Basis of Idiosyncrasies and Inconsistencies

While many in the ethics world widely hold the belief that what is needed is a 'common standard,' there is little public acknowledgment that such a standard is well nigh impossible to achieve given the wide latitude of interpretations within each ethics committee and among ethics committees. Susan Sykes, who heads the Ethics Office at the University of Waterloo and who served on the Interagency Advisory Panel on Research Ethics and its Procedural Group, has found 'large variations among REBs' (Presentation, Canadian Bioethics Conference, 31 October 2004, Fieldnotes: 162). Jim Thomas at Arizona State University, who has written extensively on the subject, has found that 'IRB members have diverse interpretations of their mission, are not equally informed about issues, and make decisions guided by procedures ranging from rigid formal rationality to more flexible substantive rationality' (SSSI LISTSERV, 30 April 2001, Fieldnotes: 763). He has also been receiving reports of 'major cluelessness, sloppy reviews, obtuseness, idiosyncratic ideological preferences replacing policy prescriptions, and expansion of purview and mandate' (SSSI LISTSERV, 20 March 2002, Fieldnotes: 765). A study on behalf of the Canadian Sociology and Anthropology Association (now named Canadian Sociological Association) includes the assessment that 'it is not necessarily the policy that is entirely problematic, it is its *interpretation* that is dangerous' (Muzzin, 2002: 5). The National Communications Association speaks of 'widely varying advice' by ethics committees and of 'alarming inconsistencies' (NCA, 2005: 206–8). Scholars have also noted 'great variations' in REB responses in content and justification of their decisions, but also in time (De Vries and Forsberg, 2002: 201). In the latter instance, there are variations in how the clock should tick once the application is submitted (Dixon-Woods et al., 2007: 8). These variations of the clock make it virtually impossible to compare and audit the length of time it takes for an ethics committee to process an application. Does one include week-ends? Does one include the time between the meetings of ethics committees (who sometimes meet with an interval of one month)?

My interviews during my own research on ethics reveal the problem of inconsistent decision-making in ethics committees. A member of an ethics committee in a mid-sized university notes that 'interpretations vary widely across the university, and across Canada, including the question of what is research' (Interview E12-M). At another REB, one member claims that the 'process now is too haphazard to be consistent in decisions' (Interview E15-S). One REB member (at another university) suggests that because all REB members are new, there is no institutional memory that might make decisions not idiosyncratic (Interview E25-S). The way out of this inconsistent and idiosyncratic world is through dialogue, not principles (Interview E13-M). Such evident idiosyncratic, arbitrary, and variable decisions, according to a researcher, are the basis of cynicism plaguing the ethics-review world (Interview R118-M). Interestingly, some researchers are hoping to dispel idiosyncratic decisions by seizing on terminologies that resonate inside the *TCPS* (e.g., 'protocol,' 'subject') so that ethics committees do not need to consider terminologies unique to each discipline. Researcher R118-M concludes that 'disciplines seize on the *TCPS* like a country such as India with 500 languages that seizes on English, but the original native language is no longer understood.'

Catherine Scott (2004) avers:

> Blatent inconsistency did not seem to trouble members of ethics committees. Projects that had been cleared during earlier stages were deemed 'dangerous' in subsequent phases. Questionnaires previously passed as satisfactory were rediscovered to be 'risky' and even venerable standardised instruments widely in use, for example the General Health Questionnaire, were found to contain items that could 'harm' research participants. (3)

Ann Hamilton (2002: 15), in her empirical study of ethics committees, found that these rules vary across IRBs, and are inconsistent. Submitting phoney proposals was a more visceral way of discovering broad inconsistencies across ethics committees. In the 1980s and 1990s, for example, Goldman and Katz (1982), Harding and Ummel (1989), and Harries et al. (1994) revealed inconsistencies. In 1990s, multi-site trials revealed inconsistencies in ethics-committee decision-making (De Vries, 2004: 7). Psychologists have documented 'censorship' of research by submitting the same application to different ethics committees with differing results (Katz, 2007; and Ceci, Peters, and Plotkin, 1985). The case of oral history research as an example of research that is technically exempt from review illustrates idiosyncratic, unpredictable, and unstable decisions by ethics committees. In some universities, this kind of research still needs to go through a review process to declare it is exempt from review. For example, oral history research that is to be conducted by an anthropologist will require review, but research done by an oral historian will not.

Idiosyncratic interpretations of ethics policies come alive in communications from ethics committees to researchers. The following section discusses a number of such letters.

Communications to Researchers/Language of (Dis)Approval[2]

Letters from ethics committees play a crucial role in presenting to the researchers the weaknesses of their proposals from the perspective of ethics. It is unlikely that REBs outright reject research proposals from the social sciences. Although the rejection rate in the social sciences falls between 1 and 2 per cent (ICL, 2006: 16) – which is quite low – many proposals go through substantial changes in numerous iterations between ethics committees and researchers before being accepted. One can ask whether those changes constitute a 'rejection' when the proposal first gets tabled. Are we also talking about 'rejection' when researchers decide to withdraw their proposals in the face of (potential or real) opposition from the ethics committee?

The first indication a researcher receives that his/her proposal will not get passed by the ethics committee is normally not through a letter but in a conversation. Catherine Scott, for example, was informed by her IRB that her proposed project had 'problems' (Scott, 2004: 93). In another case, a researcher finds out that when an IRB 'tables' a proposal, it usually means that it has been rejected (NCA, 2005: 227).

The five cases below involve graduate and undergraduate students and are emblematic of the process of going through a research-ethics review. One case left the researcher (a master's student) discouraged and, in another case, a PhD student reluctantly revised his research by having to discount all of his observations while writing his thesis (Case R093-B). R115-M went to full completion of her PhD research. R169-M is also a PhD student whose iterations with his ethics committee did not prevent him from completing his research, the same as R041-M, an undergraduate student. I discuss the outlines of each case in greater detail and highlight aspects that stand out in particular (the full text of communications from the five Canadian REBs to researchers appears in appendix C).

Case R093-B[3]

On 13 February 2003, a PhD student at a large university submitted a proposal to his REB. His planned ethnographic research involved the study of blue-collar canal workers. For several years he had worked on the canal as a summer student and became interested in conducting research in his former place of work, especially now that the place had moved from being a government employer to a private employer. In short, he wanted to study the attitudes of workers and management–worker relations that occurred as a result of privatization. As someone who had always taken an interest in participant-observation, he kept notes taken during his prior summer employment for seven years. He wanted to use those notes. He also wanted to do covert research as the best guarantee of anonymity in the workplace. It would be a participant-observational (ethnographic) study.

Several things stand out in appendix C from the exchanges between the REB and the student. First, the REB exhibited no inkling of what ethnographic research entailed. It posed unanswerable questions by asking the researcher if he knew the 'natural behaviour' of the workers. The REB put the researcher into an impossible situation. If he were going to ask research participants questions, he would need to get their consent, and therefore covert research would not be possible. On one hand, the REB (predictably) disapproved of covert research; on the other hand, it pressured him to ask questions in which case covert research would not be possible anyway.

Second, it misconstrued his research as 'deception' rather than 'covert research.' Covert research is not to be confused with deception in research. Deception involves lying at least in the initial stages of research; covert research implies the need for protection from danger, as well as ensuring complete confidentiality and absolute guarantee of the anonymity of research participants. There is a long history of highly-regarded covert research that respects the research settings and their participants.[4]

In March 2003, the student submitted a revised proposal, focusing on the objections raised by his REB. By 22 February 2004, he submitted an entirely new ethics proposal that sought consent from the workers. He would also use open-ended interviews as opposed to ethnographic research. As of 2009, he finished all of his required comprehensive exams and course work and was officially ABD (All-But-Dissertation). His thesis was actually nearing completion, based on his 2004 data collection, of course. In a communication from the student to me in July 2009, he conveyed the following:

> I think what is important to stress in your book is the fact that my data collection (my notes + years of knowledge + experiences out on the frontlines from 1997 to 2003) were not allowed to be included in my thesis because I did not obtain consent from those I interacted with. It was only in 2004 that approval was granted based on my agreement to gain consent from my subjects therefore discounting any previous data. My methodology included (overt) participant observation and interviews. I erred on the side of caution and avoided including any 'thoughts and recollections' from my days on the frontlines from 1997 to 2003 as a result of the REB. It is a shame that I cannot include the rich recollections from my first day on the job despite being so fresh in my mind because from the REB's perspective my 'fresh' recollection is likely the result of my fieldnotes. I just don't want to get into any conflict with the REB at this point and simply want to finish my PhD.

He had added a significant postscript to his communication:

> I can honestly say that the requirement of obtaining consent from my subjects in 2004 did not have a negative effect on my data collection because I was already in my eighth year of employment with the company. My immersion and acceptance into the culture occurred years earlier (which would have been nice to write about as well). [S]o my asking for consent was not deemed suspicious or odd by anyone. In fact, most were enthused that I was writing about their concerns. I actually had 2 employees call me asking to be interviewed.

Case R115-M[5]

In April 2003, a PhD student submitted her proposal to her REB. Her plans involved a study of academic writing, namely, the challenges and opportunities that academics faced when writing scholarly articles. Her chief method would involve interviews.

On 12 May 2003, the REB informed her that her project was eligible for expedited review 'since any risk to participants that might exist appears not to exceed the "minimal risk" outlined in *TCP[S]*.' The chair of the REB also informed her that 'in my opinion, your project does not appear to be in compliance with *TCP[S]* and [the University's] Policy.' The REB chair pasted all of the requirements for informed consent forms into the email he sent her and highlighted six of the twenty elements that had to be addressed. The chair had already agreed that the student could use an 'Information Sheet,' but it would have to convey the same information as the usual signed consent form. Remembering that the research involved only professors, the REB's advice that 'an Informed Consent Form must be written in language that the potential subject can understand' seemed out of place. In the context of the student's research participants, this was an exaggerated requirement.

The other REB requirement that was to be included – that 'the period of time required for subject participation' be clearly identified – was not one that was specified in either the *TCPS* or the University's Policy. The requirement fell more into the arena of anticipated courtesies on the part of the researcher rather than as an ethical breach. It is difficult during an in-depth interview to specify the exact time that will be needed. Some interviews can be as short as forty-five minutes, while others can last up to three or four hours, if not more.

A final illustrative requirement involved the REB's reminder that when 'teenaged subjects are considered by the applicant to be competent to consent without parental involvement, the applicant must provide justification for this conclusion.' It is puzzling why the REB insisted that the researcher pay attention to this requirement. It was clear from the research proposal that contact would only be with members of the professoriate.

Case R169-M[6]

In the summer of 2002, a PhD student applied for ethics approval to conduct ethnographic research in two workplaces. An analysis of the questions and comments from the ethics committee revealed that they were actually posed by the staff of the ethics office and not by the chair.

How the REB structured its reply to the researcher is, by itself, an object of interest. Its first concern was a procedural one, unrelated to ethics. Why did the student's application not go first through the dissertation committee? The student replied to the REB members, 'Yes, you are correct,' and explained that, as the research by the ergonomics group was going to start soon, 'there was little time to gather committee members and defend the proposal.'

The REB also seemed particularly concerned about the student's unexplained recruitment strategies, wanting to know whether they would be through 'a recruitment poster, presentation, word of mouth, flyer etc.' and asked for a copy of any materials used in the recruitment of research participants. The student replied, 'Interviewees will be recruited by word-of-mouth. As you suggested, I will [personally] carry out all recruitment.'

The REB's ignorance of ethnographic research revealed itself poignantly when it expressed a lack of understanding about whether the researcher would be observing 'individuals,' the 'entire group,' or 'equipment, etc.' Ethnographers attempt to capture the whole social setting, whatever comprises it. Asking the researcher to 'provide a copy of the script [he would] use to example this part of the study' is puzzling. What is the 'script' it was referring to? (As an ethnographic researcher myself, I have no idea what the REB meant by its reference to the 'script.') The query about whether 'any of the field data [would] be available to the companies and/or union' also indicated a fundamental misunderstanding about scholarship and the ingrained ethics of fieldwork.

Finally, the term 'interview protocol' would be a baffling one for social researchers, although many social researchers now resort to accommodating the use of this term so as not to distract or needlessly anger the ethics committee.

In addition to the above, the PhD student thought that the REB's question about what he (the researcher) would do if he were to witness a safety violation was an interesting one. The REB posed the question as follows, 'What happens – or what are you expected to do – in the event that you observe someone's actions that might be in violation of safety standards? How would this be handled?' The PhD student thought that it was 'perhaps reasonable for the REB to ask such a question, but it did presume that a researcher *would* do something.' He also noted that 'the wording was of interest as a "safety violation" was not the same as asking what a researcher would do if he/she witnessed a situation in which a worker was in imminent danger of injury.'

Case R041-M[7]

In this study, an undergraduate student planned to undertake a study of young athletes. The student was an athletic coach herself and wanted to conduct interviews, not participant-observation. On 25 September 2003, she forwarded her application to her REB. It went through several changes before the project was approved on 10 October – a fifteen-day turnaround time, although the student had been working on the ethics-review application for a month before submission.

The first communication (26 September 2003), on behalf of the REB, instructed the student to use an 'informed consent form,' even though the student had made it clear in her application that she would use an 'information sheet.' That letter also asked her to 'indicate when data will be destroyed/erased.'[8] There are no indications in the *TCPS* or in that University's Policy that data ought to be destroyed; the specification is that data be kept in a safe place.

The second communication (9 October 2003) informed the student that the chair of the REB 'advised me that a signed informed consent is not necessary for your type of project.' The writer of the letter apologized to the student 'for the confusion that I inadvertently created.' The REB seemed particularly interested in the 'security provision, possible use in publication' of the data and pointed out that the student had omitted to indicate when these audiotapes would be erased or destroyed.

The third communication (10 October 2003) told the student that it was the REB's 'belief' that the project 'complies with the standards outlined in the Tri-Council Policy Statements and the [University's] Policy.' It also informed the student that 'formal approval will be sent from the Office of the Vice-President (Research).' To assuage the concerns of the student about the length of time the REB took to approve her proposal, the REB listed the dates of submissions and final approval. Finally, the letter reminded the student to 're-affirm the participants' willingness to take part in [her] study and to ensure that all questions have been answered, prior to commencing the actual interview . . . [and to remind] the participant that she/he can refuse to answer a question or terminate the interview at any time.'

Case M8[9]

In the fall of 2005, a master's student submitted a proposal to her REB, wishing to do a phenomenological inquiry about high school students' understanding of respect. The class (in which the research was to take place) was an environmental education class that attempted to combine Western scientific and Aboriginal conceptions of science and the environment. The process of approval took six weeks.

The ethics committee took exception to some of the methodology of the study, and asked her to rewrite her application and then resubmit it for a second review. The supervisor accompanied the student to meet with the co-chair of the IRB, and then she and the supervisor rewrote the application based on the suggested revisions. She resubmitted the application, only to have it returned with a request for further changes. After a third resubmission, it was deemed 'ethically safe.'

The student's supervisor describes the feedback of the ethics committee as 'ferocious' and reminds us that the student 'is well trained' to conduct the research. In the final analysis, the supervisor wrote,

> [t]o say that this experience has left her disillusioned about the university as a place for knowledge production is putting it mildly. I also doubt very much, that following this experience, that either she or her teaching partner would be an advocate for doing graduate study at this institution. This concerns me, and I find myself apologizing more and more to students for an institutional practice that seems more than willing to overstep its bounds.

Although comments on the revised submission cover many pages and a wide range of topics, the REB had already approved the application.

Content

After having highlighted a number of peculiarities associated with each communication from the REBs, I wanted to learn whether there was an overall pattern that typifies the contents of all of these communications. A content analysis of these letters reveals nine primary (substantive) issues and a large number of subsidiary ones. I define primary as those issues that tend to be privileged in ethics guidelines, such as anonymity, confidentiality, and consent. Table 9.1 displays the relative prevalence of the primary issues. We can identify three categories of issues found in the communications from REBs. The category with the highest number of issues relates to research participants (occurring sixteen times in the correspondence, followed by methods (fourteen times), and consent (fourteen times). The second highest category with issues includes references in the letters to data (mentioned eight times) and anonymity (six times). The least-mentioned category with issues falls into a third group, namely, vulnerability (mentioned twice), confidentiality (twice), deception (once), and Aboriginal knowledge (once).

Table 9.1   Communications from REBs to Researchers – Relevant Primary and Secondary Issues

Primary Issues	Subsidiary Issues	R093-B	R115-M	R169-M	R041-M	M	Subtotals	Totals
Research Participant	in general		✔	✔			2	
	stated length of participation		✔	✔		✔	3	
	use of third person to avoid pressure or to report		✔	✔	✔	✔	4	16
	recruitment			✔		✔	2	
	feedback letter			✔		✔	2	
	physical safety			✔			1	
	risks					✔	1	
	power relations					✔	1	
Methods	in general	✔					1	
	ethnography	✔		✔			2	
	covert	✔					1	
	observational	✔		✔			2	
	audio-video taping			✔	✔		2	
	what is 'natural behaviour'?	✔					1	14
	asking Qs?	✔					1	
	interview schedule			✔			1	
	purpose?	✔					1	
	role of researcher(s)					✔	1	
	various aspects					✔	1	
Consent	in general	✔	✔	✔	✔	✔	5	
	consent form		✔	✔	✔	✔	4	
	statement re: decline answer Qs		✔		✔		2	14
	competence		✔				1	
	from parties			✔			1	
	photos					✔	1	
Data	in general	✔			✔		2	
	earlier	✔					1	
	data storage/ destruction				✔	✔	2	8
	data availability and dissemination			✔	✔	✔	3	

(Continued)

Table 9.1   *Continued*

Primary Issues	Subsidiary Issues	R093-B	R115-M	R169-M	R041-M	M	Subtotals	Totals
Anonymity	in general	✔		✔	✔		3	
	linking data w/ ind'ls	✔		✔			2	6
	photos					✔	1	
Vulnerability	in general	✔		✔			2	2
Confidentiality	in general			✔	✔		2	2
Deception	in general	✔					1	1
Aboriginal knowledge	in general					✔	1	1
Procedure	application process			✔	✔		2	2

Source: Based on data compiled by author and itemized in appendix C.

While the actual rank order of issues as expressed through these letters is contingent on the kinds of research proposals over which REBs have to deliberate (rather than strictly following the rank order that prevails in the ethics guidelines), it is still striking to see the relative merit REBs attach to particular issues. In the case of research participants (the most frequently occurring issue), for example, there are a large number of subsidiary issues, including the requirement for research to state the expected length of participation of research participants, to use a third person to either collect data or to witness the research, queries about recruitment practices, to provide a feedback letter, to ensure the physical safety of participants, to take into account the putative risks associated with the research, and to be mindful of potential power differentials between the researcher and the participant. This cursory overview of the first primary issue touched upon by REBs already reveals a dedication to the welfare of the research participant. Indeed, the very purpose of having ethics guidelines is to protect research participants. Nevertheless, it should be kept in mind that this desire to protect participants is sometimes articulated in a manner that does not seem relevant to the methodology being proposed.

What is a full surprise, however, is the attention that REBs give to methodology or methods of the research. There are fourteen subsidiary issues associated with this primary issue. There are questions about ethnographic techniques, covert research, observational research, audio-videotaping, the nature of 'natural behaviour,' asking questions, the interview schedule, purpose of the research, role of other researchers in the project, and an undefined aspect of methodology. It is ironic that REBs generally claim that they would only look at the methods of social research if the risk of the research were more than minimal. The actual risks of at least four of the proposed researches are minimal. Yet questions about methodology are the second most frequent ones raised by REBs.

Consent, or informed consent, is an area of concern to all five REBs (fourteen times). The REBs raise questions about the need to use a consent form, what such a form should contain (such as a statement that the participant has the right to refuse to answer a question), the competence of the participant to give consent, the need for consent from all those involved in the research, and the required consent for any use of personal photos.

A fourth area of concern for REBs relates to data (eight times). One can suppose that any suggestions emanating from REBs about data might fit more appropriately into issues related to methods. The subsidiary issues include the nature of data collected before the research has formally started, making data available to research participants, dissemination of data, data storage, and data destruction.

Considerably lower on the scale of primary ethical concerns is anonymity (mentioned six times) when REBs worry about linking data with individuals and whether anonymity can still be maintained when using photos. Closely related to anonymity is confidentiality – the two are often confused by both REBs and researchers. REBs have raised the issue of confidentiality only twice.

Deception in research (often confused with covert research) was raised only once by an REB. Similarly, only one REB mentioned the possibility of using Aboriginal knowledge. Of note are the references to the application process. Two REBs saw the importance of the application process as part of their mandate to be raised with the researcher.

The overall content analysis reveals yet another pattern (see again table 9.1). The five REBs raise between seven and nineteen issues with researchers. As was noted earlier, some of these issues are gratuitous and quite off the map in terms of their ethical relevance, but they *are* issues that REBs deem relevant to the research-ethics review process. The researchers who have been subject to the lowest number of queries by the REB (R118-M and R051-M) are, in fact, in the same university. They are also the student researchers who have gone forward and completed their research. The researcher (R093-B) who was subject to fourteen queries by the REB eventually gave up on his studies. Similarly, the researcher (M8) who received fifteen questions about the research left the university very discouraged. The REBs' ability to ask an endless number of open-ended questions with each subsequent submission of the same application is not at all unique. An anthropologist, Norman Okihiro (2000), found that each exchange of letters with his REBs raised a new issue, additional questions about in-depth interviews, or even issues beyond the pale of the original submission, such as asking him to use a pre-established consent form and asking questions about his census-like data. Moreover, for the ethics committee, there is one final enigma, 'Will he use visitors to his home to conduct research?'

The researchers find that the queries from their REBs can be stultifying rather than expressing a helpful, guiding hand. Along those lines, one wonders if researchers were to treat their research participants the same way that ethics committees treat researchers, would the members of those committees be horrified. Ethics committees will become a dynamic force of example to researchers when the committees begin treating them with the same respect as they expect the researcher to treat their own research participants. This discussion brings us to the topic of the language embedded in the communications from the REBs.

Language

If we turn again to the samples of communication found in appendix C, we will find the use of language to be particularly striking.[10] The language carries authority and a semblance of appealing to higher ethical principles. Nonetheless, the writers of these communications make extensive use of the passive voice and rely on 'words of insistence' (such as 'please clarify').

The Authoritative Voice

It is unusual for communications from the REB to the researcher to contain either the researcher's name or the specific name of the person who prepared the response to the researcher's application. In the following examples, the language of the communicator is highlighted to illustrate the authoritative tone used and that is hidden behind this anonymity. For example, an REB member might write that it is 'the *Ethics Committee*' which reviewed 'this protocol' or that 'the *Board* has reviewed the protocol for your proposed study and is requesting that you substantially rewrite and resubmit the application.' In other cases we find sentences that read, 'As *Chair of the Research Ethics Board* (REB), I have reviewed your application' and 'the reviewers, staff and Chair have determined that this application . . . ' The appeal to authority is inevitable even when it is clear that it is a single individual writing to the researcher, as in, 'as a member of the [University's] Research Ethics Board, I have reviewed your application.' One letter already had an REB number inscribed into it. The number gave it an official and authoritative voice even before the substance of the letter had been gotten to. Acronyms abound in the letters without explaining what they mean, such as *ORE* that is used without any explanation that this refers to the Office of Research Ethics.

The letter usually refers to the nameless researcher as '*the PI*' (or principal investigator), and sometimes the writer of the letter refers to the researcher as a third person, even though the letter is directed to him/her. The REB language has an influence on the language of the social researcher. The term *investigator* derives from medical usage (I also think of someone who investigates plane accidents) but, at its heart, is a term that social researchers do not use; now, however, researchers have adopted this term as one of their own and widely use it in their applications to their REBs.

Letters to researchers are deliberately used to set the stage that signals a sense of formality and authority, even intimidation. Dixon-Woods et al. (2007) found that the 141 letters they examined 'display' a sense of due process, care, thoroughness and thoughtfulness of the ethics committee. The writers of these letters use a stylized language that 'also serves[s] to deflect challenges about the pains taken by the committee, and to give a single, consistent, apparently rational account of the considerations of the committee.' They noted that many letters were poorly punctuated[11] and even rude, 'but they couch their discourse in a manner that is a display of their authority . . . ' (Dixon-Woods et al., 2007: 7–8). The 'scripting of these letters reinforces a ritualised supplicant – authority relationship,' where

> the proper role of applicants is one of docility; in responding to letters, they must make displays of obedience and deference. In particular, unless they are to resort to the appeals mechanism, applicants are obliged to accept judgements which are inherently contestable and indeterminate as incontestable and final. (Dixon-Woods et al., 2007: 9)

To further reinforce that a committee's judgments are incontestable, the same letter may contain a reminder from an REB that should the application require changes, the researcher must submit 'evidence that these changes have been made ... and [resubmit them] to the Research Ethics Committee before ethical approval for your study can be given.'

Semblance of Using Higher Principles

The REB communication leaves the unmistakable impression that the REB operates under the shadow of higher, more ethical principles. There are references and terms that invoke ethics guidelines, such as 'compliance with the Tri-Council Policy (TCP) and with the [University's] Policy.' In one instance, the REB reminds the researcher that while the email from the REB represents notification of REB approval, 'formal approval' still needs to be issued by a higher authority, namely, the Office of the Vice-President (Research).

Sometimes, too, the REB implicitly chastises the researcher. For example, a letter might state, 'Not obtaining consent from people being studied, especially if they are being questioned or if there is any intervention, goes against the spirit of the Tri-Council Policy Statement and the Committee's interpretation of it.' Dixon-Woods et al. have noted this tendency of ethics committees to make only implicit references to ethical authority:

> [t]he source of ethical authority for the [ethics committee] in coming to their conclusions is rarely explicit in the letters. The GafREC [Governance arrangements for RECs] – which provides the framework within which RECs are expected to work – is not referred to in any of the letters in our sample. Specific ethical principles or even guidelines are rarely invoked explicitly, and when they are, it is to authenticate or legitimise the decisions of the committee. (Dixon-Woods et al., 2007: 6)

Frequently, the REB couches the letters in language that makes it appear that the opinion of the REB (or the chair) is merely that – an opinion. As in, for example, '*I consider* your project to be eligible,' or 'In *my opinion,*' 'I *believe,*' or 'we *believe.*' In actual fact, this particular usage of language leaves the whole ethics-review process quite uncertain and becomes a source of anguish for researchers. What happens if a new chair comes aboard? Or a new REB member?

Along the same lines, as Dixon-Woods et al. (2007: 6) have already noted in their in-depth study of letters from ethics committees in

Britain, the source of ethical authority for the REC in coming to their conclusions 'is rarely explicit in the letters.' The letters do not refer to the framework within which ethics committees allegedly work and rarely specifically invoke specific ethical principles or even guidelines explicitly. As they further observed, the form and content of the other remaining elements of individual letters is only weakly prescribed by formal rules,

> leaving room for considerable discretion, usually exercised by the REC chair or coordinator (administrator), as to form and phrasing. Some offer a precis, then give the details in list form; others simply list (in no particular order) the issues raised; and some distinguish between essential require-ments and optional suggestions for a favourable opinion. (Dixon-Woods et al., 2007: 7)

Issues of ethics are themselves 'profoundly equivocal and contestable.' However, the ethics-review committees,

> must engage in displays of certitude deriving from institutionalised ethical norms, which are themselves products of attempts to routinise the disputable. The requirement to provide a confident statement in the face of equivocality provides some of the explanation for the authori-tative (perhaps even authoritarian) tone of some of the letters. (Dixon-Woods et al., 2007: 10)

The attributes of ethics-committee letters pointed out by Dixon-Woods and his colleagues do not conflict with my own findings that REB chairs sometimes insert phrases like 'I *believe*' in their letters to researchers. In one such case, a chair of an REB – who happens to be someone I know as very amenable to social research – defers to a higher authority by relativizing his/her own opinion about the application.

Passive Voice

Bureaucrats often resort to using the passive voice as a way to assert authority. The passive voice ignores or downplays human agency. It reinforces an 'invisible' force at work because what is needed from the reader of the letter is compliance, unquestioned compliance.[12] Letters from REBs imitate this authoritative style of writing. Dixon-Woods et al. (2007) found that the 'diligence exercised by RECs is indicated by use of a stylised language, frequently involving use of active verbs such as "considered," "queried," "questioned," "asked,"' Of the 209 sentences pertaining to the five letters from REBs (in appendix C), some seventy-two sentences (or 34 per cent) use the passive voice. This is a particularly high rate, but the responsibility also rests with the members of the committee, many of whom are researchers and who are unaccustomed to writing in the active voice. The writers of REB letters sometimes mirror the awkward language or expressions that researchers favour. It is not uncommon for many of us who are writers and researchers to play up our authority by using the passive voice.

Words of Insistence

While some researchers, as noted by Thomas (2002: 9), receive 'threatening' letters from ethics committees, the interviews and my fieldnotes reveal that very few researchers received that kind of letter. However, letters from ethics committees do contain 'words of insistence.' Words of insistence relate to urgent requests but often stand prominently alone in the text. Ironically, some words of insistence, such as 'please clarify' or 'be clear' (each phrase occurs three times in the letters) beget lack of clarity, making it hard for the researcher to understand what he/she is supposed to do. Similarly, words such as 'please justify' and 'provide justification' have a similar effect, leaving the researcher to guess what needs to be justified or how to justify it. There is no universal skeleton key (Foucault, 1980b: 118) that would allow a researcher to unlock the meaning of what the REB is after. No less curious are such terms as 'please elaborate,' 'please indicate,' or 'please explain' that typically appear after a long series of questions from the REB. There is sometimes no reference point to these comments.

This can result in mounting frustration on both sides. The REB quite genuinely seeks clarification, but the researcher has no idea what clarification the REB seeks. The chair of an REB at a large university relates the following story:

> A researcher burst into tears because I had sent a question back to her and she said, 'Do you think I'm a bad person?' and I said no. I just wanted you to answer this question (it was a yes or no question) and if the answer was no that would have been my answer and then we could work with it because there are situations where somebody can't do what the REB would like the researchers to do and then we sort of have to figure out what is the best possibility. (Interview C05-B)

A researcher's feeling of anguish about receiving a letter from the REB can be quite common, as this former researcher (and now an REB chair) describes:

> When I was doing my master's, and I did it here at [university], approaching the REB was a frightening experience. I got back a nasty letter from the REB. I thought, 'Oh my God. I'm never going to be able to do my research,' but it was with the guidance of my supervisor that I managed to get it through the REB. But they were this big mysterious group that met [and] that I had no idea who they were and I certainly didn't want to seek them out. That has changed . . . I've become more knowledgeable but also REBs have become more open to listening to students. But that's just my personal experience. (Interview C10-B)

When an REB chair is cognizant of the possible emotional consequences that might result from letters coming being sent by her/his REB, he/she urges the committee to use a consistent tone in the letters and to be sure to thank the researcher and praise the 'applicant for submitting a good application' (Interview C11-M).[13] A researcher at the same university (M8) affirms the open and good communication that exists between the REB and him/herself:

> I found there was quite a bit of back and forth and a real willingness to help me understand what wasn't clear and if it was something that I just wasn't expressing well enough that I had that opportunity to redo it until I could express it until they could see whether it was actually a problem or a deficit that I needed to think more about or whether I just hadn't expressed it well enough and they really worked with me to facilitate the process. (Interview E12-M)

A staff member expressed the same productive approach to researchers:

> We've been quite fortunate that most of our chairs have been very approachable people and are usually very personable. [The two previous chairs] both really took a kind of a proactive role of phoning people and letting them know they were approved rather than making them wait the three days till it came in the mail. And often when there were really minor issues or even when there was really major ones, phoning them[14] and saying we can sit down and talk about it and look at it [really helped]. And I think that's been really useful for people to not feel like it's something that's way

out here and you have to bow to it, but that it's more of a back and forth conversation. (Interview S47-M)

The conditions of change between a chair who is leaving and a new one coming in are self-evident. Maureen Fitzgerald (2005: 334) notes that 'many researchers know when there has been a change in the committees; they can tell by the letters they receive and the questions they are asked to address.'

It is important that the researchers become a part of the 'interpretive community' (Fish, 1980: 173). This way, 'they know how to "read" the letters so that they will be understood in particular ways. Thus, for example, what are implied to be "requests," "suggestions," "recommendations," or forms of advice will be interpreted as commandments and requirements by a competent reader.' It will be clearer which statements are intended to be 'instructions' (Dixon-Woods et al., 2007: 9). Part of the unstated task of chairs of ethics committees is to assist the researcher in reading those letters and understanding them with the same intent as bestowed upon them by the ethics-review committee.

REB Communications inside the Larger Context of the Ethics Regime

Communications from ethics committees serve several functions. They define what is ethical, demonstrate the (diligent) work of ethics committees, and specify relationships. In other words, letters are a form of 'institutional display' (Dixon-Woods et al., 2007: 7). However, the activities of ethics committees 'are brought together under a single rational plan allegedly designed to fulfill the official aims of the institution,' that is, the university. Following Dixon-Woods et al. (2007:10), 'the institutionalisation of the REC as the moral authority serves to legitimate and authorise a particular opinion for a particular application. However, the REC does so not through an appeal to the moral superiority of any ethical position, but through its place in the organisational structure and the social positioning of the parties to the process thereby implied.'

Lest the reader conclude that the process of legitimating and authorizing opinions on ethical positions is constructed from the top down, it is important to point out that researchers are complicit in this process. One function of the researcher's meeting with the ethics committee is to 'co-construct' the letter the researcher will receive from the committee.

This is much like packing the earth around a concrete foundation that will constrain the researcher:

> The organisational and institutional context in which these authorisations and permissions must be sought is highly constrained by pressures of time and other demands. Clocks begin (and cease) ticking at pre-determined times, and researchers may have financial or other important reasons for getting on with their work. In this context, researchers and RECs must work out the rules of the game that form the logic of practices, deploy or 'invest' their capital in the game, and draw on their knowledge of their positioning within that field; above all, they must accept the 'illusion,' the social reality of the game ... In particular, they must understand the roles and relationships involved in this game, and letters play a critical part in structuring these. (Dixon-Woods et al., 2007: 9)

Ann Hamilton (2002: 98) points to Foucault's 'discursive practices model' whereby the text itself is part of the 'power effects of corporate strategy discourse.' These practices sustain the exercise of power by, for example, 'the withholding by regulators of federal funds for research, ... the voluntary adoption of the federal rules by institutions ... the approval/disapproval of researchers' protocols ... and even the self-regulatory behavior of researchers themselves ... '(Hamilton, 2002: 89–90). From an outside perspective (or that of federal regulators), compliance of institutions to federal ethics codes by universities and of researchers to the authority of the ethics-review committee seems seamless. But at what costs? Underneath, there are huge ruptures that are undermining the richness and vastness of social research.

This chapter identified three issues in communications from ethics committees to researchers. First, concern for research participants, research methods, and consent constitute the committees' principal worries. Second, queries about data and anonymity comprise another, albeit lower level of concern. The remaining areas (of the least concern) deal with vulnerability, confidentiality, deception, and Aboriginal knowledge. It has come as a surprise, however, that the REBs lavish so much attention on methodology or methods of the proposed research even if the research represents a low-risk category. We have also looked at the language embodied in communications from ethics committees. The voice is one of authority and seems to appeal to irrefutably higher, more ethical principles. The communications extensively employ the passive voice and rely on 'words of insistence' (such as 'please clarify'). The style of communication brooks no resistance or argument.

Communications from ethics committees serve a number of functions. They not only define what is ethical but also demonstrate the diligence of ethics committees in arriving at their decisions. The communications are a form of 'institutional display.' Researchers see these communications as stultifying rather than helpful. Along those lines, one wonders if researchers were to treat their research participants the same way that ethics committees treat them, the members of those committees would, we are sure, be horrified. Ethics committees will become a dynamic example to the researcher when members of the committees begin treating researchers with the same respect as they expect the researcher to treat the research participant. The next two chapters focus on the adjustments that researchers make in this galaxy of research-ethics review.

10 The Underlife of Research-Ethics Review: Preparing an Application

The Seduction of Ethics points to strategies researchers use to handle the demands of research-ethics review committees, from total avoidance to full compliance, and all intermediate points of adjustment. Some of Goffman's (1961, 1967, 1974) concepts are useful in shedding light on the interactional dynamics between research-ethics review committees and researchers. We can speak of the underlife of an institution when all of its members (researchers in this case) fall under the shadow of REBs.

In the two-sided world of research-ethics review, there is a split between a relatively small number of ethics staff in universities and a large number of researchers. While some researchers and ethics staff do not view one another with suspicion – these views are not very common – the data indicate that each can view the other 'with narrow stereotypes' (Goffman, 1961: 12). The ethics staff and REBs, as we have already seen, may view researchers in a pejorative fashion; the same view can dominate the researchers' perspective towards the ethics staff and REBs.

The 'Hurt Perspective'

The 'hurt perspective' signals a tendency to blame others, directly or indirectly, for the hurt that one believes he/she has experienced. Many researchers in *The Seduction of Ethics* have adopted the hurt perspective either as a means to be pejorative about the ethics-review system or to feel keenly hurt about the research that might have once been possible but no longer is. Laura Stark (2007: 777, 785) refers to this perspective as the 'social science victim narrative.' An article by Ivor Pritchard (2002: 3) of OHRP received considerable attention from researchers who, according to him, see IRBs as 'trolls' (i.e., 'irascible, irrational, not-quite-human creatures who block the way of travellers arriving at the trolls' bridge' where a toll is demanded). Urban legends and personal experiences contribute to the hurt perspective. Analogies reinforce them.

Urban legends often set the context of the researcher's perspective towards the ethics review process. These stories, which Jim Thomas (2002: 5) refers to as memes, circulate and demonize ethics committees and can turn up during conference presentations or at other venues. For example, during the question period after presentation by Annalisa Salonius (who studied the social organization of biomedical laboratories) at the 2004 Congress of the Humanities and the Social Sciences in Winnipeg, a member of the audience related the story of 'a student whose application was turned down by the REB because she wanted to keep names not anonymous because that's what the participants wanted' (Presentation, 4 June 2004, Fieldnotes: 160). Researchers also circulate the 'green pants' story – an analogy – that I have heard several times, at least once in the United States and once in the Atlantic provinces of Canada, to denote the impossible task of predicting every harm that could come to anyone: 'You could be in a public setting, wearing green pants, and somebody with a phobia of green pants freaks out' (R095, Fieldnotes: 795). Typical of such stories is the conflicting advice received from the REB chair and its members as to whether or not a particular research project needed to be reviewed (e.g., S22-M, Fieldnotes: 722; R072 Fieldnotes: 435). Even stories about how few researchers in one's department (Interview R003-M) have gone through ethics review can attain the stature of urban legends. In the same vein, young researchers now treat ethics-breaching stories as 'memorabilia' (Presentation by Ed Gabrielle, 6 May 2005, CAREB Annual Meeting, Fieldnotes: 163). As a way of taking advantage of these horror stories, a researcher would like to know what social scientists did wrong in the past and to design a reasonable system in answer to those problems (Interview R007-M).

Surprisingly, ethics staff publicly solicit these 'war stories,' too, in an effort to find villainous projects that REBs have had to contend with (e.g., S17-S, Fieldnotes: 1105; S36-S, Fieldnotes: 1147). These solicitations inadvertently lower the curtain on any possibility for productive interaction between researchers and ethics staff. Official calls, such as the one that appeared in NCEHR's spring 2004 issue of Communiqué, wanted to include brief examples of 'challenges' in social science research (NCEHR, 5 November 2005, Fieldnotes: 1159).[1] These calls merely harden the boundary between ethics administrators and researchers. Naturally, the solicitation by researchers of frightening experiences with ethics committees also creates walls.

Personal experiences, usually solicited through my interviews or chats with researchers, reinforce the spread of urban legends (that are about someone else's experiences, usually a friend of a colleague). One researcher at a mid-sized university described his REB experience this way: '[It's a] big headache to go to REB to discuss a student's application, [it] takes a lot of time' and it takes 'too much time to work up an ethics application for small grants. Also the time line of these grants is eight to twelve weeks, and the REB does not meet regularly over the summer months; [it's] too much stress, you don't hear from REB for at least one month after their meeting, and then there are always revisions.' Besides, the same researcher told me, 'it's hard to follow REB's decision in concrete ways,' and 'a lot of researchers across the whole university now find problems with the concerns of REB with research they've always done.' He also became frustrated when the REB did not allow research participants to talk about the very things the participants raise themselves. What frustrates him in particular is that he has to go through the same risk assessment for his innocuous research as clinical trials for cancer drugs (Interview R002-M).

Other researchers complained about the amount of time it takes to prepare a proposal for the REB: 'I spend two days working on the interview schedule and one day preparing the application' (Interview R024-M). One older researcher said, 'It's too much trouble for me,' and 'ethics is too overbearing. Many are retiring [and] don't want to solve the problem of "ethics." Let others solve the problem' (Interview R118-M). When a researcher interviewed a retired professor, the retiree said, 'Have they [the REB] gone insane now?'. The same researcher insists on not using signed consent forms, but the sociology department keeps sending his application back (Interview R173-M).

Researchers also expressed considerable cynicism about the benefits of having the ethics bureaucracy. For one researcher, the university's changing of the ethics application form every three years is too much. His REB returned his application because he did not happen 'to stumble on the latest form.' Every ongoing research requires another form to be filled out each year, and for the students, that is 'big headache,' involving a lot of time. He claims that there are now fourteen people working in the Research Office, constantly creating new forms, 'but [they aren't] a lot of help' for researchers (Interview R002-M). Another researcher received a major grant, but could not receive the money until his REB approved it, but his REB would not approve it until it saw the list of questions he would be asking. He could not do this because he did not have the money to hire someone to do the initial review of literature (Interview R003-M). More than one researcher believes that the 'codes [*TCPS*] are more about protecting the institution than the research participants,' and they maintain that the problems remain for researchers anyway: 'No amount of *TCPS* can sugarcoat what we're doing; always the usual things (problems) in the past,' namely, making ethics committees and researchers believe it is about protecting research participants while, in reality, it is about protecting the university (Interview R007-M).

When researchers reflect on incumbents in other fields, they are not always happy. One said that 'famous researchers get ethics approval' (Interview R002-M), but the 'hurt perspective' comes from the comparison to journalists, who do not need to submit their plans to the REB; one has heard of a journalist going into Aboriginal communities 'pretending to be anthropologists, hurting anthropology' (Interview R007-M; Interview R173-M).

Similarly, some chairs of REBs – and a number of them were (or are still) researchers – shared the perspectives of the researchers. One chair revealed that it is 'really hard for an REB to understand complications of doing work on vulnerable populations, such as the homeless' (Interview C09-B), while another found the whole review process a 'frightening experience for the researcher' (Interview C10-B). Others sympathize with researchers, saying that they 'see the REB as a bureaucratic bump,' while 'the younger [researchers] have a jaundiced look.' Most disgruntlement comes from veteran researchers (Interview C11-M). Even when an ethics committee communicates, there is frustration on the part of the researchers who 'take one look at an attempt from the IRB to communicate, roll their eyes, and toss or delete that immediately.' 'Those are often the same ones,' says Fitch (2005: 273), 'who then complain loudly about the never-ending, senseless changes in procedures, [and] claim they were never informed that they needed approval/certification/whatever, and, above all, lament how needlessly complicated the whole thing is.' There is no doubt, another chair mentioned, that researchers see the REB as a hurdle (Interview C12-S).

While the ethics-review system and the world of researchers constitute two separate entities, the boundary between them is porous. Some chairs or other members of ethics committees were or are still researchers, after all. But, in another sense, it is important to note that researchers have no choice but to be brought into the world of the ethics regime. All sorts of interactions flow out of that new relationship. We can call the world of researchers the 'presenting culture,' which is derived from the 'home world' (Goffman, 1961: 12), which we can call the world of 'traditional' research, or more accurately, the research that, before the ethics regime came into place, did not need to go through 'ethics.' The world of research-ethics review discredits the 'home world' of researchers to secure obedience and control. This interactional device 'create[s] and sustain[s] a tension between home and institutional worlds and use[s] this persistent tension as strategic leverage in the management of people' (Goffman, 1961: 127).

The research-ethics community finds such leverage in many settings. Countless times I have personally observed presentations by social scientists at conferences sponsored by research-ethics organizations. During these presentations there have been cries of protest from attendees when a social scientist claimed that risks or harms of his/her research were either negligible or minimal. So, too, the exercises to submit application forms and annual reports – all cast in terms and on conditions foreign to social researchers – unintentionally discredit the 'home world' of researchers. The administrative incumbents of ethics offices, who are the folks without any research experience, have a major say about research. The calls for 'war stories' is another such leveraging device.

It stands to reason to think that a researcher who experiences the hurt perspective and finds that his/her research is being leveraged in the ethics-review system will experience shifts in his/her own moral career.

The Researcher's Moral Career

A career 'refers to any social strand of any person's course through life, involves image of self and felt identity, and the publicly-stated aspects of that person's self.' A moral career involves the person's self (Goffman, 1961: 127–8). The reduction of one's research plans to forms (complete with the assigning of an REB file number) where there is no overt acknowledgement that social research *does* change once the research begins is the 'rite of welcome' that greets the researcher. 'Obedience tests' ('you balk, you pay') validate the shifts in one's moral career (Goffman, 1961: 18). Every sequence of research activity is subject to regulation; there is, formally speaking, no escape (Goffman, 1961: 38). While previously the researcher strongly identified him/herself with his/her research, the research now no longer becomes part of that identity. A disruption of the usual relationship between the individual actor and his/her acts occurs (Goffman, 1961: 30). The cynicism of a researcher towards both the alleged benefits and the bureaucracy of the research-ethics review process feed these shifts in the researcher's moral career.

A number of observers of the ethics-review process agree that 'there is no evidence that the application forms, review procedures and consent materials actually' do prevent harms to subjects and patients (Derbyshire, 2006: 47). One such observer is John Mueller. He speaks of the 'minimal evidence of value' and writes that, '[g]iven the inherent low risk of social science research, even before IRBs, the absence of incidents may just indicate the baseline, not the benefits of the review committee' (Mueller, 2007: 817–18). There is a deep disquiet by researchers fuelled by cautionary tales or urban legends. The National Communication Association invited their members to send in reports of their experiences, and it concluded that it is 'hard for us not to view the IRB as a necessary evil' (NCA, 2005: 208). Commonly, researchers caricature the IRB (Dougherty and Kramer, 2005: 280–1) and describe that world as filled with disjunctures. One such example of this is 'the fill-in-the-box-oriented questionnaire [which] does not correspond to qualitative researchers' [open]-ended data-gathering approach' (Tolich and Fitzgerald, 2006: 72). IRB deadlines without recourse to decisions also trap researchers.

Reading about the researchers' cynicism about the ethics-review 'bureaucracy' is overwhelming. For example, Howard S. Becker, one of the most reputable sociologists and prominent field researchers, sees an 'ambitious bureaucracy with interests to protect, a mission to promote, and a self-righteous and self-protective ideology to explain why it's all necessary' (Becker, 2004: 415). Betsy Bach laments the red tape (2005: 261). Carl Coleman and Marie-Charlotte Bouësseau (2008: 6) refer to an OHRP study that 'found that the agency continues to nitpick consent forms ... [require] extensive documentation of compliance activities, and finds the remedy for most problems to be "more" review studies, internal monitoring procedures, education, forms ... A culture of red tape rather than a culture of ethics.' The National Communications Association found that the IRB process 'seems to have gotten out of control and become the tail that wags the dog' (NCA, 2005: 213). Another observer of the process speaks of 'overbearing regulations that stifle innovation and investigation' (Derbyshire, 2006: 35), while

Koro-Ljungberg et al. (2007: 1081) lament the '[a]lmost absolute obedi-ence' that is 'expected by IRBs, and many qualitative researchers are constantly scrutinizing whether they are following the protocol or not.' Colin D. Newman (2004: 9), citing other studies, concludes that 'boards impose unnecessarily restrictive regulations.' Raymond De Vries and Carl Forsberg (2002: 199) warn us about 'obstructionist' IRBs that are 'placing unnecessary and overly bureaucratic roadblocks in the way of research.' 'Getting through ethics,' according to Karen Szala-Meneok (2006: 2), an anthropologist who now serves as a research-ethics officer, has become the institutional discourse among all, 'it is like the thesis-defense story – just another hoop to jump through.'

When one considers the large number of publications voicing objec-tions to the ethics regime, it is striking to note the relative lack of full resistance by researchers. It might be, as Goffman (1967: 104) claims, that the behaviour of many social actors is organized to avoid embar-rassment. A new, untenured faculty member did not want to 'rock the boat,' because he/she 'might be seen as a thorn,' especially as he/she already has a tenuous relationship with the Research Office (Interview R006-M). Another researcher did not want to be labelled as a 'trouble maker' by rocking the boat as well. He repeated this perspective for my benefit: '[It's a] Power struggle, [so] don't rock the boat with bureau-crats, they make your life miserable' (Interview R003-M). One researcher admitted that it is like applying for funding. 'When you complain, you won't win and you'll be known as a troublemaker the next time around; the REB can say yes or no. That's pretty powerful' (Interview R007-M).

However, organizational explanations might be closer to the truth, as Hamilton reminds us of the insights by Alvesson and Deetz (1996):

> [This] is apparent in the way the IRB processes are 'handed down' from the federal and institutional regulators (as well as from faculty teaching methods classes) and 'passed around' by researcher among themselves. Dissent among researchers, collectively or individually, is nearly unheard of; though many researchers and some regulators do complain, they don't often act. (Hamilton, 2002: 187)

Today, there are accounts of researchers' passively resisting the ethics regime. I would suggest that the failure to resist is fully internalized, and while researchers seldom express that in action, they certainly do so through words. Ann Hamilton (2002: 283) refers to this kind of resistance as 'passive rebellion.' A high-profile researcher whose work is innovative, critical of bureaucratic establishments, and analytic, had this to say:

> I was president of the [academic society] when they introduced these damned research ethics rules ... and I fiercely (and futilely) resisted them on the grounds that they made it impossible to do any critical research, as I had done ... Any set of rules that makes you kiss arse is probably a bad thing. (R125-M, Fieldnotes: 470)

Another advocated a ceremonial public burning of consent forms and at least submitting the application form late so that the ethics committee would feel the extra pressure to be timely in its response (Interview R173-M). For some researchers, according to an ethics-staff member, another form of protest involved researchers who found a way of circumventing answers on the *TCPS* tutorial (Interview S46-S).

Whether in Canada or in the United Kingdom, researchers have expressed negative opinions about the ethics-review process. In a recent survey, the National Health Service (of the United Kingdom) found that, '78 percent ($n=130$) agreed or strongly agreed that the time needed to prepare an application inhibited social research in Health and 72 percent agreed or strongly agreed that the need to re-submit small protocol amendments was similarly inhibiting' (Richardson and McMullan, 2007: 1122).

When it comes to particular elements in ethics codes, there is, moreover, no agreement among social scientists as to what constitutes the dilemma. Some believe the problem lies with the ethics codes; others believe it is the university ethics committees. There are some who blame themselves, as Malcolm Feeley (2007: 771–4) points out: '[T]he enemy is in plain sight, and it is *here*, not "over there;" it is "us," not "them" ... We have remained all too silent as a stifling regime of regulations has been erected around us.'

One can ask why researchers did not protest when the regime was established. Part of the answer, as suggested by the AAUP (2001), is that social scientists were co-opted into the regulatory system 'from the beginning,' and that some 'social scientists opted in themselves, in part, to enhance the "scientificity" of their work, i.e., to appear more legitimate in scientific terms by succumbing to the same scrutiny as the positivists' (Hamilton, 2002: 257). Richard Shweder (2006: 5) minces no words when he says that '[researchers] have no one to blame but themselves (and their own academic administrators) for the wholesale application of the DHHS regulations to the vast majority of social scientists, [and] humanists . . . who conduct research without a reliance on federal funds.'

However, Ann Hamilton believes (2002: 14) that researchers do not call into question 'the limitations of the regulatory process itself (i.e., what regulations *can* do, or prevent), and the limitations imposed on researchers (what regulations *prevent* us from doing). The researchers are held in "intellectual captivity,"' and we fail to acknowledge regulation as a matter of choice; we seem to view it (when we see it at all) as something inevitable and unchangeable. We "confine" ourselves, build our own bars, and stay within them' (Hamilton, 2002: 14), which underscores a common sentiment that 'researchers should not allow institutional norms or expectations to limit their ethical agency' (Koro-Ljungberg et al., 2007: 1077).

The complexity of the ethics system alone would be difficult to resist. Ann Hamilton (2002: 100) reminds us that 'the instructions have become more and more detailed. More and more cumbersome, restricting, ambiguous, voluminous.' 'What power the structure has!' she exclaims:

> More accurately, what power we give to the structure!!. To gain this kind of compliance, the system must be constructed, to 'seem real' at the very least. And, it seems to be a requirement, in order for the system to operate, that the simulation 'seem right' (i.e., reasonable, important, etc.) though sometimes compliance is gained simply because the system appears unavoidable, pointless to resist, or that it is self-evident, the 'way we do things' (and eventually becoming 'the way we have always done things'). No questions asked (anymore). (Hamilton, 2002: 172)

The ominous phrase she uses (2002: 175), 'Failure to submit these items will only delay your review' and the 'managerial suggestion that resistance is futile' builds on one's inability or desire to resist. Furthermore, she points to power of the system in which,

> [w]hen questions are posed . . . they often focus on minutiae, i.e., how to revise or accomplish a procedure rather than about the need for it . . . [T]he application form demonstrates instances where common sense has been pervaded, allowing the form and the completion and submission of it, to become part of the 'ordinary' world of research. (188)

What is more, according to Hamilton,

> [r]esearchers are accomplices in their own subordination by participating in an unreasonable, ill-fitting system operated/dominated by people who often know substantially less (and often care even less than that) about (the details of) what is 'really' going on in a given situation, method, or field of research. Similarly, researchers aren't demonstrating they care enough to 'risk' changing the system. (188)

There are some sobering thoughts about ever being able to change the ethics regime. For example, one participant told me that 'we shall look constantly foolish to administrators if we always insist that the business model of research is not where we're at' (R007-M). Another spoke with hope about plans to 'make changes after you have the PhD in your pocket' (Interview R173-M). For better or worse, one must agree with a researcher who said that 'no collective resistance against REB is possible' (R003-M). There is the extra burden òf having to comply to such a research-ethics review because of the threat of loss of funding to universities while at the same time that universities are forcing researchers to produce more research grants.

It would be a misreading of the data to believe that a researcher is dishonest in his/her approach to the research-ethics review process. A researcher must juggle several ethics frameworks at the same time. These frameworks include the guidelines in the *TCPS* and the many levels of interpretations promoted by ethics committees, but also the ethical framework that is derived from his/her own experience in the research setting. Even at the point of contact between the ethics committee and the researcher or the chair of the committee and the researcher, there is much that is left open to interpretation. When, for example, a committee insists that it should be apprised of 'significant' changes after the research plan has been approved, the researcher will still not have a clear idea of what the committee has intended with that request. Unable or unwilling to appreciate that particular request (along with others), ethics committees can interpret the researcher's actions as lacking honesty.

Warming Up (or Not) to Submitting the Proposal

The ethics-review system has steadily promoted the idea that research is a 'privilege,' not a 'right,' not even an 'obligation.' The idea that research is a 'privilege' that one must earn represents a significant departure from the idea of academic freedom where faculty enjoy the right to conduct research and is altering the relationship of the researcher to his/her own work and, in particular, to the university. With the growing strength of the ethics regime, it is the regime that now has the right to accord researchers the privilege of doing research. This topsy-turvy world now has non-researchers deciding what researchers are (not) permitted to do. Veteran researchers and, to a lesser extent, novice researchers find this an uncomfortable turn of events. These events pave the way for the breaching of the norms pronounced by the ethics regime. In a survey, three out of fourteen researchers abandoned their research as a result of these obstacles (Muzzin, 2002; Fieldnotes: 566). Much is at stake.

Even in total institutions such as prisons and mental institutions, inmates engage in practices that help them to 'obtain forbidden satisfactions' (Goffman, 1961: 54). However, many practices ('secondary adjustments') do not directly challenge the staff of an institution. Of course, the world of researchers, whose work is subject to research-ethics review, is quite different from the world of inmates where secondary adjustments run counter to inmate codes of behaviour (Goffman, 1961: 54).[2] The order of the strategies in this and the following chapter falls roughly in the same chronological order that researchers use when contemplating the research-ethics review.

There are numerous reports about the anticipatory socialization even before the researcher starts his/her proposal. Catherine Scott (2004: 3) speaks about how the 'university ethics committee [develops] into a powerful and feared entity.' Significantly, only 15 per cent of 130 social-science researchers in the United Kingdom thought that the research-ethics review was a positive experience, while another 59 per cent believed it was a negative experience (Richardson and McMullan, 2007: 1123). From the outset, as Betsy Bach found, 'winning the battle or overcoming the IRB is a high stakes endeavor' (Bach, 2005: 260). The National Communications Association likens the application process to 'a game, obviously using a Ouija board . . . [N]o one knows who answers or determines approval' (NCA, 2005: 223). Even though a researcher may have gone through various incarnations, whether as an undergraduate or a graduate student or as a faculty member, 'it is impossible to build up experience and understanding of [the] IRB process' (NCA, 2005: 221).

Avoiding Review

It is surprisingly more common than assumed to find that researchers avoid the research-ethics review; but how do they avoid the research-ethics review? According to Malcolm Feeley (2007), researchers avoid the IRB whenever possible (770) and some researchers 'wholly reject control and circumvent the review process altogether ... and ... minutiae of IRB rules are not followed' (262). Researchers try to 'bypass IRBs because it has become too much trouble to accommodate apparently irrelevant processes,' and they claim that the 'dynamic nature of the research process and the experience of the human subjects may be very different from what is presented in the proposal and protocol even though there is no intent to deceive the IRB' (ICL, 2006: 6).

Based on the results of a survey of UK social science academics about the process of applying to National Health Service RECs, 45 per cent of the respondents indicated that they had modified their research design to avoid the process altogether, as illustrated by the following quotation: 'Accessed patients as citizens in the street! This is a strategy I will be using increasingly – the system is driving this kind of research underground' (Richardson and McMullan, 2007: 1122).

The norms of ethics avoidance prevail under many circumstances. For example, a report by the Professional Ethics and Policy Committee of the Canadian Sociology and Anthropology Association (PEPC, 2002; Fieldnotes: 566) reveals that one-third of research that falls under the ethics codes still has not undergone review. A report of the Annual Meeting of the Committee of Graduate Departments in Psychology, held in Sarasota, Florida, in 2006, reveals that 20 per cent of psychologists 'flew solo,' in the sense that they had not gone to their IRB for ethics approval. The main reason was the slow turnaround time, not fear that their proposals would not be approved (Anonymous, 2006a: 1).

One researcher knows that many of his colleagues in sociology 'don't go through research-ethics review – they use databases,' and he is 'surprised that there are only four of his colleagues who have gone to the REB.' 'I am sure,' he says, 'because of the pain it involves' (Interview R003-M). A sociologist conducting intellectual history research by interviewing peers has never gone to the REB with his research (Conversation R020-M, Fieldnotes: 141). Ethics staff confess that professors and departments do not forward course materials to REB for review; therefore, 'they have to be "educated"' (Interview C12-S). Two members of ethics committees I interviewed on two different campuses also admit that there might be some who avoid review (Interview E12-M; Interview E15-S).

To avoid an ethics review, a number of researchers have opted to undertake contract research off campus (Interview R092-B), ensuring that they do not use university premises for any of their research. One Quebec researcher, who uses only his contacts outside the university,

has even gone further afield and decided to conduct his research inter-
nationally, including Europe, to avoid REB review and only connects
with European researchers (Conversation R034, Fieldnotes: 143). For
some, REB avoidance involves selecting topics that do not trigger 'vulnerability issues,' such as researching juvenile auto thieves (R092-B,
Fieldnotes: 479). To circumvent review, one researcher accepts small
grants as 'consulting fees' rather than as research grants, but he finds
'it's too bad I can't hire grad students.' The same professor only takes a
grant if it is large; it is not worth his time and effort otherwise, and he
does not take small grants (i.e., $10–$20 thousand) anymore (Interview
R003-M). Another researcher's strategy is 'to avoid the irony of seeking
IRB approval, [and] use[s] anecdotal accounts . . . ' (Hemmings, 2006:
13). A professor of communications does not submit a research design
or measures for research when an organization hires him to do the
research (NCA, 2005: 221).

Another category of evading ethics review involves departments not
submitting annual reports, such as the criminologist (C12-S) who tells
me that the criminology department in her university has a seven-year
project, but has never submitted the annual report despite repeated
requests.

Another level of avoiding review involves the renaming of research
projects as 'auditing,' 'pilot,' 'quality assurance,' or 'evaluation' studies,
or replacing 'research' with 'project' (C14-M, Fieldnotes: 721). An annual
meeting of United States sociologists urged researchers not to submit their
research to the ethics committee if the research is not funded (Couch-
Stone Symposium, Fieldnotes: 351). This approach has, however, a long-
term negative impact when researchers wish to submit their work to
journals that require an ethics approval form. Another researcher who
also serves on his ethics committee argued in his committee that a colleague did not need to submit his research to the committee because
he 'didn't have a research question in mind' (R078-M, Fieldnotes: 602).
Much uncertainty prevails as to what should be submitted to the ethics
committee. For example, there is uncertainty about whether auto-eth-
nographies require ethics approval (R012-B, Fieldnotes: 434).

Engaging in Self-Censorship and Shame

Researchers, according to Kevin Haggerty and Aaron Doyle, 'seem to
be embracing a number of constraints on our knowledge production
endeavours in the name of "research ethics" that do not apply to other

knowledge production enterprises' (Email from Kevin Haggerty, 13 February 2003, Fieldnotes: 425).[3] They find that their ethics committee would find some sociological research problematic, but not when conducted by a journalist. It is easier for journalists, Haggerty claims, to produce knowledge, not having to contend with the need for anonymity, 'filming people, informing them they are being filmed, analyzing web logs on the Internet, conducting surveys, analyzing overheard conversations, using deception as a means to generate knowledge.' From the start of their research plans, researchers consider the implications of these research possibilities . . . and discard them before submitting their plans to the ethics committee.

Even when a researcher has already received approval for the research, he/she is not inclined to return to the IRB with a new strategy that has been found more useful. As one psychologist said, 'My science suffers because I cannot make necessary changes in procedure for fear of IRB delays' (COGDOP, 2007: 1). It is striking to note that, of all the researchers interviewed for *The Seduction of Ethics*, only one – a PhD student – told me about her co-researcher who 'believes that if there is a variation in interview schedule, they would be violating REB rules' (Interview R024-M). This comment indicates the extent to which young researchers themselves are increasingly being brought under the aegis of ethics committees, perhaps putting constraints on the production of knowledge. One researcher develops questions for his research as a 'natural reaction to regulations: should I ask this question, or that question?' (Interview R002-M).

Researchers experience a sense of shame and 'are sheepish coming to REB when they realize that they should have gotten approval first' (Interview C09-B). Some researchers have moved so far away from the issue of knowledge production in relation to the ethics committee that they reduce the issues to logistical ones:

The researchers typically ask, 'What form do I need? What category does this fall in?,' and of course part of the difficulty here is [that we] are currently revising the existing protocol forms for the REBs that has to go to [the University] . . . [So we] show them where the forms are and if they need help filling them out [we] give them pointers on what [they] need. When it gets to consent forms [we say], 'Have at least this and this and this and this; here's a couple of examples that you might want to follow for template purposes and what not.' But mostly it's questions about the logistics . . . like 'What do I do, where do I get the forms yada, yada, yada.' (Interview E15-S)

Starting the Study before Approval/Continuing
After Approval Time Is Finished

The starting and ending date of social research can be a bone of contention, but the fewness of replies to my query about researchers' starting the research before approval was secured or continuing (long) after the project has been deemed officially over, suggests that researchers are keeping a sharp dividing line as to how the ethics committees define such times, as opposed to the reality of the research itself about this very matter. It might be a question of self-censorship. One researcher (Presentation by S02, 3 June 2003, Congress, Fieldnotes: 151) indicated that the research was started before getting approval, while only one ethics committee chair knew of one such instance (Interview C12-S). The Bell Report (Bell, Whiton, and Connelly, 1998) mentions that IRBs claim that 33 per cent of researchers failed to get IRB approval before the start of a study (Pritchard, 2002: 10). Fifteen per cent of 130 surveyed social researchers said that they started research without ever applying, and 12 per cent started during the application process before approval was given (Richardson and McMullan, 2007: 1122). One researcher was frank and said that he usually begins his study as soon as he has applied for IRB approval. Another researcher, if asked to produce evidence that participants agreed to the study, said he does not date the data collection (NCA, 2005: 210). It is probably a common strategy, but many researchers do not indicate that 'pre-IRB-approval conversations led to research ideas and insights – and [that] the research has started!' (Feeley, 2007: 768).

Following the tradition and practice of C. Wright Mills, a sociologist who has produced enduring research, many social researchers take notes as they lead their daily lives. Some of these notes never lead to any research, while others do.[4] One REB chair was faced with a researcher who had collected his data twenty-five years earlier, and then decided to publish them (Interview C05-B). Is the starting date the same day as when he decided to analyse his data? This brings up the research of Neil Jamieson-Williams (2008) who, after twenty years of data gathering on the Wiccan Church of Canada and the Dymond Lune of Alexandrian Wiccan, decided to write them up. No wonder ethics-review committees have trouble situating the start and end dates of research. Flicker et al. (2007: 7) noted that none of the thirty surveyed ethics forms they examined were designed around the idea that community participatory research had flexible times of starting and ending dates of research (see also Boser, 2007: 1066). Moreover, ethics committees have variable perspectives about research: some claim that research is not one discrete project (Interview C03-M) and proceed to chop up the research into small pieces of data gathering, analysis, and writing (Interview R118-M). In one such case, the IRB gave the researcher a three-month window to collect data. But at the end of three months, the IRB said that the data analysis must stay under review beyond the three months even though the researcher was no longer gathering data and had moved into the analytic and writing phase. The IRB never discussed this possibility with the researcher when the original approval had been given. Some now ask the question, What happens when data sets are being reanalysed by others (NCA, 2005: 219–20; R013-S, Fieldnotes: 581)?

From the researcher's perspective, it is also difficult to ascertain when research is finished. Typically, qualitative researchers say that they 'abandoned' rather than completed their research. Qualitative researchers are not likely to know when data are no longer needed (Hamilton, 2002: 181) or when the point of theoretical or empirical saturation has been reached.

Taking Practical Steps in Preparing an Application

In the same NHS survey quoted earlier, one learns that '[t]hree-quarters of respondents either disagreed or strongly disagreed that the amount of paperwork required for submission was reasonable and 60 percent disagreed or strongly disagreed that the time between submission and approval was reasonable' (Richardson and McMullan, 2007: 1122).

Those who are faithful in creating the best application to be submitted to the ethics committee adopt several strategies: (a) turning to and/or knowing the ethics committee, the office staff, or the website, (b) relying on friends and colleagues, (c) creating strategic ambiguity, that is, providing the least amount of information or less detail, and (d) manufacturing benign fabrications. Most of these strategies betray a sophistication that can only come from experience. It is noteworthy that strategies (a) and (b) are normative – indeed, their sources are members of ethics committees. Some researchers 'throw things together at the last minute' (C12-S). A community member on an REB who was giving a public talk on the topic, however, wanted to dissuade researchers from 'cutting and pasting' their applications (Presentation by E8, 7 May 2005, CAREB Meeting, Fieldnotes: 166). Another researcher suggested, 'You have to know how a specific committee constructs and enacts concepts to really know how to frame your IRB application' (R095, Fieldnotes: 795).

When preparing an application, researchers find it helpful to know who is or who is not on the REB (Interview E12-M). Similarly, at the same university, another REB member (E13) suggested that researchers consult the ethics office website that, as it turns out, was one of the longest among Canadian universities, having a total of eighty pages. Two REB chairs recall that a researcher engaged in 'lots of dialogue' in resolving problems vis-à-vis research on the homeless (Interview C10-B). What needs to be done, according to an ethics staff member, is for researchers to go to the research office, and, if the ethics staff cannot answer the question, the staff should put them in touch with the REB chair (Focus Group REB1-S). One REB member recalls researchers coming to the REB asking how to store vast amounts of data; normally, two REB members meet with researcher to sort through such problems (Interview E27-S). Researchers may ask others how to get an ethnography study through an IRB and how hard it is 'to learn from experience of other researchers' (R073, Fieldnotes: 739). Some researchers lobby individual members of the committee (Fitzgerald, 2004: 44), although some committees forbid members to talk to researchers. But things are not as simple as that, as one researcher discovered:

> If only I had sought her out before my first meeting, I thought. She [the IRB member] would have helped me write a better application in the first place, and I might have saved myself a six-week delay. But in my heady romance with academic freedom in my department, I had forgotten there was a political game to be played – a game of talking to the right people at the right time to smooth the way to my goals. Sometimes there *are* faces behind the 'faceless gaze' of disciplinary power . . . ; the IRB was not an intangible force but rather a network of real people, and here was one right in front of me. (Johnson, 2008: 222)

And,

> . . . who knows what work they did for me behind the scenes? Silence or the appearance of cooperation can be a form of resistance . . . ; sometimes subversively negotiating around obstacles is more effective than directly confronting them [the REB]. If the goal was to get my application approved, then their means of doing so – initially going along with their IRB colleagues and then helping me get it right for the next round – may well have been the best strategy. (Johnson, 2008: 226)

Like the above-mentioned strategy, there is remarkably little information available about researchers turning to each other for help. After a presentation on ethics in research at the University of Saskatoon on 16 June 2003, I had an inkling of how difficult it is to learn from the experience of other researchers. One REB member assumed there was a mentoring process in place (for students) (Interview E13-M), but was not able to give an example. Similarly, another (E27-S) told me that researchers turn to friends at the university to find out how to fill out the form or go to the website. Advisers tell students to contact an REB member. Another faculty member advises a colleague to 'share a proposal with someone who knows, try to back up why, for example, you're not using consent forms with authoritative statements' (Interview R006-M).

As anyone who has conducted social research knows, there are sometimes large variations in research between what is planned (and submitted to the ethics committee) and what actually happens on the ground. As Carole Truman points out, '[R]esearch designs on paper . . . do not translate into practice when fieldwork actually begins' (Truman, 2003: 10). Many social researchers would agree that 'the dynamic nature of the research process and the experience of the human subjects may be very different from what is presented in the proposal and protocol even though there is no intent to deceive the IRB' (ICL, 2006: 6).

Taking this perspective, one could conclude that any formal application is a benign fabrication. Are ethics committees dealing with research that actually happens or with research in the abstract? Thus, there is also a major incongruity between formal ethics and ethics 'on the ground.' As one researcher put it, it is 'difficult to link original research plans to actual research – laughable' (R144-M, Fieldnotes: 520–1). Along these lines, some members of the audience at a session on research ethics at the Society for the Study of Symbolic Interaction (Couch-Stone Symposium, 2003), recommended that researchers should 'try the path of the least resistance; IRBs don't want to hear about inductive research; thus, strategy involves deception or being disingenuous' (Couch-Stone Symposium, 7 February 2003, Fieldnotes: 352). Another member of this audience suggested that researchers 'hide anything that might be controversial.'

Goffman in *Frame Analysis* (1974) defines 'benign fabrication' as 'the intentional effort of one or more individuals to manage activity so that a party of one or more others will be induced to have a false belief about what it is that is going on.' Such a fabrication is 'engineered in the interest of the person(s) contained by them. Or, if not done in their interest or benefit, at least not against their interest' (87).

Researchers were a lot more forthcoming about their 'doing the minimum' when filling out an application form (Interview C12-S). In some cases, it is the ethics committee that wants some things not to be 'too specific, as in mentioning the names of schools' (Interview C05-B). Interestingly, one researcher echoes the same thoughts: 'You don't list all the questions you will be asking in interviews, or maybe just general questions' (Interview R002-M). One researcher 'words her proposal loosely to allow latitude, while being specific enough to satisfy a board' (R131, Fieldnotes: 601). At a sociology conference, a member of the audience at a session on ethics suggested that you 'do not beg for questions you don't want to answer, and do put things in an innocuous way' (Couch-Stone Symposium, 7 February 2003, Fieldnotes: 352)

Aside from redesigning one's research as a 'pilot study' or as an 'audit' (as explained above), there are more significant ways that a researcher might hide some facts about his/her participants or research plans to get approval to study homeless people, without, for example, saying that three-fourths are First Nations[5] (A13-S, Fieldnotes: 230). Another researcher does not mention that he is taping the interviews (NCA, 2005: 210).

A number of insights revealed by studies on ethics-review committees shed more light on the phenomenon of benign fabrication. A National Communications Association scholar admits to adopting a stance of 'strategic ambiguity' while 'providing the least amount of information I can and still be within the confines of compliance' (NCA, 2005: 205). The impetus for ambiguity rests with IRBs who 'create an environment where researchers become less detailed in their applications' (Scott, 2005: 252–3). Here is the story of one researcher in particular:

> I realized one mistake I made in writing the application in short order: I gave too much information. In the section describing research participants, I had written that my participants would be about 5 high school teachers recruited through personal contacts, as I had already established the rapport necessary for the sensitive nature of my study. In disclosing that I knew who my participants might be – even though I had no intention of revealing the nature of my relationship to them in the study – the IRB argued that I had already breached confidentiality because *they* were now privy to that information. (Johnson, 2008: 217)

Hedging One's Bet

For researchers, submitting an application to an ethics-review committee can be a worrisome or unpleasant experience. A member of the audience attending a 2003 talk on ethics at the University of Saskatchewan remarked that researchers need to acknowledge there is a 'subculture of knowledge: what works and what does not work' (Fieldnotes: 69). Maureen Fitzgerald, an observer of the research-ethics review experience, said that 'researchers are choosing to ignore unpleasantness in filling out forms' (Fieldnotes: 79). A staff member of an ethics office (Focus Group REB1-S) spoke of a researcher who told him that he 'holds his breath each time he submits a proposal to the REB, and feels anxiety, being evaluated.' One member of an ethics committee relates the following:

> So there are still sometimes questions about . . . what exactly is the committee looking for, that sort of thing. So maybe there's not quite as much of that at least on the part of the researchers here, unless they've gone through the process personally a number of times and they have figured out what works, so to speak, and so then they just continue to use that formula. (Interview E27-S)

However, in such instances of uncertainty and unpredictability, I wonder whether researchers practise 'magic' in the same sense as Dan and Cheryl Albas found when they observed students' taking exams (Albas and Albas, 1989). Magic involved rituals of subordination while at the same time exercising control over uncertainty with a favourable outcome. We can see the use of magic as a form of insurance.[6] One of these rituals finds researchers using *performative language.*

The idea of performative language originates in the works of J.L. Austin (1962) which makes the point that 'to say something is to do something.' According to Andrew Cline (2002), who has written on the subject of performative language, to make the statement 'I promise that [something] . . . is to perform the act of promising as opposed to making a statement that may be judged true or false' (24). The use of performative language is meaningful behaviour by itself. Researchers engage in a variety of linguistics and language strategies to placate REBs. They are learning to emphasize the use of particular words, but not others.

First, whether researchers are submitting ideas or proposals to ethics committees, it is very common to find such prefatory remarks as the following: 'Let me state that I strongly share the IRB's charge and concern with promoting the implementation of ethical guidelines' (R114, Fieldnotes: 372). The National Communications Association emphasizes the importance of using 'the right language,' such as mentioning that research subjects are 'at no greater risk than they are in their normal daily activities' (NCA, 2005: 206). However, the challenge is even greater for qualitative researchers because IRBs are unfamiliar with the language of qualitative research (Hamilton, 2005: 199). Often, they must change words to meet the IRB's needs (NCA, 2005: 227). One researcher admitted to having modified her language into more 'post-positivist'[7] terms (NCA, 2005: #55: 228).

Second, the adoption of the same language that appears on application forms is an acknowledgment, on the part of the researcher, that he/she finds that language meaningful. 'Protocol,' the 'start' and 'end' of projects, the 'length' of interviews, 'written consent,' 'confidentiality,' 'anonymity,' and 'destruction of data' are powerful concepts which, to many social researchers, have no or little meaning. One researcher at a symposium goes so far as to say, 'Say anything to make the IRB happy. You have to say something. Make it up! You invent possible research findings,' and 'you must recycle the bureaucratic language (almost like plagiarism). Use the same protocol as someone else' (Couch-Stone Symposium, 7 February 2003, Fieldnotes: 352).

However, performative language can stumble over itself, and researchers are learning to avoid certain words because they experience a greater vetting of their proposal when they use a particular term, for example, 'no risks.' Hence, researchers have learned to say 'some risk.' Similarly, ethics committees are finding that students especially overstate the 'benefits' of their research that, in turn, provides an uninvited inspection of what the benefits of the research really are (Presentation by S4-M, 22 February 2004, NCEHR Workshop, Fieldnotes: 152). We also learn in a study undertaken by the Committee of Graduate Departments of Psychology (COGDOP) that 39 per cent of researchers in psychology have 'learned to describe their projects so that no red flags are raised' (Anonymous, 2006a).

Third, researchers, especially in ESL (English as a Second Language) programs, are learning to turn away from such trigger words as 'research,' and ESL researchers are gradually retraining students (and themselves) to speak of 'student learning projects,' as a means of rethinking terminologies

that speak to student work in classrooms. One student learned to his chagrin, too late, that he should not have changed the word 'volunteer work'
to 'research' (NCA, 2005: 227).

Researchers are also learning that copying or plagiarizing successful applications will hedge their bet, but others eschew any signs of
'copying and pasting.' One researcher explicitly stated, 'I don't cut and
paste. My REB application has to have a pristine, aura quality about
it' (Interview R024-M). Invoking this kind of magic (Albas and Albas,
1989) is a form of such 'insurance,' for example, when a researcher
'waited outside the REB room and was ready to answer any questions'
(Interview E25-S). Interestingly, two researchers at the same mid-sized
university each said that they 'do not want to check up on REB membership' before submitting their application (Interviews R006-M and
R007-M). Such hesitation might spring from the belief that, if you do
not pitch your application to the interests of particular REB members, it
will be less self-serving and will have a better chance, too, of being seen
as an unadulterated document.

Second-Guessing the Ethics Committee

Perhaps the greyest of all areas of interaction relates to second-guessing
the ethics committee. Experienced researchers know that 'if you give an
IRB cause to worry, it will worry' (R098, 22 November 2002, Fieldnotes:
778). A member of an ethics committee advises not to 'include stuff in
your application that will give them grief except when it's really necessary' (Interview E25-S). The key is to 'be aware what the ethics committee asks and why, and then address the question' (R072, 27 April
2001, Fieldnotes: 762). 'Researchers,' according to Gunsalus (2003a: 3),
' "guess" what might raise questions from their IRB and choose "safer"
topics.' Another suggests to make the application a 'rhetorical document'
whereby the information is presented 'in the most persuasive way.' The
inner voice, in other words, says, 'I have learned what they want to hear
and how I should say it' (NCA, 2005: 205). Similar approaches prevail in
Australia, where '[t]he applicant tells the ethics review committee what
they want to hear, as if they know from outset the nature of the problem,
the likely outcomes of the research, and its ethical considerations' ... a
necessary, but deceitful practice (Tolich and Fitzgerald, 2006: 73).

Especially if an IRB is seeking accreditation from the Association for
the Accreditation of Human Research Protection Programs (AAHRPP),
there is the ever-present issue that 'all protocols must be certified as

scientifically and methodologically valid by department chairs or their designees' who then must sign a signature box on the submission form certifying that studies are not 'silly' (Hemmings, 2006: 16). Actually, a study by a junior scholar on odour and memory was described as 'silly' and did not proceed to the IRB (Mueller, 2007: 823).

Some clearly feel that the onus is on the researcher to have a favourable response to the review. One researcher urges his colleagues not to 'use terms that make the REB inflexible, [but] give them room' (Interview E25-S). Another one states that 'it's not just the sensitive issues you are researching but also how the researcher reacts to the REB' (Interview R002-M). The same researcher advises that, 'instead of taking on a sensitive topic and to have a lot of problems with REB, it's better to change the topic [of your research].' 'Your aim,' says another researcher, 'is to try to show you can do the research. For the REB you show confidence, without worrying the REB' (Interview R024-M).

According to another researcher, 'A template will not work; each research is different, [and you] must foresee where the REB sees dangers' (Interview R007-M). 'Get to know what RECs want to know,' says another researcher in the UK, 'and tailor [the] application accordingly' (Richardson and McMullan, 2007: 1122). These adjustments are particularly true because of the inconsistencies caused by turnover of chairs and members of ethics committees, all of which yield unpredictable changes.

No doubt the inability to second-guess the ethics committee and to instill confidence that you can do the research has led at least one researcher to begin 'doubting, [even] second-guessing herself' (Interview R173-M).

Preparing for the 'News'

The reader can already infer the elaborate personal and social contexts that presage the submission of an application to the research-ethics committee. The 'hurt perspective' is the emotional context of the preparation and is built on urban legends and personal experiences. Although these experiences reinforce the idea of two different worlds, one for research-ethics committees and one for researchers, it must be admitted that their boundaries are porous. Some chairs and some members of ethics committees were or are still researchers, after all. But, in another sense, it is important to note that researchers have no choice but to be brought into the world of the ethics regime. All sorts of interactions flow out of that new relationship.

It stands to reason to think that a researcher's experiencing the hurt perspective and finding his/her research being leveraged in the ethics-review system (whereby the system discredits his/her home discipline while at the same time insisting that it is only the ethics-review system that represents 'true' ethics) will experience shifts in one's moral career. Although largely being brought into that world reluctantly, it is remarkable how muted the resistance of researchers is, indicating a feeling of powerlessness.

This chapter has dealt primarily with how researchers warm up (or not) to submitting their proposals. To that end, it looked at how researchers passively resist or avoid the review process, how they engage in self-censorship, and how they start the study before approval is gained. The chapter then turned its gaze towards the practical steps in preparing an application, the chief characteristic of which was to create strategic ambiguity and provide the least amount of information or detail possible. The chapter also explored how researchers hedge their bets and second-guess the ethics committee as to what constitutes a good application.

The next chapter considers the reaction of researchers once they have received feedback from the ethics committees. That reaction consists of both modifying their proposals and stepping into their research. But did the research go as smoothly as proclaimed by the ethics committees and, indeed, by the researchers themselves?

11 Secondary Adjustments by Researchers

Given the complexity of the ethics regime, it should come as no surprise that while some researchers embrace the social entity of ethics committees warmly and wholeheartedly, many do not. Still others resist.[1]

The challenges of submitting a proposal to the research-ethics committee come to a head after the ethics committee has returned the application to the researcher. It is unusual for the application to return without the ethics-review committee insisting on modifications. Committees rarely reject proposals, but projects may be abandoned or withdrawn if researchers cannot face the new conditions (Israel, 2005). As was noted in an earlier chapter, delays in the review sometimes play a critical role. One anthropologist at the May 2002 annual meeting of the Canadian Anthropology Society (CASCA) in Windsor taking part in a special session on ethics (Fieldnotes: 321), mentioned that the delays caused by the review process led him to drop his research plans.[2] A neophyte researcher withdrew from a project due to the strain the research ethics review caused (Halse and Honey, 2007: 343). Surprisingly, in a study in the United Kingdom, some 30 per cent of 130 social researchers claimed they abandoned research before applying and 12 per cent did the same during the application process (Richardson and McMullan, 2007: 1122).

Reactions by Researchers to Ethics Reviews

Among all the interviews I conducted with researchers, there was not one who said that complying with the review process led him/her to more thoughtful, ethical research, and many saw the process as torturous. For example, one researcher asked, 'Do I go in for a fight or do I buckle under, save myself some time?' (R007-M). The chair of one ethics committee and a member of another committee informed me that many comply but see the process as one more bureaucratic bump to endure (Interview C11-M; Interview E25-S). Another chair identifies with the researcher and 'sees the process as torture' and as 'one of the necessary evils you have to get through' (Interview E12-M). Researchers need to comply, finds one researcher (Interview R175-M), because you will 'worry about the power aspects if the REB heard you burned the ballots.' One PhD student was told by her supervisor to 'make it [her application] less volatile.' An unusual request came from one ethics committee, indicating that the researchers would be expected to go back to REB if the researched group did not want to have the results published (Interview C09-B). The researchers complied. Malcolm Feeley (2007: 770) spoke of the requirement to approach IRBs deferentially, a strategy with which Dixon-Woods et al. agree:

> Understanding what is needed to gain ethical approval involves applicants in being competent in the Bourdieusian 'game' being played, and in particular having the competence to make the appropriate displays – of docility, of deference, of submission, and understanding themselves to be supplicants. (Dixon-Woods et al., 2007: 10)

Continuing with this theme, Dixon-Woods et al. also speak of the need for the researcher to redefine him/herself not as a researcher but as a supplicant:

> [T]he proper role of applicants is one of docility; in responding to letters [from the IRB], they must make displays of obedience and deference. In particular, unless they are to resort to the appeals mechanism, applicants are obliged to accept judgements which are inherently contestable and indeterminate as incontestable and final. (Dixon-Woods et al., 2007: 9)

'Compliance, though itself often difficult,' says Ann Hamilton (2002: 259), 'remains the path of least resistance, and the need for regulation is too rarely, nearly never questioned. There is no whying. Assimilation into the regulatory system *seems* inevitable . . . ' (emphasis in original).

The most likely response from researchers is to hunker down 'in the trenches' and carry on; this 'has been a strategy for coping with IRB hassles for scholars over the years' (Mueller, 2007: 831n81). 'This strategy,' according to John Mueller, 'may provide some psychological relief to individuals, but it serves to hide the extent of the IRB problems and speaks volumes about the failure of the censors to create an ethical research environment on campus' (Mueller, 2007: 831n81). Bach (2005) also notes that the 'non-tenured [faculty] felt compelled to abide by IRB rules even as they dictate the research' (263–4).

Researchers diminish the demands of REBs as trivial. In fact, some of these changes are quite trivial (NCA, 2005: 206). One scholars advises ' . . . just go along and play the game' (NCA, 2005: 206). One researcher confides that 'researchers will follow suggested revisions in a narrow, technical sense.' He himself 'changes the questions [in order] to pass ethics review, but still asks the original questions' (Interview R002-M).

Two ethics-committee chairs (Interview C03-M; Interview C05-B) have had to deal with irate researchers after these individuals heard that their applications came back from the ethics committee with a request for emendations. These two REB chairs noted gender differences among the irate researchers: 'men get angry, women are timid.' 'Some applicants,' says one member of an ethics committee, 'reacted strongly to the refusal to his not [getting] retroactive approval' (E16-B, Fieldnotes: 1516).[3] 'Researchers,' stated another REB chair, 'play games with REBs, probably.'

A report by the Canadian Sociology and Anthropology Association mentioned that of the fourteen members reporting their experiences with ethics review, some had 'abandoned research because researchers were questioned' by the REB (Muzzin, 2002; Fieldnotes: 566). One administrator 'does not remember ever rejecting a proposal, but some "just disappear" when a graduate student did not follow up on changes' (Interview A11-S). A member of an ethics office reported that a researcher thought it was too much trouble to change the application and withdrew it, but put another one in its place (Focus Group REB1-S). One chair talked with an instructor about working up three-year course approvals, but the instructor withdrew (Interview C12-S). Several observers of the research-ethics scene have noticed that researchers have devised a variety of strategies 'to overcome persistent rejection by IRBs, including several that actually undermine the work but that have the effect of permitting graduate students to complete their doctorates' (AAUP, 2001: 64; see also Lincoln and Tierney, 2004: 222).

One begins to wonder what 'rejecting' a proposal really means. There is, of course, the obvious meaning when a proposal gets rejected outright. But does rejection of a proposal also extend to proposals that have been so seriously changed by the ethics-review committee beyond their original form that they, in effect, have morphed into different research proposal? And what do we make of the proposals which were subject to so many emendations by the ethics committee that the researcher lost heart in making those changes?

Secondary adjustment refers to any habitual arrangement in which a researcher employs 'unauthorized' means to get around the REB's assumptions regarding what the researcher should do. However, rather than seeing secondary adjustments as norm-violating behaviour, we can see these adjustments as a normal and fair response to a social context that drives researchers to re-evaluate the ethical dimensions of their own research. This point bears repeating because it must be emphasized that it is entirely erroneous to assume that social researchers purposely circumvent the dictates of their ethics committees. Downright lying is not part of the researchers' world vis-à-vis ethics committees. Seen in its proper light, the departure point of ethics committees is the *TCPS*, a document that promotes a biomedical paradigm of research. Members of ethics committees, as we have seen, also work with a 'common sense' understanding of ethics in research, which gives leeway to all sorts of opinions about ethics. Some are on target (and many social researchers admit that those are helpful in rethinking the ethical dimensions of the research), but others are taken from the ethics-committee members' own perspectives, not even in an aggregate sense, but in the sense that one individual's opinion has more weight than someone else's. As Maureen Fitzgerald (2005: 329) has found, researchers who have acquired the committee's trust by reputation or because they played the game within its rules, 'may be allowed some latitude with a later application that might have some rough spots.' Some researchers, however, refuse to play by all of the rules, and go so far as to threaten to destroy their survey if the REB does not give approval to a cherished university project. An example of this response was shown by a researcher interested in inviting and surveying Aboriginal youth to campus to study their career choices. The event was to take place within two weeks – not enough time to get ethics approval (Interview S46-S).

With so many proposals coming back to researchers with modifications, one would expect responses from researchers detailing articles in the *TCPS* to suggest to ethics committees that they should reconsider their decision – and we have already enumerated the shortcomings of the *TCPS* with regard to social research. But researchers do not do this. As some of the above quotes reveal, researchers are more inclined to follow the ethics committees' suggestions rather than referring to the *TCPS*, for example, to counter those suggestions. One wonders whether researchers are familiar enough with the *TCPS* to argue against committee findings. Of the fourteen surveyed in the CSAA report, twelve reported that they were familiar with it, but one says that he/she has 'never seen the actual document' (Muzzin, 2002; Fieldnotes: 565). At the May 2002 CASCA meeting, I was invited to make a presentation about the concerns of anthropologists with the *TCPS*; I learned that only a very few (perhaps two or three scholars) out of the forty had actually read the document.

Invariably, once researchers manage to resubmit their proposals with the asked-for modifications, they embark on their research.

Applying Secondary Adjustments

One can speak of the underlife of an institution, where its members 'severally and collectively sustain secondary adjustments' (Goffman, 1961: 199). Secondary adjustments, according to Goffman, involve practices that deviate from institutional requirements, but do not directly challenge the staff of an institution. Sociologists are interested in the character of the social relations that the acquisition and maintenance of secondary adjustments requires (Goffman, 1961: 200).

A more serious problem, however, is that '[e]thical codes, and various ethnographic accounts,' according to David Calvey (2008: 912), 'offer a sanitized picture of social research. They offer little or at best limited nuanced understanding of the emotional, biographical and shifting character of fieldwork where ethical decisions are occasioned practices.' In this light, 50 per cent of researchers did not believe that IRBs understood the nature of their research (Newman, 2004: 9). As a consequence, some researchers see 'IRBs as a bothersome obstruction to be placated, overcome, or avoided altogether' (Pritchard, 2002: 3). Significantly, Ann Hamilton adds that qualitative researchers, in particular,

> conceded so much in fact that they can no longer do their work under the rules. Perhaps inventing circumventions is somehow better, easier, involves less conflict, causes less trouble, etc. than casting off an impotent system.... Eventually the 'real' world must be 'really' encountered, i.e., experienced. (Hamilton, 2002: 259)

Changing the Research without Telling the REB

It is quite common for ethics committees to force researchers to describe their research in ways that are unfamiliar to them. 'A total of 67 per cent,' of respondents in a recent National Health Service study in the United Kingdom, 'disagreed or strongly disagreed that questions on the research ethics forms were appropriate for social research' (Richardson and McMullan, 2007: 1122). For example, one researcher initially phrased his collaborative research project as one involving 'research participants,' rather than 'collaborators.' When the research got underway, he returned to working with them as 'collaborators' (Muzzin, 2002; Fieldnotes: 565). This is a perfect illustration of what appears to be a change in the research that is actually a non-change. Similarly, even though a researcher changed questions on the interview guide (from what was originally indicated in the REB application), nothing has really changed in the research (R002-M). Such 'situationally justified actions' are quite common among social researchers.

To what extent do researchers conduct their research in spite of the modifications demanded or requested by the ethics committee? There will always be '*situationally justified actions* . . . in the field of policing . . . [a] situation being similar to what researchers . . . face in the lifeworld, [where] [r]egulations will never be able to account for every situation, and oversight can never be complete' (Hamilton, 2002: 264; emphasis in original). Besides, the decision and the power to change the demands of the ethics committees vary, depending on whether one is a junior or senior scholar. As Feeley avers,

> IRBs subject researchers to petty tyranny. Graduate students and junior scholars are particularly likely to be caught in their web – and for them, IRB tyranny is often more than petty. Senior scholars are generally more adept at avoidance, evasion, and adaptation, but they too are hardly exempt from this tyranny. (Feeley, 2007: 765)

The relevance and meaning of change during one's research project depends in part on whether one does positivistic or inductive research. The strength of inductive (qualitative) research is the researcher's changing strategies or techniques of research as new avenues of insights and analyses open up. Not changing the strategy is more the exception than the rule. No one can predict these new avenues when a researcher submits a proposal to the research-ethics committee. Whether the

changes in the course of research are minor or major is not terribly relevant for social researchers. However, from the perspective of some ethics committees who are firmly grounded in the biomedical approach,
any changes (whether minor or major) might fly against *any* approved
plans of research. According to Dixon-Woods et al. (2007), 'few options
other than to comply [with the ethics committees] are, in practice, available' and a researcher who 'disagrees therefore takes a significant risk
of an unfavourable opinion,' delays, and an intolerable appeals process. This knowledge 'makes applicants disinclined to challenge what
in many cases is challengeable' (10).

There is thus a huge gap in the understanding each party has of what
might be understood as 'change of research plans' and what constitutes
minor or major changes. Technically, researchers must refer all 'significant' changes back to the ethics committee for approval. Naturally, there
are wide differences in opinion regarding what constitutes a 'significant' change. One person who had actively participated in creating one
of the final drafts of the *TCPS* agreed that the idea of significant change
is a contentious issue (Personal Communication from E06 to author, 7
May 2005). He prefers interpreting this term in terms of any new risk
to the research participant involving a change in research plans. *The
Seduction of Ethics* shows that there is no common ground that would
even permit researchers and ethics committees to reflect constructively
on these matters. John Mueller (2007: 823) found that 'researchers and
students will predictably do just what is required, and little more ... The
committees exhibit no trust of researchers, and researchers chafe at the
actions of the committees; there is no feeling of being peers engaged in
a common mission.' One researcher confesses, 'there are many ways to
be cooperative with the IRB so that you get quick approval ... without
really following all their guidelines' (NCA, 2005: 210).

It is not unusual for researchers *not* to go back to the ethics committee
when making changes to their research. Researchers are hesitant to go
back to the Local Research Ethics Committee because either the project
will not be approved or the response will not be timely (Truman, 2003:
10). Twenty-one per cent of surveyed social researchers said they had
modified the research design after obtaining approval and then continued to conduct the research without gaining further permission for the
modifications (Richardson and McMullan, 2007: 1122). Among psychologists, 41 per cent of researchers made changes without going back to
the IRB (Anonymous, 2006a). The same researchers report that it is fear
that the IRB will not re-approve the research that prevents their going

back. Some members of the audience at the Couch-Stone Symposium advised that researchers abandon the IRB requirements altogether and stop using consent forms (7 February 2003, Fieldnotes: 352). Related to this, a young researcher explained her previous experience with her study on birders who did *not* want to sign a consent form, who said, 'I invited you into our home, made you a meal. Why would I have to sign the form?' (Interview R173-M). One PhD student was not inclined to adopt a literal approach and did not tell her (literal-minded) co-researcher that she changed the interview schedule because that would make the co-researcher believe that this violated REB policy. The same graduate student had promised the REB that interviews would last thirty minutes, but they in fact lasted three and a half hours (Interview R024-M). The graduate student must have had an uneasy relationship with her REB, who believed she was 'pestering respondents' although she had followed the usual research design when she sent her research participants a postal reminder that they still had an opportunity to fill out the survey. Another PhD student who was doing fieldwork was not permitted to collect data from one participant. As a result, he decided to ask the remaining participants in his study for their own 'recollection' of that participant (R093-B, Fieldnotes: 850). In another example, quite innovatively, Bhattacharya (2007: 1111) tells how his member-checking[4] turned into the research participant's using photos to elicit her experiences, in addition to participant observation, multiple conversations, and peer debriefings with people who knew the participant.

Increasingly, ethics committees are insisting that researchers provide an annual report of their research (and sometimes this requirement demands that a report should be forthcoming after three years or upon completion of the research). Some researchers do not respond to the request that they must get their approval renewed (S30-M, Fieldnotes: 957). What also strikes them as an 'absurdity' of IRBs is the demand for continuing reviews until 'you are no longer doing analysis of data.' Under those conditions, researchers clearly distinguish between data-gathering and analysis in an effort to keep their analysis separate from IRB monitoring (NCA, 2005: 210).

Subverting the Process

A more detailed study will be necessary to reveal how researchers are subverting the process. The subversion does tend to follow disciplines recalcitrant to ethics-review process such as political science (Hauck,

2008: 1). One way of subverting the process is for researchers to resort to making unrealistic demands of their IRBs (Bach, 2005: 259), or to submit an offhand application, just to tease the IRB. The 'invention of circumvention' is another technique employed, when researchers engaged in fieldwork often 'confess to professional misdemeanours,' namely, the ones mentioned by Gans (1982: 405).

A PhD researcher in her forties, who has been on research teams in the past, is still 'amazed at the level of subversion of researchers even after a few years' (Interview R024-M). Some researchers play the ethics committee off their own ill-founded suggestions, seen in the case of a researcher in psychology conducting research on his/her students. When the IRB said that asking students to write a five- to seven-page essay was too coercive (when classmates did not want to participate in the professor's research which would also give them points in the course), the researcher said that he/she would ask students to write a two- to three-page essay, knowing full well that *no* student would write any essay anyway (NCA, 2005: 206)!

The Social Situation of Students in the Ethics-Review Process

Students will discard the mantle of quiet resistance, maladjustments, and indifference worn by veteran researchers, partly out of obsession, out of powerlessness, and out of naivety.

The Obsession of Students Regarding Ethics Review versus Seeing Ethics Review as an Obstacle

Every instructor notes the matter-of-factness of research-ethics review in the hearts and minds of students, whether undergraduate or graduate. There is the thrill of astonishment when students learn about 'older' ethnographies, and for a few, the realization dawns that ethics review is now directing research in other, less interesting directions. But many have an obsession with ethics review (see, for example, Hamilton, 2002: 16). Too numerous are off-the-cuff comments such as, 'Did you go through ethics for that?' when a group of researchers and students informally gather to talk about past and present research ideas. The comment is intended to be humorous, but it does indicate that students accept ethics review as a necessary part of a researcher's life. Instructors are also astonished by the sense of urgency that students feel when the students feel obliged to cover every aspect of their research with ethics-review committees. An informal discussion with a professor in his/her office at the same university as the student's now requires a review by the ethics committee. Still, there is some nervousness about students wanting to pass everything through ethics review. An ethics-committee chair mentions that the typical question the committee gets from students is. Do I need to go through my department? To that chair, it seems more logistics related than ethics related (Interview C12-S). Such an approach no doubt ties into students wanting to see their research going 'through ethics' as fast as possible. 'They are,' says one REB chair, 'looking for the most efficient way to get a degree' (C09-B, Fieldnotes: 414). Still, ethics review is one more hoop to jump through. What has this to do with real ethics, one might ask? Does it breed cynicism or pragmatism rather than ethical sensitivity?

The obsession with going over every detail of the research with research-ethics review may get some students into trouble. For example, one student was required by her university to use two methods in her thesis, but the REB made it impossible for her to do participant observations (she required a written consent from all those who attended a convention where she was planning to do the observations); all she could do was interviews. As a result, the student was filled with self-doubt and she started to second-guess herself (R173-M). One student presented a research proposal to her IRB, but it took several months and repeated modifications and guarantees before the IRB reluctantly approved the proposal. The student 'nearly abandoned the project in favor of a safe and sterile study' (Lincoln and Tierney, 2004: 225). In the case of Tamara O'Doherty, a master's student, the review process took so long that the university awarded her a two-semester tuition fee waiver in the end because of the delays caused by 'actions of the Research Ethics Board' (R136-M, Fieldnotes: 404).

The Relationship between Students and Supervisors

The relationship between students and supervisors with respect to research-ethics review is uneven. In some instances, a supervisor of an undergraduate student did not mention that the student had to submit a research proposal because 'she was concerned that if submitted, the research would not have been completed by the end of the semester' (NCA, 2005: 222). Students face conflicting information from professors, administrators, and other graduate students (Couch-Stone Symposium, Fieldnotes: 352). In a report commissioned by the Canadian Sociology and Anthropology Association, respondents mentioned that 'we teach students too little about ethics and that REBs are gatekeepers' (Muzzin, 2002; Fieldnotes: 568). A member of an ethics committee mentioned that 'faculty are not diligent in helping students go through REB' (Interview E12-M).

There are a number of accounts that indicate that supervisors tend to steer students away from topics requiring ethics review (R131, Fieldnotes: 601; Pritchard, 2002: 10, citing AAUP Report of 2001). A meeting of United States sociologists urged students to do research as part of a course (Couch-Stone Symposium, 7 February 2003, Fieldnotes: 352). We also learn about a professor who is no longer encouraging students to collect data first-hand, but to do a literature search instead so that their research is exempt from ethics review (Interview R002-M). Linda Shopes of the Oral History Association learned that '[s]ome graduate advisors ... have reported that students are reluctant to undertake projects that involve oral history interviewing on controversial topics for fear that this will cause difficulties with their IRB' (Shopes, 2002: 5). As Ann Hamilton (2002: 220) observes, many graduate students and faculty members ... '*circulate advice* about what sorts of studies should be avoided (or adopted) if reasonably quick IRB approval is to happen. Their advice is based on their own individual histories with the IRB, what they feel they understand of the IRB policies, and rumor, too.'

We also learn that students, who are influenced by professors who are cynical about the ethics-review process, do not take it seriously (Interview R173-M). When a student went to her supervisor regarding a legal clause on consent, her supervisor said she was not going to fight the ethics battle on account of legalities (Interview R173-M). The whole experience can cause a PhD student to withdraw from academic work entirely. Her REB wanted her to make many changes, not just in her proposal, but in the research itself: 'I'm resigned to the fact that I can't do the work I want to do [sexual relations between teachers and students] – at least not yet ... But that's okay. As much as I love it here, I just want to get my degree and get on with my life now ... Graduate school had lost its romanticism' (Johnson, 2008: 221). The loss of innocence has become a common experience for graduate students.

Novice Innocence and Research Methods

Given the cynicism of supervisors, students often face research-ethics committees on their own, either through their applications or in face-to-face meetings. Faculty themselves 'would tell students to talk to someone on the REB' (Interview E27-S). In the absence of faculty advising graduate students about 'going through ethics,' some students implore folks on various LISTSERVS to help them (Fieldnotes: 753). A supervisor reported that 'a student tried to argue her way through research ethics review – it didn't work' (Interview R006-M). In this context, the 'system rewards deference: graduate students leave; junior faculty are not likely to have historical perspective on freedom of enquiry and will follow REBs, as do sessionals' (Mueller, 2007: 824).

There are several sources causing methods to transform in the social sciences. One of them is connected to students doing their own advocacy facing their ethics committee. Because students deal directly with ethics committees, they are not in a position to defend conventional social science methods when ethics committees challenge them on those methods. As Hamilton (2002: 257) avers, 'Some individuals (I would argue students are an especially relevant group in this situation) are susceptible to manipulation, which can lead to domination by a group or (an automated) structure.' Moreover, ethics committees feel compelled to acknowledge and overcome the 'gaps of naivety among student researchers who REBs must help out' (S30-M, Fieldnotes: 960). In this exchange, members of ethics offices or of ethics committees are helping students out with their ethical/methodological dilemmas. One chair said that it is 'never too early for students to encounter and learn about 'responsible conduct of research' (C14-M, Fieldnotes: 721). Another chair of an ethics committee informs me that 'being REB chair allows him to better teach ethics to students' (Interview C12-S). These processes ensure that students are well socialized in the ethics-review culture.

Some students are reported to have been 'a bit resentful. The students resented the extra piece of work an ethics application requires, and wanted a checklist instead' (Interview R118-M). Naturally, many REB members and staff of ethics offices are either not trained to do research or are unacquainted with social science methods. This gap in the knowledge of ethics offices determines 'the fate of students who take on interdisciplinary approach, but few REB members can step out of their own discipline' (R144-M, Fieldnotes: 520).

This and the previous chapters constitute some of the core chapters in *The Seduction of Ethics*. We see that some researchers abandon their project before it is reviewed by the ethics committee or even during the review process itself. Researchers have learned to accept the mandated changes from the ethics committee with deference – because this is the path of least resistance. Otherwise, protracted delays and appeals can ensue, dampening the research project as a whole.

The ethics committees and researchers may not see eye-to-eye on the mandated changes. Often, the changes do not speak to the nature of the research project, especially in qualitative research – the application forms, after all, normally do not contain the spirit of the social research. The proposals are, in reality, sanitized versions of research; research on the ground shifts from the image contained in the original proposal to the one desired by the ethics committee. There are thus huge gaps of understanding between the researcher and the ethics committee about social research, especially when the committee operates with a biomedical model in mind.

As a consequence, researchers tend to trivialize the proposed changes put forward by ethics-review committees. Since they cannot exhibit open contempt or resistance to the asked-for changes, they must invent circumventions, or 'secondary adjustments.' However, there are a few cases where researchers purposely subvert the process such as by looping back on the very suggestions that the committee has made.

Finally, this chapter explores the social situation of students. Students are obsessed by ethics review; some are eager to submit their proposals, while others get discouraged by the process. With respect to research-ethics review, the relationship between students and supervisors does not come easily. Supervisors convey their cynicism regarding ethics review to their students. However, there is one critical element that students inadvertently contribute to the meme of *The Seduction of Ethics*. They play a role in transforming the methods of the social sciences because they often face the demands of the ethics committees all alone. They are grateful to accept proposals from ethics committees regarding their planned strategies for the research. However, because they are not historically versed in the conventions of social research, the students are open to suggestions from committees who have a limited understanding of social research.

The next two chapters dovetail our concerns; as students increasingly adopt the perspective of research-ethics committees (and their staff) about how to do research, the opportunities to express genuine social research, rich in its diverse methods, are dwindling. As the following chapters demonstrate, all have a hand in the homogenization and pauperization of social research – ethics committees and their staff, and researchers themselves.

12 The Beleaguered Methods

I have already alluded to some of the ways in which research-ethics review has an impact on social science research. This chapter examines more closely how research-ethics review is not only redirecting social research itself but has also resulted in the decline of certain methods. As the following chapter shows, no less serious is the impact of research-ethics review on theory and on choice of research topics. It is also true that the review has resulted in the maintenance and even increase in the use of particular methods.

General Considerations about Redirecting Research

There are at least four general elements that account for the redirection of research as a result of decisions by research-ethics committees. The review process, according to Malcolm Feeley (2007: 762), 'places enormous burdens on empirical researchers and thus dramatically affects the nature and form of social science enquiry.'

First, the pressures that ethics committees put on researchers are unmistakable, but these pressures reflect the wider, structural conditions that ethics committees themselves work under. The commodification of knowledge, for example, brings new pressures to bear on academic life by 'linking student admission to faculty funding' (Lewis, 2008: 687). Researchers face competing obligations: they must pursue capital-intensive research, involve students in the most expeditious manner, and satisfy the demands of ethics-review committees. These obligations create a unique space in which, according to Julianne Cheek (2007: 1051–2), researchers are 'being worked over' by that space, rather than being allowed to position themselves to 'work within, and on' it. As the situation currently stands, researchers believe that they ought to comply with the dictates of ethics committees even though those dictates might compromise their research. They believe these compromises are a small burden to bear when measured against the need to get on with the research, get research grants, and employ students.

Second, the particular configuration of membership of ethics-review committees plays a silent hand in redirecting research. Stuart Derbyshire (2006: 46–7) points out that community members have an impact on the redirection of research, because they have 'no stake' in promoting theoretical, methodological, and ethical integrity of the research itself, because they unpack methods, theory, and purpose of research, and all of these interconnected. He finds that with the presence of community members on ethics committees, researchers 'will have to be sensitive,' thus '[r]esearch questions will be restricted to conventional, safe, and popular areas, inquiry will be characterised by deference rather than challenging established wisdom and censorship will replace academic freedom' (50). John Mueller, a noted observer of the impact of ethics committees, believes that censorship has become key rather than screening for safety (2007: 810). In some cases, researchers themselves have taken on the burden of self-censorship, as is the case with a historian who admits that 'if the ethical considerations are going to overrule the project, then I'll simply drop the project or start afresh from a more informed place' (R154, Fieldnotes: 665). What is more, according to Jack Katz (2007: 801), we find 'a miniscule set of faculty exercise oversight over a wide variety of methods.' Accordingly, 'some lines of inquiry are opened up, others are closed down.'

Third, there are forces that are redirecting research. Annette Hemmings (2006: 12) points out that the 'seemingly intractable divides [between ethical ideas in social research and principles endorsed by IRBs] ... have, in some cases, scuttled the research despite its potential benefits.' *The Seduction of Ethics* has already illustrated numerous alternate conceptions of ethics as pronounced by ethics codes and ethics committees compared to the ethics dimensions visited by social researchers. It is difficult to find a compromise between these alternating conceptions of ethics in research.

Fourth, the ethics committee's exaggerated desire to have the researcher explain the whole research exercise to participants (even though the explanation falls short of setting out surprising or uneventful aspects of the research) alters the 'real world.' Ann Hamilton points out that,

> once they [participants] are affected, researchers are, simply, no longer studying the 'real' world, but an altered research environment – an artificial

world comparable to those of the social psychological experiment and the social survey. And it is altered for no good *purpose:* not the fear of harming humans, but the fear of harming the rules, the *process* . . . I'm sceptical about changing, affecting, manipulating the natural environment and referring to the data gathered in that environment as 'empirical' data. This situation is the result of what I have called 'required but unnecessary' regulatory requirements. (Hamilton, 2002: 253–4; emphasis in original)

This context does not provide a healthy stimulus for research. Malcolm Feeley (2007: 769) has found that some researchers have abandoned their projects. C. Kristina Gunsalus' knowledge of the impact of research-ethics review testifies that research has been 'delayed, sometimes forbidden or, perhaps more commonly, abandoned' (2003a: 2). If researchers are not inclined to abandon their projects, they 'settle for more easily approved methods' (Feeley, 2007: 770). Even so, 51 per cent of surveyed social researchers in the United Kingdom have, as a result of the mandates of ethics committees, changed their research design for the worse at least once during the past five years (only 32 per cent believe they made changes for the better) (Richardson and McMullan, 2007: 1122).

Although the full effects of the redirection of research are not immediately known, there is a consensus that there may now be a 'whole generation of scholars who take this regime of censorship for granted' (Feeley, 2007: 770). In the same study of social researchers in the United Kingdom, Richardson and McMullan (2007: 1125) found that of the 131 respondents, sixteen (12 per cent) who were postgraduate supervisors or course leaders, reported that master's students are 'now qualifying without having had experience of empirical research in Health.' The following pages will deepen our understanding of the phenomenon of disappearing future empirical researchers.

The next few pages will also attest to the transformation of methods in social research. The transformation has been uneven. Some methods are now in decline, while others are on the rise. Still, some methods seem unaffected by the deepening crisis brought on by research-ethics review.

The Declining Use of Particular Methods

What constitutes the crisis brought on by research-ethics review is the decline of methods that have traditionally been at the heart of social research methods, namely, fieldwork/participant observation, covert research, action research, and the fate of data. The wounds run deep, and they cut across the grain of social research.

The Collapse of Fieldwork/Participant-Observation

A wide spectrum of researchers (many of whom are referred to in the next sections) agree that fieldwork is on the decline.

Sometimes the wounds are self-inflicted, such as when researchers are eager to appease an ethics committee or when a student does not want any undue delay in his/her graduate program. Conducting field research is far more complex and time-consuming than library or other forms of research. Among the other factors associated with the decline of fieldwork is the perception that it might involve a higher degree of risk than is the case for other types of research. Related to this, some scholars have noted even a decline in school fieldwork in a 'risk society' (for example, Cook, 2006).

The ethics regime is thus creating a new generation of students and scholars who are not familiar with doing fieldwork or participant-observation. Jack Katz (2007:804) finds that students now express 'amazement' at early ethnographies that used both methods.[1] Ann Hamilton (2002: 234), citing Punch, Becker, and others, speaks about the need for students to do research out on the street as the 'proper way' of learning about research. There is abundant advice found in qualitative methods textbooks that spells out this important need in research.

However, as Jack Katz avers (2007: 805), 'participation observation studies that ranged over hobohemia and through taxi-dance halls . . . are now routinely in violation of ethical rules because . . . they cannot meet IRB prior review requirements in a meaningful way.'[2] The 'require-ments,' according to Hamilton, 'threaten the existence of much street-style ethnography' (2005: 197, citing Weppner, 1977). There are legion accounts of researchers prevented from doing fieldwork or taking notes in anticipation of conducting research more formally, whether taking notes while leading a Bible study class in prison (NCA, 2005: 227) or doing fieldwork in a community where the researcher has conducted fieldwork during most of his/her whole academic life:

> The decisions of the REB at our university do not allow for naturalistic observation under any circumstances. Further, it is not possible to syste-matize information from seventeen years of ongoing contact with mem-bers of the community without their consent . . . [W]hat is the ethical field

worker to do to ensure that everyone they come across is informed that research is being done. Perhaps a forehead sign is the route to go! (Okihiro, 2000: 9)

The same researcher confesses that 'I am currently in a state of anomie in regards to the possibility of doing naturalistic field work' (Okihiro, 2000: 8). Some, like Rachel Hurdley, spoke of an 'unpeopled ethnography' (2010: 517). Elliott Leyton, a noted social anthropologist who has been doing important ethnographic work, admits,

> I know damned well that under the new rules I would never have been able to get funding for two of my most important critical books, *Dying Hard*, which took on [name of the company] for its poisoning of hundreds of workers; and *Bureaucracy and World View*, which critiqued [a provincial agency] for manipulating, lying to, and withholding monies from dying miners. (Email from Elliott Layton, 11 July 2003, Fieldnotes: 471)[3]

Another researcher 'balked' at one of the required changes, namely, to delete the audio recording, transcription, classroom observation, focus groups, video recording and the clarifications in writing as they 'constitute an unacceptable level of risk to the subjects.' He continues, 'I understood and accepted that I couldn't do classroom observations or focus groups, but how was I supposed to conduct an interview study without audiotapes and transcripts or follow-up email correspondence?' (Johnson, 2008: 221). Sometimes, the reluctance of ethics committees to promote or approve ethnographic research leads researchers to pursue their interest in the topic along different lines, with chagrin. A researcher dropped his original plans for field research 'in favor of proposals to study data sets already gathered and approved' (Katz, 2007: 804).

The following identifies specific changes in specific fields.

Anthropology. Some researchers have made attempts to document more systematically the fall of field research. Van den Hoonaard and Anita Connolly (2006), in their study of Canadian master's theses in anthropology over a ten-year period (1995 to 2004), explore the extent to which the theses represent a change in the number, topic, or methodology as a result of formal ethics-review guidelines that came into force in Canada in 2001. Contrary to expectations by social researchers that ethics review would discourage research, the number of master's theses in anthropology in Canadian universities actually increased between 1995 and 2004. There were 730 theses on record, averaging

73 per year. Three of the years in which the number of theses completed was higher than average occurred *after* the formal introduction of the *TCPS* in 2001.

Another surprising finding was that the proportion of master's theses *involving research participants* had actually increased. In 1995, 25 per cent (n=19) of the 290 theses involved research participants, and by the time the *TCPS* was universally adopted by Canadian universities in 2001, the proportion rose to 37.3 per cent (n=22). However, it is important to note that while students doing master's theses refer to themselves as doing 'ethnographic' or 'qualitative' research, in fact in very many instances they *solely* use interviews as a research method. This redefinition of ethnographic research is perhaps inevitable in light of the difficulty that undergraduate students experience in securing ethics approval for doing even simple participant-observation exercises for pedagogical or apprenticeship purposes. This lack of experience and training has thus prevented students from delving into ethnographic research in which interviews might simply be one component. An anthropologist (Interview R006-M) admits there are now 'serious problems' for anthropological research. He himself has had 'no chance to do extended fieldwork since his PhD along with the *TCPS*.' The pauperization of anthropology is now endemic and intrinsically connected to following ethics-review procedures. Another professor (Interview R002-M) lets his students do participant-observation in public spaces so that they can avoid ethics review. Still another professor confesses that 'given the limited amount of time to get the approval from REB, a researcher is tempted to forego the detailed revisions of a participant observation proposal (which would take up most of the summer) and be inclined to do just interviews which would more easily pass REB' (Interview R006-M).

Sociology. The kinds of qualitative research theses referred to in this chapter involve face-to-face or person-to-person interaction.[4] This approach is inductive, for it relies on data derived from interaction with research participants to enable the researcher to come up with insights, themes, and future areas of research to explore. Following the recent Discussion Paper (June 2006) prepared by the Social Sciences and Humanities Research Ethics Special Working Committee of the Interagency Advisory Panel on Research Ethics, qualitative and interpretive research

> . . . fosters the *emergence* of concepts and theories, as well as specific research strategies in the course of doing research. Qualitative and interpretative research *seeks to engage* the researcher with the data, while paying

close attention to the world of the research participants themselves. The research questions, the direction of the research, and the kinds of data to be gathered are evolving elements in this kind of research.

Qualitative and interpretive researchers typically adopt the perspective that only after a researcher has entered the world of the research participants, research field, or social setting will he or she be equipped to define and pursue appropriate research questions and issues. Although initial research questions may be outlined in the research plan, Research Ethics Boards (REBs) should be aware that it is quite common for specific questions (as well as shifts in methodological procedures) to emerge during the research project. (SSHWC, 2006; emphasis in original)

Qualitative research includes ethnography, participant-observation, field research, participatory-action research, oral history, feminist action research, and inductive research, among others.

In terms of the extent to which research participants were involved in master's theses, one can compare 1995 (six years before the *TCPS* came into force in 2001) with 2004, which is three years after the *TCPS* came into effect.[5] My study in that area (van den Hoonaard, 2006) shows that the proportion of theses that involves research participants has decreased from 31 per cent in 1995 to 8 per cent in 2004.[6] Of theses involving research participants, the decrease in the number involving fieldwork is even more stunning: 40 per cent included fieldwork in 1995, while only 5 per cent did so in 2004. These findings reflect what J. Platt (2006) found in her study of research methodologies used in Canadian sociology. Across the board there has been a noticeable paucity of books in sociology directly involving research participants. The decrease of theses in fieldwork is particularly alarming for a significant segment of sociology that must derive its material mainly from fieldwork.

Indeed, as if to reinforce the finding that fieldwork-based theses are in the decline, a researcher from a large Ontario university (Interview R016-M) had noted there has been an immense decline at the Qualitative Analysis Conferences (that has a high attendance of graduate students) of subcultural research. This is partly due to ethics review and due to the decline of participant-observation research as a research tool (R016, Notes on Presentations, 14 May 2004).[7] For sociologists, the decline in fieldwork is nothing short of drastic for a number of reasons. Master's theses were the traditional point of entry into doing fieldwork, leading to more sophisticated fieldwork for the PhD thesis and onward. The decline in fieldwork at the master's level in Canada also means that one of the key traditional theoretical perspectives, symbolic interactionism, remains unfulfilled for many sociology students.[8]

Students wanting to conduct fieldwork typically face a lengthy barrage of questions from ethics committees. For example, one student (Interview R032-M) was hoping to study an international 'secret' society. His research involved fieldwork, including interviews and some focus groups. In preparing for the ethics review, he believed his REB would worry about invasion of privacy. He had been putting together consent forms, but what 'got him down' was a long list of questions prepared by the REB. He had become too busy by then to be able to spend time on the forms (Notes on Presentations, 9 April 2005). Another researcher took fieldnotes during her shift at a call centre, but was banned by the IRB from using those notes directly. Instead, she admitted,

> I interviewed myself formally and mixed my interview among the others I conducted, later being careful to afford no more weight to my own perceptions than the others. This odd process allowed me to access my own experience, and seemed to calm the IRB considerably. (R063, Fieldnotes: 385)

A prominent Canadian researcher told me in an interview (R001-M) that he is a good field researcher and his early work always involved fieldwork. After the introduction of the *TCPS*, he refocused his approach and is now only analysing secondary databases. The Research Office, he thinks, is now 'policing' research rather than 'nurturing' it. In the United States, there is no less a pressure for researchers to abandon ethnographic research:

> The current brouhaha over IRBs has emerged since 2000 primarily from [President] Clinton's directive to federal agencies to review their protocols for human subjects protections. A few highly publicized sanctions against major research institutions reinforced the perception that institutional IRBs should be zealous. As an example suggests, sometimes the questions posed by ethics committees to ethnographers border on the absurd. (Email from Jim Thomas, 21 November 2002, Fieldnotes: 772)

A study of what master's theses say about research ethics reveals, with very few exceptions, a pro forma approach. Their statements touch the major, obligatory elements of ethics such as confidentiality, anonymity, free and informed consent, et cetera, and appendices usually offer no more than a copy of the 'consent form,' but there is not a whisper that might speak to the process and routine of seeking approval from the REB.[9] There is no *direct* indication of personal struggles with the REB or any ethical conflicts with the research. The statements, in fact, look quite bland.[10]

Nevertheless, when reading between the lines, one can get a hint of the social dynamics between the student and the REB. One graduate student, Lesley Woodman (2000: 47) speaks of the 'consent form that was *eventually* approved by the Committee' (emphasis added). She also reports that the adolescents she sought to contact found that the REB requirement to contact the legal guardian 'annoying' (48). Some had severed ties with their guardians, while others saw this as an intrusion. A number of the adolescents declined to participate in the research. Her struggles between the demands of her REB and the research participants are obvious. Karen Hindle's statement on ethics reveals the labyrinthine process of weighing the practical, legal, and ethical aspects when interviewing lawyers (2004: 62–6). Marie-José Frenette's thesis on the management of time during incarceration explains her basic acceptance of ethics codes, but points also to the shortcomings of such standardized ethics procedures (2003: 63–7). In his thesis on refugees, Gabrielle Lavigne (2002: 39) writes, 'Though this whole process [of securing ethics approval] was frustrating and it seemed that there was no end to the letters that needed writing, permissions that were needed, forms that needed preparing etc., I have to honestly say that I learned a lot.' She adds that 'the process was long.'

From my interviews and chats with academic supervisors and other academics in nearly fifty universities across Canada, it comes to light that such struggles are, in fact, quite common.[11] Even REB chairs (e.g., Interview C03-M) found there is a decrease in fieldwork. A student researcher (in a large Ontario university) had difficulty getting her proposal through ethics review because she was researching folks in the finance department of an organization and the REB considered the staff of the department to be too busy to be interrupted by a graduate student (Interview R022-B).

One of the chief challenges of 'going through ethics' is the how time-consuming it is. For example, a dean at a medium-sized Atlantic university mentioned the case of a student who was asked by a school board to do research, but the research was almost abandoned because there was not enough time for it to go through an ethics review at the university.

Eventually, the dean wrote a letter to the REB and the research started the following year (Interview R005-M).

The eventual disappearance of this characteristic aspect of sociological research will add to the blandness of sociological work in general. On a wider scale, it should be noted that a 1996 survey in *Contemporary Sociology* revealed that out of the nineteen most influential books in sociology, ten (53 per cent) were ethnographies. Among the twenty-five sociology best-sellers (i.e., those books that have sold more than 100,000 copies), thirteen (52 per cent) were ethnographies. Fieldwork is an important, relevant, and distinctive tradition in sociology (and anthropology). Its dismissal through research-ethics review indicates, indeed, a perturbing new trend.

Table 12.1 reveals the proportion of presentations at the Canadian Qualitative Research Conference which have been held in Ontario and New Brunswick since the early 1980s.[12] The conference has been the main place where qualitative researchers meet to share their findings, theories, and methodologies. Although the conference always shifts in the kinds of disciplines and theoretical paradigms it draws, one can see the drastic drop in the proportion of papers based on ethnographic fieldwork by Canadians. In 1984, some 76 per cent of the papers were based on such fieldwork, whereas in 2007, for example, only 14.5 per cent displayed findings from fieldwork. Increasingly, presentations are about theory, concepts, autobiographies, and the like. This great shift of interest occurred between 2000 and 2001 as Canada's ethics regime came into effect. In 1999, there were still many presentations based on fieldwork (32.6 per cent), but in 2002 they dropped to well below 19 per cent. In 2007, only 14.8 per cent of the presentations at the Canadian Qualitatives involved field research.

The decline in the proportion of academic presentations at conferences (such as at the Canadian Qualitatives) is a prelude to the decrease in the proportion of scholarly books that use ethnographic field research. For example, as a member of a committee devoted to assessing book manuscripts under subvention by Canada's Aid to Scholarly Publications Program, I note that between 2006 and 2008, the proportion of ethnographies declined from 31 per cent in 2006 (n=4) to 25 per cent in 2007 (n=4), and finally to 10 per cent in 2008 (n=1). Although the absolute numbers are small, they do fall in line with earlier observations about the decline in work involving ethnographic field research.

No one can simply fault the introduction of the ethics regime for such a decline in fieldwork. As *The Seduction of Ethics* indicates elsewhere, the

Table 12.1   Proportion of Studies Involving Field Research Presented at the 'Canadian Qualitatives,' Selected Years (1984–2007)

Year	Total Number of Papers (Canadian-Based)	Proportion Involving Field Research
1984	25	76.0 %
1990	47	31.9 %
1993	46	39.1 %
1995	61	49.2 %
1997	87	35.6 %
1999	86	32.6 %
Mean, 1984–99	58.7	44.1 %
2002	55	18.2 %
2004	67	17.9 %
2007	88	14.8 %
Mean, 2002–7	70	17.0 %

Source: The author's personal collection of abstracts and papers of the 'Canadian Qualitatives,' 1984, and 1990–2007.

shifts also express a trend among graduate students to speed up their thesis work – doing ethnographic fieldwork cannot achieve that objective in a timely fashion. With the subsequent fall of conducting fieldwork as part of doing graduate research, the cohort of future researchers versed in this technique will also drop, leading to even further decline. But what replaces fieldwork? As the next chapter illustrates, more and more researchers are resorting to using interviews as the *sole* research technique. (In 1984, no presentations by Canadians suggested that only interviews were used in their research; by 2007, this constituted 34.1 per cent.)

As a consequence of pressures from the social science community, Canada is aiming to change its national research-ethics codes. In November 2001, the three federal granting agencies established the Interagency Advisory Panel on Research Ethics, whose goal was to serve as a trustee of the *TCPS* and to make it a 'living document,' implying that the *TCPS* had to make more room for researchers in the social sciences and humanities. In 2003, the panel established the Social Sciences and Humanities Research Ethics Special Working Committee. Its mandate was to bring forward textual suggestions, both small and large, that would accommodate the concerns of researchers in the social sciences and humanities. In the meantime it has produced a report entitled *Giving Voice to the Spectrum* (SSHWC, 2004) that details complaints and possible suggestions for improvements. In 2006, the Committee elaborated on its desire to change the *TCPS* and made another appeal to scholars to suggest changes. Finally, in December 2009, the Interagency Advisory Panel on Research Ethics issued its first full draft of a new *TCPS*, incorporating most of the changes recommended by SSHWC into chapter 11 of the document, wholly devoted to qualitative research (PRE, 2009). However, as ethics review of scholarly research has become a more institutionalized feature and routine of life in universities, some find it hard to visualize the possibility of change.

In some respects, the insistence by ethics committees for researchers to engage in 'member-checking' has the same result (this chapter will later consider member-checking in greater detail). What is more, the boundaries between the informal and formal start of the research are quite opaque in social research. Following the long-established procedures that were also advocated by C. Wright Mills (1959), sociologists and anthropologists hoping to conduct field research take notes as they pursue their everyday lives, hoping that something will emerge from those notes that might become indispensably useful once a research project really gets underway. For REBs to categorically and summarily dismiss those notes as irrelevant and their use as 'unethical' is a bizarre position to take. Malcolm Feeley (2007: 768) notes the 'falling into disuse of fieldnotes taken before the research was approved.' Stating it more forcefully, Ann Hamilton (2005: 195) argues that 'regulatory processes corrupt real-world data.'

Once the program research becomes formally defined by the regulatory processes (such as defining the 'starting' and 'ending' date, what data are admissible and what are not), the data become 'contaminated, often with socially desirable behaviors and explanations, accounts, and attributions of participants. The natural world becomes a much more contrived one' (Hamilton, 2005: 195). According to Robert Dingwall (2008: 10), 'When we give up doing participant observation...with vulnerable or socially marginal groups because of the regulatory obstacles, then a society becomes less informed about the condition of those who it excludes.'

What never configures in the research-ethics review process is the length of time it takes to conduct ethnographic field research and how this length translates into unanticipated shifts in ethical dimensions that a researcher encounters along the way. When Vicki Smith (2002: 228) looked at fifty books and the time it took for ethnographers to complete their fieldwork and publish their results, she discovered that, on average, it took 8.14 years. A couple of other examples include Daniel Wolf's study of outlaw bikers (1991), which took fifteen years between the start of the research and its publication, and Arlie R. Hochschild's study (1989) on the division of household chores that took thirteen years of fieldwork.

There is no question today that while participant-observation as a method is dying, others who fall outside the circumscribed ethics regime are taking it over. Journalists (e.g., Barbara Ehrenreich, 2001) who put 'a higher value on the public's right to know than on the protection of the reputation of an individual' (Gunsalus, 2003a: 3) have become the ethnographers of today. Lindgren et al. (2007: 401) are asking 'how is it that journalists may conduct and publish research, but academics can't, despite the fact that journalists are more likely to point to wrong doing?' No doubt, there are many reasons why ethics-review committees 'do not dare to take on the press.' They have, according to Cary Nelson (2004: 211) a 'justified fear of the press' power.' Still, in universities, ethics committees are gradually eroding the ethics-free status of schools of journalism such as the one at the University of Missouri at Columbia that now no longer requires its students to conduct research as a way of avoiding entanglement with the research-ethics committee (SPLC, 2001). Professors of journalism such as Leon Dash (2007) assert that ethics review of what journalists do is entirely unjustified based on constitutional grounds of free speech and on the idea that journalists are beholden to their audiences, not to their 'research participants.' Anonymous reporting is one of the most discreditable things a journalist could do.

Many familiar with the research-ethics policies, such as the reviewers of the two pieces cited above (van den Hoonaard and Connolly, 2006; van den Hoonaard, 2006; Interviews with R006-M; Focus Group REB1-S), are eager to point out that the decline in ethnographic research is due to the pressures brought to bear on students and their supervisors to complete their graduate degrees in as short a time as possible; according to them, ethics policies have nothing to do with that. Although one is inclined to accept the validity of such a claim, it is nevertheless true academics are more keenly feeling the impact of ethics policies because of pressures to complete one's academic work. Canadian anthropologists at their 2002 annual meeting in Windsor, Ontario, made the point that the decline in the number of ethnographic theses is real (Fieldnotes: 321); a similar point came through at the 'Canadian Qualitatives' gathering at Carleton University in Ottawa in 2004 (Fieldnotes: 156), where participants also noted a decline in the number of studies on subcultures (Fieldnotes: 39).

Other academic gatherings, such as the 2003 Couch-Stone Symposium (held in Tempe, Arizona) were suffused with similar experiences; ethnography is becoming more and more difficult to engage in (Fieldnotes: 351). Even members of ethics committees bewail the plight of ethnographic research. One focus group (REB1-S) predicted that doing, for example, an ethnographic study of several religious communities might not be allowed in ten years, 'even though it is interesting,' and admitted that 'it would be unfortunate to lose that kind of research down the road.' 'Interview research,' according to the same focus group, 'is more manageable than participant observation which is messy, especially at the level of master's research.'

The Decline of Covert Research

As a gut reaction, covert research is something we want to stay away from. Social researchers have noted that covert research has declined primarily on account of stipulations in research-ethics regimes (see, for example, Calvey, 2008). The reluctance to approve covert research is allegedly based on the idea that it is not honourable to use people as a means of pursuing one's own hidden research agenda. The *TCPS* (section i.4) is quite clear on that score: 'Part of our core moral objection would concern using another human solely as a means toward even legitimate ends.' The case is not as clear as that, however. We already have, for example, an indication where covert research might be a possibility, as hinted by the *TCPS* itself, when the research involves 'authoritarian or dictatorial countries.' Obviously, some countries unintentionally invite covert research, when the criteria involve the type of government or regime that defies democratic standards. Should research involving democratic countries be exempt from covert research?

Ethics committees, however, confuse 'covert' research with 'deception' in research. Deception involves lying at least in the initial stages of research, and may continue throughout the research; covert research implies the need for protection from danger, as well as ensuring complete confidentiality and absolute guarantee of the anonymity of research participants and of the setting where the research is taking place. In Canada, however, there is surprisingly little in the *Tri-Council Policy Statement: Ethical Conduct for Research Involving Humans* (Medical

Research Council et al., 1998) on the subject of covert research. A notable mention relates to the 'Review of Research in Other Jurisdictions or Countries' (1.12). On one hand, 'the REB should, therefore, not veto research about authoritarian or dictatorial countries on the grounds that the regime or its agents have not given approval for the research project or have expressed a dislike of the researchers' (1.12). Such a statement implies that covert research might be a possibility. On the other hand, the *TCPS* states that 'University research should be open. It is thus unethical for researchers to engage in covert activities for intelligence, police or military purposes under the guise of university research. REBs must disallow any such research' (Subsection H, Article 1.14). Both of these assertions are not in conflict: they aver the independence of researchers to conduct research regardless of the (dis)approval of particular regimes, and the importance of not doing covert research on behalf of the 'intelligence, police or military' agencies. Thus there seems to be no restriction on scholars doing covert research on their own behalf, but only a 'small minority' of researchers are now practising covert research (Calvey, 2008: 914) while journalists, according to Robert Dingwall (2008:6), do most of the covert research nowadays, as Barbara Ehrenreich did for her book *Nickel and Dimed: On (Not) Getting By in America* (2001).

Roger Homan mentions that both covert research and deception can occur at the same time. In 1971, for example, Mexican-American women asked for contraceptives, but medical researchers gave some placebos instead (Homan, 1991: 97). There is also the risk of 'sublimated voyeurism,' shown by two psychologists who hid beneath a bed in a student dormitory (Homan, 1991: 96). With very few exceptions, these approaches to deception-cum-covert research are generally not believed to be practised outside of psychology and medical research, although there are some cases, such as anthropologist W. Caudill who, in 1958, pretended to be a patient only to observe the medical profession at work (Bloor, 2002: 179). Laud Humphreys' 1970 work on homosexual behaviour in public restrooms gained notoriety and become fodder for promoting research-ethics policies. Humphreys argued that he preserved complete anonymity, and that individuals did not suffer from the research. As Humphreys argued in his methodological appendix, his research actually helped the gay community achieve a modicum of equality and rights at a time when police raids were not only a common occurrence but also resulted in the publication of names of 'offenders' of the public order.

More recently, attempts have been made by social researchers to demonstrate that a criminal record or race is an impediment to getting employment. However, two universities, including Princeton University, blocked this kind of deception in research (Katz, 2007: 802). An ethics committee prevented a researcher, Ruth Malone, from studying the prevalence of illegal, single-stick cigarette sales in a low-income, predominantly minority neighbourhood. Although she received written assurances that law breakers would not be prosecuted, her IRB blocked the study because 'it would be unethical for the researchers to provide the occasion in which store clerks might break the law' (Katz, 2007: 804). Along the same lines, the so-called auditing studies, a research tool for revealing invidious discrimination, is also 'at risk of repression' (Katz, 2007: 805).

Covert research, of which there are three kinds in the social sciences, is a well-established practice, namely, as (1) a way of maintaining the authenticity of the observed social phenomenon, (2) a means of gaining entry to inaccessible groups, and (3) a form of 'early musings' about one's research. Ethics committees do not make distinctions among the three. As an established form of research, one recalls the study by Leon Festinger et al. (1957) of a doomsday cult that laid the foundation for such enduring and useful concepts as 'cognitive dissonance.' However, as Ann Hamilton argues (2005: 195, citing Punch, 1998: 171), ' . . . divulging one's identity and research purpose – will "kill many a project stone dead."'

As an example of the second rationale for using covert research, namely, to study inaccessible groups, one is mindful of Melville Dalton's 1959 classic study *Men Who Manage*, which debunks the myth that managers follow rational behaviour, revealing instead that they engage in 'informal, non-rational, self-protective, and clique-oriented' behaviour (Stagner, 1961: 206). The British Sociological Association, according to Emma Bell and Alan Bryman (2007: 73), leaves the door open to covert research when other methods cannot be used. What about research on corporations? Very, very few corporations allow for academic research, even non-covert research. Among the few exceptions I can think of is the corporation studied by Arlie Hochschild and reported in her 1997 book *The Time Bind: When Work Becomes Home and Home Becomes Work*. Libel, lawsuits, the inevitable fall of 'whistle-blowers,' and the power of multinationals are enough of a disincentive to conduct any kind of research in those settings. Will it be sufficient, for example, to interview ex-employees? Is that a fair approach to the study of a corporation? How fair is it to a health authority for a researcher to disguise himself as a terminally ill patient to study the workings of a health system (see, for example, Buckingham et al., 1976)?

The third form of covert research falls under the category of 'early musings,' as strange as that may be. When ethnographic researchers or those practising qualitative research find themselves fascinated by the social processes or social settings in which they are immersed (such as passing by a panhandler on the street and noting whom he is more likely to approach), they make jottings of those impressions or experiences, that is, 'early musings.' In the tradition of social scientific work (argued persuasively by C. Wright Mills in *The Sociological Imagination*, 1959), such note-taking is a means to further one's reflection and understanding of events. It is a critical aspect of doing proper ethnographic research. Studies which involved this are too numerous to mention; one can cite only a few examples to illustrate the use of 'early musings' in social research. Herbert Gans' 1967 study of the 'Levittowners' is a classic, but it started when he and his wife mortgaged a home in Levittown, and he began taking notes of the social interactions among neighbours, newcomers, and local, rural residents. Although many of these notes do not directly find their way into publications, these early musings constitute a critical component of doing solid research. Another example is Roger Homan's research, which he conducted based on his early musings. Suffering from myelitis, he was hospitalized for two months, and he found 'observation and reflection had already become habits' that he 'could not suppress.' During this time he shared his reflections with staff, and wrote a paper that he also circulated to staff (Homan, 1991: 98–9). During his hospital stay, the staff were unaware of his fascination with his surroundings while he was taking these notes.

Those early notes in the development and importance of research are comparable to the crawling stage of infants before they take their first upright steps. Just as crawling cannot be discounted as a crucial part of development, neither can the importance of one's early fieldnote musings be dismissed. Some incipient researchers are highly organized in note-taking; others are less so. But their foundation is the same: fascination with the social processes in which they are engaged in everyday life.

It is practically impossible not to use the 'early musings' stage of research. For example, my own work on airports started with my musings as an avid traveller forced to spend time in airports and observe behaviour there (van den Hoonaard and van den Hoonaard, 1992). My first book, *Silent Ethnicity: The Dutch of New Brunswick* (van den Hoonaard, 1991), started with chats with Dutch-Canadian farmers at a farmers' market long before the idea of actual research on the topic was conceived. But here is the conundrum: does a researcher need to secure post hoc research-ethics approval for those initial musings? Or is such approval out of the question? So far, experience dictates that REBs are loath to grant such post hoc approval. If no approval is forthcoming, is the researcher's choice to continue this fascination as a research project taken away because he/she did not conceive of it as 'research' ahead of time and get the requisite approval, just in case?[13]

As odd as it may seem, ethics committees are totally unaware of some forms of deception that social researchers, such as ethnographers, regularly engage in when practising their trade. Gary Allan Fine (1993) wrote a seminal piece on the taken-for-granted deceitful practices in ethnographic research. He calls them 'partial truths' or 'self-deceptions.' Field researchers are implicated in these methodological illusions and engage in impression management that can test our ethical mandates. This 'body of deceits' leads us to think about how we are able to sustain these conflicting concerns. For example, Jean Duncombe and Julie Jessop (2002) worry that faking friendship is a deceptive practice employed in the ethnographer's eagerness to build 'rapport.' We smooth over these practices.

The answer to the dilemma of doing covert research does not lie in banning it altogether. Rather, it involves a web of complex factors, such as the status of the groups being researched, and the need to establish extreme anonymity. Researchers and members of ethics-review committees must replace their gut reaction with a thoughtful consideration of the researcher's intentions and the social setting where the research is conducted. Taking our argument to another level, we note that social researchers often research collectivities, whether as communities, religious groups (including cults), or ethnic or Aboriginal groups. What are the criteria for (not) doing covert research? What if the leadership of a collectivity decides that a given setting under their jurisdiction should not be investigated? What if that setting involves injustice, violence, and so forth? Does the leadership have the right to deny access to that setting, and would the researcher have the moral right (or duty) to conduct research anyway, even if it is covert? Does the status of covert research change radically if the group has been historically disadvantaged or persecuted? Or is doing covert research the last thing a researcher should want?

Less Action Research

There are evident brakes in conducting action research, also known as participatory-action research. In Canada, we learn from Marika Morris of the Canadian Research Institute for the Advancement of Women (CRIAW) that some ethics-review boards are not allowing researchers to talk to research participants (Notes on Presentations, 3 June 2003, Fieldnotes: 150). Following Hemmings (2006: 15) in the United States, 'IRBs have considerable difficulty supporting this kind of research, even though the research shows involvement of research participants.' The ethics-review process has 'chilled the atmosphere surrounding applied [action] research' (NCA, 2005: 211). For example, we learn that a researcher 'switched to doing observational research in a chatroom, without the participation of chatroom participants. His previous applications to involve research participants were never approved' (NCA, 2005: 224). A member of an ethics-review committee (Interview E12-M) discouraged action research in the classroom because teachers who do research on their own students are 'double-dipping,' and she worries about the negative effect of students' knowledge when doing action research. The standardized consent form, moreover, constrains informal and participatory approaches necessary in action research (Koro-Ljungberg et al., 2007: 1085).

Oddly, the demands by some research-ethics review committees who are very eager to promote action research actually make it difficult for a researcher to conduct such research because 'demands for community interests to be addressed [by the RECs] will have a chilling effect on social science' (Derbyshire, 2006: 46). To improve the chances of getting action research underway, Bell and Bryman (2007: 68) make the point that they try to 'instill a therapeutic agenda on the research.' The belief also prevails that if the larger public understands the nature of action research, somehow that belief will find its way into ethics-review committees. Wiles et al. (2006: 294) suggest there is, through increased regulation, wider appreciation for action research which would mean more consumer choice and participation in research.

Destruction of Data

The formal requirement to destroy one's data has become as much a fetish as the requirement to use a consent form that must be signed by research participants. Jonathan Church et al. describe the

> fetish of the outlandish imagining of possible risk and the relentless bureaucratic pursuit of increasingly detailed research protocols, some of which may even go so far as to require that the ethnographer destroy research materials and records, making longitudinal and comparative research impossible. (2002: n.p.)

The American Anthropological Association (AAA, 2010: 1) expresses its great concern about the tendency of IRBs (in the U.S.) to ask anthropologists to 'either destroy data with identifications, including photographs, or destroy or lock up the identifications, or face not being in compliance in any future publications.' We know that for many disciplines like anthropology, sociology, and history the usefulness of research data may not be evident until much later. Not only does the destruction of data make it impossible to conduct longitudinal and comparative research but also it prevents the researcher from conducting an ongoing analysis of his/her data which the research participants have so generously contributed. Indeed, the defining character of much of social research is the constant refining of analysis as data are (re)interpreted with new insights. Social researchers would define the destruction of data as a form of disrespect towards the research participant.

It is significant to note that the call to destroy data is not reflected in national ethics policies. Rather, those policies call for safekeeping of data: 'Researchers should ensure that the data obtained are stored with all the precautions appropriate to the sensitivity of the data' (*TCPS*, Article 3.2).

Curtailment of Survey Research

An observer of developments in the field of research-ethics review would indeed anticipate that survey research, as one of the hallmarks of quantitative research, would be the least affected by ethics policies. From a number of accounts, it appears that survey research is also being curtailed. Questionnaires, once a standard research tool, are disappearing according to someone who is closely involved with the research-ethics process at a medium-sized Canadian university (R054-M). The National Communications Association makes the point that in some research, the survey could not be conducted nationally because the IRB believed that 'the simple recounting of the death of a family member required psychological counselling (severe psychological risk) and wanted the researchers to offer access to psychological counselling' (NCA, 2005: 214). The need to have a team of psychologists stand by on a national level is a condition that no survey researcher can fulfil.

No less interesting is a recent study of how the legal wording of cover letters (as mandated by ethics review) involving students affected the response rate in surveys. I already referred to the study by Grayson and Myles (2005) that found that if impersonal, legally worded cover letters get a response rate of 100, friendly and personal letters would get 128. The wording of cover letters has a significant impact on the reliability of survey data. The higher the response rate to a survey, the greater the probability that the sample represents the population. York University and Dalhousie University REBs approved more ideal, warm cover letters; the University of British Columbia and McGill University required more legally stringent ones. The response rates were 43 per cent, 38 per cent, 33 per cent, and 20 per cent, respectively. Another instance that involved the difficulty of promoting survey research concerned a PhD student who had contacted young gay men through clubs, but was required by an ethics committee to gain their parents' consent for them to be interviewed, as a result of which he actually could not do that research.[14] Crow et al. (2006: 89) present similar reasoning about the inability to pursue survey research. And as Paul Grayson (2004: 10) sums it up: 'survey research is being killed.'

In light of these restrictions, researchers are increasingly considering online survey methods, obviating restrictions noted by ethics committees. However, new discrepancies are emerging with this type of survey, and researchers must contend with them while at the same time developing proper 'protocols' (see, for example, Buchanan and Hvizdak, 2009).

In summary, the ethics-review process is redirecting social research in very significant ways. We are witnessing the collapse of fieldwork and participant-observation research in such fields as anthropology and sociology. Covert research (often confused with 'deception' in research) has become a rarer phenomenon. What adds poignancy to this finding is that covert social research was used not only to gain entry to inaccessible groups but also allowed the social researcher to make more extensive use of his/her 'early musings.' Moreover, covert research allowed the researcher to retain the authentic conditions of the social settings. Action research is also experiencing a decline of sorts. The insistence that data be destroyed deeply affects social research and interrupts the ongoing process of discovery and insights, even beyond its symbolic value to research participants who have given so much of their time to research. The ethics-review process has also meant that researchers have had to curtail survey research.

The significance of this redirection of research speaks to the commodification of research, including academic research. This trend demands that research, especially when it is conducted by students, must move forward at a quicker pace (and therefore creates the tendency to select methods more easily understood and approved by ethics committees). The ethics-review process also forces research into smaller conceptual sizes which does injustice to the holistic concept of research plans. We have also learned that the concepts of ethics that prevail in ethics committees are at variance with normal notions of ethics in social research. The final outcome is that the observed natural, social world is being manipulated by having to fictitiously spell out to research participants every step of the research process, despite the fact that the researchers themselves might not be aware of all these steps.

This redirection of social research leads to one conclusion: the ethics-review process has homogenized social research and pauperized the social sciences. Will the topics and methods favoured by the research-ethics review process, which I discuss in the next chapter, bring a measure of relief to this redirection?

13 On Theory, Topics, and Favoured Methods

While the previous chapter demonstrated how particular methods in social research are waning, this chapter shows us some important new shifts in social research primarily as a consequence of research-ethics review. The chapter explores how the ethics-review process is reshaping the theoretical orientations of social research, often as a result of the rise of neo-positivism and the criterion of 'scientificity' demanded by ethics committees. No less drastic are changes related to the choice of research topics: what ethics committees allegedly want are topics that are pleasant, safe, and non-sensitive, and that have social, rather than analytical, merit. Finally, the chapter touches upon the favoured methods of research, namely, the interview, member-checking, and the focus group. Still, by themselves, these methods do not offer a solution to the dilemma facing social science research. Social research needs the full panoply of methods in its arsenal to keep research vibrant . . . and alive.

Shaping Theoretical Orientations

There is not much space or time left for theoretical orientations in the social sciences. During the period that '[e]thics committees grew out of a positivist tradition of biomedical research' (Halse and Honey, 2005: 2153) and the current resurgence of neo-positivism, it stands to reason that social science theories, especially those based in qualitative research, did not have much time for their efflorescence. 'The positivist biomedical model of research ethics,' according to Halse and Honey, 'has had exceptional discursive power and has been taken up and imposed on disciplines such as the social sciences and humanities, even when these disciplines employ radically different epistemic frames and forms of data collection and analysis' (2153). They also argue that it is this 'shroud of scientific neutrality and universal certainty that crafts an illusion that ethics approval means ethical research, begetting a compliance approach to research ethics and to the ways that researchers think through ethical questions' (2153).

In Canada's case, formal drafts of the *TCPS* suffused with biomedical paradigms began circulating in the mid-1990s. In 2009, Canadian researchers were starting to see drafts of the second version of the *TCPS*. In effect, there was a fourteen-year paradigmatic hiatus in the life of the *TCPS* which allowed ethics-review committees to look askance at qualitative research. Of course, through the exigencies of the popularity of qualitative research, many ethics committees have come face-to-face with it and have had to recognize its relevance in the research world. And in December 2009, Canada produced the first complete draft of a new *TCPS* (PRE, 2009) which now includes a full chapter devoted to qualitative research.

The story in the United States is even bleaker for qualitative research. Here, the 'Federal Policy for the Protection of Human Subjects' became law in 1983 (although a draft had existed since 1979). Because the central core of the law that negatively affected social research still remains (in 2010), we can subscribe to a twenty-six-year paradigmatic hiatus. The length of this hiatus covers more than one generation of social researchers – enough time for the Policy to have had its profound effect on the social sciences.

The current re-emergence of neo-positivism (called the third positivism) in the public and scholarly domain is bound to halt any move to liberate the Policy from its biomedical shackles. The *Dictionary of Philosophy* says that the third positivism is occupied with 'the philosophical problems of language, symbolic logic, the structure of scientific investigations . . . ' In other words, neo-positivism has been easily gaining strength because it permits reconciliation in 'the logic of science with mathematics, the course of formalisation of epistemological problems' (*Dictionary of Philosophy*, 2009). As a consequence, Julianne Cheek (2007: 1052) argues that qualitative and other social researchers are working in 'increasingly conservative and potentially hostile contexts.' In this light, Cheek maintains that '[w]e are seeing the evolution and emergence of new and potent combinations of methodological fundamentalism and understandings of evidence, ethics, and research enquiry' (1053), which are resulting in a 'backlash against diverse forms of research' promoted by direct government intervention (1055). The recent drive by researchers and research administrators to return to 'evidence-based' research is yet another illustration of the rise of neo-positivism. The proof, or evidence, is in numbers, not text. Some scholars aim at colonizing qualitative research with quantitative approaches by holding out a 'promise.' For example, Paluck (2010: 59) avers that 'over the past few decades, a productive exchange in political science has explored the idea that qualitative research should be guided by the logic of mainstream quantitative and experimental methods.' Imbedded in her argument are the concepts of the logic of regression, experimentation, and causal inferences – concepts that are antithetical in conventional inductive or qualitative research.

Since 2002, U.S. authorities have been 'scrubbing' databases in the field of education, ridding them of qualitative research findings. Tara Star Johnson offers the following assessments:

> An even more appalling and less subtle condemnation of qualitative research's legitimacy is apparent within the What Works Clearinghouse (WWC; Institute of Education Sciences, U.S. Department of Education, n.d.), established in 2002 by the U.S. Department of Education's Institute of Education Sciences with a purpose of helping 'the education community locate and recognize credible and reliable evidence to make informed decisions,' as 'few resources exist to help education decision makers differentiate high-quality research from weaker research' (Institute of Education Sciences, U.S. Department of Education, n.d., para. 1). (2008: 226)

How do these epistemic frameworks make a difference in the way ethics committees adjudicate social science research proposals? Franklin Silva (2008: 326) notes that what an ethics committee chair and staff look for in a good ethics application are the marks of scientificity. Betsy Bach (2005: 261) argues that 'IRBs see their role to critique theory and methods, rather than ascertain risks.' Lincoln and Tierney (2004: 222) find that qualitative work is more likely to undergo full committee review than other kinds of research; and that 'at some institutions, qualitative, phenomenological, critical theorist, feminist, action research, and participatory action research projects have been summarily rejected as "unscientific," "ungeneralizable," and/or "inadequately theorized."' In their participant observation study of ethics committees, Parker et al. noted that,

[i]nstead of making fine-grained criticisms of the research design, the number of subjects, the control groups or the statistical methodology, they would make ostensibly vaguely couched yet obviously pointed comments such as, 'I'm not sure about the science,' and 'Wouldn't the study be more valid if . . . ?' (2005: 19)

Sometimes, the bent to have theory trump data yielded distinctive decisions by ethics committees. A researcher at a mid-sized university (Interview R173-M) learned that 'if the focus group(s) did not affirm her themes [i.e., theory] that she got from interviews, she would have to remove her analysis from her data.' Her ethics committee 'policed the discipline by not allowing the perspective of the research participant to enter the data.' Along those lines, the researcher should have 'no room for serendipitous sampling' in his/her research (Fieldnotes: 65) and must abandon theoretical sampling, one of the key concepts in qualitative research.

Changing Topics of Research

This section is devoted to the changing topics of research as a result of deliberations by ethics-review committees. It constitutes a subsection that discusses some of the general topics that ethics committees are encouraging the researcher to veer away from. There is also a discussion about the specific topics of research that ethics committees (and now researchers) are reluctant to address. The consequences of these topical shifts entail choosing to study topics that interest research-ethics committees, rather than those that purely meet the criteria of curiosity-driven research. Finally, we cover a number of current and prospective changes of topics in research.

A policymaker and researcher (Interview R013-S) pointed out that REBs are reluctant to consider research on unpleasant or negative topics such as gambling, illegal behaviour, or sexual conduct (Presentation by R013, 21 May 2005, Fieldnotes: 158). Ethics committees are often tempted to look at the social merit of research proposals, although, according to Steven Breckler of the Science Directorate of the American Psychological Association, 'ethics committees generally do not have the capacity to assess a range of methods – nor is it their mandate' (Anonymous, 2006a: 3). A researcher (Interview R002-M) reminds us that when you have a 'sensitive topic' even in the title, 'there will be panic on the REB.' He advises that instead of taking on a sensitive topic and having 'a lot of problems with the REB,' it is 'better to change your topic.' The conundrum of sensitive topics is related to the idea of risk and the tendency to exaggerate risks. In a nutshell, these researchers are suggesting that a research topic should be a pleasing, non-sensitive one and should possess social merit.

From my numerous interviews, emails that I received from both administrators and researchers, and fieldnotes taken during public presentations on ethics in research, it is apparent that the following topics will either elicit closer scrutiny or be rejected altogether: research on vulnerable people, students studying children, pedophilia, Aboriginal research and child or wife abuse, minors, the use of medicinal (herbal) plants, sexuality, drug users, illegitimate activities, or infidelity among professors.[1] Researchers are discovering that 'stringent guidelines silence under-represented populations' (NCA, 2005: 204). One researcher asked herself, 'was I crazy to choose to study *prisoners*? But I wanted to research something that was important to me' (NCA, 2005: 227). In her work on website games, Amy Bruckman (2002: 221) chose to exclude those under eighteen years of age from her study, though ironically this meant excluding the group that was most dedicated to gaming, because those under-18 year-olds would have required parental approval to participate in the research. Yvonna Lincoln and William Tierney (2004: 227) noted that '[a]nother difficulty that seems to be appearing in some of the cases is the reluctance of IRBs to approve research with children, in some cases, despite school board approval and encouragement of such research.' Adam Hedgecoe (2008: 883), a British researcher who sees value in maintaining the ethics regime, found that the impediment of pursuing particular topics 'is a far more detailed and nuanced threat to British sociological research than the general worries about ethics review being a form of "censorship" and committees not being able to "handle" ethnography.' Debbie S. Dougherty and Michael W. Kramer (2005a: 187) learned that '[s]ome lists of protected populations include everyone except un-incarcerated white males ages 18–65 and white females after menopause, but before retirement.' 'By expanding definitions,' they claim, 'IRBs serve as gatekeepers to what can or cannot be studied either implicitly or explicitly.'

Sometimes, the redirection of topics to be researched has an important theoretical impact. Christine Halse and Anne Honey tried to capture the theoretical complexity in their research on 'anorexic' teenage girls by including participants who defined themselves as such and those who met specific medical criteria. What they found in their submission to the ethics committee was that the committee had 'narrowed the research focus by excluding a range of potential participants (e.g., girls who rejected their diagnosis) and (re)configured the study's aim to illuminate the diversity among all anorexic teenage girls:

> The result was a disconcerting paradox: the act of defining the research population erased the particular and individual differences among potential participants, ignoring 'the plurality of modes of being human, and differences among humans' ... and, in doing so, disregarded one of the four fundamental principles of humanist research ethics policy – respect for persons. (Halse and Honey, 2005: 2154)

Even titles of proposed researches are subject to review by ethics committees; one asked a researcher to make the title of a study more vague. They suggested 'Interaction of Demographic Variables with Target Communication Behaviors,' rather than 'Gender Differences in Politeness of Requests' (NCA, 2005: 216). The demands associated with specific topics were sometimes alone sufficient to abandon the research. For example, an ethics committee insisted that studies of conflict resolution required the researcher to have a 'licensed therapist on hand.' The researcher thought that was asking too much, saying that no therapist is required, and there were dozens of studies to that effect (NCA, 2005: 207).

Research on sexuality has inherent IRB limitations, according to some researchers. 'Most of my research,' says one researcher, 'involves anonymous self-reports which ... would be exempt from IRB review.' However, the application was upgraded to expedited review based on the topic alone. He believes that IRB reviewers are distrustful of motivations for research on sexuality (NCA, 2005:225). Annette Hemmings (2006: 14–15) reports the case of 'Jane,' who had what she thought was a foolproof way of avoiding risk for students in sexual harassment research, but the IRB moved her study up to full review, and student and supervisor had to attend the meeting where they were 'grilled' by the IRB. Jane decided to change to another topic and method of her research 'rather than face another round of review.' Jonathan Church et al. (2002) report how an undergraduate student had wanted to study a 'gentleman's club' and the life-world of exotic dancers but was faced with numerous questions from the ethics committee, including how she would protect the anonymity of the dancers and what she would do if she came across illegal activities. And what would happen if, one night, her interview notes were stolen? In the end, she did not pursue her research. A final example involves an investigation of sexual dynamics in the classroom that was 'hard to get through IRB approval' (Johnson, 2008).

As a consequence of these topical shifts and as I noted elsewhere, researchers are now increasingly seeking out 'safer' topics to study. Significantly, researchers are also diverting their attention away from studying marginalized people and groups (Fieldnotes: 64): ethics review, they find, is too difficult. Equally noteworthy is the current trend to study 'library' topics (R054-M, Fieldnotes: 364). A sociologist at Marquette University (R131) is now steering students away from certain topics to expedite IRB passage (Fieldnotes: 601) and Jonathan Church et al. (2002) mention that an undergraduate student activist in AIDS prevention decided not to study that area in view of IRB experience.[2] As another example, Crowe et al. (2006: 89) are irritated by the fact that some groups have become inaccessible for research and mention that, 'people with dementia ... are hugely under-represented because we can't get consent' and are 'thereby rendered "hidden people."' The same difficulty applied to

> the inapplicability of seeking consent from parents for research into aspects of their children's lives about which they may not know led to the abandonment of plans to conduct 'a postal survey of school children related to alcohol consumption where we felt to go for a kind of absolutist position around informed consent basically made large-scale postal surveys not do-able. (89)

Furthermore, Crow et al. continue, 'More challenging research simply did not get done, at least in research undertaken by students whose tutors increasingly steer them towards topics that are "as mundane and as normal everyday kind of things as possible"' (89). These pressures are widespread throughout many countries that have developed ethics policies related to social research. Stuart Derbyshire (2006: 46) talks about a 'pressure [on RECs] to make research "legitimate in the eyes of the community"' that 'will result in local sensibilities regarding the proprietary of the inquiry ... having veto power over inquiry.' Jack Katz (2007: 803) mentions a host of studies that the IRB has banned researchers from pursuing, such as an IRB at Cal State campus that blocked a proposed study of university admission practices while another IRB banned the publication about the deplorable health benefits at Native-run casinos after an advocate for Indian tribes claimed that the study had not gone through IRB review. Katz also found 'critical social research projects aimed at protecting gay men and poor minority youth have been successfully repressed,' much like the UC-San Francisco IRB that blocked an observational study that would have examined compliance by bathhouses with public health regulations.

The overall effect of researchers not being able to undertake the study of sensitive topics has been negative. Ann Hamilton found that

> [m]any investigators, particularly students and faculty with whom I've spoken from 1999 to 2002, have said there is something more interesting they would explore if they 'could get it past the IRB' or they are breaking the rules occasionally, or circumventing the process in order to do something of greater interest and importance to them. (2002: 253)

In the end, Pat Sikes (2008: 249) avers that such control 'does not advance critical and innovative research' and leads researchers to play it safe. No less serious is the impediment to socially relevant and critical sociology (Feeley, 2007: 766; compare also Katz, 2007: 802). To follow through on her ideal of choosing a worthwhile topic, one student required considerable stamina for 'several months and repeated modifications and guarantees' related to her topic of research before an IRB reluctantly approved a proposal. Such was the case for Colleen, who nearly abandoned her project in favour of a safe and sterile study. In the study, Colleen wanted to explore how direct feedback from Grade 6 students to teachers on their performance in the classroom might be used for professional development. All the teachers would be volunteers in the research (Lincoln and Tierney, 2004: 225).

Robert Dingwall (2008: 9–10), an observer of the process of research-ethics review in Britain, refers to an online survey to encourage self-reporting of deviant behaviour in 350 hospitals. However, this research would have meant getting 1,600 signatures and 9,000 pages of documentation, in addition to having 300 occupational health examinations and criminal records checks of colleagues who were co-investigators. It became a limited study. This study could have prevented 'at least seven patients from dying each year,' in addition to spotting numerous health care infractions.

Given these current changes in topics, one wonders what the prospects are for new topics in research. We are beginning to see researchers occupying ill-defined spaces in research (at least from the ethics review perspective). The new topics involve the use of technology and the arts. Internet usage by the public is advancing at such great speed, with new formats emerging on a regular basis (Facebook, Twitter, Delicious, etc.), that it has become a problem for ethics committees to consider the new media which can involve radical notions of anonymity (pseudonyms on the Internet have become monikers and are 'identified' with particular posters of information), and a complete lack of confidentiality involving unabashedly personal and intimate accounts (SSHWC, 2008b). Researchers, I expect, will be exploring the intricacies of biotechnology (such as nanotechnology) that are currently out of reach of ethics policies. The rise of research in the field of dramaturgy, the arts, and music accompanies these zones still empty of ethics review (SSHWC, 2008c).

The Rise of Other Favoured Methods

With the ongoing collapse of the research methods outlined in the previous chapter, there is an equivalent rise of other methods. These other methods, primarily the blanched interview method, account for the homogenization and pauperization of the social sciences.

The Interview as a Sole Method of Research

Thanks to talk show hosts and 'celebrity interviews,' we have become the 'interview society' (van den Hoonaard, 1994b), but it is far more important to see the interview as a method that members of ethics committees are familiar with. There are some striking features of qualitative methods employed in sociology theses during the period before and after the *TCPS* was implemented in 2001. First, there is a slight increase in the proportion of master's theses where interviews are the primary means of gathering data. Before 2002, the average was 63 per cent of theses; after 2002, this proportion averaged 66 per cent. However, theses using qualitative methods have increased significantly over time, from 26 to 34 per cent. A closer inspection of qualitative theses shows that interviews account for most of these. A researcher (Interview R006-M) confessed that among the various circumstances that moved research away from participant observation in the field to doing interviews alone was the role that research-ethics review played. In many respects, these developments in sociology parallel those found by van den Hoonaard and Connolly (2006) with respect to anthropology: a homogenization of research methods (i.e., interviews) across the disciplines (van den Hoonaard, 2006).

The REBs' insistence on researchers doing interviews can lead to awkward moments in research. The Professional Ethics and Policy Committee of the Canadian Sociology and Anthropology Association (Muzzin, 2002: 2) asked researchers, 'Have you renounced any research that you were planning because you anticipated the Ethics Review Board [sic] at your institution would question the status of your research with respect to the Guidelines?' One researcher offered the following answer to this question:

> I have spent time trying to find ways to describe my research which would be acceptable to the ethical review and would not construct my research collaborators as passive objects. One way I attempted to do this was not to call the interactions 'interviews.' Some shift in the process was involved in this and it didn't work. Part of my research involves dialogues with experts around issues in the area/field. I have to call these 'interviews' when they are not. (Muzzin, 2002: 2)

The interview represents even the one-to-one interaction in which some medical researchers find themselves when conducting their research. According to a researcher (Interview R118-M), the interview is the closest many come to the experimental procedure. It is a method that can be encapsulated by an interview 'guide' or 'protocol.' A focus group of ethics committee members (Focus Group REB1-S) believes that interview research is simply 'more manageable than participant-observation.' According to a researcher (Interview R118-M), the use of a tape recorder makes something more definitive, like a biomedical approach. It has a clear beginning and end. It is a ritualized method that still places the researcher as an expert of sorts. What is demanded by ethics committees is a Gesellschaft-type interview rather than a Gemeinschaft-type (Fieldnotes: 65). The former emphasizes a contractual arrangement between the researcher and the participant while the latter sees the interview as a community-building exercise which builds on mutuality and trust. From the perspective of the social researcher, however, there is no interview without participant observation of the surroundings and circumstances of the interview and interview participant. A good interviewer takes fieldnotes of those surroundings and circumstances. The ethics committee is unaware of this untold dimension of the interview, for it never enters into the ethics-review process.

There is, however, a more ominous aspect to the interview as a method, as it is increasingly conceived by new generations of researchers across many disciplines. Researchers have now become distant from the interview participant through (1) the use of computer-based analysis, (2) interviews performed by numerous research assistants or other researchers, (3) the development of coding even before the interview takes place (or coding done by third-party researchers), and (4) the process of transcription that is either left uncorrected or that is corrected by those who stand outside the research process itself. All of these elements create a significant distance between the primary researcher and the research participant.

The interview method is increasingly exhibiting a superficial level of analysis. As my own studies of Canadian master's theses in anthropology and sociology have shown, researchers or students rely on presenting interview data on the basis of findings related to the interviewed individual (van den Hoonaard and Connolly, 2006; van den Hoonaard, 2006); there is no attempt to correlate or sort through commonalities, patterns, or differences among the interviews. They do not attempt to relate findings to larger cultural processes to make sense of the interview data, nor do they try to bring in potentially relevant insights from the literature that stretches beyond the confines of the study. Such studies are as dry as a pickle left in the hot sun.

It should be noted that interviews are normally part of any ethnographic research or fieldwork, but always in addition to the other collected data. In ethnographic research, it was common to see interview data complementing other, more substantive data, and quite rare that researchers relied only on interviews (in 1997, for example, none of the theses only used interviews). Certainly the rise of the formal interview is a more recent phenomenon in ethnographic research. The exclusive reliance on interviews represents a new phase in the so-called ethnographic forms of research. The proportion of theses employing *only* interviews has risen steadily each year since 2001, going as high as 48 per cent of theses in anthropology in 2004. If we assume that 2004 represents the first year that saw the completion of theses that underwent research-ethics review after the formal adoption of the *TCPS* in 2001, the proportion of research using interviews only will likely rise considerably higher after 2004 (van den Hoonaard and Connolly, 2006). A recent thesis by Michele McIntosh (2009: 62) similarly demonstrates the pervasiveness of the interview as a research tool. Her search through six databases (ERIC, PsychINFO, Sociological Abstracts, Sage, Web of Science, and CINAHL) reveals a stunning rise in interview-based research. In each of the three decades (1960–9, 1970–9, 1980–9) prior to the rise of research-ethics review, these databases recorded each year a total of 42, 150, and 133 researches involving interviews, respectively.

In the two following decades (1990–9, 2000–9), one sees that the numbers leaped to 3,296 and 17,456, respectively. It strikes one as far-fetched to attribute this phenomenal rise to research-ethics review, but at least one might agree that the dramatic increase in the use of the interview chronologically follows the requirement for research-ethics review.

First, the practice of such sole reliance implies a considerable *narrowing of understanding* of the world of the research participants. Macdonald (2002: 69) alluded to the 'expanding critique of ethnographic practice' when she highlighted the increasing use of personal accounts and dialogue in anthropology. However, she favours the coupling of 'firsthand observation with interviews and with historical data and analysis of texts and imagery' (72). In a classic piece comparing participant-observation and interviewing, Becker spoke of participant-observation as providing more complete data:

> An observation of some social event, the events which precede and follow it, and explanations of its meaning by participants and spectators, before, during, and after its occurrence ... Participant observation can thus provide us with a yardstick against which to measure the completeness of data gathered in other ways, a model which can serve to let us know what orders of information escape us when we use other methods. (1969: 322)

As strange as it may seem, there seems to be a growing awareness of the limitations of the interview method among members of research-ethics committees who have a professional background in counselling work. One such member (Interview E13-M) admits that, 'what bothers me in qualitative research is the use of interviews as a consulting technique.'[3] In this light (Interview R002-M), a graduate student who did not have the full support of the ethics committee was not allowed to interview Aboriginal inmates by prison officials; she had to use datasets.

Most recently, there is the urge by supervisors to discourage students from doing interviews so as not to go through ethics review and instead to enrol in journalism courses (Interview E12-M). Speaking for myself (just like R118-M), I am increasingly *not* using tape recorders when interviewing participants, believing that the strictures of research-ethics review will be less cumbersome that way.

Member-Checking

At a time when feminists and other social researchers believed in the importance of 'giving voice to the voiceless,' there were good reasons to ask the researched whether the researcher had accurately rendered their experiences and whether the researcher had managed to fully capture those experiences (Sandelowski, 2008: 501). Ethics-review committees are latching onto these ideas because they make common sense. However, in practice it means that researchers must return the transcribed interview to the research participant who must review it for inaccuracies and infelicitous statements. Ethics committees are now trying to find other uses for member-checking. One IRB stated that researchers 'needed to allow our participants to read and edit the transcripts' so that the transcripts would be admissible in court. The researcher, however, gave good reasons not to do that and the IRB changed its position (NCA, 2005: 226). Some ethics committees also see member-checking as an extension of consent; the consent process is not complete until the research participant has vetted the transcript (Crow et al., 2006: 92). Researchers face retrospective withdrawal of research participants from the research (Hedgecoe, 2008: 881) that can lead to serious difficulties in the research itself (Crow et al., 2006: 92).

There is, however, a darker side to member-checking. Bhattacharya (2007: 1103–5) claims that the alleged value of member-checking is reduced by the trust the research participant has in the researcher. One researcher who studied aging activist women found that her research being was overruled by member-checking. She relates how an interview participant worked on the transcript for eight hours and it came back 'entirely different.' The participant's 'personal thoughts were gone;' it was just the 'party line.' The research had become 'something else.' Impeded by an orthodox ethics committee and an overly compliant supervisor, the researcher was not allowed to start writing until the research participants agreed with the themes she was planning for her analysis. When some research participants did not have the time, energy, or desire to go over the transcripts, the researcher lost those participants (whose number was already dwindling because the ethics committee required that the researcher to get a personal consent from everyone in a convention where the women had gathered and had invited the researcher). As the women were scandalized by such a request, they did not want to sign such a form, which blocked the researcher from doing participant observational research (Interview R173-M).

A further complication relates to how research participants see their own spoken word as text. All of us speak in grammatically and syntactically incorrect ways, and when an individual sees the transcript of his/her own interview punctuated by such notations as [silence],

[ah], [uh], and so on, would that not produce the unintended effect of interviewees withdrawing their consent? Interviewees may be under the impression that researchers will use the whole interview and therefore might be more vigilant about their transcripts. However, researchers, by many accounts, use only 10–30 per cent of interviews when writing up their research.[4] In essence, putting a transcribed interview through member-checking gives the wrong impression of the research: while the researcher generally captures only a small part of the interview in the final results, the research participant is inadvertently led to believe that the whole transcript will be published.[5]

One sociologist (R167-M) reported her frustration to a colleague when she heard that her ethics-review committee wanted her to go back to every person she has quoted in her report to check whether each quote is accurate (Fieldnotes: 147). This requirement is not too dissimilar from the one posed by another ethics-review committee that insisted that the researcher needed a confidentiality statement for every quote she used in her project (Presentation, 3 June 2003, Congress of the Humanities and the Social Sciences, Halifax, NS, Fieldnotes: 151).[6]

The Focus Group

The final research method favoured by ethics-review committees, focus groups, has been around since the 1950s, but it was primarily developed as a business/marketing tool to explore the potential receptivity to products. Later, the focus group as a research tool became widely accepted in the social sciences (see Morgan, 1997, for detailed information). In the past decade, thanks to research-ethics review committees, the use of focus groups has grown further. Before the *TCPS* was adopted in 2001, there was only one year that saw a thesis using focus group research in sociology, but in 2004, 6 per cent of master's theses used mainly focus groups (van den Hoonaard, 2006).

However, despite its growing popularity as a research tool that originated as a business practice, the method is now starting to develop dark shadows. Members of the National Communications Association reported that a new IRB chair did not approve a focus group project because the researchers 'had no way to guarantee that the *participants themselves* would maintain confidentiality' (NCA, 2005: 211). In the previous year, it had been approved. The next year, video-taping a focus group was not allowed 'because researchers, participants, students, the transcriptionists and perhaps others could tie what was said to specific individuals' (NCA, 2005: 211–12). In another example, researchers were not allowed to organize a focus group to promote diversity of opinion in the conversations – that was seen as unfair because it would exclude other potential participants. Besides, participants could not be held to the promise of confidentiality, and not all focus groups would be treated equally because graduate student facilitators would only take notes for two groups, not all three (NCA, 2005: 212). Accordingly, the IRB's demand qualitatively changed the research itself (NCA, 2005: 212).

As research-ethics committees learn about the decisions by other committees regarding confidentiality and particularly internal confidentiality, there is a growing awareness of problems of confidentiality associated with focus group research, because no one can guarantee that the information shared within a focus group will not be taken by one of the participants beyond the group itself (Interview C25-M).

The adoption of the *TCPS* coincides with other developments within academia. Research-ethics review unites these developments and is, at the same time, their most visible expression. Developments might hinge on the waxing popularity of some research techniques, such as focus groups, with the consequent decline of other methodologies. There is also the increasing availability and attraction of secondary datasets which already have anonymized data and do not require the ethics-review process. In terms of the graduate students themselves, there is now a greater urgency for them to complete their work in as little time as possible. While some might choose the course-based master's degree, others will be urged (or might convince themselves) that a methodology with speedier results is preferable to engaging in fieldwork that might well stretch over a long period of time. Departmental audits as well as quality assurance programs might also lead to completing master's theses in a shorter time frame. These are some of the contingent factors that mutually sustain the influence of the *TCPS* in the manner described in this chapter.[7]

This chapter shows us some important new shifts in social research primarily as a consequence of research-ethics review. It shows how the review process is reshaping theoretical orientations of social research, often as a result of the rise of neo-positivism and the criterion of 'scientificity' demanded by ethics committees. No less drastic are changes related to the choice of research topics: what is wanted are topics that are pleasant, safe, and non-sensitive, and they must have social, rather than analytical merit. Finally the chapter touches upon the favoured methods of research: interviews, member-checking, and the use of focus groups. Although favoured by ethics committees, these methods have a darker side. Researchers are now driven to conduct interviews without delving more deeply into the cultural, scholarly, and social aspects of their findings. Member-checking has become the exigent correlation when doing interviews that can disallow researchers to frame their own analysis. Finally, the emphasis on increased use of focus groups is now being tempered by other considerations, including the issue of confidentiality.

Taking together the previous and current chapter, one is compelled to declare that social research has become homogenized: the many disciplines within the social sciences, such as anthropology, sociology, social work, education, interdisciplinary studies, and so on are relying on similar methods of research, however few they are. And given this homogenization of research methods, ethics committees are pauperizing the social sciences. There is great potential for us to lose the richness of data that can only be secured by particular methods and approaches.

The march towards research-ethics review is a relentless one. The next chapter shows how the wider linkages of the research-ethics world make that march a sure-footed one. There are too many obligations and institutional linkages to wish it away. We either need to state the position of social research more clearly and persuasively, or face an extinction of sorts.

It becomes obvious to anyone who lives in the research-ethics world that two kinds of hierarchies prevail, one of them relates directly to the work of research-ethics review committees, and the other to the researchers. In these cases, one can speak of *vertical ethics* when a system of ethics at one level is actively engaged with other levels of ethics, such as for example, when a departmental ethics committee works with a university-wide ethics committee. Vertical ethics functions to bind several institutional levels of ethics to one another. It is a hierarchy of ethics that spirals up or down the system. A system of vertical ethics exists separately for ethics-review committees and for researchers themselves, but both systems overlap. This chapter explores the vertical linkages of ethics committees and researchers, and also how they overlap.

Vertical Ethics from the Perspective of Research-Ethics Committees

Vertical ethics is deeply imbedded in the system of research-ethics committees and staff. This system of vertical ethics is one of accountability. Contrary to the 'commonly voiced misperception that IRBs are accountable to no one' (Fitch, 2005: 275), ethics committees are bound by upward ties: national ethics codes, a national ethics office and secretariat, and even 'university administrators have a stake in human subjects' oversight being carried out effectively' (Fitch, 2005: 275). Susan Boser (2007: 1070) makes the same observation, namely, that 'IRBs do not operate in a vacuum. Research-ethics committees constitute merely one level. Below it, one might find departmental-level committees that triage research applications according to risk, for example.' At a higher level, one might find a senior-ranking administrative officer being responsible for maintaining the function of ethics committees and answering appeals. At a more distant level, ethics committees must be seen to follow scrupulously national guidelines or legal requirements. University-wide ethics committees must also pay attention to directives from centralized agencies. In the United States, this is the Office of Human Research Protections, while in Canada, it is the Panel and Secretariat on Research Ethics. As Boser (2007: 1070) avers, these agencies 'work under federal regulations that specify protocol, structures, and procedures, with the institutions themselves subject to fiscal consequences for failure to comply with regulations.'

Jim Thomas suggests that this hierarchy of ethics works like a *franchise* with a 'complex mix of interests and missions' (Thomas, 2002: 3; also Presentation at Couch-Stone Symposium, 7 February 2003, Fieldnotes: 351). Ann Hamilton (2002: 12) herself notes that there is a 'steady stream of calls for actual issuances of "updates" [issued by federal authorities] . . . also evidenced by the steady pressure on the regulatory organization from inside and out.' The policy initiative for change originates from a central authority, although there might be resistance at the lower levels. One REB chair had this to say:

> And they [the federal agency] said well, 'it didn't adequately provide guidance about what to do if you were doing participant-observation.' [Our own statement] was more critical of the *TCPS* than anything so, as our little act of resistance, we left it in there this time. We've added other things like documenting the consent and we left it in. So what are the implications of them [the federal agency] doing that with, you know, holding an axe over the university's head in terms of funding and 'get it to us by August 1st or else.' You know, there's a lot of information, [but] I think we may regret some of the things that we've gone along with down the road. Like we're doing it under pressure with, you know, limited resources . . . I hope that we haven't given away too much. We've tried not to, but I just wonder what it's going to turn out like . . . (Interview C03-M)

The same chair complained that when her REB was reviewed, it was 'not a good experience [and we] had to move closer to the positivist model' of research. A senior administrator at a small university confesses that it's 'scary to think that research ethics ought to be in the hands of bureaucrats as opposed to academics' (Interview A11-S).

Still, there are some REBs who set time aside to become acquainted with documents originating from the Interagency Panel on Research Ethics (PRE), spending one meeting going over the consultation item (Interview C11-M). Sometimes, according to another chair, after the REB meeting there is 'a free flow of comments about for example stuff from PRE or NCEHR [National Council for Ethical Human Research]' (Interview S47-M). Some REBs consider themselves quite proactive, checking with the Secretariat on Research Ethics of PRE when writing their own policy (Interview C12-S).

The fear of program shutdown results in IRBs 'bend[ing] over backward to make sure all "t's" are crossed' and leads to 'overzealous demands that impede research and discredit the IRB [in the eyes of researchers],' a sort of 'death penalty' (ICL, 2006: 6). Observers of this system of vertical ethics have noted that the sanctions in the United States, for example, do not necessarily protect participants from harm, but rather protect alternative purposes such as funding, avoiding litigation, and even the regulatory system (Hamilton, 2005: 196). IRBs fear being punished for not following the federal regulations that leads IRBs 'to become overzealous in policing social science research' (NCA, 2005: 219). In Canada, there is the ongoing fear that grant money will be withheld. These audits[1] of ethics-review committees mainly reveal procedural facets[2] that place importance on *pro forma* compliance instead of the review of fundamental ethical issues (ICL, 2006: 6). Vertical ethics is making IRBs, who are seeking accreditation, afraid to delegate anything, slowing down and centralizing the review process (Anononymous, 2006a, Fieldnotes: 278). But, ultimately, asks one REB chair, 'whose interests does the REB serve' (InterviewC25-M)? Is it the researcher, the ethics committee, or the central agency?

All in all, local ethics committees have a hard time dealing with 'higher demands' due to the extremely tight deadlines to comply (Interview C03-M). As a result, some chairs and members of ethics committees in Canada do not bother looking at interpretations from the Interagency Advisory Panel of Research Ethics (PRE) (Interview C05-B) – there is simply no time. The considerable workload prevents a careful reading of documents from PRE in Ottawa (Interview E15-S). One member of the REB has not read *Giving Voice to the Spectrum* (Interview E27-S),[3] which is a key document setting out the ethical dimensions of qualitative and ethnographic research, while two other chairs have no idea what has happened since this document came out (Interviews C09-B and C10-B). Another REB member complains that the 'PRE stuff is not brought to the attention of REB members' (Interview E12-M). She says of the ethics galaxy that it's 'hard to know what's happening in this world.' One must expect that these pressures of time (and lack of resources or personnel) to do things properly might correlate with many not having taken the time to read the *TCPS*. Thus, to garnish more resources, smaller REBs have fallen away and been taken over by centralized ones (Interview C10-B).

Increasingly, one is seeing the intrusion of legal considerations into those of ethics, such as when an IRB insists that researchers 'provide evidence' that they have received publishers' permission to use the wording or phrases in already-published survey measures when planning to collect survey data, even when the wording is slightly changed, for example, from 'spouse' to 'romantic partner.' The IRB wants to see that permission (NCA, 2005: 207).[4]

While not formally part of the auditing or regulatory structure, the public, too, exercises pressure on ethics committees to make research legitimate in the eyes of the community. Pat Sikes (2008) discovered that despite REC approval, her British study on teachers' sexual relations with students got a lot of distorted media attention that reflected back on her university and REC. The public's anger was visceral.

Vertical Ethics from the Perspective of Researchers

While researchers also must contend with a system of vertical ethics, that system looks quite different. The ethics committee continues to play the critical role, but increasingly, so do other institutions that want to make sure that researchers follow ethics standards. In this light, one finds departmental ethics committees, as well as more and more editors of scholarly journals who now insist that the researcher supply the journal with an ethics certificate once the research has reached the publication stage. That system of vertical ethics can include such modest requirements as to include a statement to the effect that the ethics committee has approved the research (plus an REB file number) in ads and posters used to solicit research participants. This requirement seems only to serve the purpose of allowing the ethics committee to assert its public authority; most likely readers of that ad or poster may just leave scratching their heads not knowing what REB or the file number stand for. There are still other partners in the system of vertical ethics for researchers, such as when research-grant committees take a closer look at the ethicality of applications (even though such judgments are typically rooted in ethics-review committees). Professional codes also constitute part of that hierarchy, although their authority and power are fading in light of the rising importance of ethics-review committees.

As we already know, the system of vertical hierarchy extends, or applies, to researchers whose research must not only satisfy departmental ethics committees but also those committees at the university or school board level. This hierarchical system of vertical ethics becomes more pronounced as the nature or style of research becomes more complex and requires, for example, approval from ethics committees at the school board level. An ethics staff member at a small university reported that parents had to give consent before videos could be taken of their school children (Focus Group REB1-S). Tilley and Gormley (2007: 372), two researchers in the Faculty of Education at Brock University, remind us of the vertical ethics that applied to the study of a school within a prison. Prison officials, university officials, federal, provincial, and local authorities had to be approached, as well as the principals, parents, and teachers (Interview E27-S). In the case of several elementary schools, a chair of an REB mentioned that a proposal had to go through several education boards (Interview C05-B). Another researcher, Betsy Bach (2005: 261), reported that another researcher's process involved nine applications, about 500 emails to REB members, and eleven months of submissions. Still another researcher (R008-S, Fieldnotes: 464) notes the different levels she had to negotiate when she tried to get ethics approval of her work that included the Nova Scotia Department of Corrections.

Groups in vulnerable contexts become the most difficult to research, at least when walking the path of vertical ethics. In one curious case, vertical ethics made it impossible for a graduate student to maintain anonymity. In her research on deaf children in sports, she was required to secure ethics approval not only from each school but also from school boards, athletic departments, and the Maritime School for the Deaf in Amherst, Nova Scotia. The small contingent of deaf children in the province meant that it would not be a difficult task to know who the children were (Kennedy, 2005). It is not uncommon for researchers to need to approach multiple REBs when researching vulnerable groups such as these and who might be spread out over several jurisdictions (Interview E25-S). In another instance, a graduate student was not allowed to study Aboriginals in prison. Prison officials did not allow the research despite the fact that his research already had ethics approval, albeit from other sources (Interview R002-M). All of these instances do not mean that ethics approval should not be sought. Rather, it means that researchers need to know that vertical ethics can complicate many research paths and can clearly extend beyond the university ethics committees themselves.

But vertical ethics extend even further. In Canada, the Social Sciences and Humanities Council (SSHRC) Grants Committees are increasingly touching the issue of ethics when debating research proposals for grants, something that ought to be left to REBs.[5] Ironically, REBs sometimes focus on the quality of the methods – something that ought to be left to the SSHRC Grant Committees. In another arm of the federal research-grants program (according to one REB chair), the Canadian Institutes for Health Research (CIHR) wants REBs to do a preliminary review of grant applications before CIHR will consider the grant. Once CIHR has approved the grant, it then undergoes a formal review by the REB. The main considerations are methods and ethics (Interview A11-S). One of the readers of an early draft of *The Seduction of Ethics* commented that, in her experience, particularly in CIHR reviews, assessors address the issue of ethics and, if there are any significant ethical issues identified, one is not funded.

The courts are now implicated, too, such as in the case of the graduate student Russell Ogden, formerly of Simon Fraser University (now at Kwantlen University College), whose notes about his master's research on assisted suicides and euthanasia were subpoenaed once by a coroner and at least twice by a Crown prosecutor (see, for example, Mueller, 2007: 828–9; SSHWC, 2004: 30). Ogden's steadfast refusal to hand over confidential notes was eventually recognized by a court, but only after considerable personal anguish and after his university was found negligent in defending his research (see also Presentation by Ogden, 6 March 2004, Fieldnotes: 155).[6] His refusal to break the confidentiality of his research participants earned him the respect of the participants in his subsequent research projects.

In a 1980s case in the United States, the police ordered Mario Brajuha, a graduate student in sociology at SUNY-Stony Brook, to turn over his fieldnotes after a suspicious fire broke out at the restaurant where he was conducting research for his dissertation (Thomas, 2002: 2). On 5 April 1984, a decision by federal Judge Jack B. Weinstein of the Eastern District of New York ruled that '[s]erious scholars cannot be required to turn over their fieldnotes in a grand jury investigation when the government fails to establish "substantial need" for them to do so.' The case went through appeal and back to the lower court, but it eventually accepted Brajuha's edited notes as fulfilling the subpoena. While the American Sociological Association thought that the case resulted in 'a positive solution,' it also believed that 'questions remained about what constituted "scholars' privilege" and the types of research that may be protected' (ASA, 2004).

Even within universities there are countervailing forces that sometimes pull the researcher in opposite directions. At Kwantlen University College, the REB approved the above-mentioned Russell Ogden's study of euthanasia, but the president of the University College rescinded that approval. As John Mueller (2007: 833) noted, 'Universities have revealed themselves to be, at the best, quite useless..., not willing or able to defend the institution and the researcher at the same time. Too often university administrations serve as accomplices in the abuse [of researchers], ignoring their own decisions and policies.' At another university, the school of journalism requires its researchers to have at least four signatures before his/her approved project reaches the university IRB, but only the IRB's signature, the fifth one, itself counts (R137, Fieldnotes: 733). At a Canadian mid-sized university, a student had run out of time to conduct his research and the Dean of Arts intervened to help speed up the REB's decision-making process (Conversation with R005-M, Fieldnotes: 140). It is not uncommon for a university's School of Graduate Studies to get involved (Interview C05-B). The payment of interview participants[7] has now led to a situation where researchers have to collect a receipt as demanded by the university's Accounting Office, but that violates the anonymity imposed by the REB (Interview R003-M).[8]

A more recent phenomenon (see, for example, C14-M, Fieldnotes: 942; Focus Group REB1-S), as mentioned above, requires researchers to submit an ethics certificate to scholarly journals to show that their respective ethics committees have approved the study.[9] Increasingly, researchers come to the REB with quality assurance studies for which journals might still require an ethics certificate (Interview S46-S); these studies normally do not require ethics review at the university level. One member of an REB offers this advice when dealing with researchers who approach him when they need an ethics approval for a journal (E16-B, Fieldnotes: 1516). He simply declines to review the project because, first, 'there is no longer any opportunity to protect participants,' and, second, a decision by the REB to approve the publication of research would look like approval to publish, and 'REBs should have nothing to do with this for reasons of academic freedom.' Some REBs, however, write 'a no-objection letter.'

Such requests for certificates, however, can take an unusual turn. One such case involves Tim Seifert, a senior professor at Memorial University of Newfoundland, and his graduate student, Christa Hedderson, who wanted to publish their study of skateboarders aged fourteen to eighteen (Seifert and Hedderson, 2008) with the *Journal of Sport Behavior.* When they submitted it for publication, the journal refused to accept it based on the fact that an adult witness had not been present to watch Christa as she observed the under-sixteen-year-old youth at the skateboard park. One of the reviewers wrote that in order to be published, they should have had

> someone at the skate park who [was] an adult to oversee what the researcher [was] doing (such as someone who works in a skateboard shop and who knows the kids, etc.) . . . there wasn't an adult at the skate park in this role. Additionally, all consent was oral, so there is no record of consent. I feel very strongly about adhering to the legal and ethical guidelines set by human subjects [*sic*] and that this [*sic*] data should not be published.[10]

Their study had passed ethics review at their own university.

A more peculiar instance concerns the editor of the *Journal of Applied Communications Research (JACR)* who stipulated that the authors of the article 'obtain either IRB approval or a statement that the project was not subject to IRB review' (Dougherty and Kramer, 2005a: 184).[11] We also learn of a researcher's friend's research that could not get published in a journal because her data started as personal journal entries before the IRB gave its approval (R131, Fieldnotes: 601). In other instances, journal editors prefer to have subjects anonymized (Dingwall, 2008: 7), as in the case of an oral historian who had completed a study of publicly identified community health activists only to have a major journal remove their names upon publication (Dingwall, 2008: 7). Malcolm Feeley (2007: 765) notes that 'journals that publish such [unapproved] research risk severe sanctions – even if it can be demonstrated that no harm to subjects occurred.'

The Intermeshing of Both Systems of Vertical Ethics

The above-mentioned comments might mean that each of the systems of vertical ethics for ethics committees and researchers do not overlap very much. Each side has its own vertical ethics to take care of. However, they do overlap substantially sometimes, such as when an application in

Alberta (Canada) also has to be submitted to the Privacy Commissioner and to Scientific Review Committee who must signify approval of the research (Interview C10-B), or when the university involves both the ethics committee and researcher in publicly contentious research projects or projects that might provoke litigation. In Manitoba, the Provincial Health Information Privacy Committee must approve all research in the province involving health research and it will not consider proposals unless already approved by the REB (Interview A11-S). However, when the projects do overlap, the researcher can also profoundly feel its negative impact, perhaps threatening the whole structure upon which his/her research stands. In the United States, as Fitch (2005; 273) argues, research is more complicated and risky now when 'the litigious, media-saturated culture ... raises the stakes on any decisions made about the studies conducted by employees of research institutions, many of them funded by tax dollars and thus subject to scrutiny from any number of angles.'

A deepened public concern about human subjects also causes these two hierarchies to mesh together. This concern, usually from the political right, according to Lincoln and Tierney (2004: 220), discredits everything related to postmodern theorizing, 'including constructivist theories of knowledge, postmodern epistemologies, Foucauldian analyses, post-structural investigations, action and participatory action research, and other kinds of research associated frequently or primarily with qualitative and/or interpretive research.' One researcher, in an interview, mentioned that all 'over the world people are questioning research, with political issues added on to it, not just ethics' (Interview R007-M). These public concerns, it seems, will not diminish the pressure on researchers and REBs to reshape research in unpredictable ways, touching on academic freedom. The two vertical ethics systems mesh in still other ways. An applied ethicist, in a public presentation at the 2003 bioethics conference in Calgary, noted that local ethics committees blame researchers, researchers blame the national ethics policies, but the national ethics regime blames these ethics committees and researchers (A06-B, Fieldnotes: 151).

Ideological and Practical Linkages

According to Iara Guerriero who has done very extensive research on the problem of research-ethics governance in Canada, there are at least thirty-one bodies and agencies engaged in this governance, some formal, some informal (Personal Communication, 5 June 2009). Aside from the numerous governmental agencies (with some buried inside other agencies), there are two prominent non-governmental organizations that nourish the life of ethics-review committees, namely, NCEHR (the National Council on Ethics in Human Research) and CAREB (the Canadian Association of Research Ethics Boards). Their annual gatherings are normally held, respectively, in February and May and attract members of ethics-review committees, administrators, staff, and sometimes researchers, in addition to a roster of guests mainly from North America who are considered experts in the field of ethics. The origins of these two groups are entirely different. At the request of the Medical Research Council of Canada (MRC) and with funding from MRC and Health Canada, the Royal College of Physicians and Surgeons of Canada established the National Council on Ethics in Human Research (NCEHR) in 1995, although its early foundations date back to 1989.[12] NCEHR filled an important vacuum. Although its basis was an interest in promoting ethics in medical research, it currently has undertaken a large number of visits to universities to assess the work of REBs. In April 2010, NCEHR lost its funding support and as of July 2010 was inactive. The Canadian Association of Research Ethics Boards (CAREB) is a 'grassroots national membership organization intended to represent the interests of all Canadian REBs and to reflect REB perspectives and concerns.'[13] Here, too, the MRC had a hand in helping to create this organization in March 2001 to monitor the work of REBs and to create 'a mechanism for improving the networking between REBs, and by building a community of Canadian REBs.'

Participants at the annual conferences of both NCEHR and CAREB conferences do share a common perspective whereby staff and members of ethics-review committees take cues from the presentations and seminars at the conferences.[14] Since 2004, when the full effect of the *TCPS* became obvious and relevant, attendance has always been over 210 participants (Participant Listings for NCEHR and CAREB, 2002–2008). More than a quarter of the attendees at the NCEHR meetings (normally held in February) attend the CAREB gatherings that are held a few months later.[15] The participants are mainly the staff of ethics offices, although there are representatives of the Interagency Advisory Panel on Research Ethics and other agencies. The participants at the CAREB meetings reflect a similar composition. During the 2005 and 2008 NCEHR conferences, 63.8 per cent and 70.5 per cent of attendees (out of 265 and 224), respectively, were women, which generally reflect the composition of ethics staff. As far as CAREB meetings go, 67.6 per cent and 74 per cent, respectively, were women (out of 210 and 200) who attended the conferences in 2005 and 2008. CAREB's narrow focus on REBs accounts for the larger proportion of women.

Thus, we can infer that the staff in research-ethics offices learn about many cues regarding the handling and adjudication of applications. These cues extend far beyond what is specified in the *TCPS* (given its large number of gaps). Indeed, when one explores the LISTSERVs of NCEHR and CAREB, it is these staff members who raise practical, mundane questions, primarily about procedures. Having followed these LISTSERVs since at least 2001, I have never seen an ethics question or comment addressed to researchers resolved, although there are occasional posted expressions of frustration by researchers when a member of the ethics staff 'gets it all wrong.'

The topics addressed at NCEHR and CAREB meetings do involve attendees and presenters from the United States. In 2005, four American presenters attended the 2005 NCEHR conferences, and three attended the 2008 conference, while only one American each attended the 2005 and 2008 CAREB conferences.[16] The conferences generally placed American presenters in the plenaries.

The NCEHR conferences in 2005 and 2008 strongly reflected the biomedical orientation of topics. In 2005, 35 per cent of agenda topics dealt primarily with biomedical research, which was quite similar to the 2008 conference.[17] The second highest number of presentations dealt with the process of research-ethics review (30 per cent and 20 per cent) (all figures correlate, respectively, with 2005 and 2008). Sessions on law and/or ethics in general covered 15 per cent of the presentations in both conferences. Increasingly though, one found sessions devoted to presenting topics related to NCEHR as an organization, usually in plenaries (5 per cent and 15 per cent). Presentations that dealt with ethics in the social sciences were far less numerous (15 per cent and 20 per cent). However, I may have exaggerated the content of the social-science presentations because I have included presentations dealing with research in First Nations (Aboriginal, Native) communities. Thus, social science topics are a distant minority on the NCEHR programs.

The two CAREB conferences (2005 and 2008) were shorter in length than the NCEHR conferences and relied less on non-Canadian presenters. Topics related to the process of the research-ethics review occupied an important place in both programs (42 per cent and 24 per cent). Presentations on topics of interest to medical researchers constituted

17 per cent and 35 per cent, respectively, of the programs in 2005 and 2008. Like the NCEHR meetings, there was very little on the program that spoke to social science research (8 per cent and 18 per cent); and most of those sessions involved research in First Nations communities. Topics that dealt with law and/or ethics covered 17 per cent and 18 per cent of the conference. All sessions were plenaries. There was hardly anything about CAREB itself.

When comparing the two sets of conferences, there were more American presenters at the NCEHR meetings than at the CAREB ones. CAREB also looked more like a 'home-grown' Canadian meeting focusing less on American-style ethics and review processes than was the case with NCEHR. At both conferences, however, there were no critical challenges posed about the ethics-review system itself. No critical self-reflection about the work and nature of ethics committees. Participants of both conferences lived in a bubble of compliance. Unlike academic conferences, there were no voices of dissent, nor were any expected.

It is clear that the system of research-ethics review constitutes a membrane of interrelated institutions and activities. Vertical ethics is what we call the connective tissue between all levels of the membrane. While research-ethics committees and researchers share many parts of vertical ethics, one can also claim that the vertical ethics that binds committees to other levels can also be quite different from that of researchers. For ethics-review committees, the primary vertical ties involve other ethics-review committees, federal or national offices, and non-profit organizations that annually drive the ideological and practical aspects of the ethics-review system. The two annual conferences (of NCEHR and CAREB) not only reinforce the ideological content of the system of research-ethics review but also prioritize the model of biomedical research as *the* accepted model for ethics review to the disadvantage of social research models. This ideological world does not entertain insights and views critical of the research-ethics review system. For researchers, those ties are more closely tied to university administrators, grants committees, editors of peer-reviewed journals, and (to a much lesser extent) professional code of ethics. There is no question, though, that both systems of vertical ethics intersect, gradually displacing the world of research as they do.

15 Will the Social Sciences Wither Away or Is There an Alternative?

Don't be lulled into unconsciousness.
George Feenstra

We return to the analogy of the tundra. When social researchers try to plot their way through the ethics tundra by following the biomedical exigencies of ethical research, they lose their way. The ethics codes tend to cast their guidelines in a way that direct the gaze of biomedical researchers to a point on the horizon. Any experienced traveller knows that the tundra cannot be traversed using a beacon as a straight line: there are innumerable bogs, ponds, rock formations, and outcrops that can obstruct the direction of even the most seasoned adventurer Without intimate knowledge of the tundra, one can become lost. Taking the analogy to a higher level, one expects to see ethics guidelines in the same light, a form of direction-giving in the landscape of ethical research. However, the ethics codes offer little in the way of direction for social researchers. And, yet, ethics codes are so persuasive and seductive, that they can lead many astray.

One can see formal research-ethics codes in light of their seductive quality, luring countless administrators, researchers, scholars, and policymakers into their ambit. Several societal trends drive this seduction: moral panic, the belief that people are vulnerable, the questioning of science and scholarship, and the societal drive for accountability. This seduction has led to systematic changes in the way social research is conducted, altering its methods and frameworks. These inevitable changes have led to a homogenization of research methods and the pauperization of the social sciences. Disciplines have begun to resemble each other. The richness of conventional social research has been lost as researchers have tried to fit their approaches to the technical demands of ethics codes.

While lamenting the particular effects of research-ethics codes on social science research, one cannot take a stand on whether ethics codes should be either retained or dismissed. To hope for, or to engineer, the collapse of ethics codes (because they do not serve the social sciences well) is unrealistic. The codes express the temper of the times and are here to stay. This book has simply tracked their impact.

Is there no relief from the gloom for the social sciences? Relief is perhaps not possible. Research-ethics review derives its dynamics from its own, internal processes, particularly as they relate to its fledgling bureaucratic habits. Its modus operandi is secretive and undemocratic. It can create 'danger myths' that distort its assessment of social research. There is an unquenchable devotion to the goodness of its own regulation, accompanied by surges of self-aggrandisement and power. Its moral cosmology mitigates against the moral agency of researchers and research participants. The epithet directed at researchers is 'trust but verify'; the epithet for research participants is 'they need our protection and they are vulnerable.' Ethics pointillism (which magnifies every detail of an application and exaggerates the extent to which research projects pose a threat to research participants) ensures that each research application is carefully vetted, but on what grounds?

It is worrisome to see that the decisions by ethics committees are grounded more in personal reflection and the disciplinary paradigm of their individual members than in a collective, consensus-building consultative process. Sometimes, too, there is no intimate familiarity with ethics codes and with the research design and theories of research applications. The internal structure of the research-ethics review system is a destabilizing one for researchers despite its claims of having authority. Its discursive regime offers texts laden with authority, embedded in a semblance of higher ethical principles. It resorts to the use of the passive voice. It uses words of insistence rather than words of assistance. It is a system of social regulation of research.

The internal dynamics of the research-ethics review gain energy from wider social-structural dynamics. The belief that humans are vulnerable is grounded in the culture of fear about science; worries about accountability are another driving force behind these regulations. Although technically independent, ethics-review committees are lodged in university administrations that pursue agendas independent of those of researchers. The research-ethics review is linked to a system of vertical ethics in which national guidelines and regulations give it authority. It also connects to numerous agencies and bodies that have thought about ethics and research. The rise of neo-positivism gives credence (again) to the value of hypothesis-driven research as opposed to inductive research. In Canada alone, the business of academic ethics is a $35 million industry; when you include three other countries (United States, United Kingdom, and Australia), the industry amounts to some $500 million, with an inordinate amount of costs borne by cash-strapped universities. The reciprocal obligations, contradictions, and inherent permutations of such a large industry are nearly impossible to escape.

Yet, there is an escape ... of sorts. Ethnographic fieldwork is fleeing into the hands of journalists who have largely remained free of the ethics-review constraints that researchers commonly face. Undercover police and security personnel now engage in the kinds of research previously reserved for social researchers. Anthropologists (and other social researchers) are fleeing to the military and corporate sectors where researchers are invited to bring about understanding of culture and markets, respectively. Biomedical researchers are filling the vacuum and resorting to narrative research and, in the process, establishing ethics guidelines for other narrative researchers.

The internal and external systems are the reasons why there is a cacophony of complaints. Social researchers buttress their complaints with acts of defiance that operate just below the surface of attention by ethics committees. Some researchers fully avoid ethics review, others comply to a certain extent, and still others faithfully try to comply. The moral career of researchers, however, depends on the perceived obedience to the new regime of the ethics review.

One can worry about the decline of particular research methods, although not wholly due to this rising regime (but also fostered by careerism, grantsmanship, and the push to speed one's way through graduate studies). Whether it be the traditional social research involving fieldwork, covert research (not to be confused with deception in research), and the decline of national surveys, or a committees' self-assigned mandate that all data be destroyed, each one of these speak against the kinds of social research discussed in chapter 12 of this book. It has also become more difficult to pursue some topics of scholarly interest, such as those involving children, minors, abuse, illegal activities, and sex-oriented topics. The topics must not only be 'safe' but also bring a 'social benefit.' Conventional theoretical orientations are falling under the axe of neo-positivism. Paradoxically, one hears the subjective voice of research-ethics committees, while the voices of researchers and research participants are silenced. The ethics chill has arrived.

The favoured methods of research in the research-ethics review regime pale in diversity and richness in comparison to conventional social research. The method of stand-alone interviews can miss the cultural and social character of life. The regime also advocates member-checking, but may do so at the expense of critical analysis of collective representation of social data. Similarly, advocating the use of the focus group as an acceptable research method can push social research away from the diversity and richness of other methods. Will the social sciences whither away? Social forces seem to relegate the social sciences at least to the margins.

Puncturing the Gloom

History shows us that moments of change occur abruptly, like birds changing their direction in mid-flight. There are several alternatives that can puncture the gloom about the fate of social research and the disenfranchisement of researchers. First, one must rely on the creativity of social researchers themselves that cannot be stilled by uniform obedience. Members of ethics-review boards might want to step beyond the ritualism and fetishism of application forms, consent forms, and checklists. Both sides (i.e., researchers and members of ethics-review committees) can replace gut reaction with a mindful consideration of the researcher's intentions and the social setting where the research is conducted. If the data presented in *The Seduction of Ethics* are any guide to the future, there seems to be enough concern among chairs and members of research-ethics committees about the current state of affairs to press for changes in the direction of restoring the lustre inherent in the diversity and richness of social research. The responsibility lies on the shoulders of universities, REBs, and researchers to puncture the gloom.

Universities need to question themselves about how the tasks and responsibilities of research-ethics committees are to be reformulated and reassigned. The question is whether universities will be satisfied with ethics committees merely undertaking 'convenience work' rather than pursuing ethical research paths in collaboration with researchers. One hopes that universities and research-ethics committees will take lessons from such cases as Ogden's at Simon Fraser University and Kwantlen University College that express conflict of interest among university administrations, ethics boards, the courts, researchers, and research participants.

Aside from allocating additional resources to the tasks of research-ethics committees, universities need to have a clearer idea as to the intent of well-functioning committees: are they meant to be low-grade taskmasters devoting their (already scarce) resources to, in effect, 'grading' the applications from researchers, or are they there to instil the engagement of higher-grade ethical principles? To be sure, higher-grade principles in ethics need not involve more paperwork. Paperwork, as we have seen, distracts committees from doing ethics work and researchers from pondering ethical considerations. In this connection, universities can enter into a dialogue with their ethics-committee chair and discover ways to find a more effective division of labour between the chair and the other members of the ethics committee.

As mentioned earlier, universities' holding research grants in abeyance while researchers are seeking ethics approval for their research can act as a brake in the universities' desire to speed up the research-ethics review process.

Researchers must undertake the responsibility of knowing the ethics code that formally governs their work, whether it is the *TCPS*, the 'Common Rule,' or another national instrument, so that they can engage in a direct and knowledgeable discussion with ethics committees, university administrations, and national policymakers about their own perspectives and needs.

Researchers will be well advised to come together among themselves to engage in strategic collaboration with research-ethics committees and to inundate the academic literature with their perspectives about the ethics-review process. Researchers should not allow themselves to become passive recipients of ethical knowledge and ethics reviews; researchers should attach themselves to a more active model. The more senior the scholar, the more important and relevant such a task is.

Research-ethics committees should have the same obligation and standards of treating researchers with which they expect researchers to treat research participants. The treatment of researchers can be dismissive; it constitutes one of the hidden paradoxes of what ethics committees do. The committees see themselves as concerned about ethical conduct in research, despite a good dollop of bureaucratic control and social regulation of research, but they might consider expressing their relationship with researchers as one of the foremost ethical actions they can take as a dynamic force of example. Such self-designations as 'ethics queen' or 'ethics czar' run counter to any attempt to establish an ethical relationship with researchers.

REBs need to have a dialogue about the relationship between their chairs and their members. No less challenging is to abandon a number of practices that they instituted vis-à-vis the social sciences during the implementation of the first *TCPS* or the 'Common Rule' so that they now can turn for guidance to the second *TCPS*[1] or subsequent versions of the 'Common Rule' that incorporate new aspects fundamental to social science research. Probably, the most significant task for ethics committees, however, is to resist offering, suggesting, or insisting that students adopt the committees' own ideas about methodology. The only acceptable source for students who want to imbibe knowledge about methods of research rests with their supervisors and within their disciplines. When ethics committees insist that students conform to their fragmented or incomplete knowledge and discipline-specific techniques of research, the decline of social science methods and frameworks is the inevitable result.

The power structure inherentin our current systems of ethics review is an antithetical one. The ethics task masters reinforce subtly and not-so subtly this power structure. Power structures beget power struggles – hardly a beneficial element when universities, committees, and researchers engage in the discovery of ethical guidelines. Such discovery is especially important when ethical horizons are being pushed further and further back from our ken. The amount of work undertaken by ethics committees and researchers keeps those horizons away, unexplored. Such busyness lulls them into unconscious action – the antidote to a life of active reflection about things that matter.

Cooperation, not competition, will allow universities, researchers, and research-ethics committees to bring the horizon closer to all of us. One is tempted to recommend strategic opposition to the prevailing power structure, but such an approach defeats itself. Public and political sentiments reinforce the continuing prevalence of national research-ethics regimes. The regimes are here to stay even when the diversity and richness of social research must suffer as a consequence.

One ventures to offer the idea that the spirit of being of service in all matters pertaining to research ethics might be an answer. Such service finds its highest expression in humble, active, and consensual attitudes and behaviours among all parties who wish to embark on a road already fraught with power, conflict, and prestige. Indeed, the success-ful wayfarer crossing the tundra must rely fully on consensual attitudes and behaviours in order to traverse an area that is fraught with surprise and unexpected twists and turns. We can ill afford bureaucratic rou-tines to lull us into unconsciousness.

Appendix A: Methodology

The Seduction of Ethics is not a strictly qualitative-research study. While it does rely on qualitative research as its core, the book also invokes historical and international-comparative data, as well as other techniques of gathering data. With the help of a grant from the Social Sciences and Humanities Research Council of Canada (Grant No. 410-2003-0318) I embarked on an ethnographic study of the interactions between Canada's Research Ethics Boards and social science researchers in 2003. I completed the research in the summer of 2008 and focused on analysing the data in the fall of 2008. By February 2009, I was ready to discuss the data and began writing *The Seduction of Ethics*. In July 2009, after a two-month hiatus, I completed the first draft.

I attempted to cast a wide net across Canada's national ethics regime, using a variety of research strategies and relying on as many participants as possible with as many divergent views. During these five years of research, I increasingly relied on ten strategies that would allow me to understand the metabolism of the research-ethics review. Each of these strategies occupied my attention in varying intensity. While each strategy is conceptually distinct, there are nonetheless many interconnections among them. When a particular strategy provided findings and hunches, I would often resort to other strategies to either echo what I thought was germane or to confirm that it was not. Often, a strategy might indicate a wealth of data that could only be procured through another strategy.

1. Participant-Observation

With the initial goal of analysing fifteen Research Ethics Boards (REBs) across Canada, I had hoped to conduct participant-observations during the REBs regular sessions. Some REBs proved to be impregnable, not allowing any opportunities for participant-observation and also leaving no time to their staff to be interviewed by the researcher. Other REBs, while still not allowing participant-observation during the meetings, were sufficiently interested in the research to allow all of their members (and office staff) to be interviewed. A few others, namely five, opened their doors to being observed in 'action,' two of which offered a full inspection of their records and applications (with the consent of their researchers) and cooperated in a wonderful manner (these involved three small, one medium-sized, and one large university). At one meeting, a stack of my first book on ethics, *Walking the Tightrope* (2002), was waiting for me at the assigned place at the table and I was asked if I would please autograph them. I took extensive notes during these formal meetings, often preceded by conversations and/or interviews with REB chairs, researchers, and staff. Before sending the book manuscript to press, I shared chapter 8 with these REBs asking them to assure me that I had sufficiently protected their anonymity.

Three of the universities allowed me to take the minutes of their previous meetings outside the REB meeting itself for my analysis, while four permitted me to keep a copy of the agenda. I had formal meals with members of two REBs; three offered to pick me up at the hotel. The care of researchers in general, and of me as an outside researcher, was particularly striking among the small universities (see below for a definition of small, medium-sized, and large universities).

Attending conferences and symposia on ethics in research allowed me to observe and learn about research ethics from their particular perspectives. Especially important were those sponsored by the National Council on Ethical Human Research (NCEHR) and by the Canadian Association of Research Ethics Boards (CAREB), and by numerous professional societies, including the Canadian Anthropology Society (CASCA) held in Windsor (May 2002); the Couch-Stone Symposium in Tempe, AZ (February 2003); the Canadian Bioethics Society Conference in Calgary (October 2004); and the Canadian Institutes of Health Research Strategic Training Initiative and the Quebec Population Health Research Network in Montreal (May 2005). In the end I listened to over sixty presentations at these and other conferences. In some cases, I was invited to make a presentation about some aspect of my own growing research or about the development of Canadian national policy. Between 2003 and 2009, inclusive, I made forty-one formal presentations throughout Canada, the United States, Argentina, Slovenia,

Brazil, Australia, Denmark, and China. I also participated in several roundtable discussions. I took note, like any lecturer, of the specific questions and comments that came my way. As a result, I had to cull my findings from some 1,700 pages of fieldnotes.

2. Interviews, Conversations, and Chats

Somewhat more contrived are the interviews I conducted. I would formally request a place, date, and time. Less regimented, however, are conversations and chats ('research moments'): I would simply approach the intended research participant and ask for an opportunity to talk with him/her on behalf of my research; more typically, chats would arise more spontaneously. After someone had learned I was doing research, he/she would, without being asked, volunteer something about his/her own experiences with REBs or IRBs. The number and types of disciplines represented are diverse, despite my focus on the experience of social science researchers (in the fields of criminology, sociology, social work, business, psychology, demography, philosophy, history, Aboriginal studies, education, communication, anthropology, social justice, counselling, botany, fine arts, English-as-a-Second Language, and so on).

With one or two exceptions, I have disguised all research participants in *The Seduction of Ethics*. Interestingly, a number of research participants, including some REB chairs, researchers, and staff were not interested in seeing the 'Information Sheet' about my research. In one case, moreover, I had forgotten to bring the sheet along, and I held the interview without much ado.

For the most part, I held the interviews in the academic offices or work rooms (if I were interviewing two people at the same time), sometimes in restaurants, sometimes in my hotel room. An interview in the university's cafeteria proved too difficult to tape, and I returned with the interview participant to his office where he so very kindly repeated his insights about research-ethics review. In another case, I started the interview in the lobby of the hotel where I was staying, but when the noise from the hotel's registration desk got too overwhelming, we moved to the glass-partitioned lounge. One interview participant asked me to come back the following day and then acted as a guide to his favourite part of a rocky beach, sharing with me his world views and his workday manners, a most thoughtful and meaningful gesture. Throughout all the interviews, there was not one discourtesy; all participants were eager to help.

Table A.1   Summary of Research Participants

	Researcher	Chair of REB	Member of REB	Staff in ethics office	University administrator	Editor or member of an academic journal	Total
Interviews	9	9	6	4	3		31
Conversations and chats	130	3	4	31	5		173
Presentations	39	2	7	8	5	1	62
Focus group		1	1	2			4
Totals	178	15	18	45	13	1	270

Appendix D offers a typical line of topics covered in my interviews. As the research progressed, I offered additional conversational topics and sometimes talked about my initial research findings, offering something as corroboration or to think about. Sometimes, the direction of the interview, conversation, or chat would flow in the opposite direction when the research participant asked me about recent policy initiatives (Fieldnotes: 324).

Table A.1 offers an overview of my research activities. The 31 people I formally interviewed included 9 researchers, 9 chairs of REBs, 6 other members of REBs, 4 staff members in the ethics or research offices, and 3 senior-level administrators. The longest interview lasted two and a half hours, the shortest forty-five minutes. On average, though, interviews lasted one hour and fifteen minutes. All of this material resulted in 444 pages of formal-interview data and numerous other pages of data.

When one considers the overall contacts with the 'research-ethics' landscape, I have reached 270 people, 66 per cent of whom were researchers, 6 per cent REB chairs, 13.6 per cent members of REBs (excluding the chairs), 7 per cent staff in ethics offices, 5 per cent administrators, and 0.4 per cent editors of an academic journal (all percentages are rounded). These contacts include people from the United States, England, Australia, and South Africa. Many of these contacts reached me through email or through a LISTSERV.

Throughout my research there was, as expected, an extensive email exchange, some through the NCEHR (National Council of Ethical Human Research) and CAREB (Canadian Association of Research Ethics Boards) LISTSERVs, while other emails were directed to me

Table A.2   Cross-Section of Research Participants According to Canadian Universities and Organizations Represented in *The Seduction of Ethics*

Type of Institution	Western Canada	Prairies	Ontario	Quebec	Atlantic Provinces*	Totals
Large universities	1	3	3	4	0	11
Medium-sized universities	2	2	6	1	3	14
Small universities	9	3	5	1	6	24
Total universities	12	8	14	6	9	49
Non-university research centres	1	0	9	0	1	11
Non-university REBs	1	1	1	1	0	4
Total non-university	2	1	10	1	1	15

*There are no 'large' universities in the Atlantic provinces.
Source: The size of the universities is drawn from SSHRC Report, 'Research Capacity' (29 October 2001; unpublished).

personally or were a result of my contacting nearly 100 researchers. In all, these exchanges involved about 160 people and hundreds of emails. When identifying a person by name, I have sought their approval for every one of their specific, identifiable comments and insights appearing in *The Seduction of Ethics*. Many comments, however, were so generic or universal that they might have come from anyone interested in research ethics. Some sought my advice as to how they could approach their IRBs in a constructive manner in the hopes of change.

A cross-section of universities and organizations across Canada is displayed in table A.2. I found research participants in forty-nine universities (representing 71.4 per cent of all universities and colleges in Canada), as well as in fifteen non-university organizations. When sorting the universities into small, medium, and large universities, the spread is fairly representative (the sorting of universities is based on the classification scheme developed by SSHRC: small universities have fewer than 250 faculty, medium-sized universities have 250–499 faculty, while large universities have more than 499 faculty).

3. The Focus Group

Given the pressures of work on the part of REBs, it was not easy to convene a focus group, but in March 2006 I did convene a group at a small university in Ontario, consisting of an REB chair, a member of the REB, and two staff members of the ethics office.

4. Reports, Memos, Cases, and a Poem

Throughout the length of the research, researchers and members of REBs sent me reports, either of their activities or about the actions taken by their respective academic societies. Of particular interest to me were memos and cases. The former contained the accounts of the experiences of researchers, albeit in an abbreviated form. The latter, however, were the full-fledged telling of these experiences. In this context, researchers shared with me letters from their ethics committees. I selected five sets of those exchanges for inclusion in this book. Researchers also included the history and/or fate of their interactions with their ethics committees. I am grateful to each one for sharing these experiences. As will be seen from the contents of *The Seduction of Ethics*, some of the authors explicitly asked that their names be associated with my reporting of those accounts. A poem also constituted an interesting part of the researchers' experiences with REBs.

5. Role of Conferences, Workshops, and Symposia

Aside from their value as sites for participant-observation, the materials produced by conferences and symposia proved to be invaluable for the analysis of conference themes and programs and to see who typically participates in the conferences sponsored by NCEHR and CAREB. My findings allowed me to assess the degree to which these venues were helpful in assisting REB members and their staff develop decisions.

I have already mentioned my participation in a number of annual meetings of various academic and professional bodies. As well, the Congress of the Humanities and the Social Sciences (Toronto, Halifax, Winnipeg, Saskatoon), the Canadian 'Qualitatives,' and a regional conference of the American Sociological Association were helpful venues for learning more about the interaction between ethics-review committees and researchers. Over the five-year period, I attended twelve such conferences. In half of the cases, I presented on behalf of the Interagency Advisory Panel on Research Ethics; in the other half, as someone presenting his research findings.

6. Textual Analyses

Textual analyses took several paths. First, I compared the texts of both earlier and current policies at one university, noting tone and emendations. Second, I took advantage of my three-year stint as the Sociology Book Review Editor of the *Canadian Review of Sociology and Anthropology* (now *Canadian Review of Sociology*) to examine the 200 books that crossed my desk, to realize that only 27 involved research participants. This finding was particularly relevant for my discussion of how research methods have changed under the purview of the research-ethics review. Third, I also studied a number of annual reports submitted by REBs to various university senates. Fourth (as mentioned earlier), a number of researchers across Canada shared with me letters they received from their respective research-ethics boards, often including their own detailed replies.

7. Experience in Canada's National Research-Ethics Regime

Between 2001 and 2005, I served as founding member of Canada's Interagency Advisory Panel on Research Ethics (PRE); I also served as the first chair of the Social Sciences and Humanities Working Group on Ethics (SSHWC) from 2003 to 2005. This organizational experience laid an important foundation for my own understanding of the landscape of the national research-ethics regime. As such, I many documents came under my purview. Given the confidential nature of many of these documents, I only used those that were already (or later) published in a public venue. During this time, too, I limited my research activities to gathering public documents, reports, and academic and other literature, hoping to avoid any perceived potential conflict of interest between my duties as a member of PRE and as an academic researcher. The views in my book do not reflect the viewpoints of PRE.

In the course of my research, I was in contact with Mr Michael O'Higgins who was spearheading a British advisory group to review the NHS Research Ethics Committee (2004) and, in April 2008, I spoke at the invitation of OHRP to an advisory group in Washington, DC.

8. Survey Data

Just before I received a grant from the Social Sciences and Humanities Research Council of Canada, I was asked by PRE to make a presentation on 'expedited review' to the 2003 NCEHR Annual Conference. I contacted twenty-one universities and asked them to relate to me their experiences with expedited review (van den Hoonaard, 2003a). I found ample opportunity to use the resulting survey data when I was writing a portion of *The Seduction of Ethics*.

9. Theses Sources

Between 1994 and 2004, during my short period of abeyance in contacting research participants while I was a member of PRE, I examined the contents and nature of Canadian master's theses in anthropology and sociology. This time period represents five years before and five years after the *TCPS* came into effect (i.e., 2001). This examination resulted in my publishing two papers in the *Journal of Empirical Research on Human Research Ethics* (van den Hoonaard, 2006; and van den Hoonaard and Connolly, 2006). During this time, various universities asked me to serve as an external examiner for PhD theses. I also had a number of graduate students pursuing ethics in research for their degree or course work.

10. Publications

Numerous are the published publications concerning ethics and research. I have relied primarily on three types of publications: those issued by governmental agencies, those available through special issues of academic and professional journals, and the approximately 600 journal articles and books on the topic. Of the latest, there are nearly eighty articles that specifically described the relationship between research-ethics committees and researchers. *The Seduction of Ethics* concentrated on this latter group.

11. LISTSERVs and Blogs

I have relied on the availability of websites and blogs dealing with the issues of ethics and research. In Canada, two LISTSERVs are available. The National Council on Ethical Human Research (http://ncehr-cnerh. org/english/listserv.php) has frequently proven to be a valuable source of information. In the preamble to its LISTSERV, the NCEHR listserv describes its contents as being particularly useful for researchers, among others:

> The NCEHR List Serv [*sic*] is a Canadian-based resource for networking and sharing of information and best practices. It is open to professionals with direct and significant involvement in the protection of research participants.

Subscription

The List Serv [*sic*] is open to Canadian members of Research Ethics Boards (REBs), research administrators, researchers conducting human research and professionals involved in clinical activities in Canada. Others will be admitted to the list depending on the extent of their expertise and involvement in human subjects research. NCEHR reserves the right to approve or decline subscription.

Confidentiality

Although the List Serv [*sic*] is restricted, it should be considered a public forum. Therefore, authors must abstain from communicating confidential information. (accessed 24 January 2009)

The other Canadian LISTSERV, although referred to less frequently, belongs to the Canadian Association of Research Ethics Boards (careb-accer@careb-accer.org). As someone known to have a long-standing research interest in ethics and research, I regularly participated in both of these LISTSERVs.

In the United States, at least four LISTSERVs and blogs offer the most recent debates and issues on ethics and research. I found the Institutional Review Blog at http://www.institutionalreviewblog.com/ to be one of the most useful blogs. This blog is largely critical of the use of IRBs. The AAAS Scientific Freedom, Responsibility and Law Program (SFRL), in conjunction with the AAAS Committee on Scientific Freedom and Responsibility, publishes on-line 'Professional Ethics Report (PER)' at per@listserv.aaas.org. Since 1988, this quarterly newsletter has reported on news and events, programs and activities, and resources related to professional ethics issues, with a particular focus on those professions whose members are engaged in scientific research and its applications.

Although they fall strictly outside the realm of ethics and research, there are two additional American LISTSERVs that have been sources of insights. The first one belongs to the Society for the Study of Symbolic Interactionism (I joined the LISTSERV on 10 July 2003 and indicated that I would be participating in it both as a member of the Society and as a researcher on the topic of ethics and research (Fieldnotes: 309). The second one belongs to the Oral History Association of America at su.edu. This LISTSERV actively pursues the condition and fate of oral history research on IRBs, along with its other professional interests.

Appendix B: Applications Considered Annually by Selected Research Ethics Boards in Canada*

University	No. of applications	% which are social science	% which are expedited	Size of university (i.e., number of researchers)
A Selection of Large Canadian Universities				
U of Alberta			30–40%	685
U of Calgary	approx. 400–500			515
U of Manitoba	818	48.4%*		527
McGill U (2 REBs)	127			598
U of Ottawa	265 (2005)	64.9%		684
U of British Columbia	777			880
U of Western Ontario	900 (2005)		90%	657
A Selection of Medium-Sized Canadian Universities				
Carleton U	ca 200			340
Concordia U	163			401
Dalhousie U	ca 215	60%		343
U of Guelph	350–400 (2006)	16% (?)	95%	257
Laurentian U	122 (2005–6)		68.0%	264
McMaster U	227			272
Memorial U of Newfoundland	120		25–30% of medical res.	439
Queen's U			83.5%	416
U of Regina	04–05: 176		90–95 %	306
Ryerson U.	169		99.4%	351
U of Saskatchewan	Social Sci REB: 300			414
U de Sherbrooke	125			306
Simon Fraser U	386 (2002)		97%	393
U of New Brunswick	153 (2002)		99%	319

University	No. of applications	% which are social science	% which are expedited	Size of university (i.e., number of researchers)
A Selection of Medium-Sized Canadian Universities				
U of Victoria	700–800		80–90%	454
U of Waterloo	800		92%	351
U of Windsor	301	13.6%	68.4%	304
A Selection of Small Canadian Universities				
Athabasca U	95	100%		63
Bishops U	8	25%		87
Brandon U	50			117
U of Cape Breton			90–100%	56
Fraser Valley U	47 (2004)			109
Lakehead U	124			159
U of Lethbridge	approx. 100	100%	99%	
U of Vancouver Island	49		90%	
Okanagan U College			0%	116
Saint Mary's U	250	58.6%		156
St Francis Xavier U	ca. 100		10–15%	102
St Thomas U	6			73
Trinity Western U	100	85.2%		66
U of Northern BC	135 (2005)		14.8% (2005)	88
Wilfrid Laurier U	200–240		98%	208

*Applicable years vary but they normally cover any year between 2004 and 2008.
**Psychology, sociology, education, nursing, and so on.
Sources: (1) For statistics regarding number of applications: Research Offices/Services in related universities. (2) For the size of the university: SSHRC Report, 'Research Capacity' (29 October 2001; unpublished). (3) For the particular information on the number of applications: Ethics Research Offices in relevant universities.

Appendix C: Samples of Communications from Ethics Committees to Researchers*

Case R093-B

The Ethics Committee reviewed this protocol and had the following comments:

(1) The PI should clarify the purpose of the research and what his main research questions are. For example, what about worker-management relations is of concern to him? The four dissertation questions (protocol states there are three) in the Purpose and Objectives section are unclear.

(2) The PI is requesting to use data on blue-collar canal workers that he collected three years ago during his employment with the same company he will be working for and proposing to conduct research this summer, but no details about the data are provided. Please elaborate on what is contained in the past data. Does the company know that you were collecting data three years ago? How was the data collected? Over what period of time was data being collected? What were the circumstances in which the data was [*sic*] collected?

(3) The PI would like to collect more data from the same company through participant observation (naturalistic) this summer, but he does not want to tell them that he is conducting research. The PI argues that the subjects' 'natural behaviour would change and consequently contaminate the data'–what is their 'natural behaviour'?

---

*Errors of spelling, grammar, and syntax have been retained unless there was an unavoidable misunderstanding

(4) Since the PI will also be working in the environment that he will be observing, presumably he will be interacting with the workers. Will the PI be asking the workers questions?

(5) When intervention by the researcher occurs, can the data collection methodology still be considered naturalistic observation? Arguably, at the moment of intervention, the behaviour observed would not have been engaged in anyway had the researcher not been present, so can the workers behaviour be considered 'natural.' Not obtaining consent from people being studied, especially if they are being questioned or if there is any intervention, goes against the spirit of the Tri-Council Policy Statement and the Committee's interpretation of it. Please refer to Article 2.3 on Naturalistic Observation in the Tri-Council Policy Statement available from the following website: http://www.nserc.ca/programs/ethics/english/index.htm. Could the researcher respond to the previously raised points?

(6) Although the PI claims that he will be coding all aspects of the work environment so that no person or place can be identified, what could happen if a worker was identified and linked to sensitive data? Some data being collected is most likely sensitive, maybe even potentially damaging to a person's career, which leaves the workers at the company vulnerable. Also, not only are individual workers vulnerable, but more important, this labour force as a collective is vulnerable. Writing about labourer's feelings about management is tricky for 'subjects.' The Committee is concerned about how the workers and the labour force as a collective will be protected. When deception is used in any study, a strong case for why it is necessary needs to be made; an especially strong case needs to be made for a study that is not considered minimal risk because it involves a vulnerable population. Please justify further why you think deception should be used in your study.

Case R115-M

As Chair of the Research Ethics Board (REB), I have reviewed your application ([title of research project]–REB#...) for its compliance with the Tri-Council Policy (TCP) and with the [University's] Policy. On the basis of the review, I consider your project to be eligible for expedited review since any risk to participants that might exist appears not to exceed the 'minimal risk' outlined in TCP.

In my opinion, your project does not appear to be in compliance with TCP and the [University's Policy]. There are a few minor matters to address. Specifically, although Tri-Council policy permits the principal investigator to bypass use of an Informed Consent Form, the elements normally found in consent forms must be conveyed to participants through the project-related information they receive before they agree to participate. In your case, at least two of these elements have not been included in your 'Information Sheet for Participants.'

So that you may make the minor additions with only minimal effort, I am taking the liberty of pasting the 'Requirements for Informed Consent Forms' below this material. I have highlighted those elements that appear to be missing. You might find one-or-two more that are missing when you review them.

. . .

(a) An Informed Consent Form must be written in language that the potential subject can understand.
(b) A statement identifying a person not directly involved in the research, for example the Department Chair or Faculty Dean, who may be contacted should the subject have concerns about the research.
(c) The period of time required for subject participation.
(d) Where applicable, (for any research involving questionnaires or interviews), a statement informing subjects that they may decline to answer specific questions.
(e) When teenaged subjects are considered by the applicant to be competent to consent without parental involvement, the applicant must provide justification for this conclusion.

Please revise your Information Sheet to include the above noted omissions (and any others I might have missed) and return the revised documents to me via e-mail. I thank you in advance for your compliance with my request.

Case R169-M

(a) The response to Q 5 in the ORE 101 [Office of Research Ethics] indicates that this project is [R169-M]'s PhD research. If this is the case, isn't it standard practice for a PhD proposal to be reviewed and approved by the student's dissertation committee before the research is initiated? Please clarify this.

(b) (i) Have you received written confirmation from the two companies that they support the conduct of this study at their locations. If so, may I have a copy of the letters? I realize that [your Department] has a relationship with Company A and Company B through previous studies but would appreciate confirmation that the companies do not anticipate any safety issues due to the researcher's presence on the floor for several hours 2–3 times per week for a 4–5 month period. (ii) Further, are workers given time off work to participate in the one hour interviews? (iii) Could you comment on whether there is a union at either company that would have to be consulted on any issues (I presume so sin[c]e [sic] this is mentioned in the information letter)? How did you go about getting support of the union?

(c) I could not tell from the [Office of Research Ethics] application or proposal what process you intend to use to recruit volunteers from each of the two companies and within each of the three groups. For example, will it be through a recruitment poster, presentation, word of mouth, flyer etc? I would need a copy of any materials used of recruitment. Also, please indicate who will be responsible for recruitment i.e., will it be [R169-M] vs. someone in the company? In order to ensure arm's length in recruitment, it is preferred that [R169-M] do this

(d) Queries about the Information Letter and Consent Form for Interview.

(e) (i) It is not clear what and who is being observed during the 2–3 hours sessions. How much of each observational interval is focused on individuals vs. equipment etc. If it's individuals, is it only those ones who participate in the interviews or the entire group? (ii) how are the workers advised about the observational period so that they understand the procedures and do not worry about the implications for their job. Please provide a copy of the script you will use to example this part of the study to the workers. (iii) how do you determine whether or not the groups you plan to observe are all willing to have this take place? (iv) what happens if a worker does not want to be involved in the observational component of the study? (v) will any of the field data be available to the companies and/or union? If not, how is this conveyed to workers so that they won't worry about this? (vi) what happens – or what are you expected to do – in the event that you observe someone's actions that might be in violation of safety standards? How would this be handled? (vii) will any videotaping of the sessions be done?

(f) Comments on the Interview Protocol.

(g) Comments on the Feedback Letter. I could not find any feedback letter. Please draft a prototype and send this for ethics review.

Case R041-M

26 September 2003

As a member of the [University's] Research Ethics Board, I have reviewed your application titled ' XXX.'

I believe your project complies with the standards outlined in the Tri Council Policy Statement and the [University's] Policy with a few minor exceptions. These exceptions must be addressed before ethical approval for this project can be given.

One of the pages included in the 'Instructions for Applying for Review of Research Involving Humans' document, is a page titled 'Requirements for Informed Consent Forms' On this page, the information that must be contained on an Informed Consent Form is listed. The required information that does not appear on your Information Sheet includes:

1. Name of a person not directly involved with the study who the participant can contact if she/he has any concerns about the study. The REB considers your supervisor to be involved with this project.

2. A statement indicating how participants will receive information about the outcomes of your study. Although you indicate that a participant is entitled to this information, you do not indicate how this will be done.

3. A statement indicating that interviews will be audiotaped – if that is what you plan to do. In addition, you should indicate when data will be destroyed/erased.

4. In your proposal, you indicate that the size of your accessible population is quite small. Given that, it might be useful to include a statement indicating how confidentiality of participants will be protected. For example, will pseudo-names [*sic*] be used to identify participants in your final report? Obtaining informed consent is a

two-step process. First, it involves informing the potential research participant about the study. And second, it involves documenting the participant's informed agreement to participate. One copy of the Informed Consent Form should be given to the research participant and a second signed copy should be retained by the researcher.

Evidence that these changes have been made must be submitted to the Research Ethics Committee before ethical approval for your study can be given.

All the best in your research endeavours . . .

9 October 2003

I received your revised ethics submission and have reviewed your case with [Dr XXX], Chair of the [University's] Research Ethics Board.

He advised me that a signed informed consent is not necessary for your type of project. I apologize for the confusion that I inadvertently created on this matter. However even if an Information Sheet is used rather than a Consent Form, all of the elements included in the 'Requirements for Informed Consent' list (refer to application package) must be addressed.

After reviewing your revised Information Sheet, the following information still appears to be missing from your document:

1. A statement to identify a person not directly involved in the research, for example the Department Chair or Faculty Dean, who may be contacted should the participant have concerns about the research. As I mentioned previously, the [University's] REB committee considers a supervisor to be directly involved with his/her student's project.
2. Although information is provided in terms of the procedure that will be used to collect data, who will have access to the records, security provision, possible use in publication, you have omitted to indicate when these audiotapes will be erased or destroyed. Although all identifying information can be removed from the transcripts of these tapes, it is difficult to remove this information from the audiotape itself. Evidence that these changes have been made must be submitted to the [University's] Research Ethics Committee before ethical approval for your study can be given.

10 October 2003

With these revisions, I believe your project, [title of project], complies with the standards outlined in the Tri Council Policy Statements and the [University's] Policy.

Please consider this e-mail to represent notification of REB approval of your project. Formal approval will be sent from the Office of the Vice-President (Research).

In terms of your concern about the time-delay in obtaining ethical approval for your study, the [University's] REB committee attempts to expedite the review process whenever possible.

Please note the actual turn-around times for your project:

September 25th – Received copy of your ethics application in campus mail
September 26th – E-mail sent to you outlining required changes
October 8th – Received e-mail from you with revised document
October 9th – E-mail sent to you outlining requested changes that had not been completed
October 10th – Received e-mail from you with revised document
October 10th – Ethical approval for project granted

Finally, I would encourage you to re-affirm the participant's willingness to take part in your study and to ensure that all questions have been answered, prior to commencing the actual interview. In addition, remind the participant that she/he can refuse to answer a question or terminate the interview at any time. I wish you all the best in your research endeavours . . .

Case M

The Board has reviewed the protocol for your proposed study and is requesting that you substantially rewrite and resubmit the application.

The HREB only comments on research methodology when the ethical issues are of a nature and extent that compromise the ethical conduct of the research. The reviewers, staff and Chair have determined that this application needs to be substantially reworked and resubmitted. The following specific comments are provided as feedback on your initial application and are intended to inform you about some of the Board's concerns and to assist you in rewriting your application.

(a) Co-investigators: The role of Ms XVY the vice-principal, is explained in the application, but the consent letter also refers to the participation of Mr THTH, but his role is unclear. Item 4 does not identify any co-investigators. Please revise your response to item 4 and explain in the application who Mr THTH is and what his role will be in the research.

(b) Methodology: (i) It is not clear in item 9 what criteria/measurements will be used for assessing 'respectful or disrespectful attitudes and behaviour' and if these criteria will be made known to the subjects. This requires careful consideration, both in terms of ethics and credibility for the research. Will this be a value judgment made by you or based on some prior established criteria? Please explain. (ii) In 9b, you state that two focus groups will take place during class time and will be conducted by a third party. Please clarify who will be conducting the research 'focus groups.' (iii) We are concerned that the focus group activity for research purposes only will take place during class time (conducted by a third party) and that all students will be required to take part in the group discussions, with or without their consent to participate in the research. This compulsory attendance compromises voluntary participation in the research (and the legal responsibility for teacher supervision). Please explain clearly why it is necessary to conduct the focus groups during class time and provide justification. (iv) We recommend reading the 'Action Research Guidelines' available on our website to clarify the distinction between the researcher and teacher roles. Please consider the suggestion in these guidelines that information gathering be limited to activities that are conventional classroom practices and that permission is sought to make use of selected portions of these classroom data for research purposes in addition to their primary use to assess student learning. In this case, student journals and teacher observations of students would be retained, while the research only portion (i.e., videotaped class discussion) would not. (v) The use of photographs requires additional clarification both when describing the methodology in Section C of the application and especially in the consent letter. It needs to be made clear that the use of photographs has implications for limiting the anonymity and confidentiality of participants who will be identifiable in the final report. Explicit consent for the use of photos must be sought in the consent form. Furthermore, assurances must be given in the consent letter that no photographs will be used which include anyone in the background who has not given explicit consent.

(c) Recruitment: In item 10 you state that the participants will be recruited by the vice-principal. Please attach a script of what the third party will say to students in explaining the project and note that the vice-principal has a power-over relationship with the students.

(d) Inconvenience: In item 10, you indicate that there are 25 students in the class, all of whom would be required to participate in whole-class videotaping that utilizes three hours of class instructional time. The videotaped 'focus group' is only intended for research purposes, so inconvenience to the students is three hours. Since it cannot be assumed that all students will consent to be research participants and that the focus groups only serve the purpose of your research project, this seems like an unjustified intrusion into the instructional time of all students in the class (approximately 10 per cent of the total instructional time). See comments regarding the use of photographs, under Methodology above.

(e) Potential Risks: (i) students could feel demeaned or embarrassed if they were judged as having 'disrespectful attitudes and behaviours.' (ii) students may feel self-conscious or inhibited by being photographed, taped, observed (and judged). (iii) stigmatization could result from students who were viewed as 'disrespectful.' Reconsider your responses to the items in 13, and in item 14, please describe how the possible risks identified above will be addressed and minimized.

(f) Power-over: (i) In item 18iv., describe how the dual-role relationship between yourself and the students will be explained to participants. (ii) In item 22, you state that a third party will inform students about the research and collect consent forms. The vice-principal is in a position of power over the potential participants. Please explain how you will deal with this. (iii) The Action Research Guidelines include several suggestions for mitigating power-over in addition to the use of a third party for consent. For example, they suggest that the consent letter includes a statement acknowledging the potential for unintended coercion to participate and a statement to mitigate this potential effect.

(g) Informed Consent: (i) The students have a choice about whether
their data will be used for research purposes but they do not
appear to be given a choice about being involved in the research
study (recorded, photographed, observed, interviewed). How
would the course be taught differently (if at all) if it were not part
of this research study? All students will take part in the research
activities and be treated equally since you will not know who is
participating and who is not until the end of term. What impact
does this have on participants[1] rights to voluntary consent? (ii) In
item 19, you indicate that parents will not be informed about the
project. We wonder why that would be and if the School District
would allow this. We believe that at a minimum, a letter should
be sent to parents to inform them about the research project (and
perhaps seek their consent).

(h) Indigenous Community: While we agree that this study does not
need Indigenous community approval, please be aware that much
of the publicly-available information on First Nations cultural
knowledge and traditions did not enter the literature without
consent of the knowledge holders (this is a general comment, not
a comment on any of the authors mentioned). It would be reassur-
ing if there was some indication that you are aware that sharing
Indigenous knowledge (especially by non-Aboriginal people) is
sometimes controversial and that sensitivity will be used in sharing this information.

(i) Ongoing Consent: As there will be a gap of several months
between the initiation of the project and identification of participants, participants should be asked to confirm their willingness
to have their data used for research purposes after grades have
been submitted and the identity of participants is revealed. Please
revise your response to items 23a and b.

(j) Dissemination: Will the results of your study be shared with the
school, School District, parents and participants? If so, item 31
needs to add 'directly to participants' and the consent letter needs
to state this and inform student/participants how they may obtain
or request the results of the research. (As a suggestion, you could
make a copy of the thesis generally available to the entire school
community, possibl[y] [sic] by placing a copy in the school/com-
munity library.)

(k) Consent Form: Please include an Information Letter or Consent
Form for parents. The Consent Form should say that all students

will be participating in the course but they have the right to consent or not to the use of the data that will be collected about them.

(l) Para 7: Explain Mr THTH's position in the school and what role will he play in the research. Also state how much time will be involved for participation in the research.

(m) Para 8: Possible risks should be reconsidered (see earlier comments) and indicated.

(n) Para 9: Indicate that participation will not advantage or disadvantage students in the course.

(o) Para 11: Explain Ms. XYZ's position in the school and her role in the research project. Address power-over relationships.

(p) Para 12: Explain how the photos will be used in the study and the resulting limitations to confidentiality.

(q) Para 14: Be clear about when you would be happy to talk to students about your project – after it is completed? Be clear that the signed consent form should be returned to XX – the third-party (not to you).

(r) The consent form should request students to not tell you if they are participating in the research, as you cannot know until after you have completed their grades for the course.

(s) Address data storage and destruction.

(t) Address ongoing consent.

(u) Provisions for explicit consent to use student photographs needs to be included in the consent form.

Appendix D: Interview Guides

Note: In qualitative research, the researcher tries to follow the lead of the interview participant, with the idea of discovering his/her perspective and what is meaningful to that person. A general opening question is usually a good start if it is broad enough.

Interview Guide for Chairs of Research Ethics Boards

General

How did you go about learning how to do ethics review of research? Was there a training session? What were your expectations? Did your later experiences confirm those expectations? Were your experiences different? Describe to me the usual procedure for considering proposals for their ethical dimensions.

About Social Science Applications

What stands out for you in applications coming from social scientists? What sorts of principles or standards guide your assessment of these applications? [Probe especially whether these standards are derived from quantitative research.] What takes up most of your time? How do social science proposals differ from other submissions? What advice would you give to social researchers' submitting proposals to your REB?

About Qualitative Research Proposals

How do qualitative research proposals differ from other submissions? What sort of questions do their applications generate for you?

What questions go back to these researchers? What is the nature of the feedback of those researchers to your questions? If there are complaints, how would you describe them? (If applicable) are those complaints the results from misunderstanding of what REBs attempt to do?

Interview Guide for Researchers

General

What has your experience been in submitting proposals to Research Ethics Boards? What stands out for you in your experience?

Learning the Ropes

How did you go about learning how to prepare your proposal for research-ethics review? [Follow through on such possibilities as training session, expectations, learning the ropes from colleagues, etc.]

Experiences

How did the process of submitting your proposal look like? What sorts of questions came back to you? Was it a frustrating process? In what way? Or, did you find the process quite satisfactory? What advice would you give to social researchers' submitting proposals to your REB? If you have heard stories about the experiences of researchers going through ethics-review, how did your own experience match up with those stories?

About Qualitative Research Proposals

Are qualitative research proposals different from other, quantitative, proposals? In what way? Would you say that research-ethics review has reshaped (or not) your methodology? Your topic of research? If so, in what way? What sort of questions did you get back from the REB about your proposal? How did you go about providing feedback to those questions? If there are complaints, how would you describe them? (If applicable) are those complaints the results from misunderstanding of what you do as a researcher (and as a qualitative research in particular)?

End Result

Did you ever give up (re)submitting a proposal? In what concrete way do you think that research-ethics review has changed the way you do research now?

Notes

1 Introduction

1 My book assumes a knowledge of why research is important and the steps that academics must go through in the research process. However, all of this may be new to some readers, such as students and those outside of the university. Most of the public may feel that the primary job of a professor is to teach. Teaching comprises only one aspect of a professor's job. He/she is expected to carry out many managerial functions in the university, as well as to conduct research. Promotion is contingent upon research. It is up to the professor to come up with his/her own ideas about what is to be researched (some believe that 'they' tell a professor what to research). Once the researcher has a topic, he/she must often get funds to support the research and go through an ethics-review process at the university. The length of time to get research published varies considerably. The book you are currently holding in your hand, took six years of research, followed by two years to get it published. One of my other books took ten years from beginning to end. These time frames are not unusual.

2 A recent article by Claudio Aporta (2009) shows how indispensable Inuit knowledge is when experiencing tundra wayfaring.

3 Dr Gunsalus has kindly given me her permission to use this quotation from her work (Email from CKG, 21 June 2009 to WCvdH).

4 See, for example, C. Kristina Gunsalus et al. (2007), Citro et al. (2003), and AAUP (2006).

5 I have adopted the following codes when I refer to my research participants: **R**=researcher; **C**=chair of REB; **E**=member of REB; **A**=Administrative staff; **S**=staff of ethics office; **J**=editor or member of an editorial board of an academic journal; **B**=big university; **M**=mid-sized university; **S**=small

liberal arts university. In this case, E28-M refers to the twenty-eighth member of an REB who participated in my research, coming from a mid-sized Canadian university.

6 'Fieldnotes' refer to my own nearly 1,900 pages of notes taken during the course of my research.

7 Feminist research is having a particular, unintended impact on some prescriptive judgments by ethics committees. For example, member-checking is now becoming a pervasive requirement imposed by these committees and, in many cases this becomes a serious problem for conducting critical research. So, too, is the resulting broadening definition of research, which means more projects fall under ethics committees to review (see, e.g., Muzychka et al., 1966).

8 The works of Ivor Pritchard (2001a, 2001b, 2002), a member of the United States Office of Human Protection, constitute an exception.

9 Rose Wiles et al. (2006: 289) found it hard to probe researchers' personal research practice, such as when they explored confidentiality and how to handle anonymity. An undergraduate student, Colin D. Newman (2004), reported that none of the thirty-nine researchers in his study submitted failed research proposals to him.

10 Of the thirty-two ethics committees approached by Maureen Fitzgerald, only nineteen allowed themselves to be observed. For some, the researchers had to sign confidentiality agreements. In 1988, 30 per cent of committees had closed meetings, 4 per cent were open to the public, and 66 per cent were open to requests for a researcher to attend (Fitzgerald, 2004: 35–6). In New Zealand, however, regional committees are considered public or open (Fitzgerald, 2004: 41).

11 Maureen Fitzgerald (2004: 39–41) gives detailed characteristics of closed and open committees.

12 De Vries and Forsberg (2002: 202) faced this issue when they surveyed IRBs, not individual IRB members.

13 I owe a debt to Jill Adams, Department of Sociology, University of Victoria, Canada, who used the term 'metabolism,' albeit in another context.

14 The 2009 survey is online at www.surveymonkey.com/s,aspx?sm=N1v1MJ vyg3USMopDAOQV3g_3d_3d

2 An Archaeology of Research-Ethics Review

1 I derived this thumbnail sketch from 'The Nuremberg Code,' accessed 23 February 2006, from www.dallasnw.quik.com/cyberella/Anthrax/ Nuremberg.htm. Tim Seifert (2005) also has detailed descriptions of the Nuremberg proceedings.

2 'The Day that Alvin Gouldner Punched a Guy,' accessed 20 July 2009 from http://orgtheory.wordpress.com/2007/09/24/the-day-alvin-gouldner-punched-a-guy/

3 Parts of the section on 'Moral Panic' are derived from a paper I presented at the 'Canadian Qualitatives' (van den Hoonaard, 2000) and later revised for my edited volume (van den Hoonaard, 2002).

4 I remind the reader that a deductive template does not necessarily invalidate social research. For example, historians sometimes approach their work with theoretical validation in mind and that work can be very good.

5 In my estimation, Christine Halse and Anne Honey (2007) offer one of the most concise and insightful analyses of the developments of research-ethics review.

6 The United Nations Conference on Science and Technology, held in Vienna in 1979, recommended such medical councils, followed by a similar suggestion from the World Health Organization (Charbonneau, 1984: 21).

7 My introductory chapter in van den Hoonaard (2002) provides the essential elements of this section. This section, however, also reflects the vast changes recently taking place in Canada's research-ethics regime. I wish to express my gratitude to Francis Rolleston, one of the founding members of the Medical Research Council of Canada that developed early ethics guidelines for his invaluable assistance.

8 Valerie Fabrikant, an engineering professor at Concordia University in Montreal, murdered two colleagues in 1992 who, he felt, had slighted him and had not given him recognition for his contributions to their research.

9 The Tri-Council Working Group consisted of ten voting and two non-voting members. In all, the Group included six medical researchers, two lawyers, a psychologist, a philosopher, a bio-engineer, only one social scientist, and an anthropologist, Dr Michael Asch, whose expertise includes political relations between Indigenous peoples and Canada.

10 As of June 2009, no university had been penalized for not abiding by the requirements of the 'Memorandum of Understanding.'

11 Already in December 1994, for example, I had voiced complaints about the early draft of the *TCPS* (van den Hoonaard, 1994).

12 Both Schrag (2009a) and Ann Hamilton (2002) have the most detailed history of ethics-review developments in the United States; the latter is a fine critical analysis of this history. Schrag's book, *Ethical Imperialism* (2010), came off the press the same time that *The Seduction of Ethics* went to the University of Toronto Press.

13 *Miss Evers' Boys*, the 1997 HBO television film adaption of David Feldshah's play about the Tuskegee Study, offers dramatic insights into the lives of all those involved in this experiment.

14 Cary Nelson's estimate comes close to this figure: in 2000, there were 4,000 IRBs in the U.S., mainly in universities, hospitals, and private research facilities (Nelson, 2004: 209).

15 For example, the university lawyer is not permitted to serve on REBs mandated by the *TCPS*.

16 I am grateful to Dr Richard Neuman, Professor of Pharmacology, Co-Chair, Human Investigation Committee, Faculty of Medicine, Memorial University, for these observations (Email from R. Neuman to W.C. van den Hoonaard, 15 Jan. 2009).

17 See, for example, www.ncehr-cnerh.org/pdf/publications/focus/FOCUS_ReportCOI_ washington_2004_e.pdf

18 For example, the 2005 FOCUS Conference in Montreal promoted an interest in the International Conference on Conflict of Interest, Washington, DC. It indicated sessions as '*Behavioral* and Social Science Research' (in Canada, social research is normally referred to without the 'Behavioural' component), advocated accreditation (there is a far stronger movement about accreditation in the United States than in Canada), and urged attendees to connect with AAHRPP, a United States organization exclusively set up to promote certification of IRBs).

19 Adam Hedgecoe (2009) offers a detailed overview of the origins of Research Ethics Committees in the United Kingdom between 1967 and 1972, on which I draw for details in this section. Please also read Carole Truman (2003).

3 The Criticisms of Research-Ethics Review

1 I owe a particular debt of gratitude to Ann Hamilton's insightful and well-articulated PhD dissertation, 'Institutional Review Boards: Politics, Power, Purpose and Process in a Regulatory Organization' (2002), for elevating some of these issues into a theoretical perspective.

2 Twenty-seven per cent of 130 surveyed United Kingdom social scientists claim the irrelevance of ethics regime for social scientists (Richardson and McMullan, 2007: 1123).

3 This list of thirty-one *federal* agencies includes PRE and its various subcommittees and task forces, NCEHR and its various committees, CAREB, the CIHR Office of Ethics, the Management Committee of the three funding agencies, the SSHRC Office of Ethics and Integrity, Health Canada, the Roundtable of Experts, and other governmental and non-governmental bodies, including those whose mission deals only with research in Aboriginal communities (the term 'First Nations' is the aggregate term

for Canada's Indigenous non-Inuit peoples.). I thank Dr Iara Guerriero, a Brazilian post-doctoral fellow who worked (2008–9) at the Atlantic Centre for Qualitative Research and Analysis at St Thomas University, Fredericton, New Brunswick, for having come across all of these agencies and bodies while conducting her own research on ethics and qualitative health research in Canada.

4 OPRR stands for the Office for Protection from Research Risks, Department of Health and Human Services, National Institutes of Health, Washington, DC.

5 While official statistics indicate that this university is mid-sized, the university appears to the REB chair as a small one (as it did to me, the researcher).

4 What Is the Normative Ethics Framework for Social Researchers?

1 This section contains segments from van den Hoonaard (2008b) published in Brazil.

2 The current use by biomedical researchers of more neutral terms in informed consent forms such as 'studies,' 'trials,' or 'research' point to the lingering worries about experimentation.

3 Over the past few years, however, biomedical researchers are increasingly using the term 'research participant,' rather than 'subject' – such a switch indicates the dynamic nature of change in research ethics across Canada, and possibly elsewhere, too.

4 Elsewhere, I have argued about the difficulty of maintaining anonymity of research participants in ethnographic research, either advertently or inadvertently (for example, W. van den Hoonaard, 2003b).

5 I am grateful to Sean Kennedy of the Department of History at the University of New Brunswick (Personal communication, 20 May 2008) for drawing my attention to a new French law regarding access to public archives that has left some historians concerned about (a) the fact that some archives, it seems, may never be opened, and (b) that the definition of 'private life' is being expanded. In the past, researchers used to sign a declaration indicating they would not write about a private life in a damaging way. See Ministre de la culture, 2008.

6 Susan Cox (W. Maurice Young Centre for Applied Ethics at the University of British Columbia) is co-principal investigator on a project in the health field, 'Centring the Human Subject in Health Research: Understanding the Meaning and Experience of Research Participation.' The purpose of the project is to explore the meanings and experiences of being a human

subject in various types of health research. The project is described at
www.ethics.ubc.ca/research/projects/participation.htm.

7 I have featured these three studies in a paper I presented in Brazil at a
   World Health Organization Conference (van den Hoonaard, 2007) that was
   subsequently published in Portuguese (van den Hoonaard, 2008a).

8 This refers to a 376-page study about the first five minutes of interaction.

9 Katja M. Guenther (2009) offers a fine discussion about the problematique
   of confidentiality and about whether or not real names ought to be used in
   published research.

10 'People who work and live on the street, as a general rule, do not like, let
    alone permit, photographs to be taken of them. Some do not like the idea
    of their lives being reduced to tourist attraction, while others see photo-
    graphs as an aspect of police surveillance' (Hasan, 'Aferword,'1999: 326).

11 Diamond describes one person who disliked and distrusted him: 'Suzy
    [a nursing assistant] disliked me, or perhaps distrusted me. No doubt
    many staff and residents in whom I did not confide could see right through
    me and knew that something was going on that I was not telling' (135).

5 Structure and Composition of Research-Ethics Committees

1 My estimation of the direct costs is based on (a) the number of university
   and hospital ethics committees in Canada (perhaps 300); (b) the costs
   to run an ethics office that are based on the salary of two staff members
   ($44,800 including fringe benefits, each) who also attend one or two
   conferences per year ($1,500 each) and office supplies ($3,000) (subtotal:
   $28.68 million); (c) the chair's salary, which runs from a free service offered
   by a retired faculty member to as much as 35 per cent of a professor's or
   doctor's salary (subtotal: $5.25 million); (d) the costs of the central admin-
   istration of the *TCPS* (i.e., the Interagency Advisory Panel on Research
   Ethics and its secretariat) (subtotal: $1.4 million). The total direct costs
   amount to $35.33 million. Excluding the costs of the Interagency Advisory
   Panel on Research Ethics and its secretariat, the 300 universities and hospital REBs bear $33.93 million of these costs, or $113,100 per REB. If we
   assume there are seventy-six REBs in universities, we can estimate the
   costs to run them totals $8,595,600. (I have, however, excluded the costs
   of setting up a university ethics office and the running of various other
   federal ethics agencies and non-profit bodies related to ethics in research,
   such as NECHR, CAREB, Health Canada. Some of their costs are absorbed
   by regulatory agencies or fees.) I have also excluded the potential hourly
   cost for each committee member, which is normally absorbed by his/her

salary of \$100/hour for seven-hour meetings once a month. Membership numbers vary considerably, but I conservatively estimate ten per committee (some committees have twenty-seven members, others around ten, or even lower), but these indirect costs amount to an estimated \$2,100,000.

2 Lewis (2008: 692) has an important section on public nature of universities and its officers, for example, REBs which ought to redefine the chair's position as something to be open to scrutiny.

3 At the same university, a researcher suggested that the REB chair is a 'power monger' (R045, Fieldnotes: 147).

4 Some of the REBs also handle biomedical research.

5 At least two psychologists, David Rennie and Janet Stoppard, have clearly explained that the inductive approach in psychology is still very much on the margins (Rennie, 2002; Rennie et al., 2002; Stoppard, 2002).

6 Of the three advertisements posted in 2009 for recruiting administrative assistants or managers of research-ethics offices, the Ontario Institute for Cancer Research and the BC Children's Hospital did not list knowledge of research (or research methods) as a requirement for the position; in the case of the third position (with the University of Alberta), the ad listed 'extensive knowledge of research methods, standards, and regulatory requirements ...' (emphasis added). Retrieved 21 July 2009 from www...oicr/JobDescription.asp?JobNumber=609999, www.bcchildrens.ca, and www.careers.ualberta.ca/competition.aspx?id=A10698505, respectively.

7 I wish to express my thanks to Ms Rebecca Anderson for having taken part in this survey.

8 In New Zealand, incidentally, the ethics committee must have a majority of lay people (R157-B, Fieldnotes: 400).

9 What sparked Colin Newman's interest in devoting his master's thesis to the study of REBs was the rejection by his REB of another projected study. That rejection and the difficulties experienced by other researchers at his university become the subject of a new thesis.

10 I have used the term 'committee' (as in 'ethics committee' or 'ethics-review committee') to refer to these boards, because 'committee' is a more generic term that seems to apply to the use in other countries.

11 Every week, perhaps several times a week, at least 210 people across Canada sit around a table or in front of a computer monitor reviewing, on average, nearly 100 research proposals for expedited review. I have included these figures for the sole purpose of illustrating the large scope of research proposals in Canada. My own University Research Ethics Board evaluated, in 2002, some 89 research proposals from a faculty pool of 500 professors and many more students. A medium-sized university,

it probably attracts a medium number of grants. Using the conservative figure of 0.178 research projects per faculty member, we come to a total of 5,874 research projects all across Canada with a total of 33,000 researchers. If 85 per cent of those projects go through expedited review, we have 4,993 projects, averaging 96 per week.

12 As a researcher, I was truly reluctant to bother the ethics committees and staff with my queries. I recall that there was one REB chair I was unable to reach; he did not call me back (Fieldnotes: 146). In regard to appendix B (number of applications): there are indeed some gaps in the information. In this case, too, I was hesitant to burden the ethics office with queries. I tried to derive information from other sources, published and unpublished.

6 The Moral Cosmology of the Ethics-Review World

1 I shall treat the role of both conferences in a separate section of another chapter. Jim Thomas (2002: 10) advocates the study of these conferences.

2 A reader of an earlier draft of *The Seduction of Ethics* was offended that ethics committees believed they should teach him about ethics. He informed me that 'you may think otherwise, but in these matters I'm a complete Protestant. I don't need anyone telling me what is ethical.' This is a sentiment echoed by many researchers I interviewed.

3 The 2009 movie *District 9* illustrates the perfunctory and paternalistic role of consent forms used by the South African authorities requiring the signature of aliens about to be dislocated to another location from their current slum.

4 My introductory chapter in *Walking the Tightrope* (van den Hoonaard, 2002) forms the basis of this discussion about the use of consent forms in Nunavut and by Dr Grace Getty.

5 I deliberately use the term 'vulnerable context' rather than 'vulnerable people.' After all, there are both 'strong' and 'weak' people in all kinds of social settings that can more aptly be described as 'vulnerable.' The term 'vulnerable people' is a stereotype.

7 Procedural Routines: The Application Form and the Consent Form

1 Foucault uses the expression 'radical deafness' to refer to Marxists who are so faithful to the old positivism that 'there was a radical deafness to new questions asked by science' (Rabinow, 1984: 53).

2 The one exception is a university who asks the researcher to write a one- or two-page memo detailing how he/she visualizes the ethics dimensions of the research. Ethics staff then sit down with the researcher and consult on dimensions he/she missed.

3 I taught an ethics course at the University of New Brunswick, focused on ethical reflection, rather than on how to fill out an application form for research-ethics review. If the reader is so inclined, he/she can get in touch with me at will@unb.ca to receive details about this course.

4 The reader should imagine doing an oral history of his/her family, and before interviewing a grandparent, asking the grandparent to sign a consent form. This act alone would create an entirely different atmosphere for the interview, disrupting the moments of trustworthiness.

5 I have been unable to locate the actual research which allegedly uses signed consent forms for the first time. I ask readers to help me locate this particular reference.

6 As an example, I cite Ann Hamilton's study (2002: 166): 'The University of Utah's informed consent template is five pages long; University of Texas at Austin's form has expanded during the past two years, from about one and a half pages to 10 pages as of May 2002; and the University of California at Berkeley's model is barely one page in length. UC Berkeley's form is titled "Low-risk Adult Survey/Interview Form" and is more targeted to social science concerns.'

7 One small university in the Canadian Maritimes allows Aboriginal students to have picture consent forms that they develop with the Aboriginal Elders.

8 It is quite possible that the cases of the survey by the political scientist refer to the same study. It is not uncommon in the scholarly literature to find repeated examples of the most extraordinary demands of ethics-review committees.

9 This tale appears in my 'Introduction' to van den Hoonaard (2002).

8 The Meeting: Making Agendas and Decisions

1 Actually, a sixth REB was not averse to being observed during its meetings, but it believed that studying just one meeting might give me a lopsided view of how that REB works. I can now well sympathize with that opinion, reflecting on my own experience with the remaining REBs.

2 To protect the anonymity of the universities, I used pseudonyms and without mentioning the number of faculty, except to say the universities are

small, mid-sized, or large (appendix B indicates what these sizes entail across Canadian universities).

3 COGDOP (Chairs of Graduate Departments in Psychology) found that to avoid conflict of interest, 50 per cent of IRBs should be non-researchers, but the problem of getting the public to meetings would slow down the process (COGDOP, 2006; Fieldnotes: 542).

4 There are differences between the way female and male community members consider applications. According to Don Sinclair, a community member in a large REB, women 'try to figure out the research participants, while men follow their own voice' (Presentation, CAREB, 7 May 2005, Fieldnotes: 166).

5 Chapter 6 details the REB's cosmology about researchers. The discussion on researcher – REB relations in this chapter's section is largely confined to what I have been able to gather from my participant-observation of the four REBs.

6 In another participant-observation study, members joked about workload as measured by thickness of files (Fitzgerald, 2005: 329).

7 One could say that researchers making such declarative statements is akin to signing one's 'death warrant.'

8 The case: A student had started to interview 6-7 professional people about their work and had asked for oral consent, rather than written consent. The research proposal had gone to an REB in the relevant Faculty, but the Chair of that REB, in effect, never got back to the student or the supervisor. Despite numerous attempts by the student, the REB did not respond. With time pushing on, his supervisor said he should go ahead with the research and get oral consent, because the written consent form had not yet been considered. Now, the student has finished the thesis and is going to defend it next week. What to do? This case had now risen to the university-wide REB for resolution.

9 Fitzgerald notes that ethics committees develop 'worst-case scenarios' and make decisions based on hypothetical possibilities (2005: 328).

10 One researcher, upon learning that REB decisions are based on personal experiences and not policy, concluded that that was a very dangerous or irrelevant practice (Interview R002-M). A researcher (Interview R006-M) informed me that an REB can ask 'irrelevant' questions. He gave the example of an anthropologist doing research in Northern Ireland, but being told to be 'very careful about asking religious questions,' whereas, in fact, these were not dangerous questions at all.

11 I am indebted to Ms Janice McKendrick for sharing this insight with me (Fieldnotes: 522).

12 Section 5 of the 1998 *TCPS* focuses on the need to include research involving women. This particular need, however, evolved from a medical
research stance which habitually excluded women from clinical trials. The
case of including pregnant women poses interesting questions by itself
(Article 5.2 of the *TCPS* speaks about 'presumptive or automatic exclusion
from research on the basis of sex or reproductive capacity').

13 There is one solitary 'odd' paper that defends the *TCPS* in light of qualitative research and dismisses the 'myths' held by qualitative researchers
about the *TCPS*. Ironically, it used the term 'protocol' (Ells and Gutfreund,
2006: 361) – a term unfamiliar to qualitative researchers.

9 An Idiosyncratic and Inconsistent World

1 Elsewhere in *The Seduction of Ethics,* I discuss the problem of 'member
checking' that is rapidly becoming a new fad among REBs, sometimes
with detrimental results to research participants (who must now commit
more time to the research) and to the research (which can preclude a sound
analysis of a group of interview data).

2 I am very grateful to all five researchers who have not only given me their
approval to cite these materials but also have made suggestions.

3 This case is found in Fieldnotes (804-851) and consists of the exchange of
correspondence between the REB and the researcher, in addition to sup-
plementary notes and emails between the researcher and me.

4 Jean Duncombe and Julie Jess (2002) make the interesting point that
researchers can fake friendship as a means of securing rapport with the
research participant. Yet ethics committees take no note of this kind of
interaction when researchers submit proposals to them.

5 Fieldnotes (337-341) provide the data for this particular section. They contain
two pages of a brief correspondence between the REB and the researcher.

6 Details of this case rely on Fieldnotes (366-371) containing the REB's letter
to the researcher, the latter's response to his REB, and exchange of emails
between the researcher and me.

7 Fieldnotes (620-631) contain a number of communications from the REB,
in addition to a description of her undergraduate research proposal.

8 The REB also refers to the need to use 'pseudo-names' rather than
'pseudonyms.'

9 Fieldnotes (706-711) provide a lengthy letter from the student's REB; there
is no information about the student's actual response to that letter, except
for a few notes appended by the student's supervisor. The student's name
is anonymous.

10 The following section takes quotes from Appendix C. To designate the source of every quote in this section would be quite cumbersome for the reader. I refer the reader to the Appendix.

11 This is interesting given that REB members tend to function as manuscript editors when poring over research applications.

12 Ironically, even the cited passage from Dixon-Woods et al. (2007) uses the passive voice – a style of writing that is very much ingrained in scholarly writing.

13 The reader will note that the REB chair makes a critical difference in setting a good tone for the researchers. This chapter and appendix C convey a disappointing experience by the researcher under an earlier chair. This particular excerpt of my interview comes from the new chair of the REB. Different indeed!

14 A reader of an early draft of *The Seduction of Ethics* commented that the attitude expressed in this quote is still 'very patronizing because it assumes that the researcher is waiting breathlessly for the "The Decision."'

10 The Underlife of Research-Ethics Review

1 Both researchers and ethics staff maintain the wall between the two worlds, such as when the chair of an REB does not permit REB members to hold conversations with researchers about their research applications, or when researchers maintain the wall by not wanting to know the names of REB members.

2 The sources of these observations are published writings on the topic, fieldnotes of personal observations of several LISTSERVs, and interviews. In all, 23 researchers, 5 ethics-staff members, 3 ethics committee members, including chairs, and 1 administrator from some 25 universities in North America, including 3 large, 9 mid-sized, and 7 small universities in Canada.

3 I return later to the theme of self-constraints when I discuss researchers changing the topic of research.

4 On a return trip from South America, I sat next to a tango dancer for ten hours in a plane. I appreciated the opportunity to speak with him on which occasion he happily consented to be interviewed about his experiences with doing the tango ('The floor is my canvas'). After returning home I converted my notes into a transcription that I then forwarded to him. He sent the transcription back and had made notations that amplified our earlier exchanges. These amended transcriptions now sit in a file along with other notes. I have no idea if I will ever use them for research. I ask the reader to tell me if my 'research' has already begun. Or does it begin

when I make a formal proposal to a grant committee, or to an REB? What if I decide not to ask for a research grant, and as I decide to take up tango as a hobby and take fieldnotes at the same time? How do I indicate the start date of the research to the ethics committee?

5 Except for the Inuit (formerly known as 'Eskimos' by colonizers), the term 'First Nations' is the aggregate term for Canada's Native (Indigenous) peoples.

6 Sadly, too few interview participants contributed ideas as to the use and nature of 'magic' by researchers in applying for approval for research. I suspect that the term itself might have provoked an unsavoury understanding whereas sociologists like Dan and Cheryl Albas see 'magic' in a unique sense: secular folks applying rituals that they see as foreshadowing a good outcome (such as wearing a particular sweater when writing exams). Of course, students themselves will not have used the term 'magic.' Hopefully, another researcher can explore this topic more fruitfully than I have.

7 I think the researcher had meant to say 'positivist' rather than 'post-positivist.' The latter would include qualitative research, and, from the context, one gathers that is not what the author had intended to say. It is a common error.

11 Secondary Adjustments by Researchers

1 A portion of this chapter was part of a paper I presented at the 2009 Canadian Qualitatives at the University of Waterloo.

2 My own student who was interviewing researchers about ethics while researching children eventually had to submit three revised information sheets between 3 and 12 September 2003. By 10 October the Chair of the REB had approved her project... five weeks (R041-M, Fieldnotes: 613–19).

3 This involved the case of a researcher doing a qualitative assessment study (for which he did not need ethics approval). When he submitted an article with his findings to a journal, the journal insisted on seeing a certificate of ethics approval. The REB could not retroactively give the approval.

4 Member-checking occurs when a researcher asks the research participant to evaluate or check the transcript of an interview.

12 The Beleaguered Methods

1 In my own experience, giving lectures in Australia and England generated among the students considerable interest in and wonderment about these 'early' ethnographies (which until the early 1990s were quite common).

2 See also Paul G. Cressey's 1932 study, *The Taxi-Dance Hall.*

3 Elliott Leyton, *Dying Hard: The Ravages of Industrial Carnage* (Toronto: McClelland and Stewart, 1975); Elliott Layton, with Don Handelman, *Bureaucracy and World View: Studies in the Logic of Official Interpretation* (St. John's, NL: Institute of Social and Economic Research Press, 1978).

4 A note about what qualifies as 'qualitative research' when examining the theses held by ProQuest Dissertations: while I used a liberal interpretation of what constitutes qualitative research, I have drawn the line at any research that does not directly engage research participants. For example, I omitted 'content analysis' from this category, even though the researcher would indicate that as 'qualitative research.' Similarly, some theses explained that they used 'qualitative analysis' of documents. One thesis called a study of movies 'qualitative,' but did not directly engage research participants. These three approaches do not engage in interaction with research participants. However, theses that used, e.g. both interviews and content analysis were deemed to be 'qualitative.' Questionnaires fell into the quantitative camp, because they lacked the essential inductive quality necessary to make them 'qualitative.' In any case, the issue of whether content analysis is qualitative or not might be a moot point for research that goes directly into doing routine content analysis of e.g. movies, photographs, or texts, etc., would not be presented to an REB for approval.

5 The number of master's theses in sociology (excluding French-language theses in Quebec) has actually increased over the years. Over the ten-year period (1995–2004), Canadian universities produced some 968 master's theses, or almost 97 per year.

6 2002 and 2005, when I served as the Sociology Book Review Editor for the *Canadian Review of Sociology and Anthropology,* some 200 books passed through my hands. Only 27 (13.5 per cent) dealt with research participants (Fieldnotes: 38).

7 After such a declaration was made by a participant in this Qualitative Analysis Conference, I went through all available previous programs and found that the proportion of presentations dealing with stigmatized, subcultural groups has not appreciably declined after the introduction of the *TCPS*. Before 2001, the proportion ranged from 9.4 per cent to 22.3 per cent; after 2001, it varied between 16.3 per cent and 22 per cent.

8 The methodology attached to symbolic interactionism emphasizes the importance of fieldwork and interviews in an effort to capture the meanings that people attach to the things they say and do. These meanings not only define social interaction, but also emerge out of that interaction.

9 I refer to the obligatory, larger picture of ethics as 'the big E,' while the process of seeking routine ethics approval from REBs as the 'little e.'

10 There is one happy exception to such bland statements. Guillermo Senn (2004), in his study of the sterilization of Quechuan women between 1995 and 1998, gave a three-page discourse on the nature of ethics in his own research, citing a number of authorities, including Descartes' 1637 concept of moral agency!

11 Using the categorization of the Social Sciences and Humanities Research Council of Canada, the 47 universities break down into 12 large, 15 medium-sized, and 20 small universities.

12 a regular attendee of the Qualitative Research Conference (more popularly known as the 'Canadian Qualitatives'), I have amassed a large number of programs and abstracts which I used for the findings in table 12.1. Although presentations by researchers from outside of Canada also exhibited a similar pattern, I have only incorporated data based on researchers whose home base was Canada so as to trace more carefully the putative impact of the introduction of Canada's research ethics regime on social research, and on ethnographic/fieldwork in particular. I used the abstracts of the papers to carefully note the methodology. If I could not deduce the fieldwork methodology from the abstract, I did not enter that datum.

13 The matter of taking away the researcher's choice was raised by Ted Palys, 31 July 2003.

14 I took this information from an earlier research project where I identified the research participant as 'No. 26.' I am unable to retrace this source.

13 On Theory, Topics, and Favoured Methods

1 I base this sample list on the following sources: Presentation at Couch-Stone Symposium, February 2003, Fieldnotes: 353; Interview R168-M, Fieldnotes: 148; Interview R002-M; R007-M; NCA (2005: 204); and Interview C12-S.

2 The issue of students studying their own lives and interests (known as 'me-search' as opposed to 'research') is an entirely different matter. However, this was not the reason why the IRB turned down the research.

3 He actually prefers Likert-type questions, not in-depth interviews. It makes 'confidentiality easier.'

4 My own draft of an unpublished book, an ethnography of cartographers entitled *The Dark Side of the Moon: Women and Men in Cartography*, contains numerous interviews. Later reflecting on those reported interviews, I realized I used only 7 per cent of the material in the transcriptions.

5 It is important to distinguish among different types of interviews. For example, an oral historian (R103, Fieldnotes: 359) at Georgetown

University does digital recordings of oral histories of Palestinian refugees and either mails the interview participant a CD data copy of the recording or burns a CD on the spot. When I was doing my own research on the history of Dutch families in New Brunswick (van den Hoonaard, 1991), I taped all the interviews and sent them to each family as a keepsake of their own histories.

6 Interestingly, these rather insistent demands come from two Canadian ethics-review committees which are widely known among social researchers to be the most ardent in misunderstanding ethnographic-qualitative research.

7 I wish to thank one of the *JEHRE* reviewers for bringing some of these points to my attention. This reviewer had attended a conference where he or she had 'listened sympathetically to a university PhD student describe her arduous attempts to conduct qualitative health research in a correctional facility stymied first by a university REB and corrections gatekeepers, and later log-jammed by a health ethics committee. At this point of her PhD no data had been collected. Her conference paper was her two-year ethics moral career.'

14　Macro-Structural Linkages

1 Between June 1998 and March 2000, NIH/OPRR conducted ten on-site investigations (Hamilton, 2002: 124).

2 The audit statistics are as follows: 28 per cent relate to poor or missing standards of procedure, 21 per cent concern poor minute keeping, 13 per cent speak to quorum failures at meetings, 11 per cent critique consent elements of research, and 12 per cent fault IRBs for poor review of research by IRBs (ICL, 2006: 6).

3 This is a reference to SSHWC (Social Sciences and Humanities Research Ethics Special Working Committee) (2004).

4 It appears that psychologists (and their journals) are more attentive to copyrighting questionnaires and research 'instruments' than is the case among sociologists and anthropologists. Whether a researcher adopts the whole 'instrument' or part of it, or modifies it, all of this requires legal consent.

5 In the six years that Deborah K. van den Hoonaard and I successively served on SSHRC Standard Grants Committees, we noted a steep rise in the way committees are intervening in the ethicality of proposals.

6 If researchers involved in the process of research-ethics review needed a 'Rosa Parks,' then surely Russell Ogden deserves that title.

7 The payment of research participants is common in psychological research, but, until recently, very uncommon in the social sciences. In this sense, the social sciences are becoming psychologized as far as these kinds of payments go. Researchers can now inflate their research grants to account for these new measures, which signifies an increase in status as well.

8 The case involved participants in a focus group who would be given $50 each.

9 Although there is no wide agreement among journals about how such certificates ought to be provided (in a survey of fifteen medical journals, for example) or whether or not publications require REB approval (C09B, Fieldnotes: 411).

10 I am grateful to Dr Tim Seifert who generously shared with me all of his correspondence from and to the *Journal of Sports Behavior*. He has consented to the use of all this information in *The Seduction of Ethics*.

11 There are dissimilar arguments as to what constitutes research when 'applicants may need the imprimatur of the REC in order that their particular project be determined to be "research"' (Dixon-Woods et al., 2007: 9). IRBs can conveniently define 'research' as something that is intended for publication (ICL, 2006: 8). However, why do IRBs regard in-course research projects for pedagogical reasons as 'research' especially as there is no intent to publish them?

12 NCEHR Council Origins, retrieved 23 November 2010 from http://ncehr-cnerh.org/en/about-us/council-origins.html

13 CAREB Frequently Asked Questions, retrieved 23 November 2010 from www.careb-accer.org/?q=node/4

14 The source of learning about participants at these venues is the relevant participants' lists, in addition to my own fieldnotes of these gatherings.

15 In 2005, there were 265 participants at the NCEHR conference, of these 74 (27.9 per cent) attended the CAREB Conference which had an attendance of 210. In 2008, there were 224 participants at the NCEHR gathering, of these 59 (26.3 per cent) attended the CAREB conference which had an attendance of 200 participants.

16 NCEHR and CAREB are organizations well worth a study each in its own right. Lack of space permits only a brief outline of its activities and conferences. The availability of complete records for the conferences in 2005 and 2008 led me to choose these particular conferences as examples in this section. I have attended the NCEHR conferences since 2002, several times as a presenter myself. The distribution of topics does not seem dissimilar to those other years. I have attended CAREB conferences only since 2004.

17 When I was unsure about the nature of a presentation I did not manage to attend, I checked the background of the speaker to obtain the topic's orientation. For example, a session on research in First Nations communities was oriented more towards biomedical research when the presenter turned out to be collecting genetic material among First Nations people.

15 Will the Social Sciences Wither?

1 The reader can find the proposed version of *TCPS.2* at www.pre.ethics. gc.ca/english/newsandevents/newsreleases/draft_2nd_ed_of_TCPS.cfm. The proposed version was open to consultation until the end of July 2009. It contains many new elements that recognize the characteristics of social science research.

References

AAA (American Anthropological Association). 2010. 'Institutional Review Boards and Anthropology' Retrieved 23 November 2010 from www.aaanet.org/cmtes/ethics/IRB.cfm

AAUP (American Association of University Professors). 2000. *Institutional Review Boards and Social Science Research*. Retrieved 28 January 2008 from www.aaup.org/AAUP/comm/rep/A/protecting.htm

– 2001. 'Protecting Human Beings: Institutional Review Boards and Social Science Research.' Retrieved 28 January 2008 from www.aaup.org/IRBCdoc.htm

– 2006. 'Report: Research on Human Subjects: Academic Freedom and the Institutional Review Board.' American Association of University Professors. Retrieved 26 September 2006 from www.aaup.org/AAUP/comm/rep/A/humansubs.htm

Ad Hoc Advisory Group. 2005. *Report of the Ad Hoc Advisory Group on the Operation of NHS Research Ethics Committees*. London: Department of Health. Report No. 268110.

Albas, Daniel, and Cheryl Albas. 1989. 'Modern Magic: The Case of Examinations.' *Sociological Quarterly* 30(4): 603–13.

Alderson, Patricia. 1999. *On Doing Qualitative Research Linked to Ethical Healthcare*. London: The Wellcome Trust.

Aldred, Rachel. 2008. 'Ethical and Political Issues in Contemporary Research Relationships.' *Sociology* 42(5): 887–903.

Alvesson, M., and S. Deetz. 1996. 'Critical Theory and Postmodernism: Approaches to Organizational Studies.' In S. Clegg, C. Hardy, and W. Nord, eds., *Handbook of Organizational Studies*, 191–217. Thousand Oaks, CA: Sage.

Anonymous. 2006. 'Research Ethics Boards and Research in Practice.' A personal memo.

Aporta, Claudio. 2009. 'The Trail as Home: Inuit and Their Pan-Arctic Network of Routes.' *Human Ecology* 37: 131–46.

ASA (American Sociological Association). 2004. 'History Update, Chapter 1, Part 4.' Retrieved 7 July 2009 from www.asanet.org/cs/root/leftnav/centen nial/centennial_publications/a_history_of_the_asa_1981_to_2004/history_update_chapter 1_part_4

Austin, J.L. 1962. *How to Do Things with Words: The William James Lectures Delivered at Harvard University in 1955.* Ed. J.O. Urmson. Oxford: Clarendon.

Australia. 2006. *Draft of the National Statement on Ethical conduct in Human Research: Second consultation.* Developed jointly by the National Health and Medical Research Council, the Australian Research Council, and the Australian Vice-Chancellors' Committee (January).

Baarts, Charlotte. 2009. 'Stuck in the Middle: Research Ethics Caught between Science and Politics.' *Qualitative Research* 9: 423–39.

Bach, Betsy Wackernagel. 2005. 'The Organizational Tension of Othering.' *Journal of Applied Communication Research* 33(3): 258–68.

Baumrind, Diana. 1964. 'Some Thoughts on Ethics of Research: After Reading Milgram's "Behavioral Study of Obedience."' *American Psychologist* 19: 421–23.

Becker, Howard S. 1969. 'Participant Observation and Interviewing: A Comparison.' In G. J. McCall and J.L. Simmons, eds., *Issues in Participant Observation: A Text and Reader,* 322–31 Reading, MA: Addison-Wesley.

– 2004. 'Comment on Kevin D. Haggerty, "Ethics Creep: Governing Social Science Research in the Name of Ethics."' *Qualitative Sociology* 27(4): 415–6.

Beecher, Henry. 1959. 'Experimentation in Man.' *Journal of the American Medical Association* 169: 461–78.

– 1966. 'Ethics and Clinical Research.' *New England Journal of Medicine* 74: 1354–60.

Begley, Sharon. 2002. 'Science Journal.' *The Wall Street Journal,* 1 November: B1

Bell, Emma, and Alan Bryman. 2007. 'The Ethics of Management Research: An Exploratory Content Analysis.' *British Journal of Management* 18(1): 63–77.

Bell, J., J. Whiton, and S. Connelly. 1998. *Evaluation of NIH Implementation of Section 491 of the Public Health Service Act, Mandating a Program of Protection for Research Subjects: Final Report.* Arlington, VA: Bell Associates.

Berger, Peter L., and Thomas Luckmann. 1966. *The Social Construction of Reality.* New York: Doubleday.

Bhattacharya, Kakali. 2007. 'Consenting to the Consent Form: What Are the Fixed and Fluid Understandings between the Researcher and the Researched?' *Qualitative Inquiry* 13(8): 1095–115.

Bloor, Michael. 2002. 'The Ethnography of Health and Medicine.' In Paul Atkinson, Amanda Coffey, Sara Delamont, John Lofland, and Lyn Lofland, eds., *Handbook of Ethnography*, 177–87. London: Sage.

Boser, Susan. 2007. 'Power, Ethics, and the IRB Dissonance over Human Participant Review of Participatory Research.' *Qualitative Inquiry* 13(8): 1060–74.

Bosk, Charles L., and Raymond G. De Vries. 2004. 'Bureaucracies of Mass Deception: Institutional Review Boards and the Ethics of Ethnographic Research.' *Annals of the American Academy of Political and Social Science* 595(1): 249–63.

Brainard, Jeffery. 2000. 'Spate of Suspensions of Academic Research Spurs Questions about Federal Strategy: A U.S. Agency, Its Own Future Uncertain, Unsettles College Officials with its Crackdown.' *Chronicle of Higher Education* 96(22): A29–30, A32.

Bravo, Gina, Marie-France Dubois, and Mariane Paquet. 2004. 'The Conduct of Canadian Researchers and Institutional Review Boards Regarding Substituted Consent for Research.' *IRB: Ethics & Human Research*, 26(1): 1–8.

Bruckman, Amy. 2002. 'Studying the Amateur Artist: A Perspective on Disguising Data Collected in Human Subjects Research on the Internet.' *Ethics and Information Technology* 4(3): 217–31.

Buchanan, Elizabeth A., and Erin E. Hvizdak. 2009. 'Online Survey Tools: Ethical and Methodological Concerns of Human Research Ethics Committees.' *Journal of Empirical Research on Human Research Ethics* 4(2): 37–48.

Buckingham, R., S. Lack, B. Mount, L. MacLean, and J. Collins. 1976. 'Living with the Dying: Use of the Technique of Participant Observation.' *Canadian Medical Journal* 115: 1211–15.

Burawoy, Michael. 2005. 'For Public Sociology: Address to the American Sociological Association, San Francisco, August 15th, 2004.' *American Sociological Review* 70(1): 4–28.

Calvey, David. 2008. 'The Art and Politics of Covert Research.' *Sociology* 42(5): 905–18.

Campbell, Rebecca, Adrienne E. Adams, Sharon M. Wasco, Courtney E. Ahrens, and Tracy Sefl. 2010. '"What Has It Been Like for You to Talk With Me Today?": The Impact of Participating in Interview Research on Rape Survivors.' *Violence Against Women* 16(1): 60–83.

Canadian Social Work Review. 2006. Forum on Ethics 23 (1–2).

Casper, M. 1998. *The Making of the Unborn Patient*. New Brunswick, NJ: Rutgers University Press.

Ceci, Stephen J., Douglas Peters, and Jonathan Plotkin. 1985. 'Human Subjects Review, Personal Values, and the Regulation of Social Science Research.' *American Psychologist* 40(9): 994–1002.

Chalmers, Donald, and Pettit, Philip. 1998. 'Towards a Consensual Culture in the Ethical Review of Research.' *Medical Journal of Australia* 1658: 528.

Charbonneau, R. 1984. 'Ethics in Human Research.' *The IDRC Reports* 13(1): 20–1.

Charmaz, Kathy. 1999. 'Stories of Suffering: Subjective Tales and Research Narratives.' *Qualitative Health Research* 9(3): 362–82.

Cheek, Julianne. 2007. 'Qualitative Inquiry, Ethics, and Politics of Evidence: Working Within These Spaces Rather Than Being Worked Over by Them.' *Qualitative Inquiry* 13(8): 1051–9.

Church, Jonathan T., Linda Shopes, and Margaret A. Blanchard. 2002. 'For the Record: Should All Disciplines Be Subject to the Common Rule? Human Subjects of Social Science Research.' *Academe* 88(3): 62–9. Retrieved 8 February 2008 from http://aaup.org/AAUP/pubsres/academe/2002/MJ/For+the+Record/FTR2.htm

CIOMS (Council for International Organizations of Medical Sciences). 2002. *International Ethical Guidelines for Biomedical Research Involving Human Subjects.* Retrieved 9 July 2006 from www. cioms.ch/frame_guidelines_nov_2002.htm

Citro, Constance F., Daniel R. Ilgen, and Cora B. Marrett, eds. 2003. *Protecting Participants and Facilitating Social and Behavioral Sciences Research.* Washington, DC: National Research Council of the National Academies.

Clarke, Dawne. 2005. 'The Research Process among Researchers with Varying Epistemological Approaches.' PhD diss., Department of Sociology, University of New Brunswick.

Cline, Andrew R. 2002. 'Understand and Act: Classical Rhetoric, Speech Acts, and the Teaching of Critical Democratic Participation.' PhD diss., English and Political Science, University of Missouri-Kansas City.

COGDOP (Council of Graduate Departments of Psychology). 2006. 'Data on Problems with Ethics Review.' Report of the Council's Annual Meetings, Sarasota, FL, 9–13 February.

Cohen, Stanley. 1972. *Folk Devils and Moral Panics.* New York: St. Martin's Press.

Coleman, Carl H., and Marie-Charlotte Bouësseau. 2008. 'How Do We Know that Research Ethics Committees Are Really Working? The Neglected Role of Outcomes Assessment in Research Ethics Review.' *BMC Medical Ethics* 9(6): doi:10.1186/1472-6939-9-6.

Commonwealth of Australia. 2007. 'National Statement on Ethical Conduct in Human Research.' Retrieved 20 April 2008 from www.nhmrc.gov.au/publi cations/syNOPSes/_files/e72.pdf

Conn, Lesley Gotlieb. 2008. 'Ethics Policy as Audit in Canadian Clinical Settings Exiling the Ethnographic Method.' *Qualitative Research* 8(4): 499–514.

Connolly, Kate, and Adella Reid. 2007. 'Ethics Review for Qualitative Inquiry: Adopting a Values-Based, Facilitative Approach.' *Qualitative Inquiry* 13(7): 1031–47.

Cook. Victoria A. 2006. 'Geography Fieldwork in a "Risk Society."' *Area* 38(4): 413–20.

Couch-Stone Symposium. 2003. Organized by the Society for the Study of Symbolic Interactionism. Tempe, AZ, 7 February.

Cressey, Paul G. 1932. *The Taxi-Dance Hall.* Chicago: University of Chicago Press.

Crow, Graham, Rose Wiles, Sue Heath, and Vikki Charles. 2006. 'Research Ethics and Data Quality: The Implications of Informed Consent.' *International Journal of Social Research Methodology* 9(2): 83–95.

Curtis, Jenefer. 1999. 'The Business of Ethics.' *Globe and Mail* Saturday, 21 August: D1, D4.

Dalton, Melville. 1959. *Men Who Manage.* New York: John Wiley and Sons.

Dash, Leon. 2007. 'Journalism and Institutional Review Boards.' *Qualitative Inquiry* 13(6): 871–4.

Deetz, S. 1995. *Transforming Communication, Transforming Business: Building Responsive and Responsible Workplaces.* Cresskill, NJ: Hampton Press.

Dematteo, Dale. 2002. 'The "Moral Imperative" of Prenatal HIV Testing and Treatment: Public Policy Explored through the Experiences of Affected Women.' Master of Science thesis, Department of Public Health, University of Toronto.

Derbyshire, Stuart W.G. 2006. 'The Rise of the Ethics Committee: Regulation by Another Name?' In James Panton and Oliver Marc Hartwich, eds., *Science vs Superstition: The Case for A New Scientific Enlightenment,* 35–50. London: Policy Exchange Limited and University of Buckingham Press Limited.

De Vries, Raymond. 2004. 'How Can We Help? From " 'Sociology in" to "Sociology of" Bioethics.' *Journal of Law, Medicine & Ethics* 32(2): 279–92.

De Vries, Raymond, and Carl Forsberg. 2002. 'What Do IRBs Look Like? What Kind of Support Do They Receive?' *Accountability in Research: Policies and Quality Assurance* 9(3–4): 199–216.

Diamond, Timothy. 1992. *Making Gray Gold: Narratives of Nursing Home Care.* Chicago: University of Chicago Press.

Dictionary of Philosophy. 2009. 'Positivism.' Retrieved 16 June 2009 from www.marxists.org/reference/subject/philosophy/help/mach1.htm

Dingwall, Robert. 2008. 'The Ethical Case against Ethical Regulation in Humanities and Social Science Research.' *21st Century Society* 3(1): 1–12.

Dixon-Woods, M, E. Angell, R.E Ashcroft, and A. Bryman. 2007. 'Written Work: The Social Functions of Research Ethics Committee Letters.' *Social Science & Medicine* 65(4): 792–802.

Dougherty, Debbie S., and Michael W. Kramer. 2005. 'A Rationale for Scholarly Examination of Institutional Review Boards: A Case Study.' *Journal of Applied Communication Research* 33(3): 183–8.

Duncombe, Jean, and Julie Jessop. 2002. '"Doing Rapport" and the Ethics of "Faking Friendship."' In Melanie Mauthner, Maxine Birch, Julie Jessop, and Tina Miller, eds., *Ethics in Qualitative Research,* 107–22. London: Sage.

Duneier, Mitchell. 1999. *Sidewalk.* Photographs by Ovie Carter. New York: Farrar, Strauss and Giroux.

Ehrenreich, Barbara. 2001. *Nickel and Dimed: On (Not) Getting By in America.* New York: Metropolitan Books.

Ellard, John H., and Keith S. Dobson. 2007. 'Implementation of the Tri-Council Policy Statement: Ethical Conduct for Research Involving Humans in the Context of Non-medical Research: What is Happening?' Paper presented at the Annual Meeting of the Canadian Society for the Study of Higher Education, Saskatoon, SK, 30 May.

Ells, Carolyn, and Shawna Gutfreund. 2006. 'Myths about Qualitative Research and the Tri-Council Policy Statement.' *The Canadian Journal of Sociology* 31(3): 361–73.

Eyre, Linda. 2007. 'Whose Ethics? Whose Interests? The Tri-council Policy and Feminist Research.' *Journal of Curriculum Theorizing* 23(2): 91–102.

Feeley, Malcolm M. 2007. 'Presidential Address: Legality, Social Research, and the Challenge of Institutional Review Boards.' *Law & Society Review* 41(4): 757–76.

Feroz, B. 2006. 'Reflections on Ethical Challenges for a Doctoral Student: A Participatory Action Research Dissertation and Institutional Review Board.' Paper presented at the Second International Congress of Qualitative Inquiry, Urbana-Champaign, IL, 4–6 May.

Festinger, Leon, Henry W. Riecken, and Stanley Schachter. 1956. *When Prophecy Fails.* New York: Harper and Row.

Fine, Gary Alan. 1993. 'Ten Lies of Ethnography: Moral Dilemmas of Field Research.' *Journal of Contemporary Ethnography* 22(3): 267–94.

Fish, Stanley. 1980. *Is There A Text in This Class? The Authority of Interpretive Communities*. Cambridge, MA: Harvard University Press.

Fitch, Kristine L. 2005. 'Difficult Interactions between IRBs and Investigators: Applications and Solutions.' *Journal of Applied Communication Research* 33(3): 269–76.

Fitzgerald, Maureen H. 2004. 'Open and Closed Committees.' *Monash Bioethics Review* 23(2): 35–49.

– 2005. 'Punctuated Equilibrium, Moral Panics, and the Ethical Review Process.' *Journal of Academic Ethics* 2(4): 315–38.

Flicker, Sarah, Robb Travers, Adrian Guta, Sean McDonald, and Aileen Meagher, Aileen. 2007. 'Ethical Dilemmas in Community-Based Participatory Research: Recommendations for Institutional Review Boards.' *Journal of Urban Health* 84(4): 1099–3460.

Flowers, Amy. 1998. *The Fantasy Factory: An Insider's View of the Phone Sex Industry*. Philadelphia: University of Pennsylvania Press.

Foucault, Michel. 1972. *The Archaeology of Knowledge and the Discourse on Language*. Translated by A.M. Sheridan-Smith. New York: Pantheon Books.

– 1980a. *Power/Knowledge: Selected Interviews and Other Writings, 1972–1977*. Hassocks, Sussex, UK: The Harvester Press.

– 1980b. *The History of Sexuality*. Vol. 1. New York: Vintage.

– 1984. 'On the Genealogy of Ethics: An Overview of Work in Progress.' In Paul Rabinow, ed., *The Foucault Reader*, 340–72. New York: Pantheon.

– 2003. *Abnormal: Lectures at the Collège de France, 1974-1975*. Translated by Graham Burchell. London: Verso.

Freeman, Derek. 1983. *Margaret Mead and Samoa: The Making and Unmaking of an Anthropological Myth*. Cambridge, MA: Harvard University Press.

Frenette, Marie-José. 2003. 'Aménager son temps en milieu carceral: Récits de détenus en longue durée.' Master's thesis, University of Ottawa.

Gans, Herbert J. 1967. *The Levittowners: Ways of Life and Politics in a New Suburban Community*. New York: Random House.

– 1982. *The Urban Villagers: Group and Class in the Life of Italian-Americans*. New York: Free Press.

Glasser, Irene. 1988. *More than Bread: Ethnography of a Soup Kitchen*. Tuscaloosa: University of Alabama Press.

Glen, David. 2007. 'Anthropologists in a War Zone: Scholars Debate Their Role.' *Chronicle of Higher Education* 54(14): A1.

Goffman, Erving. 1961. *Asylum: Essays on the Social Situation of Mental Patients and Other Inmates*. Garden City, NY: Anchor Books.

– 1967. *Interaction Ritual: Essays on Face-to-Face Behavior*. New York: Pantheon.

– 1974. *Frame Analysis: An Essay on the Organization of Experience*. New York: Harper and Row.

Goldman, J., and Katz, M.D. 1982. 'Inconsistency and Institutional Review Boards.' *Journal of the American Medical Association* 248(2): 197–202.

Goode, David. 1979. 'The World of the Congenitally Deaf-Blind: Toward the Grounds for Achieving Human Understanding.' In Howard Schwartz and Jerry Jacobs, eds., *Qualitative Sociology: A Method to the Madness*, 381–96. New York: The Free Press.

Goode, Erich, and Nachman Ben-Yehuda. 1994. *Moral Panics: The Social Construction of Deviance*. Oxford: Blackwell.

Grayson, J. Paul, and Richard Myles. 2005. 'How Research Ethics Boards Are Undermining Survey Research on Canadian University Students.' *Journal of Academic Ethics* 2(4): 293–314.

Guenther, Katja M. 2009. 'The Politics of Names: Rethinking the Methodological and Ethical Significance of Naming People, Organizations, and Places.' *Qualitative Research* 9(4): 411–21.

Gunsalus, C. Kristina. 2003a. 'Human Subject Regulations: Whom Are We Protecting From What, and Why? Working to Align Incentives with Ethical Goals.' *Professional Ethics Report* 16(2): 1–3. Retrieved 27 February 2008 from www.aaas.org/spp/sfrl/per/per33.htm

– 2003b. 'Human Subject Regulations: Some Thoughts on Costs and Benefits in the Humanistic Disciplines.' Illinois Public Law Research Paper No. 03-02. Retrieved 13 June 2008 from http://papers.ssrn.com/sol3/papers.cfm?abstract_id=394040

Gunsalus, C. Kristina, Edward M. Bruner, Nicholas C. Burbules, Leon Dash, Matthew Finkin, Joseph P. Goldberg, William T. Greenough, Gregory A. Miller, Masumi Iriye, and Deb Aronson. 2007. 'The Illinois White Paper – Improving the System for Protecting Human Subjects: Counteracting IRB "Mission Creep".' *Qualitative Inquiry* 13(5): 617–49.

Halse, Christine, and Anne Honey. 2005. 'Unraveling Ethics: Illuminating the Moral Dilemmas of Research Ethics.' *Signs: Journal of Women in Culture and Society* 30(4): 2141–162.

– 2007. 'Rethinking Ethics Review as Institutional Discourse.' *Qualitative Inquiry* 13(3): 336–52.

Hamburger, Philip. 2005. 'The New Censorship: Institutional Review Boards.' *The Supreme Court Review* 2004: 271–354.

– 2007. 'Censorship and Institutional Review Boards: Getting Permission.' *Northwestern University Law Review* 101(2): 405–92.

Hamilton, Ann. 2002. 'Institutional Review Boards: Politics, Power, Purpose and Process in a Regulatory Organization.' PhD diss., University of Oklahoma.

– 2005. 'The Development and Operation of IRBs: Medical Regulations and Social Science.' *Journal of Applied Communication Research* 33(3): 189–203.

Harding, T., and M. Ummel. 1989. 'Evaluating the Work of Ethical Review Committees: An Observation and a Suggestion.' *Journal of Medical Ethics* 15(4): 191–4.

Harries, U. J., P.H. Fentem, W. Tuxworth, and G.W. Hoinville. 1994. 'Local Research Ethics Committees: Widely Differing Responses to a National Survey Protocol.' *Journal of the Royal College of Physicians of London* 28(2): 150–4.

Hasan, Hakim. 1999. 'Afterword.' In Mitchell Duneier, *Sidewalk*. Photographs by Ovie Carter, 319–30. New York: Farrar, Strauss and Giroux.

Hauck, Robert J-P. 2008. 'Symposium: Protecting Human Research Participants, IRBs, and Political Science Redux.' Retrieved 7 April 2008 from *APSANet*. www.apsanet.org/section_788.cfm

Hazelgrove, J. 2002. 'The Old Faith and the New Science: The Nuremberg Code and Human Experimentation Ethics in Britain 1946–73.' *Social History of Medicine* 15: 109–35.

Hedgecoe, Adam. 2008. 'Research Ethics Review and the Sociological Research Relationship.' *Sociology* 42: 873–86.

– 2009. '"A Form of Practical Machinery": The Origins of Research Ethics Committees in the UK, 1967–1972.' *Medical History* 53: 331–50.

Hemmings, Annette. 2006. 'Great Ethical Divides: Bridging the Gap between Institutional Review Boards and Researchers.' *Educational Researcher* 35(4): 12–18.

Hindle, Karen L. 2004. 'Professionalism and Client Autonomy in the Law Office: Lawyers' Perspectives on Their Relationships with their Clients.' Master's thesis, Queen's University.

Hirtle, Marie, Martin Letendre, and Sebastien Lormeau. 2004. *Final Report: A Comparative Analysis of Process Requirements for Canadian Research Participant Programs*. Ottawa: Biotika.

Hochschild, Arlie R. 1983. *The Managed Heart: Commercialization of Human Feelings*. Berkeley: University of California Press.

– , with Anne Machung. 1989. *The Second Shift*. New York: Penguin.

– 1997. *The Time Bind: When Work Becomes Home and Home Becomes Work*. New York: Henry Holt.

Holland, Kate. 2007. 'The Epistemological Bias of Ethics Review: Constraining Mental Health Research.' *Qualitative Inquiry* 13(6): 895–913.

Homan, Roger. 1991. *The Ethics of Social Research*. London: Longman.

Horowitz, Irving Louis, ed. 1967. *The Rise and Fall of Project Camelot: Studies in the Relationship Between Social Science and Practical Politics*, Cambridge MA: The MIT Press.

Humphreys, Keith, Jodie Trafton, and Todd H. Wagner. 2003. 'The Cost of Institutional Review Board Procedures in Multicenter Observational Research.' *Annals of Internal Medicine Online* 139(1): 77.

Humphreys, Laud. 1970. *Tearoom Trade: Impersonal Sex in Public Places.* Chicago: Aldine.

Hurdley, Rachel. 2010. 'In the Picture of Off the Wall? Ethical Regulation, Research Habitus, and Unpeopled Ethnography.' *Qualitative Inquiry* 16(6): 517–28.

ICL (Illinois College of Law). 2006. 'The Illinois White Paper – Improving the System for Protecting Human Subjects: Counteracting IRB Mission Creep.' Retrieved 1 May 2008 from http://papers.ssrn.com/sol3/papers.cfm?abstract_id=902995

Indian National Committee for Ethics in Social Science Research in Health. 2000. *The Ethical Guidelines for Social Science Research in Health.* Retrieved 9 July 2006 from www.hsph.harvard.edu/bioethics/guidelines/ethical.html

Institutional Review Blog. News and Commentary about Institutional Review Board Oversight of the Humanities and Social Sciences. Retrieved 25 January 2010 from www.institutionalreviewblog.com.

Israel, Mark. 2004. *Ethics and the Governance of Criminological Research in Australia.* Sydney: NSW Bureau of Crime Statistics and Research.

– 2005. 'Research Hamstrung by Ethics Creep.' *The Australian News,* 12 January: 30.

Israel, Mark, and Iain Hay. 2006. *Research Ethics for Social Scientists.* London: Sage.

Jamieson-Williams, Neil. 2008. 'The Ethnographer as Knave: Juggling the Ethical Issues of Using Unanticipated Data.' Paper presented at the 25th Annual Qualitative Analysis Conference, University of New Brunswick, Fredericton, NB, 21–24 May.

Johnson, John M., and David L. Altheide. 2002. 'Reflections on Professional Ethics.' In Will C. van den Hoonaard, ed., *Walking the Tightrope: Ethical Issues for Qualitative Researchers,* 109–28. Toronto: University of Toronto Press.

Johnson, Tara Star. 2008. 'Qualitative Research in Question: A Narrative of Disciplinary Power With/in the IRB.' *Qualitative Inquiry* 14(2): 212–32.

Katz, Jack. 2007. 'Toward a Natural History of Ethical Censorship.' *Law & Society Review* 41(4): 797–810.

Kellner, Florence. 2002. 'Yet Another Current Crisis: The Ethics of Conduct and Representation in Fieldwork-Dependent Social Science.' In Will C. van den Hoonaard, ed., *Walking the Tightrope Ethical Issues for Qualitative Researchers,* 48–62. Toronto: University of Toronto Press.

Kennedy, Joyce Ellen. 2005. 'Grey Matter: Ambiguities and Complexities of Ethics in Research.' *Journal of Academic Ethics* 3(2–4): 143–58.

Kierkegaard, Søren. 1966. *On Authority and Revelation: The Book on Alder; or, a Cycle of Ethico-Religious Essays.* Translated and with Introduction and Notes by Walter Lowrie. New York: Harper and Row.

Koerner, Ascan F. 2005. 'Communication Scholars' Communication and Relationship with Their IRBs.' *Journal of Applied Communication Research* 33(3): 231–41.

Koro-Ljungberg, Mirka, Marco Gemignani, Cheri Winton Brodeur, and Cheryl Kmiec. 2007. 'The Technologies of Normalization and Self: Thinking About IRBs and Extrinsic Research Ethics with Foucault.' *Qualitative Inquiry* 13(8): 1075–94.

Kotarba, Joseph A. 1979. 'The Accomplishment of Intimacy in the Jail Visiting Room.' *Qualitative Sociology* 2(2): 80–103.

Lavigne, Gabrielle. 2002. 'Indochinese Refugees, Ste-Thérèse, Québec, 1979–1982: Twenty Years Later.' Master's thesis, Laurentian University.

Levine, Felice J. 2001. 'Weighing in on Protecting Human Research Participants: Let Our Voices Be Heard.' *ASA Footnotes* 29(1): 2.

Lewis, Magda. 2008. 'New Strategies of Control: Academic Freedom and Research Ethics Boards.' *Qualitative Inquiry* 14(5): 684–99.

Lewis, Oscar. 1966. *The Culture of Poverty.* New York, NY: W.H. Freeman.

Lincoln, Yvonna S., and Gaile S. Cannella. 2004. 'Dangerous Discourses: Methodological Conservatism and Governmental Regimes of Truth.' *Qualitative Inquiry* 10(5): 5–14.

Lincoln, Yvonna S., and William G. Tierney. 2004. 'Qualitative Research and Institutional Review Boards.' *Qualitative Inquiry* 10(2): 219–34.

Lindgren, James, Dennis Murashko, and Matthew R. Ford. 2007. 'Foreword: Symposium on Censorship and Institutional Review Boards.' *Northwestern University Law Review* 101(2): 399–403.

MacDonald, S. 2002. 'British Social Anthropology.' In P. Atkinson, A. Coffey, S. Delamont, J. Lofland, and L. Lofland, eds., *Handbook of Ethnography,* 60–79. London: Sage.

Mäkelä, Klaus. 2006. 'Ethical Control of Social Research: Rules of Research Ethics and Their Interpretation.' *Nordisk Alkohol & Narkotika Tidskrift* 23 (English Supplement): 5–19.

McCambridge, Shauna, and Michael Owen. 2007. 'Resolving the Ethics Debate: Is Education the Solution?' PowerPoint Presentation, Annual Meeting of the Canadian Society for Studies in Education, Saskatoon, SK, 27 May.

McDonald, Michael, and Eric Meslin. 2003. 'Research Ethics as Social Policy: Some Lessons from Experiences in Canada and the United States.' *The Tocqueville Review/La Revue Tocqueville* 24(2): 61–85.

McIntosh, Michele Janet. 2009. 'Participants' Perspectives of Risk Inherent in Unstructured Qualitative Interviews.' PhD diss., University of Alberta.

McKendrick, Janice. 2006. 'Submission to S. Sykes, Chair of the SubGroup on Procedural Issues for the *TCPS* (ProGroup).' 8 March.

Mead, George Herbert. 1964. 'The Genesis of the Self and Social Control.' In Andrew J. Reck, ed., *Selected Writings: George Hebert Mead*, 267–93. Indianapolis: Bobbs-Merrill.

Mead, Margaret. 1928. *Coming of Age in Samoa: A Psychological Study of Primitive Youth for Western Civilization*. New York: Morrow.

Medical Research Council, Natural Sciences and Engineering Research Council, and the Social Sciences and Humanities Research Council (MRC et al.). 1998. *Tri-Council Policy Statement on Ethical Conduct for Research Involving Humans*. Ottawa: Public Works and Government Services Canada.

Milgram, Stanley. 1963. 'Behavioral Study of Obedience.' *Journal of Abnormal and Social Psychology* 67: 371–8.

Mills, C. Wright. 1959. *The Sociological Imagination*. New York: Oxford University Press.

Ministre de la culture (et de la communication). 2008. 'Loi No.2008-696 du 15 juillet 2008 relative aux archives.' *Journal officiel de la République française*, 16 juillet. Texte 2 sur 161.

Morgan, David L. 1997. *Focus Groups as Qualitative Research*. Thousand Oaks, CA: Sage.

Morier, Gilles B. 2006. 'Memorandum Regarding the Society of Research Administrators (SRA) International Annual Meetings in Quebec City, October 14–18, 2006,' dated 28 July, to CAREB members.

Mueller, John H. 2007. 'Ignorance Is Neither Bliss Nor Ethical.' *Northwestern University Law Review* 101(2): 809–36. Retrieved 20 March 2008 from www.law.northwestern.edu/lawreview/v101/n2/809/LR101n2Mueller.pdf

Muzychka, Martha, Carmen Poulin, Barbara Cottrell, Baukje Miedema, and Barbara Roberts. [1996] 2003, 2004. 'Feminist Research Ethics: A Process.' Retrieved 20 April 2008 from www.grace-network.org/store/Docs/5_96_Feminist_Research_Ethics_-_ENG.pdf

Muzzin, Linda. 2002. 'Report of the Professional Ethics and Policy Committee (October).' Presented at the Annual General Meeting of the Canadian Sociology and Anthropology Association, Dalhousie University, Halifax, NS, 3 June 2002.

NAIM (National Association of IRB Managers). 2001. 'The Certification Process.' Retrieved 25 May 2002 from www.naim.org/cert.htm

National Commission for the Protection of Human Subjects of Biomedical and Behavioral Research. 1979. *The Belmont Report: Ethical Principles and Guidelines for the Protection of Human Subjects of Research*. Washington, DC: Department of Health, Education, and Welfare.

NCA (National Communication Association). 2005. 'Communication Scholars' Narratives of IRB Experiences.' *Journal of Applied Communication Research* 33(3): 204–30.

Nelson, Cary. 2004. 'The Brave New World of Research Surveillance.' *Qualitative Inquiry* 10(2): 207–18.

Nelson, Connie H., and Dennis H. McPherson. 2004. 'The Task for Ethics Review: Should Research Ethics Boards Address an Approach or a Paradigm?' *NCEHR Communique* 12(2): 11–22.

Newman, Colin D. 2004. 'Analyzing Research Ethics: I Wish I Didn't Know Now What I Didn't Know Then.' Honour's thesis in Psychology, Acadia University.

Ogden, Russell. 2004. 'When Research Ethics and the Law Conflict.' Paper presented at the Annual Meeting of NCEHR, Aylmer, QC, 6 March.

Okihiro, Norman R. 2000. 'Should I Wear a Sign on My Forehead? New Ethical Dilemmas for Extended Field Work.' Paper presented at the CASCA Annual Meetings, University of Calgary, 4–7 May.

Paluck, Elizabeth Levy. 2010. 'The Promising Integration of Qualitative Methods and Field Experiments.' *The Annals of the American Academy of Political and Social Science* 628: 59–71.

Pappworth, Maurice H. 1962. 'Human Guinea Pigs: A Warning.' *Twentieth Century Magazine* 50(4): 66–75.

– 1967. *Human Guinea Pigs: Experimentation on Man.* London: Routledge and Kegan Paul.

Parker, Damon R., Michael James, and Robert J. Barrett. 2005. 'The Practical Logic of Reasonableness: An Ethnographic Reconnaissance of a Research Ethics Committee.' *Monash Bioethics Review* 24(4): 7–27.

Peters, Michael A. 2004. 'Educational Research: "Games of Truth" and the Ethics of Subjectivity.' *Journal of Educational Enquiry* 5(2): 50–63.

Platt, J. 2006. 'How Distinctive Are Canadian Research Methods?' *Canadian Review of Sociology and Anthropology* 43(2): 205–31.

Pool, Gail. 1998. 'CSAA Response to the *Code of Ethical Conduct for Research Involving Humans.*' *Society/Société* 22(1): 1–5.

Power, M. 1994. *The Audit Explosion.* London: Demos.

– 1997. *The Audit Society: Rituals of Verification.* Oxford: Oxford University Press.

PRE (Interagency Advisory Panel on Research Ethics). 2001. 'Draft Statement with Regard to Teleconference, 18 November.'

– 2009. 'Draft 2nd Edition of the Tri-Council Policy Statement: Ethical Conduct for Research Involving Humans (TCPS).' Available at www.pre.ethics.gc.ca/english/newsandevents/newsreleases/draft_2nd_ed_of_TCPS.cfm

Pritchard, Ivor. 2001a. 'Protecting Human Beings: Institutional Review Boards and Social Science Research.' *Academe* 873: 55–67. Retrieved 30 March 2008 from www.aaup.org/statements/Redbook/repirb.htm

– 2001b. 'Researching for "Research Involving Human Subject": What Is Examined? What Is Exempt? What Is Exasperating?' *IRB: Ethics & Human Research* 23(3): 5–13.

– 2002. 'Travelers and Trolls: Practitioner Research and Institutional Review Boards.' *Educational Researcher* 31(3): 3–13.

Punch, Maurice. 1986. *The Politics and Ethics of Fieldwork.* London: Sage.

– 1998. 'Politics and Ethics in Qualitative Research.' In Norman Denzin and Yvonna Lincoln, eds, *The Landscape of Qualitative Research: Theories and Issues,* 156–84. Thousand Oaks, CA: Sage.

Rabinow, Paul. 1984. 'Introduction.' In Paul Rabinow, ed., *The Foucault Reader,* 3–29. New York: Pantheon.

Rasmussen, Lisa. 2009. 'Problems with Minimal-Risk Research Oversight: A Threat to Academic Freedom?' *IRB: Ethics and Human Research* 31: 11–16.

Rennie, David L. 2002. 'Making a Clearing: Qualitative Research in Anglophone Canadian Psychology.' *Canadian Psychology* 43(3): 139–40.

Rennie, David L., Kimberly D. Watson, and Althea M. Monteiro. 2002. 'The Rise of Qualitative Research in Psychology.' *Canadian Psychology* 43(3): 179–89.

Richardson, Sue, and Miriam McMullan. 2007. 'Research Ethics in the UK: What Can Sociology Learn from Health?' *Sociology* 41(6): 1115–132.

Roberts, Lynne, and David Indermaur. 2003. 'Signed Consent Forms in Criminological Research: Protection for Researchers and Ethics Committees but a Threat to Research Participants?' *Psychiatry, Psychology, and the Law* 10(2): 289–99.

Robin, Ron. 2004. *Scandals and Scoundrels: Seven Cases That Shook the Academy.* Berkeley: University of California Press.

Rothman, David R. 1991. *Strangers at the Bedside: A History of how Law and Bioethics Transformed Medical Decision Making.* New York: Basic Books.

Sandelowski, Margarete. 2008. 'Member Check.' In Lisa M. Given, ed., *The Sage Encyclopedia of Qualitative Research Methods,* 501–2. Los Angeles: Sage.

Schrag, Zachary, M. 2009a. 'How Talking Became Human Subjects Research: The Federal Regulation of the Social Sciences, 1965–1991.' *Journal of Policy History.* 21(1): 3–37.

– 2009b. 'Finnish Group Warns Against Unnecessary Bureaucracy.' *Institutional Review Blog.* Retrieved 7 July 2009 from www.institutionalre viewblog.com/2009/06/finnish-group-warns-against-unncessary-bureaucracy

– 2010. *Ethical Imperialism: Institutional Review Boards and the Social Sciences, 1965-2009.* Baltimore, MD: Johns Hopkins University Press.

Schwartz, Howard, and Jerry Jacobs, eds. 1979. *Qualitative Sociology: A Method to the Madness.* New York: The Free Press.

Scott, Catherine. 2004. 'Ethics and Knowledge in the Contemporary University.' *Critical Review of International Social and Political Philosophy* 6(4): 93–107.

Seifert, Tim. 2005. '(Re)interpreting the Tri-Council Policy Statement.' Paper presented at the Doctoral Seminar Series, Faculty of Education, Memorial University of Newfoundland, 17 March. Retrieved 28 May 2008 from www.mun.ca/research/researchers/Seiferts_Talk_TCPS.pdf

Seifert, Tim, and C. Hedderson. 2008. 'Intrinsic Motivation and Flow as a Natural High: An Ethnographic Study of Skateboarding.' Unpublished paper.

Senn, Guillermo. 2004. 'Under the "First World" Scalpel: The Sterilization of Quechua Women between 1995–1998.' Master's Thesis, University of Ottawa. ProQuest No. AAT MR01602.

Shea, Christopher. 2000. 'Don't Talk to Humans.' *Linguafranca* 10(5): 1–14.

Shopes, Linda. 2002. 'Oral History Interviewing, Institutional Review Boards, and Human Subjects.' Paper presented to the Organization of American Historians Meeting, Washington, DC, 13 April.

Showalter, Halle. 2005. 'Towards a Process-Based Policy: Report of an Internship at the Center for Pediatric Bioethics at the Seattle Children's Hospital.' Master's thesis, University of New Brunswick.

Shweder, Richard, A. 2006. 'Protecting Human Beings and Preserving Academic Freedom: Prospects at the University of Chicago.' *American Ethnologist* 33: 507.

Sieber, Joan E., Stuart Plattner, and Philip Rubin. 2002. 'How (Not) to Regulate Social and Behavioral Research.' *Professional Ethics Report* 15(2): 1–4.

Sieber, Joan E., and Reuel M. Baluyot. 1992. 'A Survey of IRB Concerns about Social and Behavioral Research.' *IRB: A Review of Human Subjects Research* 14(2): 9–10.

Sikes, Pat. 2008. 'At the Eye of the Storm: An Academic('s) Experience of Moral Panic.' *Qualitative Inquiry* 14(2): 235–53.

Silva, Franklin Leopoldo e. 2008. 'Methodological Procedures and Ethical Decisions.' *Ciênca & Saúde Coletiva* 13(2): 324–28.

Sin, Chih Hoong. 2005. 'Seeking Informed Consent.' *Sociology* 39(2): 277–95.

Smith, Dorothy E. 1986. 'Institutional Ethnography: A Feminist Method.' *Resources for Feminist Research/Documentation-sur-la-recherche feministe* 15: 6–13.

Smith, Vicki. 2002. 'Ethnographies of Work and the Work of Ethnographers.' In Paul Atkinson, Amanda Coffey, Sara Delamont, John Lofland, and Lyn Lofland, eds., *Handbook of Ethnography*, 220–33. London: Sage.

SPLC. 2001. 'Graduate Student Contests Review Board's Authority to Approve Journalism Research.' Student Press Law Center Report 23 (Fall).

Springer. 2009. 'Inuit Trails Represent Complex Social Network Spanning Canadian Arctic.' *ScienceDaily* (15 February). Retrieved 15 February 2009 from www.sciencedaily.com/releases/2009/02/090204112237.htm

SSHWC (Social Sciences and Humanities Research Ethics Special Working Committee). 2004. *Giving Voice to the Spectrum: Report of the Social Sciences and Humanities Research Ethics Special Working Committee.* Ottawa: Interagency Advisory Panel and Secretariat on Research Ethics. Retrieved 20 April 2008 from http://pre.ethics.gc.ca/english/workgroups/sshwc/SSHWCVoiceReportJune2004.pdf

– 2005. 'Reconsidering Privacy and Confidentiality in the TCPS: A Discussion Paper.' Discussion paper prepared for the Federal Interagency Advisory Panel on Research Ethics (PRE) for a national consultation. Available online at http://pre.ethics.gc.ca/policy-politique/initiatives/docs/sshwc_consultation_eng.pdf

– 2006. 'Qualitative Research in the Context of the TCPS: A Discussion Paper.' Ottawa: Interagency Advisory Panel and Secretariat on Research Ethics. (Draft April 11).

– 2007. 'Qualitative Research in the Context of the TCPS: A Follow-up to the *Giving Voice to the Spectrum* Report and a Discussion Paper.' Ottawa: Interagency Advisory Panel and Secretariat on Research Ethics.

– 2008a. 'On Privacy and Confidentiality: Recommendations from the Social Sciences, Humanities and Creative Arts Research Communities.' Ottawa: Interagency Advisory Panel and Secretariat on Research Ethics. February

– 2008b. 'Internet Research and the TCPS: Recommendations from SSHWC.' Ottawa: Interagency Advisory Panel and Secretariat on Research Ethics. February.

– 2008c. 'Creative Practices: A Chapter for Inclusion in the TCPS.' Ottawa: Interagency Advisory Panel and Secretariat on Research Ethics. February.

– 2008d. 'Qualitative Research: A Section for Inclusion in the TCPS.' Ottawa: Interagency Advisory Panel and Secretariat on Research Ethics. January.

Southwick, Ron. 2002. 'Pentagon Considers Tighter Control of Academic Research.' *The Chronicle of Higher Education* 48(34): A24. Retrieved 22 November 2010 from http://chronicle.com/article/Pentagon-Considers-Tighter-/2647/

Southwick, Ron, and Richard Monastersky. 2001. 'Research Groups Plan to Accredit Colleges That Conduct Studies on Human Subjects.' *The Chronicle of Higher Education* 47(38): A22. Retrieved 22 November 2010 from www.careernetwork.com/article/Research-Groups-Plan-to/13520/

Stagner, Ross. 1961. 'The Politics of Management: A Review of Dalton's *Men Who Manage*.' *Journal of Conflict Resolution* 5: 206–11.

Standing Committee on Education. 2007. 'REB Community Member Educational Needs: a PRE Pilot Project: Report.' Ottawa: Interagency Advisory Panel on Research Ethics. Retrieved 22 November 2010 from www.pre.ethics.gc.ca/pdf/eng/FINAL%20ENGLISH%20PDF%20PAPER%20VERSION%2025%20September%202007.pdf

Stark, Laura. 2007. 'Comment on the Presidential Address: Victims in Our Own Minds? IRBs in Myth and Practice.' *Law & Society Review* 41(4): 777–86.

Stoppard, Janet M. 2002. 'Navigating the Hazards of Orthodoxy: Introducing a Graduate Course on Qualitative Methods into the Psychology Curriculum.' *Canadian Psychology* 43(3): 143–53.

Szala-Meneok, Karen. 2006. 'Some Reflections on the Sometimes Conflictual Relationship between Researchers and Research Ethics Boards.' Unpublished document.

Taylor, Judith, and Matthew Patterson. 2010. 'Autonomy and Compliance: How Qualitative Sociologists Respond to Institutional Ethical Oversight.' *Qualitative Sociology* 33: 161–83.

Thomas, Jim. 2002. 'Re-examining Human Subjects Protections in Ethnographic Research: Unpacking the Memes of Over-Zealous Oversight.' Paper presented at the Midwest Sociological Society Annual Meetings, Milwaukee, 7 April.

Tilley, Susan A., and Louise Gormley. 2007. 'Canadian University Ethics Review: Cultural Complications Translating Principles into Practice.' *Qualitative Inquiry* 13(3): 368–87.

Tilley, Susan A., Kelly D. Powick, and Snežana Ratković. 2009. 'Regulatory Practices and School-Based Research: Making Sense of Research Ethics/Review.' *Forum: Qualitative Social Research* 10(2): Art. 32. Retrieved 1 June 2009 from www.qualitative-research.net/index.php/fqs/issue/view/31

Tolich, Martin, and Maureen H. Fitzgerald. 2006. 'If Ethics Committees Were Designed for Ethnography.' *Journal of Empirical Research on Human Research Ethics* 1(2): 71–8.

Tri-Council Working Group. 1996. 'Code of Conduct for Research Involving Humans.' Ottawa: Tri-Council Working Group.

Truman, Carole. 2003. 'Ethics and the Ruling Relations of Research Production.' *Sociological Research Online*. 12. Retrieved 12 March 2008 from www.socresonline.org.uk/8/1/truman.html

van den Hoonaard, Deborah K. 2004. 'Widowers' Stories: Older Men Talk about Losing Their Wives.' In W.L. Randall, D. Furlong, and T. Poitras, eds., *Narrative Matters 2004 Conference Proceedings*, 1022–1033. Fredericton, NB: Narrative Matters Conference Planning Committee.

van den Hoonaard, Will C. 1991. *Silent Ethnicity: The Dutch of New Brunswick*. Fredericton: New Ireland Press.

– 1994. Letter to Dr Douglas K. Martin, Secretary, Tri-Council Working Group on the Ethics of Research Involving Humans, 6 December.

– 1994b. 'Disacquiring Perspectives in Interviewing: On Avoiding the Trapdoor Effect.' Paper presented at Qualitative Research Conference, University of Waterloo, Waterloo, ON, 19–22 May.

– 2000. 'Research Ethics Review as a Moral Panic.' 17th Qualitative Analysis Conference, University of New Brunswick and St. Thomas University, Fredericton, NB, 18–21 May.

– 2002. 'Introduction: Ethical Norming and Qualitative Research.' In Will C. van den Hoonaard, ed., *Walking the Tightrope: Ethical Issues for Qualitative Researchers*, 3–25. Toronto: University of Toronto Press.

– 2003a. 'A Blessing in Disguise? The Practice and Ambiguities of Expedited Review.' Plenary, Annual Conference of the National Council for Ethics for Research on Humans, Ottawa, 28 February.

– 2003b. 'Is Anonymity an Artifact in Ethnographic Research?' *Journal of Academic Ethics* 1(2): 141–51.

– 2006. 'Trends in Canadian Sociology Master's Theses in Relation to Research Ethics Review, 1995-2004.' *Journal of Empirical Research on Human Research Ethics* 1(4): 77–88.

– 2007. 'Bursting the Bubble: The Relationship between Researcher and Research Participants.' 1st International Seminary to Strengthen the Capacity to Analyze Ethical Aspects of Health Research in Social and Human Science, Sao Paulo, Brazil, 16–18 October.

– 2008a. 'A explosão da bolha: relações entre pesquisador e participantes pesquisados.' (Bursting the Bubble: The Relationship between researcher and Research Participants). In Iara Coelho Zito Guerriero, Maria Luisa Sandoval Schmidt, and Fabio Zicker, eds., *Ética Nas Pesquisas Em Cências Humanas e Sociais Na Saúde*, 83–101. Sao Paulo: Aderaldo and Rothschild.

– 2008b. 'Re-imagining the "Subject:" Conceptual and Ethical Considerations on the Participant in Health Research.' *Ciência & Saúde Coletiva* 13(2): 371–9.

– 2009. 'The Underlife of Research Ethics Review: Secondary Adjustments in the World of Researchers.' Paper presented at the 26th Canadian Qualitatives, University of Waterloo, Waterloo, ON, 30 April.

van den Hoonaard, Will C., and Deborah K. van den Hoonaard. 1992. 'Awaiting Fate: Is there Life at Airports?' InterArts Lecture Series, Faculty of Arts, University of New Brunswick, Fredericton, NB, 20 February.

van den Hoonaard, Will C., and Anita Connolly. 2006. 'Anthropological Research in Light of Research-Ethics Review: Canadian Master's Theses, 1995–2004.' *Journal of Empirical Research on Human Research Ethics* 1(2): 59–70.

Victor, Jeffrey S. 1998. 'Moral Panics and the Social Construction of Deviant Behavior: A Theory and Application to the Case of Ritual Child Abuse.' *Sociological Perspectives* 41(3): 541–65.

Wax, Murray L. 1982. 'Research Reciprocity Rather than Informed Consent in Fieldwork.' In Joan E. Sieber, ed., *The Ethics of Social Research: Fieldwork, Regulation, and Publication,* 33–48. New York: Springer-Verlag.

Wax, Murray. L., and J. Cassell. 1981. 'From Regulation to Reflection: Ethics in Social Research.' *American Sociologist* 16(4): 224–29.

Webster's Seventh New Collegiate Dictionary. 1965. Toronto: Thomas Allen and Son.

Weppner, R.S. 1977. *Street Ethnography.* Thousand Oaks: Sage.

Wiles, Rose, Vikki Charles, Graham Crow, and Sue Heath. 2006. 'Researching Researchers: Lessons for Research Ethics.' *Qualitative Research* 6(3): 283–99.

Wolf, Daniel. 1991. *The Rebels: A Brotherhood of Outlaw Bikers.* Toronto: University of Toronto Press.

World Health Organization. 2000. *Operational Guidelines for Ethics Committees that Review Biomedical Research.* Retrieved 9 July 2006 from www.who.int/tdr/publications/publications/ethics.htm

Woodman, Lesley A. 2000. 'A Grounded Theory of Conflict between Child Care Counsellors and Adolescents in a Juvenile Justice Facility.' Master's thesis, University of Victoria.

Wright, David. 2004. 'Creative Nonfiction and the Academy: A Cautionary Tale.' *Qualitative Inquiry* 10(2): 202–6.

Index